(M

MALAYSIAN ECLIPSE

Economic Crisis and Recovery

CONTRIBUTORS

Chin Kok Fay (MEc, Malaya) is a Lecturer in the Faculty of Development Sciences, National University of Malaysia (UKM), Bangi, Selangor, Malaysia.

Natasha Hamilton-Hart (PhD, Cornell) is a postdoctoral fellow in the Research School of Pacific and Asian Studies, Australian National University, Canberra, ACT, Australia. From December 2000, she will be Assistant Professor in the Southeast Asian Studies Programme, National University of Singapore. Her forthcoming book, *Asian States, Asian Bankers,* investigates the political economy of central banking in Southeast Asia.

Jomo K. S. (PhD, Harvard) is Professor in the Applied Economics Department, University of Malaya, Kuala Lumpur, Malaysia. His major book publications include *A Question of Class*, *Growth and Structural Change in the Malaysian Economy*, *Southeast Asia's Misunderstood Miracle* (with others) and *Malaysia's Political Economy* (with E. T. Gomez).

Laura Kaehler is a PhD candidate in the Anthropology Department, City University of New York (CUNY) Graduate Center.

Lee Hwok Aun (MA, SOAS) is a postgraduate student at the School of Oriental and African Studies, University of London.

Liew San Yee (MEc, Malaya) is Part-time Lecturer in the Faculty of Business and Accounting, University of Malaya, Kuala Lumpur, Malaysia.

Rajah Rasiah (PhD, Cambridge) is Professor of Industrial Organisation, Institute of Malaysian and International Studies (IKMAS), National University of Malaysia (UKM), Bangi, Selangor, Malaysia. During 1999-2000, he has been on secondment as Dean of the Faculty of Economics and Business at Universiti Malaysia Sarawak, Kota Samarahan, Sarawak, Malaysia. His major publications include *Foreign Capital and Industrialization in Malaysia.*

MALAYSIAN ECLIPSE

Economic Crisis and Recovery

edited by
Jomo K. S.

ZED BOOKS LTD
London and New York
2001

MALAYSIAN ECLIPSE
was first published in 2001 by
Zed Books Ltd
7 Cynthia Street, London N1 9JF, UK
and Room 400, 175 Fifth Avenue, New York, NY 10010, USA

Distributed in the United States exclusively by
Palgrave, a division of St Martin's Press, LLC

Printed and bound in Malaysia

A catalogue record for this book is available from the British Library

ISBN 1 84277 022 5 Hb
ISBN 1 84277 023 3 Pb

CONTENTS

TABLES

FIGURES

GLOSSARY

ADB	Asian Development Bank
AIM	Amanah Ikhtiar Malaysia
APEC	Asia Pacific Economic Co-operation
BAFIA	Banking and Financial Institutions Act
BIS	Bank of International Settlements
BLI	bank loan inflows
BNM	Bank Negara Malaysia
CDRC	Corporate Debt Restructuring Committee
CIC	Capital Issues Committee
CLOB	Central Limit Order Book
CPI	consumer price index
EPF	Employees Provident Fund
FCI	foreign capital inflows
FDI	foreign direct investment
FPI	foreign portfolio investment
GATS	General Agreement on Trade in Services
GDP	gross domestic product
GFCF	gross fixed capital formation
GNP	gross national product
GSP	General System of Preferences
HPAEs	high performing Asian economies
HRDF	Human Resources Development Fund
ICOR	incremental capital-output ratio
IFC	International Finance Corporation
IMF	International Monetary Fund
IMP2	Second Industrial Master Plan, 1996-2005
IOFC	international off-shore financial centre
IS	import-substituting
KLCC	Kuala Lumpur City Centre
KLCI	Kuala Lumpur Composite Index
KLSE	Kuala Lumpur Stock Exchange
KUB	Koperasi Usaha Bersatu (Malaysia)

LMW	licensed manufacturing warehouse
LTCM	Long-Term Capital Management
M1	currency in circulation plus demand deposits
M2	M1 plus savings deposits
M3	M2 plus deposits placed with other banking institutions
MAS	Malaysia Airlines
MFA	Multi-Fibre Arrangement
MHR	Ministry of Human Resources
MIMOS	Malaysian Institute of Microelectronic Systems
MISC	Malaysian International Shipping Corporation
MSCI	Morgan Stanley Capital International
MTUC	Malaysian Trade Union Congress
NEAC	National Economic Action Council
NFPE	non-financial public enterprise
NEP	New Economic Policy
NICs	newly industralising countries
NIEs	newly industralised economies
NPL	non-performing loan
OECD	Organisation for Economic Cooperation and Development
OEM	original equipment manufacturing
PNB	Permodalan Nasional Berhad
PPI	producer price index
R&D	research and development
RER	real exchange rate
RFSMIs	Rehabilitation Fund for Small and Medium Industries
SE	Southeast
SES	Stock Exchange of Singapore
SIJORI	Singapore-Johore-Riau (growth triangle)
SME	small and medium enterprise
SMI	small and medium-scale industry
TNB	Tenaga Nasional Berhad
TNC	transnational corporation
UEM	United Engineers Malaysia
UK	United Kingdom
UMBC	United Malayan Banking Corporation
UMNO	United Malays National Organisation
UNCTAD	United Nations Conference on Trade and Development
US(A)	United States (of America)
VAR	vector auto-regression
WTO	World Trade Organisation

NIA

ACKNOWLEDGEMENTS

After editing *Tigers in Trouble* during the first half of 1998, I decided to continue working to understand and explain the economic crises of 1997-98, especially as it has impacted on Malaysia. I was frustrated by the policy influence of the old orthodoxy, represented by the International Monetary Fund (IMF), which was exacerbating the situation in the region. However, I was also uncomfortable with some of the critical responses to this orthodoxy, which seemed oblivious to the complexity of the situation, and often preferred instead to think in terms of conspiracies and bogeymen, be they currency speculators, hedge funds, Jews or even the likes of George Soros.

A new orthodoxy was also rapidly emerging, one which was turning the earlier East Asian miracle arguments on their head. The close business-government relations said to characterise East Asia had come to be acknowledged in the eighties and early nineties as responsible for the synergies underlying rapid growth in the region. Then, in the aftermath of the crisis, and with the failure of economic orthodoxy to anticipate and address the situation and its eventual gravity, a new explanation had to be found. The crisis was instead blamed on cronyism and other East Asian sins such as the 'Asian values' supposedly responsible for the erstwhile East Asian miracle.

The new orthodoxy was seductive, especially for me personally. People who had previously ignored or condemned our work were suddenly claiming that our earlier critical exposes of Malaysian political economy (e.g. Gomez and Jomo 1997) had anticipated the crisis. For others, our other critical work on the inferiority of the Southeast Asian miracle (Jomo *et al.* 1997; Jomo 2001a, 2001b) was also said to have foretold a crisis just waiting to happen. After all, after Mexico's tequila crisis of early 1995, I had engaged in public debate warning of the possibility of capital inflow reversals and financial crisis in Southeast Asia, and had lamented the withdrawal of the capital controls introduced in Malaysia in early 1994. Yet, it would be a pretentious lie to suggest that we had really anticipated the outbreak of the crises from the second half of 1997, how they unfolded and their severity.

Allow me to go back in time a little to explain how I was forced to re-engage issues I had long left behind. When I started as an undergraduate in

1970, I asked to join Berkeley College at Yale because its Master then was Robert Triffin, the famous international monetary economist. But soon after that, the Bretton Woods system collapsed in 1971, when Nixon unilaterally declined to honour earlier US commitments. The post-Bretton Woods international monetary arrangement was developed in an ad hoc fashion, largely in response to new crises — quite unlike how Bretton Woods was designed.

But it was only many years later that I would come back to such concerns, initially in the wake of the 1985-86 crisis in Malaysia, after the debt crisis began in Poland in 1981 and spread to Latin America and other heavily indebted developing countries. I then revisited the work of many at Yale whom I now regret not paying enough attention to while I was a student. I had been a research assistant to and student of Carlos Diaz-Alejandro, who later warned of financial crashes in the wake of financial liberalisation in Latin America in the mid-1980s. I have also since learnt a great deal from the writings of Jim Tobin, Joe Stiglitz and Paul Krugman — three others I first met at Yale in the early 1970s. Similarly, while at Harvard in the mid-1970s, I also remember listening to interesting discussions of crises by Ken Galbraith and Charles Kindleberger at MIT. But despite my respect for them, I was never really very interested in international monetary economics then.

When the recent crisis forced me to relearn the subject, I was returning to a very different world. Along the way, many friends have helped me along and I must thank them all. Many were involved in helping me prepare *Tigers in Trouble*. The crisis has also forced a renewed appreciation of the work of John Maynard Keynes. In this regard, the students of the late Hyman Minsky have been especially important. Through their work and communications, Yilmaz Akyüz, Manuel Agosin, C. P. Chandrasekhar, Chang Ha-Joon, Jayati Ghosh, Kasian Tejapira, Khoo Khay Jin, Joseph Lim, Manuel Montes, Anwar Nasution, Jose Antonio Ocampo, Prabhat Patnaik, Sakakibara Eisuke, Ammar Siamwalla, Ajit Singh, Joe Stiglitz and Lance Taylor have all helped me better understand this crisis. In the current political situation, I am more reluctant to list the Malaysians and others with a Malaysian connection who have been especially helpful to me. In these times, one can never be sure how such connections will be seen and interpreted. Some — especially those with whom I have disagreed — are not even aware of how influential they have been. I thank them all nonetheless, but can probably safely mention R. Thillainathan and Mahani Zainal Abidin since our differences are well-known.

Most chapters in this volume are based on work originally written for others. I wish to thank all those concerned for kindly agreeing to let me use the material in this volume. Chapters one and eight draw from material for a Ford Foundation project on the social impact of the East Asian crisis led by Chalongphob Sussangkarn, director of the Thai Development Research Institute; in this connection, Sauwalak Kittiprapas has been especially helpful as well. Chapter two has been revised from an article originally published by Routledge in the *Journal of the Asia-Pacific Economy*. Chapter three is revised from material for a project for the Japanese Ministry of Finance undertaken by the University of Sydney's Research Institute for Asia and the Pacific (RIAP). The project was led by John Matthews, while the current RIAP director is Stephanie Fahey. Chapter four draws from material for an East-West Center project led by Chung H. Lee, of the University of Hawaii. Chapters five, six and seven use material prepared for a project led by Stephany Griffith-Jones and Jacques Cailloux of the Institute of Development Studies at the University of Sussex. Chapter nine is revised from a much longer paper for the G24 group of developing countries in the Bretton Woods institutions whose research co-ordinator is Dani Rodrik of Harvard University. I remain most grateful to all of them for their permission, encouragement and critical feedback.

Many others have also helped this work, for which I am most thankful. All the other authors were very co-operative throughout. I am especially grateful to Robert Molteno, Anne Rodford, Farouk Sohawon, Mohammed Umar and others at Zed Books for their consistent co-operation and support. As usual, Foo Ah Hiang was efficient and careful in transforming messy manuscripts into this book. Liew San Yee helped with the preparation of many tables, figures and references. Din Merican has been generous with his books and time to offer feedback on drafts. Anisa Muzaffar kindly prepared the index and glossary besides helping proof-read. Azman Mokhtar and Tan Eu Chye also cast their sharp eyes over most chapters before the book went to press.

On the evening of Friday, 9 May 1998,[1] I reluctantly attended my first — and last — ever policy discussion with Finance Minister Anwar Ibrahim. Though I had come to know him in the seventies, I had had little to do with him after he joined the ruling party and government in 1982. After I arrived late for the meeting from an earlier workshop with some Southeast Asian colleagues, he summarised the preceding discussion and asked for my views. With little hesitation, I criticised the government's deflationary fiscal and monetary policies from late 1997, urging instead Keynesian-type reflationary policies while prioritising potentially (internationally) competitive productive capacities and equity considerations. I was pleasantly surprised by the support from my economist colleagues at the meeting, including those whom I had previously considered to be far more orthodox. I was also impressed by Anwar's openness to the criticisms as well as his lucid and spontaneous explanation of the policy dilemmas faced by the government.[2] He displayed a good grasp of the issues faced, and highlighted the difficulties for national monetary policy in the face of the huge amount of ringgit held in Singapore, then estimated to be around RM25-30 billion — contrary to the impression of Anwar's stupidity, incompetence and pro-IMF/Western slavishness given by Mahathir's recent historical revisionism.[3] At that meeting, Anwar also sought to explain and even defend the Prime Minister's various policy initiatives as the crisis unfolded despite the obvious antagonism to Mahathir among most in his audience.

Most importantly, in the following weeks, Anwar announced various policies to reflate the economy along the lines suggested, i.e. well before September 1998, although one could well argue that the policy reversal probably began even earlier, from late March 1998, when the central bank's *Annual Report* for 1997 was announced. It is necessary to emphasise this because developments and pronouncements since September 1998 have coloured memories and perceptions. Anwar has since been presented by Mahathir and his media as a stooge of the IMF and other foreign interests.

Despite my previous differences with Anwar and my criticisms of the IMF's role and of government economic policies under his watch, I find this misrepresentation dishonest and offensive because of the political ends to which it has been deployed. Although the events of the last two years and other constraints have made it impossible to finish the book I had originally planned, this volume nevertheless makes the point that Malaysian economic policy-making is desperately in need of open discussion and debate.

Thankfully, despite the circumscribed limitations of officially sanctioned public discourse, the sea change in Malaysian society that has occurred since the economic crisis began in mid-1997, and especially since Anwar's sacking from the cabinet on 2 September 1998, has begun to liberate Malaysian — and especially ethnic Malay — public culture and discourse in ways no one previously imagined. I would like to think that the forces set in motion by recent events are irreversible, though it is yet unclear where we will go from here, and not all outcomes will necessarily be 'Pareto-superior'. All this would not have been possible if not for the sacrifices Anwar has chosen to make despite the high personal costs to him and his family as well as the comfortable alternative options he had. For this, we should all be grateful.

Hence, in spite of our obvious policy disagreements, I would like to dedicate this volume to Anwar and all others before and after him who have sacrificed and will sacrifice so much to enable the people of this land to build a new, better and just Malaysia, including my children and my mother, who had to endure my frequent absences and inattention as I struggled to finish this book.

2 September 2000

Notes

1. In a letter to the *New Straits Times* in August 1998, just weeks before he was sacked, I criticised Anwar's speech at Universiti Putra Malaysia (UPM) decrying economists with outmoded ideas, which as reported in the press, seemed to be an unwarranted attack on our calls for heterodox approaches in light of the failure of contemporary orthodoxy as well as the implications of the hegemonic Washington consensus.
2. The discussion in the meeting room then moved from the economic to the political. I was surprised by the criticisms of Prime Minister Mahathir being made by those gathered who were not identified with the Anwar camp. I still remember one particular appeal to Anwar to 'lead us out of this darkness' caused by Mahathir. I was even more surprised by Anwar's response. Although he could have maintained a discreet silence, Anwar tried to explain the reasoning behind some of Prime Minister Mahathir's controversial public remarks and to relate this to his earlier explanation of government policy dilemmas. Just before the meeting wound up, I registered my disagreements with the main thrust of the preceding political discussion. Despite my well-known criticisms of Mahathir's policies and role, I urged unity of the leadership in the face of the challenges facing the country at the time. Although only one other person supported this position, Anwar did not indicate any approval for the majority view before closing the meeting to rush to meet a guest.

   Perhaps somewhat naively, I have since been of the view that although there were many who were keen for Anwar to take advantage of the situation then to move against Mahathir, there is no evidence that Anwar wanted to or was prepared to do so. Much is often made of Anwar's anti-corruption campaign while Mahathir was away in mid-1997, of the foreign media promotion of Anwar (as an urgently-needed, worthy successor to Mahathir in the second half of 1997 in contrast to its unsympathetic coverage of Mahathir's contrarian remarks), of Anwar's hospitality to some Indonesians who had turned against Soeharto in May 1998, of his vociferous criticisms of 'corruption, cronyism and nepotism' ('KKN') at Pulau Sibu, Johor, earlier that month, and of then Anwar associate, UMNO Youth chief Zahid Hamidi's thinly veiled criticisms of the Mahathir leadership at the UMNO annual party conference in late June 1998.

However, it should be clear to any objective analyst that, even considered together with other evidence of disagreement and dissent between Anwar and Mahathir, none of this indicates any conspiracy, let alone a strategy, to oust Mahathir. After all, as Mahathir confidante Daim noted at the UMNO general assembly after Anwar's sacking, Anwar not once, but twice (in 1995 and 1997) recruited Daim's help to deter Mahathir from retiring earlier. Why should Anwar then turn on Mahathir, his erstwhile patron, when he could have succeeded him effortlessly earlier?

What is the evidence that Anwar conspired with his camp to oust Mahathir? After Anwar was sacked, he claimed, in mid-September 1998, that he was responsible for the Zahid criticisms, but investigations by many suggest that his role was indirect and tangential at most. But even if he was the author of those criticisms, what was the strategy? After more than sixteen years of close association with Mahathir, could Anwar have seriously believed that Mahathir would resign due to some muted Malaysian echoes of the far more strident public criticisms of Soeharto which led to the Indonesian president's resignation on 21 May 1998? Unless one assumes Anwar to be politically naive, this account is hardly persuasive.

My own impression is that as the economic situation deteriorated in the second half of 1997 and Mahathir's policy initiatives and rhetoric caused the situation to deteriorate, Anwar became more receptive to the community and business media, and to foreign, including IMF, policy advice. In this, he was strongly, but quietly supported by many other government officials. For example, when Anwar was considering cutting government spending by 10 per cent after the first 1998 Budget announced in October 1997, then Government Economic Adviser, Daim Zainuddin, the main person responsible for economic liberalisation from the mid-1980s, is said to have suggested a cut of twice as much, leading to the compromise 18 per cent announced in early December 1997.

As this book will show, the government was caught between a rock and a hard place. While Mahathir was causing the exchange rate to decline further, the IMF/market alternative would accelerate and exacerbate economic contraction by cutting government spending and tightening monetary policy. Beginning with the UEM-Renong episode from November 1997, Anwar probably also resisted Mahathir-Daim pressyres to bail out some politically well connected business interests, thus inevitably exacerbating the divide. However, recognising the adverse economic and political effects of the December 1997 policy reversals, Anwar began to reverse himself again in the second quarter of 1998 to reflate the economy. However, it is also likely that by that time, Mahathir had been shocked by Soeharto's surprise resignation only a week after they had met in Cairo in mid-May 1998. The foreign media enthusiasm for Anwar to replace him and the increasingly independent and critical stance of the Anwar camp must have worried the aging premier. While Mahathir had probably long been aware of the machinations of those conspiring against Anwar, it seems likely that the Soeharto resignation was the straw that broke the camel's back, causing him to move to eliminate Anwar politically. The rest, as they say, is history.

One can see why this view would not sit comfortably with either camp. For the Anwar camp, it has become increasingly important to emphasise long-standing differences between the two, and to offer evidence of earlier dissent and opposition to Mahathir by Anwar. Ironically, those against Anwar are more than likely to exaggerate their differences as well, especially to suggest that Anwar had long opposed Mahathir and was conspiring to oust his erstwhile patron. The main casualty of such self-serving accounts is the truth as well as our understanding of errors in policy-making.

3. For the most sophisticated effort so far, see Mahathir Mohamad "When stability is vital for growth", *New Straits Times*, 23 August 2000; "Move that helped economic recovery", *New Straits Times*, 24 August 2000; "How ringgit trading was stopped", *New Straits Times*, 25 August 2000.

To demonstrate Anwar's supposed ignorance, the article suggests that Anwar did not understand that 'off-shore ringgit' did not involve ringgit physically overseas. Mahathir — or his ghost-writer — then mocks Anwar for ordering his Customs officers to confiscate ringgit cash being taken out of the country, little remembering that the events took place after the imposition of capital controls, by which time Anwar had been sacked and Mahathir had appointed himself Finance Minister. My own impression at the May 1998 meeting would not confirm the article's insinuations about Anwar's understanding of the offshore ringgit market.

The article is otherwise loyal to the Mahathir explanation of the crisis as due solely to currency speculators, especially hedge funds, often colluding in conspiratorial actions against Malaysia. Needless to say, little evidence is offered to support the principal claims of the article. As this volume will try to show, the crisis can be explained by the nature of the market without resorting to conspiracy theories. Unfortunately for Mahathir, his dogmatic insistence on such unpersuasive explanations has undermined the credibility of his other, often legitimate concerns and arguments. His credibility has been further eroded — especially in the eyes of most ethnic Malay Malaysians — by his regime's duplicitous persecution of Anwar.

INTRODUCTION

By mid-2000, it seems likely that the Malaysian economic recovery since early 1999 will continue for some time to come despite some prophecies to the contrary. This would confirm the characterisation of the 1998 downturn as being V-shaped rather than U-shaped, or W-shaped for those predicting another imminent downturn. After five quarters of economic contraction from the first quarter of 1998 until the first quarter of 1999, Malaysian economic recovery has proven to be more impressive than in Thailand and Indonesia. However, thus far, it has been more modest than in South Korea despite the Northeast Asian economy's more severe financial crisis and more onerous IMF policy conditionalities imposed. Thus, 1998 can be said to be the year when the Malaysian economy — not unlike others in the region — was eclipsed temporarily by the currency and financial crises that began in mid-1997.

However, understanding of this Malaysian eclipse has been confounded by several factors, not least the rejection of heterodox economic theories and views, including the earlier Keynesian orthodoxy, with the ascendance of neo-liberal economic dogma in the last two decades. The political crisis in Malaysia since September 1998 has also coloured and confused popular understanding of the economic issues involved and the policy options available due to the Mahathir regime's influential portrayal of his erstwhile deputy as a stooge of the International Monetary Fund (IMF) and other Western interests. Misunderstanding has been further compounded by the declining appreciation of economic history, not least among economists, e.g. of different types of economic crises and their causes. This problem has been exacerbated by the short-termist priorities of the dominant economic considerations accompanying the resurgence of finance capital globally and in Malaysia.

There have been at least three major sources of misunderstanding of the recent 1997-98 crisis of the Malaysian economy. The first has been to see the recent crisis in cyclical terms, like earlier crises in 1974-75 and in 1985-86 (and, of course, before that). This view has characterised the 1997-98 crisis as the latest manifestation of eleven or twelve year business cycles in Malaysia. While there certainly are cyclical elements in the latest crisis, there is little basis for taking this particular cyclical view.

While macroeconomic and product business cycles have certainly not been eliminated by recent technological and productivity developments, the recent crisis was mainly precipitated by a financial crisis in the wake of an externally induced currency shock in the region after the Thai baht collapse. It is, of course, then quite correct to see the recent financial crisis in cyclical terms as the inevitable deflationary downside — accelerated by herd panic — to the asset price inflation induced by reversible short-term foreign capital inflows. But this implies a different kind of cycle from those significant in earlier crises.

Careful study of the earlier crises would suggest important differences between the crises of mid-1970s and mid-1980s (Jomo 1990) as well as even more important differences with the latest crisis. One important similarity, however, has been the downturn in the international prices of at least some major primary commodity exports in all three instances. Furthermore, it can be argued that temporary downturns in electronics business cycles exacerbated all three crises. Although fiscal elements featured in both earlier crises, they were not significant this time round. And whereas a significant and rapidly growing element of the public debt in the mid-1980s crisis involved foreign borrowings, external private debt did not feature prominently a decade earlier. There are also other important differences as well as parallels, but this volume is not primarily interested in comparing and contrasting the various economic crises. However, some consequences of the earlier 1985-86 crisis — most notably, improved prudential regulation —were important in limiting the impact of the latest crisis.

The second major source of misunderstanding is far more influential. While there are some differences in the perspectives associated with financial markets (as reflected by the business media) and the International Monetary Fund, both have advocated fairly predictable monetarist positions. Their phobias about fiscal and monetary irresponsibility discouraged counter-cyclical budgetary responses to recessionary tendencies and insisted on higher interest rates to stem capital flight and counter inflationary trends (e.g. due to currency devaluation) as well as stricter banking regulation in the midst of the crisis which exacerbated liquidity problems for the real economy.

Refusing to recognise how poorly conceived and sequenced financial liberalisation had contributed to the crisis, they claimed the high moral ground by suggesting that the crisis was due to moral hazard, especially crony capitalism. Most of this volume rejects the view that the crisis in Malaysia was principally caused by cronyism, though chapter 1 fully acknowledges the role of inappropriate policy responses — often motivated by such considerations — in exacerbating the crisis in Malaysia. One might add that cronyism was probably also crucial in precipitating the Malaysian political crisis which exploded in September 1998, discussed in chapter 8.

Thirdly, this political crisis has greatly obscured understanding of the 1997-98 economic crisis in Malaysia and its ramifications. There had long been extensive documentation of what is now called cronyism in Malaysia (e.g. Gomez 1990; Gomez 1991; Gomez 1998; Gomez 1999; Gomez and Jomo 1999; Searle 1999). Coined by the growing middle class opposition to then Filipino President Marcos in the mid-1980s after the assassination of opposition leader Ninoy Aquino, the term only caught the popular imagination and inflamed greater opposition to the Mahathir regime after Indonesian President Soeharto's unexpected resignation on 21 May 1998. As chapter 1 shows, cronyistic considerations strongly influenced government policy responses to the crisis in the second half of 1997.

Each time then Deputy Prime Minister Anwar Ibrahim contested the government's policy response to the crisis, he became further estranged from his erstwhile mentor and patron, Prime Minister Mahathir. When he did not readily agree to bend the stock market rules in November 1997 to facilitate a bail-out for a conglomerate associated with the powerful ruling party Treasurer, the lines began to be drawn. After securing full cabinet support in Mahathir's absence in early December 1997, Anwar was associated with a series of orthodox fiscal and monetary reforms[1] (including spending cuts [mainly for extravagant so-called mega-projects], higher bank statutory reserve requirements, tighter definition of non-performing loans and allowing interest rates to rise). These measures almost certainly exacerbated the recessionary tendencies already setting in throughout the region. Hence, it appears that Anwar approved of the tighter fiscal and monetary policies from late 1997, in line with market expectations as much as IMF recommendations.

But to be fair, by June 1998, Anwar had increased public spending, especially to provide credit for investments in food agriculture, by small businesses and the poor (micro-credit). He also sought to increase liquidity by reducing reserve requirements as well as banking margins. With an estimated 25-30 billion Malaysian ringgit in Singapore, the Malaysian monetary authorities could not expect to altogether prevent interest rates from rising with the much higher rates available in the island republic. As chapter 4 shows, although interest rates rose after the crisis began, and especially from December 1997, the increase never exceeded three percentage points or 300 basis points.

And as chapter 7 shows, the rise in Malaysia was far less than in Thailand, and for that matter, in the rest of the region. Interest rates in Malaysia were well below Thailand's from mid-1997 until September 1998, after which Thai rates fell below Malaysia's without the aid of controls. While the Malaysian authorities now claim that the September 1998 measures enabled interest rates to be brought down, actual comparison with Thailand shows Malaysian interest rates to be lower before September 1998 and higher after that.

And as the same chapter shows, capital controls had previously been introduced in 1994, while Anwar was Finance Minister, so there is little reason to believe that he was dogmatically committed to full capital account convertibility. Hence, he also began to reverse his earlier policies, at least from the second quarter of 1998, when government spending started to rise again despite reduced tax revenue, and monetary policy began to be relaxed.

The political fall-out from the 1997-98 crisis has thus greatly politicised subsequent analysis and interpretation of the crisis as well as its consequences and implications. On 2 September 1998, then Finance Minister, Deputy Prime Minister and heir apparent Anwar Ibrahim was sacked from the cabinet and then from the ruling party for alleged sexual misbehaviour. However, Anwar was soon accused of having instituted IMF-type policy measures in Malaysia from late 1997 and blamed for causing the 1998 recession and exacerbating its consequences for the Malaysian economy through such policy measures. Several major public policy pronouncements since then (e.g. the 1999 official *White Paper*) have been skewed to support this kind of interpretation of the causes and consequences of the crisis.

Hence, while Anwar was undoubtedly more inclined to cater to 'market sentiment', his post-September 1998 demonisation by Mahathirists as an IMF stooge and agent of the West is certainly not supported by his economic policy record. Some Anwar critics would argue that he always sought popularity, which would explain his apparent pro-market stances in a job where to behave otherwise would invite approbation and adverse comment by the powerful and influential financial media. These may well be valid criticisms, but they are of a different order altogether, and have very different political implications.

In any case, the Mahathirist depiction of Anwar has politically coloured the debate over the causes of the crisis and economic policy responses. Some Anwar sympathisers have naively endorsed monetarist and other criticisms of Mahathir, and reject all Mahathir's criticisms of global economic inequities. Meanwhile, critics of globalisation and financial liberalisation have supported Mahathir's actions as if the Mahathirist caricatured demonisation of Anwar was true and Mahathir had always been critical of economic liberalisation, both domestically and internationally, forgetting his actual economic policy record over the last two decades. There have been many variations on both themes, but one consequence has been simplistic economic debates that have been misleadingly personalised.

Earlier work (e.g. Gomez and Jomo 1999; Jomo 1994) has shown, as this volume will, that while Mahathir initiated the turn to economic liberalisation from the mid-1980s, with considerable help from then new Finance Minister Daim Zainuddin, Anwar largely continued these policies in the 1990s. Both have been populists, albeit of different types, and have at different times, deployed nationalist and anti-Western rhetoric. While Anwar has largely abandoned old-style anti-Western rhetoric, perhaps to assuage a West long suspicious of his Islamic credentials, Mahathir has continued to invoke it in the 1990s, especially after the outbreak of the recent crisis. Besides such differences in personal and political style, Anwar has had a record of greater interest in social safety net and poverty reduction policies in contrast to Mahathir's more trickle-down approach to growth, modernisation and progress, through more intimate government-private business relations (Mahathir's 'Malaysia Incorporated', now vilified as cronyism).

When cronyism was joined with corruption and nepotism as the three enemies of Anwar's Malaysian *reformasi* movement, inspired by the events in Indonesia leading to Soeharto's resignation on 21 May 1998, Anwar was unwittingly set on a collision course with Mahathir. In retrospect, there are many reasons to believe that Anwar did not fully realise what he was getting into then, and was probably carried away by the naive enthusiasm and euphoria of his impatient Malaysian supporters riding the crest of the Indonesian *reformasi* wave after its surprise success in forcing Soeharto's ouster.

Contrary to *ex post* Mahathirist claims, there is no persuasive evidence that Anwar had any — let alone a good — coherent plan or program to accelerate his succession to, let alone depose Mahathir. Instead, with the benefit of hindsight, it seems likely that heightened popular expectations (especially among Anwar's many supporters) about the imminence of regime change in Malaysia after the May 1998 events in Indonesia provided momentum for increasingly public dissent. The unprecedented affront (but not real threat) of Anwarist condemnations of *KKN* (corruption, cronyism, nepotism) may well have nudged a previously unfazed (and perhaps ambivalent) Mahathir into the waiting arms of Anwar's enemies, some of whom had long resented and conspired to eliminate the 'upstart' heir apparent. The rest, as they say, is history, with some of it figuring in chapter 8's discussion of the politics of capital controls.

Roots of the Crisis: The Book Outline

This volume takes various approaches to understanding the crisis and policy responses to it. The first six chapters explore different dimensions of the origins of the crisis. Chapter 1 by Jomo serves as an overview chapter, outlining how the Thai baht devaluation on 2 July 1997 led to currency crises in Southeast Asia, which, in turn, precipitated financial crises in the region and led to sharp recessions during 1998. The macroeconomic focus of the chapter is set against a review of official policy responses to the crisis in the crucial second half of 1997 and thereafter.

The chapter will show that the economic crisis began as a currency crisis due to strong pressure on the dollar-pegged ringgit after the reversal of the yen-dollar relationship from mid-1995 and the floating of the Thai baht, which had been under pressure since 1996. The initial ringgit devaluation after an abortive and expensive defence of the currency accelerated the asset price deflation after the stock market reached a peak in February 1997. This asset price collapse quickly threatened the banking system with Malaysia's high level of indebtedness, including heavy exposure to property and share purchase loans.

The currency crisis from July 1997 put considerable pressure on the ringgit. After an aborted defence, which is believed to have cost over RM9 billion (then over US$3.5 billion), the ringgit was also floated, following the Thai baht, Indonesian rupiah and Filipino peso. The ringgit devaluation lowered the foreign exchange value of Malaysian assets, especially share prices. This, in turn, triggered a vicious cycle of asset price deflation involving flight of foreign as well as domestic portfolio capital. Lower asset prices also caused lending institutions to make margin calls, requiring additional collateral. Foreign lenders became more reluctant to 'roll over' their short-term loans. Interest rates also tended to rise for a variety of reasons, exacerbating the effects of reduced liquidity in the financial system.

Of course, the ringgit devaluation also raised the prices of consumer as well as producer imports, particularly during 1998. Food prices seem to have been especially adversely affected, reflecting the high import content in the national food bill. The effects of higher producer prices due to currency devaluation are difficult to generalise about. For example, although electronic exports are reputed to have a very high import content, the ringgit devaluation would actually have the effect of reducing the cost of value added in Malaysia. And in so far as internal transfer pricing is the norm within transnational production chains, it is actually quite possible that currency devaluation would encourage increased output. But there are a variety of other relations that would have different outcomes and effects from higher producer import prices due to currency devaluation.

Early official responses seemed to smack of hubris, 'denial' and 'bailing-out' well-connected corporate interests, which inadvertently served to exacerbate the growing problems, including declining confidence in official policy. While the policy reversal from late 1997 may have served to signal some checks on 'cronyism', they also exacerbated the deflationary consequences of declining domestic and regional demand. Thus, what began as a currency crisis soon generated a financial crisis, which in turn led to recession. Hence, these different aspects of the 1997-8 economic crisis were distinguished in order to be able to more carefully consider their respective social impacts.

Ironically, instability in the region subsided from around September-October 1998, after the Russian crisis, LTCM collapse and Wall Street scare of August 1998 caused the US Treasury to agree to a strengthening and stabilisation of the yen and other East Asian currencies. In Malaysia, however, the imposition of selective capital controls and the pegging of the ringgit to the US dollar at RM3.8 from 2 September 1998 had a similar effect, though with the benefit of hindsight, the Malaysian initiative may well have been somewhat unnecessary.

The exchange rate instability that followed the July 1997 currency floats must have made planning especially difficult for enterprises with various types of international exposure. Thus, the quasi-dollarisation of the ringgit may have helped many enterprises with international exposure to plan better. Looser monetary policy from mid-1998 as well as central bank directives to increase lending by eight per cent per annum from September 1998 and then for 1999 as well as served to restore liquidity to the system.

Although Malaysia recovered more strongly than Thailand and Indonesia during 1999, its recovery only began in the second quarter. Available evidence does not allow either proponents or opponents of the Malaysian capital control measures to conclusively prove that they enhanced or undermined recovery. However, it is generally agreed that the Malaysian approach has probably limited the reforms and restructuring which might otherwise have proven necessary if recovery was far more subject to international pressures and expectations.

The speed of recovery — certainly swifter than many predicted — suggests the partly cyclical nature of the crisis. Businesses, workers and families appear to have weathered the crisis reasonably well, thanks in part to the high savings rate, relatively low public debt, docile labour force, relative political stability, and reasonable human resource base. Nonetheless, various structural problems — such as heavy dependence on foreign direct investments, intermediate goods and technology, and declining international competitiveness — persist. Badly-needed structural and institutional reforms, particularly to the financial system, have not been forthcoming. Instead, the forced bank mergers appear intended to consolidate the financial power of some of the politically better connected.

This book will thus begin by pulling together various aspects and episodes in the economic crisis in Malaysia, leading to severe GDP contraction, price inflation and modest increases in unemployment. The impacts on different economic sectors of the recession and the dissipation of ringgit value will be considered. The overall economic contraction was most pronounced in the second half of 1998. Sectors vulnerable to crises of confidence, job losses or sudden currency depreciation, such as construction and manufacturing, were the worse affected, suggesting the significance of Keynes's 'animal spirits' for understanding the impact of this crisis. Also, the highly leveraged suffered under the burden of high interest rates while low-income households were hurt by reduced transfer payments.

The second chapter by Rajah Rasiah argues that first-order macroeconomic fundamentals in Malaysia before the crisis did not give much cause for concern (with the important exception of the persistent current account deficit in the early and mid-1990s). Not all was well, however, especially if one looked at 'second-order fundamentals' reflecting and determining the potential for sustained growth, industrialisation and economic welfare gains. In other words, impressive growth performance before the crisis was not sustainable indefinitely.

While this does not mean that the crisis was primarily due to weak economic fundamentals, as alleged in some quarters when the crisis first began in mid-1997, it does mean that Malaysia was not rising adequately to meeting the new challenges of sustaining rapid growth, structural change and industrialisation in the face of new external and internal constraints. Most importantly, it appears that the economy had not developed its industrial and technological capabilities rapidly enough in the face of increasingly intense international competition.

Besides technological and human resources bottlenecks, the chapter recognises that the financial system was not ensuring that rapid capital accumulation meant commensurately enhanced productive capacities. Part of the problem, of course, was the abuse of government-business relations for the aggrandisement of a politically connected few, i.e. cronyism. But again, it needs to be emphasised that while cronyism was taking a debilitating toll on the Malaysian economy and would severely compromise government policy responses to the crisis, as it unfolded, this book does not identify cronyism as the principal cause of the crisis.

In chapter 3, Natasha Hamilton-Hart and Jomo take a longer view in looking at changing governance of the banking sector from the sixties, focussing particular attention on the role of central bank, especially in ensuring prudential regulation. The review also considers some implications of banking liberalisation in the decade before the crisis, and their likely contribution to creating conditions that rendered Malaysia prone to crisis in 1997. The following chapter by Chin Kok Fay and Jomo focuses and elaborates on this last period, especially Malaysia's financial vulnerabilities from the mid-1990s, and considers the intimate relationship of banking to the stock market in Malaysia during this time.

Unlike the three worst affected economies (namely Thailand, South Korea and Indonesia), the Malaysian financial system has been less bank-based, with a far greater role for the capital market. The chapter points to how the unsustainable virtuous cycle of asset price inflation — which may have boosted growth slightly during the boom period through the wealth effect and its limited multipliers in Malaysia's very open economy — could so readily become its anti-thesis, a vicious cycle of asset price deflation. Reduced liquidity due to the financial crisis must, in turn, have exacerbated recessionary tendencies.

After reaching a peak of around 1300 in February 1997, the decline of the Malaysian stock market index was greatly exacerbated by the currency crisis as well as its repercussions for the banking system. It had fallen by about four-fifths — or 80 per cent — to reach its nadir of 262 on 2 September 1998, on the day after the announcement of capital controls. With the relatively much higher stake of foreign portfolio investors in the Malaysian capital market, especially on the first or main board of the Kuala Lumpur Stock Exchange (KLSE), came its greater collapse.

The proportionately very high capitalisation of Malaysia's share market meant that the adverse wealth effect of this collapse was probably greater than elsewhere in the region. Likewise, the recovery of the stock market since September 1998 has also probably had a significant positive wealth effect, reflected in increased domestic consumer demand. Besides the stock market, the property sector was also adversely affected by asset price deflation, with significant consequences for the banking sector, e.g. with the declining value of collaterals, etc. The reversal of the sector's fortunes has also adversely impacted on the construction sector, as well as supplier industries. The casualties have included employment by as well as the very survival of construction and supplier firms.

Both chapters 3 and 4 underscore the significance of Malaysian banking reforms of the late 1980s in limiting the most dangerous consequences of poorly conceived and sequenced financial liberalisation at both national and international levels. Fortunately for Malaysia, after the Malaysian banking crisis of the late 1980s, when the share of non-performing loans in the system rose to almost 30 per cent, the authorities significantly strengthened prudential regulation, e.g. through the Banking and Financial Institutions Act (BAFIA), 1989.

Although this regulation was subsequently undermined by various liberalisation measures, it nevertheless served to protect Malaysia to a greater degree than in the more crisis-hit countries. While prudential regulation weakened in the face of continued financial liberalisation in the 1990s (e.g. bank supervisions are reported to have been conducted biennially rather than annually from the mid-1990s just before the crisis), the institutional reforms in the wake of the banking crisis of the late 1980s put Malaysia in much better stead than other rapidly liberalising economies with more bank-based financial systems.

Hence, unlike Thailand, Korea and Indonesia, Malaysia did not need to seek emergency IMF credit facilities, and thus did not have to accept accompanying conditionalities. Thus, Malaysia avoided the forced closure of banks and financial institutions that occurred in the other three economies, which exacerbated panic and undermined confidence in the domestic financial systems. While Malaysia did briefly adopt tighter fiscal and monetary policies from late 1997 until early 1998, the depth of the recession in 1998 was probably due to other factors as well, most notably the negative wealth effect of the stock market collapse.

The fifth chapter by Jomo elaborates on the crucial role of reversible short-term capital inflows in the recent crisis. Recognising Malaysia's better prudential banking regulation (in the aftermath of the banking crisis of the late 1980s) and lower exposure to short-term bank borrowings from abroad, it suggests that the larger role of Malaysia's stock market probably contributed more to worsening its crisis than elsewhere in the region. The increased role of foreign portfolio investment inflows during the 1990s meant that capital flight — exacerbated by herd panic in response to regional contagion — would wreak a devastating toll on the Malaysian stock market and real economy.

Capital inflows into Malaysia increased substantially in the mid-1990s. Although portfolio investment inflows abated after February 1997, bank borrowings grew tremendously in 1996 and the first half of 1997, i.e. just before the crisis. While additional credit availability due to capital inflows could have stimulated total spending with increased domestic investments, such inflows also supported a consumption boom (with high import content) as well as speculative asset price bubbles (involving shares and property). Such increases in demand were unsustainable as capital flight caused the bubble to begin to deflate from early 1997 before it accelerated with the onset of the regional currency crisis.

Such a combination of increased capital inflows, credit expansion and exchange rate appreciation had raised aggregate demand more rapidly than GDP, further increasing the current account deficit. Capital inflows — encouraged to finance this deficit — tended to raise foreign reserves and domestic credit availability as well as exchange rates, although sterilisation measures mitigated some of these consequences while adding new problems. By sterilising capital inflows, the Malaysian monetary authorities may have presumed that the consequently greater external deficit could be sustained, perhaps not recognising that sterilisation merely displaced the problem and postponed the day of reckoning.

Malaysian exposure to foreign bank borrowings was relatively much less than in the three economies most adversely affected by the crisis, namely Thailand, Indonesia and South Korea. Although foreign bank borrowings rose rapidly during 1996 and the first half of 1997, exposure to foreign loans was still relatively lower in Malaysia. Commercial banks in Malaysia may have been particularly hard hit by the currency crisis. Although private sector lending from abroad grew tremendously in the year and a half before July 1997, private corporations were largely constrained from borrowing heavily overseas. Hence, it is likely that financial institutions accounted for much of the foreign credit to private borrowers in Malaysia. In so far as they sought to profit from arbitrage and related opportunities, it is likely that they were also hurt by the currency and term mismatches suffered by their counterparts in the rest of the region.

Critically, unlike the other three, Malaysian external liabilities did not exceed its foreign exchange reserves. Also, it seems that three quarters of corporate foreign borrowings were accounted for by three partially privatised state-owned enterprises. Hence, Malaysia was not forced to seek emergency credit from the IMF (in the absence of available alternative sources), and therefore, never really had to accept conditionalities often imposed by the Fund on such distressed economies. This not only meant that Malaysia enjoyed greater degrees of freedom than the others, but also that the impact of the crisis on the Malaysian economy was less to begin with.

The sixth chapter by Jomo with Liew San Yee and Laura Kaehler confirms the much greater volatility of foreign portfolio investment flows, compared to foreign direct investments and even foreign bank borrowings. It uses a variety of methodologies to measure and otherwise demonstrate such dif-ferentiated capital flow volatility, pointing the finger at the most likely principal culprit, foreign portfolio investments, which are even less mobility-constrained than short-term bank borrowings. There is a need for even more detailed and careful analysis, differentiating various types of portfolio flows. For instance, it has been suggested that the investment behaviour (including investment duration) of pensions funds, mutual funds and hedge funds are significantly different, while some are pointing to further differentiation within these broad categories. More careful understanding would be crucial to appropriate policy making intended to reduce the volatility of capital flows.

The next chapter looks at Malaysia's unique policy response, namely the capital controls introduced from September 1998.[2] While chapter 7 by Jomo considers various economic issues in this regard, none of this should detract from the significance of the Malaysian government's willingness to boldly experiment with capital controls from September 1998. The Mahathir regime's willingness to do so, with relatively little immediate adverse effect, has exposed the lie of its ideologically driven monetarist critics who prophesised unmitigated disaster. However, as chapter 7 suggests, the discussion of capital controls needs to go well beyond the simple debate over capital account liberalisation, which the Malaysian authorities had long been committed to despite the imposition of temporary controls (taxes on inflows among others) in early 1994 in response to sudden and massive portfolio capital flight. The introduction of such controls under Anwar Ibrahim's watch at the Treasury underlines the fact that Mahathir's conflict with his erstwhile deputy had little to do with capital controls *per se*, though of course, the nature and design of the control measures were quite different.

The Malaysian introduction of capital controls fourteen months after the crisis began in July 1997 has been compared to closing the stable doors long after the horses have bolted. While the controls constrained further capital flight, many would argue that little more outflow was likely after the collapse of stock market capitalisation by four-fifths over eighteen months from its earlier peak in February 1997. Besides doubts about the efficacy of introducing such controls so long after the outbreak of the crisis, it is generally agreed that such controls are better imposed before a crisis to discourage undesirable inflows rather than after a crisis has started.

And while one might have concurred with the need for drastic measures after the turbulence of August 1998 (Russian, LTCM and Wall Street crises), there seems to be far less justification for them in retrospect. This was especially true after the 20 per cent devaluation of the greenback against the yen in early October 1998, which strengthened all other East Asian currencies (except for the pegged ringgit and Hongkong dollar), and transformed the intended ringgit appreciation into an effective depreciation. As chapter 7 shows, interest rates in Thailand, which had remained much higher than in Malaysia before September 1998, fell below Malaysian rates from October 1998, suggesting that the Malaysian control measures were no longer necessary to keep interest rates down.

Opponents of the capital controls introduced in September 1998 have tended to exaggerate its likely adverse effects, which have not really been as manifest as they were wont to claim. On the other hand, proponents of the control measures are not able to demonstrate that the controls were responsible for either a speedy or a strong recovery. The three worst affected economies all registered positive growth in the first quarter of 1999, whereas Malaysia only came out of the recession from the second quarter. And while the recovery in Malaysia has been stronger than in Thailand and Indonesia, South Korea has performed better thus far. And even if Malaysia were to perform better than South Korea, it still has to be demonstrated that this was due to the capital controls, which have largely been amended and dropped except for the dollar peg and related currency controls since September 1999.

Most importantly, as lessons are drawn from the recent experience to reform for the future, the chapter highlights the range of capital control instruments available and their likely different effects as well as the likely circumstances for their introduction and deployment. A fuller discussion of such matters is crucial in devising appropriate capital control instruments to serve particular policy objectives. In retrospect, the Malaysian initiative looks rather late, inappropriate and unnecessary, but hardly the disaster threatened by its most vociferous critics from financial centres in the West. In contrast, 'market wisdom', the coercive power of market sentiments and their ideological peddlars, as well as the IMF conditionalities imposed on the most crisis-affected economies are now widely recognised to have exacerbated, rather than ameliorated the financial crisis, thus worsening the recession in the region in 1998.

The chapter also provides some support for the aborted Japanese government proposal (associated with then Vice Finance Minister for International Affairs, Sakakibara Eisuke) in the third quarter of 1997 for an Asian regional monetary facility. Rejected by the West, the IMF and, surprisingly, China, such regional initiatives are deemed necessary as the prospects for fundamental international monetary and financial reform remain bleak. Despite the official rhetoric about the need for a new international financial architecture from around August 1998, when the previously East Asian financial crisis threatened briefly to go global, reform efforts seem increasingly unlikely to materialise. However, to serve the region well, regional initiatives should complement national efforts, be both market-based and flexible, besides minimising the potential for moral hazard.

The eighth chapter by Jomo with Lee Hwok Aun continues some themes from the first chapter's review of the macroeconomic impact by focussing on other social impacts, especially those affecting economic welfare. As both the opening macroeconomic chapter and chapter 8 on social impacts show, the adverse consequences of the crisis were consequently more limited than in the other two more hard-hit Southeast Asian economies, Thailand and Indonesia. Owing to better pre-crisis prudential regulation, including restrictions on foreign borrowing, the banking crisis in Malaysia was more limited and better managed, partly thanks to avoidance of IMF tutelage.

Full employment before the crisis and the huge presence of foreign workers, many of whom were not documented and probably not counted as well, have limited its adverse impact on Malaysian workers. Many Malaysian workers also appear to have opted for lower wage incomes rather than job losses, though the significance of such choices is difficult to estimate. The poor quality of labour statistics in Malaysia also frustrates assessment of the impact of the crisis on Malaysian workers. Unfortunately, other indicators of human or economic welfare in Malaysia are not much better.

Most social safety net initiatives in Malaysia in response to the crisis are associated with Anwar's tenure at the Finance Ministry. In any case, at least some of them have been criticised as poorly conceived (e.g. financing to boost food agriculture) while there is no evidence of performance evaluation to assess the effectiveness of such spending. With crucial general elections in late 1999 and controversial ruling party elections in May 2000, there has been considerable suspicion that much recent discretionary government spending has been abused for political ends to protect the *status quo*.

Instead, there is considerable evidence of many important government initiatives to protect politically well-connected business interests. As chapter 1 showed, these have included official initiatives to:

- set up a RM60 billion 'bail-out' fund to rescue selected shareholders;
- change stock market rules to check 'short-selling';
- change share market and other rules to facilitate 'bail-outs' and 'rescues';

- use public funds (including the Employees Provident Fund (EPF), Petronas and Khazanah) to buy over assets at above-market prices; in some cases, this has involved virtually renationalising assets (including those recently privatised) on generous terms.

Not surprisingly, the survival of the Mahathir regime has been widely seen as crucial for such policy initiatives to protect business cronies.

But it should be recognised that the regime's survival (e.g. during the November 1999 elections) has also been due to other factors, including its ability to present itself as the more attractive alternative through a variety of means, including its control of the media and its seeming ability to 'deliver' economically. Most importantly, the Mahathir regime successfully portrayed itself as protecting national economic interests more generally, e.g. through capital controls and related economic measures to lower interest rates, provide credit, restore liquidity and otherwise stimulate economic recovery.

The concluding chapter offers a comparative perspective on crisis and recovery in the East Asian region by comparing the Malaysian experience with those of the three most-affected economies, namely Thailand, Indonesia and South Korea, all of which sought IMF emergency credit facilities and were thus subjected to its conditionalities. The first part reviews the causes of the crises in the region. Macroeconomic indicators in the four economies are reviewed to show that despite some problems (mainly persistent current account deficits in Thailand and Malaysia), the crises cannot be attributed to macroeconomic profligacy. Instead, the reversal of short-term capital inflows is blamed. Malaysia was less vulnerable thanks to pre-crisis restrictions on foreign borrowings as well as stricter central bank regulation, but was more vulnerable due to the greater role of its capital market compared to the other three. The role of IMF policy conditionalities and financial market expectations in exacerbating the crises is also emphasised.

The second part of chapter nine advances the emerging discussion of economic recovery in the region. It asserts that recovery in the region, especially in Korea and Malaysia, has been principally due to successful Keynesian reflationary efforts. The recovery suggests that the emphasis by the IMF and the financial media on the prior necessity of corporate governance reforms has been misguided, i.e. such reforms are not a pre-condition for economic recovery. Instead of the neo-liberal-inspired reforms proposed, reforms should create new conditions for further catching up throughout the region. The chapter ends by outlining an agenda for international financial system reform in the interests of the South, although it remains pessimistic about reform prospects.

Prospects

As is well known, the 1997-98 economic crises gave rise to distinctively different regimes in the three most adversely affected economies, namely Thailand, South Korea and Indonesia. Yet, to varying degrees, all three new regimes have been obliged to accept many externally imposed reforms in order to secure and sustain emergency credit facilities from the IMF. Although there was never any real need for Malaysia to require such aid or to accept such conditionalities for any other reason, the Malaysian authorities did briefly implement such monetary and fiscal policies favoured by financial markets from late 1997. However, such policies began to be reversed from the second quarter of 1998, and more dramatically, from September 1998, with the sacking of the incumbent Finance Minister and the imposition of capital controls as well as several related monetary measures.

Meanwhile, relatively successful early policy responses to the financial crisis may well have served to contain the potential spread of a banking crisis in Malaysia. Danaharta was established in the second quarter of 1998 (while Anwar still headed the Treasury and Ahmad Don presided over the central bank) to remove large non-performing loans from the worst affected banks and financial institutions. This — together with recapitalisation of de-capitalised banks by a companion agency, Danamodal — served to restore liquidity to the banking system. Such prompt and successful action probably reduced the adverse impact of the financial crisis on the real economy. Although the central bank set an eight per cent credit growth target for 1998 and 1999, actual growth was rather modest, staying below two per cent despite a massive increase in credit for share and residential property purchases and a decline in lending for manufacturing and other productive purposes.

Of greater concern in the long term is the changed nature of bank loan portfolios. Although banks may have become more careful about lending for property purchases, lending limits for share purchases have been raised to help boost the stock market, with positive wealth effects contributing to renewed domestic demand, helped along by expansionary fiscal policies. Similarly, consumer credit has been officially encouraged, particularly for vehicle purchases to resuscitate the automotive industry and residential property purchases. Meanwhile, bank lending for productive purposes, especially manufacturing, have dropped drastically.

But strict pre-crisis prudential regulation as well as less exposure to foreign borrowings may well have been crucial in averting a more serious banking crisis. While there is little evidence of abandonment of the prudential regulatory framework or a renewed foreign borrowing spree in Malaysia for the time being, recent lending trends must be a cause for concern. Not only is additional property lending being generously provided (e.g. second residential property loans for civil servants), lending limits for share purchases have been raised and consumption credit may be rising as well. All this, of course, is at the expense of loans for productive purposes, whether manufacturing, agriculture or mining. Seen against the decline of foreign direct investment interest in Malaysia since 1996, the trend is ominous, as emphasised in Rajah Rasiah's second chapter.

Although more robust and less vulnerable than in the worst crisis-hit economies with their more bank-based financial systems, Malaysia's banking system has not been required to play a more developmental role in promoting industrialisation. Instead, over-exposure to the property sector and increasing lending for stock purchases served as the nexus for banks to fuel asset price inflation in Malaysia even before considering the contribution of net capital inflows during the nineties before the crisis. The ability to deploy the banking sector more effectively to finance productive investments may well be crucial in determining Malaysia's future ability to sustain rapid growth.

Not surprisingly, there is still much doubt as to whether the Malaysian economy will be able to resume — let alone improve upon — its pre-crisis growth trajectory despite the impressive recovery after 1998. The recent international phenomenon of manufactured commodity price deflation has enhanced doubts about the likely welfare gains from further export-oriented industrialisation. Recent trends seem to suggest that generic manufactured goods not enjoying strong intellectual property rights — and associated monopoly rents — are as vulnerable to price pressures as primary commodities.

Consequently, productivity gains have not been translated into commensurate welfare gains for producers. The advent of China, India and others as lower cost producers in similar production niches in global commodity chains threatens a 'race to the bottom' with the intensification of competition. Much will therefore depend upon whether Malaysia will be able to constantly reposition itself ahead of its competition. It is unclear how sustainable short-term successes in particular niches will be in the medium to long term.

Economic policy priorities generally continue to remain in the recovery mode. And while much of the recovery so far has come from fortuitous export booms, especially in electronics, the official emphasis continues to be on domestic-led economic recovery. Such domestically oriented economic policies have had some effect, e.g. as reflected by the revival of consumer spending and related manufacturing output. Hence, it is difficult to identify the new developmental thrusts of post-crisis economic policy. At this point, it appears that the government is fairly undiscriminating in trying to attract all possible investments despite the relevant minister's claim that manufacturing investment approvals have declined due to greater government selectivity.

Before the crisis, there seemed to have been a greater emphasis on attracting higher value-added investments in view of full employment, the high and fast-growing presence of foreign workers and the official desire to progress more rapidly up the technological ladder. But this seems to have been suspended, at least temporarily, perhaps due to the exigencies of economic recovery. Consequently, it now seems as if Malaysia is once again interested in the kinds of investments it seemed to have become averse to just before the onset of the crisis. However, it seems quite likely that Malaysia will revert to its policy of more selective high technology, high productivity investments as recovery proceeds. But even during the earlier pre-crisis phase, there was little evidence of enough commensurate efforts in education, training and human resource development more generally as well as stricter supportive labour migration policies.

Many of the costly misplaced priorities and burdensome liabilities of the last two decades may well continue to take their toll on Malaysian competitiveness beyond the short term. Most worrying is the modest pace of human resource development with widening gaps in skills and other technological capabilities behind Singapore, Taiwan and Korea. Malaysia's modest entrepreneurial capabilities have been additionally retarded by ethnic and crony political biases. The historical domination of the economy from the colonial era by foreign investment has been extended well into the post-colonial period, encouraging accumulation on the basis of 'know-who' types of rent-seeking rather than entrepreneurial 'know-how'. Meanwhile, the costs of doing business in Malaysia have risen unnecessarily with the privatisation of potentially profitable utilities, infrastructure and other essential services.

Notes

1. In a long article serialised over three days in the *New Straits Times* (23-25 August 2000), Mahathir has provided a self-serving summary of Anwar's policy errors without acknowledging widespread popular frustration with the failure and bias of his own policy responses which only seemed to exacerbate the situation, especially by causing the ringgit to devalue further. The following excerpt, from

the first day, is a nonetheless useful summary of some the policy measures introduced in late 1997 under pressure from the market and with IMF advice:

However, instead of providing relief, the Central Bank, on April 27, 1998 announced the following measures to tighten the situation even further:

(i)   The minimum risk weighted capital ratio of the finance companies (who were the worst affected by the crisis) was raised from 8.5 per cent to 9.00 per cent.

(ii) The minimum capital funds of the finance companies was raised from RM5 million to RM300 million to be complied with by end June 1999 and subsequently to RM600 million by end 2000.

(iii) The single customer limit of the financial institutions was reduced from 30 per cent to 25 per cent of the financial institutions' capital funds.

On the fiscal side, the Minister of Finance reduced Government expenditure by 21 per cent. This virtually stopped development work altogether, as salaries, which make up 80 per cent of the Government's budget, could not be cut.

No developmental expenditure meant no contracts for many construction companies and their suppliers. This, together with the other measures of the Central Bank, meant bankruptcy for many companies.

The sum effect of all the above measures was that the banks and businesses which were already suffering from the currency crisis, were pushed into a situation of dire distress.

What the Minister of Finance, together with the Central Bank, had done was to implement a virtual IMF without the IMF loans; namely a combination of tight monetary and fiscal policy, raising the interest rate to defend the exchange rate, attempting to strengthen the banking system through more stringent prudential standards and cutting down public expenditure to improve the current account balance.

As a result of the implementations (*sic*) of these standard IMF prescriptions, Malaysia's economy plunged deeper into recession.

Business was almost at a standstill and the Government revised downwards the expected revenue from corporate taxes for the following year. The foreign media praised the Minister of Finance for implementing a virtual IMF policy.

Everyone was gleefully predicting that the time was near for Malaysia to go to the IMF for help and to surrender economic control to the IMF. Malaysia, it was felt, had no choice but to open up its economy to foreigners without conditions.

There would be rich pickings for foreign capitalists, including those who had invested in the hedge funds.

2. In the *New Straits Times* (25 August 2000), Mahathir has provided a useful summary (p. 16) of the policy measures introduced after he sacked Anwar and appointed himself Finance Minister:

The following chronology of events reflect (*sic*) the fast gear that was engaged by the Executive Committee of the NEAC to revive the economy:

–   Sept 1, 1998: The statutory reserves requirement was reduced from eight per cent to six per cent, injecting RM8 billion into the financial system.

- Sept 3, 1998: The BNM intervention rate was reduced from 9.5 per cent to eight per cent per annum to bring about an equivalent lowering of interest rates across the board in the financial system. The liquid asset ratio requirement was also reduced from 17 per cent to 15 per cent, freeing RM8 billion of liquid assets that could be sold by the financial institutions to fund their operations. The requirement for commercial banks to maintain their vostro balances with the Central Bank was uplifted and this provided extra liquidity to the banks of more than RM1 billion.
- Sept 8, 1998: Loans for the purchase and construction of houses costing RM250,000 and below were exempted from the 20 per cent limit on lending to the broad property sector to further stimulate the construction sector.
- Sept 15, 1998: The maximum margin over the quoted Base Lending Rate was reduced from four percentage points to 2.5 percentage points to lower the lending rate for companies and individuals so as to facilitate viable projects and encourage consumption as well as reduce the interest servicing burden of companies.
- Sept 16, 1998: The SRR was reduced from six per cent to four per cent, releasing another RM8 billion into the economy.
- Sept 23, 1998: The limit for financial institutions on lending for the purchase of shares and unit trust funds was increased from 15 per cent to 20 per cent of total outstanding loans so as to encourage investment in the KLSE.
- Sept 25, 1998: The non-performing loan classification was lengthened from three months to six months to provide borrowers with some breathing space to regularise their accounts.
- Oct 5, 1998: The BNM intervention rate was reduced from eight per cent to 7.5 per cent per annum, to lower further the general interest rate level in the system.
- The maximum margin of financing of 60 per cent imposed on loans for the purchase of residential properties and land was abolished, so as to give a boost to the property sector which had a serious overhang as a result of the crisis.
- Oct 13, 1998: The Loan Complaints and Monitoring Unit (LCMU) was established in Bank Negara Malaysia to assist borrowers facing difficulties in securing financing.
- Nov 10, 1998: The BNM intervention rate was reduced from 7.5 per cent to seven per cent per annum to reduce further the interest rate level in the financial system.
- Nov 19, 1998: The Government established a RM750 million 'Rehabilitation Fund for Small and Medium Industries', to provide financial assistance to viable small and medium industries (SMIs) which were facing temporary cash flow problems.
- Nov 20, 1998: The minimum monthly repayment of credit cards was reduced from 10 per cent to five per cent to promote consumer spending.
- Nov 21, 1998: Every banking Institution was required to set up a 'Special

Loans Rehabilitation Unit' to assist borrowers who had problems repaying their loans. The maximum margin of financing of 85 per cent for passenger cars costing RM40,000 and below was abolished.

– Dec 5, 1998: BNM reduced the maximum lending rate under the Small and Medium Industries Fund and the Special Scheme for Low and Medium Cost Houses from 10 per cent to 8.5 per cent.

However, instead of providing relief, the Central Bank, on April 27, 1998 announced the following measures to tighten the situation even further:

(i) The minimum risk weighted capital ratio of the finance companies (who were the worst affected by the crisis) was raised from 8.5 per cent to 9.00 per cent.

(ii) The minimum capital funds of the finance companies was raised from RM5 million to RM300 million to be complied with by end June 1999 and subsequently to RM600 million by end 2000.

(iii) The single customer limit of the financial institutions was reduced from 30 per cent to 25 per cent of the financial institutions' capital funds.

On the fiscal side, the Minister of Finance reduced Government expenditure by 21 per cent. This virtually stopped development work altogether, as salaries, which make up 80 per cent of the Government's budget, could not be cut.

No developmental expenditure meant no contracts for many construction companies and their suppliers. This together with the other measures of the Central Bank, meant bankruptcy for many companies.

The sum effect of all the above measures was that the banks and businesses which were already suffering from the currency crisis, were pushed into a situation of dire distress.

What the Minister of Finance, together with the Central Bank, had done was to implement a virtual IMF without the IMF loans; namely a combination of tight monetary and fiscal policy, raising the interest rate to defend the exchange rate, attempting to strengthen the banking system through more stringent prudential standards and cutting down public expenditure to improve the current account balance.

As a result of the implementations of these standard IMF prescriptions, Malaysia's economy plunged deeper into recession.

Business was almost at a standstill and the Government revised downwards the expected revenue from corporate taxes for the following year. The foreign media praised the Minister of Finance for implementing a virtual IMF policy.

Everyone was gleefully predicting that the time was near for Malaysia to go to the IMF for help and to surrender economic control to the IMF. Malaysia, it was felt, had no choice but to open up its economy to foreigners without conditions.

There would be rich pickings for foreign capitalists, including those who had invested in the hedge funds.

1

FROM CURRENCY CRISIS TO RECESSION

Jomo K. S.

History has shown that there are many types of currency crises, financial crises and recessions. There is no simple straightforward relationship among the three. In the late 1980s, Malaysia experienced a severe banking crisis after a recession, which had relatively little to do with currency crisis (Jomo 1990). In fact, it appears that the depreciation and then peg of the Malaysian ringgit against the declining (against the Japanese yen) US dollar from late 1985 enabled Malaysia to recover. Export-led industrialisation with foreign direct investment from Japan and the other East Asian newly industrialised economies (especially Taiwan and Singapore) experiencing higher production costs, partly due to their appreciating currencies, were crucial to recovery then.

The 1997-8 crises in East Asia had several common features, particularly with the importance of reversible capital flows, contagion and the deflationary policy responses imposed by the IMF. Yet, as we shall see, Malaysia's experience was different in several important regards. Thailand, South Korea and Indonesia have had much more bank-based financial systems compared to Malaysia's more capital market-oriented system. Partly due to the banking system collapse of the late 1980s, when the ratio of non-performing loans almost reached 30 per cent at the worst point, the prudential regulatory system which emerged in its aftermath was not completely undermined by the pressures for liberalisation in the early and mid-1990s. Crucially, although they grew tremendously in 1996 and the first half of 1997, loans from foreign banks were less important than in the other three crisis-affected economies.

This introductory chapter will show how the currency crisis, triggered by the collapse of the Thai baht in July 1997, led Malaysia into financial crisis and then economic recession. This sequence was not inevitable, but instead, was very much influenced by the nature of Malaysia's financial system and economy, as well as government policy responses as the situation changed, which significantly exacerbated the crisis. Several factors associated with the financial crisis — e.g. loss of investor confidence, sudden and massive capital outflows, credit crunch — had various adverse effects on the real economy and thus, on growth, employment, inflation and social welfare. Like the early debate on the origins of the regional crisis, initial discussion on the economic crisis in Malaysia tended toward extremes of either denial or exaggerated alarm.

There is now no denying that the Malaysian economy experienced a severe downturn from late 1997, with economic contraction through 1998, as the currency crisis developed into a financial crisis, and then, economic recession. However, it is now also generally agreed that the Malaysian economy and population were not as adversely affected as their counterparts in Thailand, South Korea and Indonesia. Though comparative analysis of the nature and impact of the crisis in the region has been left to the last chapter, it has to be emphasised that the financial crisis was not as severe in Malaysia. While the pre-crisis level of indebtedness in Malaysia was very high, the level of foreign exposure was far less — as a share of GDP, and especially, as a share of export earnings. Unlike the others, the level of foreign liabilities did not exceed Malaysia's foreign exchange reserves. After the severe banking crisis of the late 1980s, Malaysian prudential regulation was improved and had not been as badly undermined by liberalisation pressures as in the other three economies. There is an ongoing debate about the actual effects of the unusual Malaysian policy responses associated with capital controls from September 1998 taken up in a later chapter.

From Miracle to Debacle

Labour shortages and the 1988 withdrawal of privileges under the General System of Preferences (GSP) from the first-tier East Asian newly industrialised economies (NIEs) of South Korea, Taiwan, Hong Kong and Singapore encouraged relocation abroad of production facilities from these NIEs. Meanwhile, reforms, selective deregulation as well as new incentives made relocation in Southeast (SE) Asia as well as China more attractive. Malaysia's resource wealth and relatively cheap labour have also sustained production for export of agricultural, forest, mineral and, more recently, manufactured products.

Much of the wealth generated was captured by the business cronies of those in power, who in turn contributed to growth by re-investing in the 'protected' domestic economy, mainly in import-substituting industries, commerce, services, real estate, privatised utilities and infrastructure. Thus, the export-led growth from the late 1980s was soon accompanied by a construction and property boom, fuelled by financial interests favouring such 'short-termist' investments — involving loans with tangible asset collateral, which bankers like — over more productive, but also seemingly more risky investments in manufacturing and agriculture. The exaggerated expansion of investment in such 'non-tradables' also exacerbated current account trade deficits.

Although high growth was sustained for a decade, with modest fiscal surpluses in the nineties, monetary expansion was not excessive and inflation was generally under control. Nevertheless, some other indices have been awry. Foreign savings supplemented the already high domestic savings rates in the country to further accelerate the rate of capital accumulation. Sadly, the additional funds probably encouraged greater property and share purchases, which do not add to productive capacity, but instead raised asset prices. With the heavy foreign domination of most internationally competitive industries in the country (more so than in most countries in the world except neighbouring Singapore), Malaysian investments tended to dominate domestic and primary production.

Thus, the current account deficit — which exceeded RM12 billion every year during 1994-96 — was financed by net capital inflows of foreign savings. Consequently, Malaysia's savings-investment gap was 5 per cent of GNP in 1997. Before the nineties, the gap had been partially bridged by foreign direct investment (FDI), though high levels of FDI and foreign debt had both caused growing investment income outflows abroad. In the nineties, especially in mid-decade, the current account deficit was increasingly covered by short-term capital inflows. Much of these inflows consisted of portfolio investment in the stock market, with larged surges in 1993 and again from 1995 until mid-1997, and with serious adverse consequences following their hasty exit, first in early 1994 and especially from the latter half of 1997.

As noted earlier, capital inflows — into the stock market as well as through bank borrowings — helped bridge current account deficits. These current account imbalances were mainly due to the growing proportion of non-tradeables being produced in Malaysia with imported inputs and equipment. Much of this economic activity involved infrastructure as well as property construction. The authorities seemed lulled into a false sense of complacency by their successful efforts to 'sterilise' such inflows in order to minimise excessive growth in money supply and consequent consumer price inflation. However, the high investment rate, with considerable funds going into the property and stock markets, instead fuelled asset price inflation, mainly involving real estate and share prices.[1] Consequently, by mid-1997, several related problems had emerged from the rapid growth of the previous decade.

The Malaysian economic boom from the late eighties was helped by the significant depreciation of the ringgit against the US dollar from late 1985. Indonesia, Thailand and Malaysia undertook significant devaluations of their currencies against the US dollar as the greenback declined against the yen. As a consequence, while one Malaysian ringgit was equivalent to a hundred yen in 1994, it could only secure half that amount of yen by 1997. Meanwhile, the Korean won, the new Taiwanese dollar and the Singapore dollar also appreciated against the US dollar, and hence, even more against the ringgit.

Contrary to the central bank's claim that the ringgit had been pegged to a basket of the currencies of Malaysia's major trading partners, for all intents and purposes, it had been virtually pegged to the US dollar for many years. The currency had long been trading within a limited band against the greenback — not unlike the other currencies in the region. By continuing to peg their currencies against the US dollar, they failed to adjust to the new circumstances, allowing their currencies to appreciate with the greenback against the yen and other yen-linked currencies in the region. The appreciation of the region's currencies rendered them even less cost competitive, adversely affecting exports and also growth itself.

Such quasi-pegging offered certain advantages, particularly the semblance of stability — including low inflation — so much desired by financial interests. This growing orientation towards financial sector concerns, often at the expense of the real economy, reflected the political weakness of export manufacturer interests in Malaysia — especially in terms of influencing economic policy-making. Almost all internationally competitive non-resource based industrial capability is foreign-owned. The 1990 and 1994 devaluations of China's *yuan* or *renminbi* currency put greater price competitive pressure on the emerging second-tier or second-generation Southeast Asian newly industrialising countries (NICs), including Malaysia.

In mid-1995, the decade-long decline of the US dollar against the yen was reversed after the greenback fell to 79 yen in June. Apparently, then

US Deputy Treasury Secretary Lawrence Summers and then Japanese Finance Vice-Minister for International Affairs Sakakibara Eisuke agreed to let the yen weaken in an attempt to stimulate the flagging Japanese economy. According to Sakakibara, the two sides gave little consideration then to other possible ramifications of the reversal, especially with regard to the East Asian region.

The problem was exacerbated by the failure to 'progress' more rapidly to higher value-added production, mainly due to inadequate or misallocated public investments in education and training as well as limited indigenous internationally competitive industrial capabilities. As the dollar strengthened with the US economy, especially against the Japanese yen from mid-1995, the ringgit and other regional currencies followed suit, adversely affecting Southeast Asian export competitiveness.

The impact of these exchange rate appreciations varied with the countries' respective cost, output and export profiles. With exports, and growth more generally, most adversely affected in Thailand, the property market, construction activity, stock market and financial institutions were also put under strain, setting up the pegged Thai baht as the choice target in the region for currency speculation. Several currency attacks from 1996 severely depleted the Bank of Thailand's reserves, eventually forcing it to let the baht float from 2 July 1997.

With the baht down, currency speculators turned their sights on the other economies in the region that were perceived to have maintained similarly unsustainable US dollar quasi-pegs for their currencies. Both the Indonesian and Filipino monetary authorities gave up defending their currencies after very brief defence attempts. Only the Malaysian central bank put up a more spirited — and expensive — defence of its currency.

The Malaysian ringgit had vacillated around RM2.5 against the US dollar during the first half of 1997 (see Table 1.1). After the Thai baht was floated on 2 July 1997, like other currencies in the region, the ringgit was under strong pressure, especially because, like Thailand, Malaysia had maintained large current account deficits during the early and mid-nineties. The monetary authorities' efforts to defend the ringgit actually strengthened it against the greenback for a few days before the futile ringgit defence effort was given up by the third week of July. Before that, the ringgit rose to RM2.47 against the US dollar from RM2.53, before the authorities finally gave up ringgit support operations after hefty losses. The aborted ringgit defence effort is widely believed to have cost over nine billion ringgit, then worth almost US$4 billion.

Table 1.1
Malaysia: Ringgit Exchange Rates with US Dollar and
Japanese Yen, Annual, 1984-2000, Monthly, January 1997 – March 2000

Year	RM equivalent for one unit of		Month	RM equivalent for one unit of		Month	RM equivalent for one unit of	
	US$	¥		US$	¥		US$	¥
1984	2.34	0.0099	Jan-97	2.49	0.0212	Sep-98	3.81	0.0284
1985	2.48	0.0105	Feb-97	2.49	0.0202	Oct-98	3.80	0.0313
1986	2.58	0.0154	Mar-97	2.48	0.0202	Nov-98	3.80	0.0316
1987	2.52	0.0175	Apr-97	2.50	0.0199	Dec-98	3.80	0.0324
1988	2.62	0.0204	May-97	2.51	0.0211	Jan-99	3.80	0.0336
1989	2.71	0.0197	Jun-97	2.52	0.0220	Feb-99	3.80	0.0326
1990	2.70	0.0188	Jul-97	2.57	0.0223	Mar-99	3.80	0.0312
1991	2.75	0.0205	Aug-97	2.75	0.0233	Apr-99	3.80	0.0318
1992	2.55	0.0201	Sep-97	3.01	0.0249	May-99	3.80	0.0312
1993	2.57	0.0232	Oct-97	3.29	0.0271	Jun-99	3.80	0.0315
1994	2.62	0.0257	Nov-97	3.39	0.0271	Jul-99	3.80	0.0317
1995	2.51	0.0268	Dec-97	3.77	0.0291	Aug-99	3.80	0.0335
1996	2.52	0.0231	Jan-98	4.40	0.0338	Sep-99	3.80	0.0354
1997	2.81	0.0232	Feb-98	3.82	0.0304	Oct-99	3.80	0.0358
1998	3.80	0.0300	Mar-98	3.74	0.0291	Nov-99	3.80	0.0363
1999	3.80	0.0351	Apr-98	3.73	0.0283	Dec-99	3.80	0.0370
			May-98	3.81	0.0283	Jan-00	3.80	0.0362
			Jun-98	3.99	0.0285	Feb-00	3.80	0.0347
			Jul-98	4.15	0.0295	Mar-00	3.80	0.0356
			Aug-98	4.20	0.0290			

Source: Bank Negara Malaysia, *Quarterly Economic Bulletin*, Table V.6.

It was widely believed that the ringgit had become slightly overvalued by the 'quasi-peg' against the US dollar as the American economy and dollar had strengthened significantly in recent years.[2] Hence, the ringgit was expected to depreciate to around RM2.7-2.8 against the dollar, the supposed 'equilibrium' exchange rate based on calculations taking account of purchasing power parity, etc. However, the Malaysian ringgit fell precipitously after mid-July 1997, reaching RM4.88 to the US dollar in early January 1998, its lowest level ever; this represented a collapse by almost half within less than half a year from a high of RM2.47 in mid-July 1997. The stock market fell even more severely. The main Kuala Lumpur Stock Exchange (KLSE) Composite Index (KLCI) dropped from over 1,300 in the first quarter of 1997 to less than 500 in January 1998, around 300 in August 1998 and 262 on 2 September 1998, after the announcement of the capital control measures.

The sudden and massive collapse of the ringgit — politely referred to in the financial community as 'overshooting' — by about two ringgit, much more than the anticipated 'correction' to RM2.7-2.8 against the US dollar, raises serious questions about the very nature of the international monetary system. Foreign and domestic speculators also contributed to the collapse, further exacerbating the panic.

Such behaviour generally constituted self-interested reactions to perceived and anticipated market trends, rather than as part of some conspiracy, as sometimes alleged. As investors scrambled to get out of positions in ringgit and other regional currencies, the currencies fell further, and, with them, the stock and other markets, constituting a rapid vicious cycle. With financial liberalisation, fund managers increasingly have an almost infinite variety of investment options to choose from, and can move their funds much more easily than ever before, especially with the minimal exit restrictions Malaysia and other countries in the region had prided themselves on. The operations and magnitude of hedge fund operations, as well as other currency speculators, have undoubtedly exacerbated these phenomena, with disastrous cumulative consequences.

Like the currencies of other crisis-hit economies, the ringgit fluctuated wildly until mid-1998, weeks before the ringgit was fixed at RM3.8 against the US dollar on 2 September 1998. Much of the downward pressure on the ringgit was induced by regional developments as well as by adverse perceptions of the regional situation. There is also evidence to suggest that inappropriate political rhetoric and policy measures by the political leadership exacerbated the situation.

A Crisis of a New Type

The Southeast Asian currency crises from mid-1997, in turn, precipitated a financial crisis, especially for banking systems in the region, which led to severe recessions throughout the region in 1998, after at least a decade of sustained and rapid economic growth and industrialisation. Once considered by the World Bank (1993) as an impressive example of successful development, the Malaysian economy was transformed from an economic 'miracle' into a 'debacle' in 1998.

There have been many competing explanations for this unprecedented crisis. Many popular accounts, especially in the Western dominated international media, have portrayed the crisis as primarily one of crony capitalism (Jomo 1999). Others have focussed on the vulnerability of the national financial systems in the region with growing international financial liberalisation (e.g. Jomo 1998). Many observers have also highlighted the large current account deficits which Thailand and Malaysia had during most of the early and mid-nineties. Such deficits were largely financed by their net capital account surpluses during this period.

Many observers immediately assumed that the crises were due to poor macroeconomic management, as suggested by the second generation of theories seeking to explain currency crises. Except for large current account deficits and worsening savings-investment gaps, Malaysia's macroeconomic fundamentals were generally sound prior to the crisis (see Tables 1.2 and 1.3). Over the previous decade, Malaysia had enjoyed rapid growth, stable inflation, falling unemployment and fiscal surpluses. As such, the first generation of currency crisis theories — which focused on public sector debt related to fiscal deficits — were also clearly irrelevant for explaining the financial crisis in Malaysia.

However, it also soon became clear that all the governments affected had been maintaining decent macroeconomic balances except for balance of payments current account deficits, especially in the case of Malaysia and Thailand. These had been bridged by massive capital inflows, mostly of a short-term nature, in the form of portfolio investments and also foreign borrowings. The debt — including foreign borrowings — mainly involved the private sector. Continued high growth and savings rates in the region further enhanced their credit standings, as did the low consumer price inflation rates despite huge financial inflows. Thus, monetary and financial policies in the region were largely encouraged by the international financial community.

Once it was clear that the region's macroeconomic balances were not seriously awry, various commentators, including US Federal Reserve Board chairman Alan Greenspan, began to focus on alleged cronyism and its supposed consequences as the new explanation for the crises. Nebulous catch-all terms — such as cronyism and Asian values as well as business practices — seemed to provide ready-made explanations for the crises. Differences in organisations, relations, practices and norms — which had previously been credited with the East Asian miracle by some commentators — were now condemned as the sources of the financial debacle. Popular versions of the political economy of rent seeking are now readily invoked and deployed in the post-crisis discourse as if to explain all, while in fact, often explaining nothing.

Table 1.2
Malaysia: Growth, Inflation and Unemployment Rates, 1984-1999 (%)

Year	Growth*	Inflation (CPI)	Unemployment
1984	7.8	3.6	6.3
1985	-1.0	0.4	7.6
1986	1.2	0.6	8.7
1987	5.2	0.8	8.2
1988	8.9	2.5	8.1
1989	9.2	3.9	7.5
1990	9.7	2.0	5.1
1991	8.7	4.4	4.3
1992	7.8	4.7	3.7
1993	8.3	3.5	3.0
1994	9.2	5.0	2.9
1995	9.5	3.5	2.8
1996	8.6	3.4	2.5
1997	7.7	2.7	2.4
1998	-6.7	5.3	3.2
1999	4.3	2.8	3.0

Note: * GDP growth rate (%) at 1978 constant prices.
Sources: Bank Negara Malaysia, *Annual Report*, various issues, for growth and unemployment figures.

Table 1.3
Malaysia: Key Macroeconomic Variables, 1985-2000 (percentages)

	1985	*1986*	*1987*	*1988*	*1989*	*1990*
GDP growth rate (%) at 1978 prices	-1.0	1.2	5.2	8.9	9.2	9.7
Share of GDP (at current prices)						
Gross national savings	25.6	25.5	31.5	31.2	28.8	30.3
Consumption expenditure	67.4	67.9	62.7	63.7	66.1	65.6
Private	52.1	51.0	47.3	49.4	52.1	51.8
Public	15.3	16.9	15.4	14.3	14.0	13.8
Gross capital formation	29.8	26.3	23.0	24.1	29.8	33.0
Private	15.8	14.3	13.8	15.4	18.9	21.9
Public	14.0	12.1	9.1	8.7	10.9	11.2
Balance of Payments (net)						
Current account	-2.0	-0.4	8.3	5.2	0.7	-2.1
Official long-term capital	3.2	3.0	-3.1	-5.6	-2.4	-2.4
Private long-term capital	2.2	1.8	1.3	2.1	4.4	5.3
Balance of long-term capital	5.5	4.7	-1.8	-3.5	2.0	2.9
Basic balance	3.5	4.3	6.6	1.7	2.7	0.8
Private short-term capital	1.1	-0.1	-3.1	-3.2	1.5	1.1
Errors and omissions	-0.5	1.8	0.2	0.3	-1.0	2.5
Overall balance	4.1	6.1	3.6	-1.2	3.3	4.5
Implicit capital inflows	6.1	6.5	-4.7	-6.4	2.6	6.6
Short-term capital inflows	0.6	1.8	-2.9	-2.9	0.6	3.7
Reserves (months of retained imports)	5	7	7	5	4	4
Services balance as % of GNP	-14	-13	-11	-12	-12	-9
Current account as % of GNP	-2	-1	9	5	1	-2

Notes: (1) Short-term capital inflows = Private short-term capital + Errors and omissions.
　　　　　　Implicit capital inflows = Balance of long-term capital + Short-term capital inflows.
　　　　(2) Figures for 1999 and 2000 are computed based on Bank Negara Malaysia, *Annual
　　　　　　Report 1999*, Table A.6, p. 19 and *Economic Report 1999/2000*, Table 2.3, p. xiii.

Table 1.3 (continued)
Malaysia: Key Macroeconomic Variables, 1985–2000 (percentages)

1991	1992	1993	1994	1995	1996	1997	1998	1999	2000[a]
8.7	7.8	8.3	9.2	9.5	8.6	7.7	-6.7	5.4[a]	5.8[b]
29.2	31.6	34.6	33.6	33.9	37.1	37.3	39.6	36.6	33.4
65.9	63.3	60.9	60.4	60.3	57.1	56.2	51.5	53.0	54.9
52.2	50.3	48.3	48.1	47.9	46.0	45.3	41.5	41.6	43.8
13.7	13.0	12.6	12.3	12.4	11.1	10.9	10.0	11.4	11.1
36.4	36.6	38.9	40.2	43.6	42.5	43.1	26.8	22.2	22.3
24.0	22.3	24.9	27.6	31.2	31.3	31.8	15.6	11.2	11.0
12.3	14.3	14.0	12.6	12.4	11.2	11.3	11.2	11.0	11.3
-8.6	-3.7	-4.6	-7.6	-9.7	-4.4	-5.6	12.9	14.0	11.1
-0.5	-1.9	0.6	0.4	2.8	0.3	1.6	0.8	0.8	n.a.
8.1	8.8	7.5	5.5	4.7	5.0	5.1	3.0	3.0	n.a.
7.6	6.9	8.1	6.0	7.5	5.3	6.8	3.7	3.8	n.a.
-1.0	3.1	3.4	-1.6	-2.3	0.9	1.2	16.7	17.8	n.a.
3.8	7.9	8.1	-4.3	1.1	4.1	-4.6	-7.3	-7.3	n.a.
-0.3	0.1	5.4	1.7	-0.9	-2.5	-0.4	4.8	4.8	n.a.
2.5	11.1	17.0	-4.2	-2.0	2.5	-3.9	14.2	15.3	n.a.
11.2	14.8	21.6	3.3	7.8	6.9	1.7	1.2	1.3	n.a.
3.5	8.0	13.5	-2.6	0.3	1.6	-5.0	-2.5	-2.5	n.a.
4	6	8	6	4	4	3	6	5.9	n.a.
-10	-10	-10	-9	-9	-8	-9	-8	-8.9	-9.2
-9	-4	-5	-8	-10	-5	-6	14	16.9	14.2

Notes: [a] Forecasted by Bank Negara Malaysia.
        [b] At constant 1987 prices.

Sources: Bank Negara Malaysia (BNM), *Quarterly Economic Bulletin*, Table VI.1, VIII.1;
          BNM, *Annual Report*, various issues, for GDP figures.

Thus, a popular explanation of the East Asian crisis emphasises corruption, cronyism as well as lack of transparency, resulting in moral hazard, with adverse consequences for the economy. This diagnosis, however, fails to provide a satisfactory explanation of why the crisis — which started in Thailand — spread to the rest of the region so quickly, leading to massive disruption of the economy. Crony capitalism — which has existed for some time — fails to explain how Malaysia sustained rapid growth for four decades after independence in 1957 without experiencing an earlier financial crisis of comparable magnitude. More importantly, as pointed out by UNCTAD (1998), this explanation also ignores the similarities with the financial crises in developed and developing economies, which have been occurring with increasing frequency since the late 1970s.

Despite ongoing debates about the significance of macroeconomic fundamentals and crony capitalism in contributing to the East Asian economic crises since mid-1997, there is now little disagreement that they began as currency and financial crises. It will be argued here that the currency and financial crises in Malaysia became a crisis of the 'real economy' owing to the government's policy responses, especially due to financial market pressures and the IMF. Related work (Montes 1998; Jomo 1998) shows that the crises have been due to the undermining of previous systems of international and national economic governance due to deregulation and other developments associated with financial liberalisation and globalisation. Thus, the erosion of effective financial governance at both international and national levels created conditions that led to the crises.

Industrial policy or selective state intervention in Malaysia has been of much poorer quality and considerably less effective than in the first tier newly industrialised East Asian economies of South Korea, Taiwan and Singapore for various reasons. Instead, there has been much more state intervention motivated by other (non-developmentalist) considerations, especially in Malaysia and Indonesia (Jomo *et al.* 1997). Such interventions — now often cited as evidence of 'crony capitalism' — bear some of the responsibility for the vulnerability of the second-tier Southeast Asian NICs to the factors that precipitated the financial crisis in the region in mid-1997. Even more importantly, such interests have influenced government policy responses in ways that have exacerbated the crisis. In other words, while 'crony capitalism' does not really explain the origins of the crisis, except in so far as crony financial interests were responsible for the financial policies from the mid-nineties which led to the crisis, it has certainly exacerbated the crisis in Malaysia.

It is worthwhile to emphasise at the outset that Malaysia's experience differs from those of other East Asian crisis-hit economies in at least four respects. First, although prudential regulation had deteriorated with growing financial liberalisation, especially since the mid-eighties, the situation in Malaysia was not as bad as elsewhere in the region. Second, although the Malaysian banking system had contributed to asset price inflation, and was thus severely affected by the crisis, Malaysian banks and corporations had far less access to international borrowing than their counterparts in other crisis-affected economies. Unlike the others, foreign bank loans did not figure as significantly in the story of the Malaysian crisis, whereas capital market flows, especially into and out of the stock market, figured more prominently. Third, as a consequence of its reduced exposure to private bank borrowings from abroad, Malaysia was not in a situation of having to go cap in hand to the International Monetary Fund (IMF) or to others for emergency international credit facilities. Fourth, for most of the second half of 1997, and again from mid-1998, the Malaysian authorities deliberately pursued unconventional measures in response to the deteriorating situation, with rather mixed results.

Hence, while there are important parallels between the Malaysian experience and those of its crisis-affected neighbours, there are also important differences. It is tempting to exaggerate the significance of either similarities or contrasts to support particular preconceived arguments when, in fact, the nature of the experiences do not allow strong analytical or policy conclusions to be drawn. For example, whereas South Korea, Thailand and Indonesia experienced positive growth in the first quarter of 1999, Malaysian economic recovery only began in the second quarter. Critics were very quick to blame Malaysia's unorthodox measures for its later recovery. Conversely, the Malaysian regime has been equally quick to claim success for its approach on the basis of limited evidence of a stronger recovery since then, which critics have just as readily attributed to a technical rebound, the externally-induced electronics boom and 'unsustainable' government measures.

Policy Responses: Deepening the Crisis

Conventional policy making wisdom — including IMF prescriptions — cut government spending in the wake of the crisis to further transform what had started as a currency crisis into a full-blown financial crisis, then into a crisis of the real economy as the Southeast Asian region sharply went into recession in 1998.

The ringgit's collapse was initially portrayed by Malaysian Prime Minister Mahathir as being exclusively due to speculative attacks on Southeast Asian currencies. In a study published in mid-April 1998, the IMF acknowledges that currency speculation precipitated the collapse of the baht, but denies the role of currency speculation in the collapse of the other East Asian currencies. While currency speculation *per se* may not have brought down the other currencies, the contagion effect undoubtedly contributed to the collapse of the other currencies in the region not protected by the large reserves held by Japan, China, Taiwan, Hong Kong and Singapore. Contagion — exacerbated by the herd-like panicky investment decisions of foreign portfolio investors who perceived the region as much more similar and integrated than it actually is (e.g. in terms of trade or investment links, or even structural characteristics) — quickly snowballed to cause massive capital flight.

As acknowledged by Mahathir, the ringgit probably fell much further than might otherwise have been the case due to international market reactions to his various contrarian statements, including his tough speech in Hong Kong on 20 September 1997, at a seminar before the joint World Bank-IMF annual meeting. Arguing that 'currency trading is unnecessary, unproductive and immoral', Mahathir argued that it should be 'stopped' and 'made illegal'.

Most damagingly, he seemed to be threatening a unilateral ban on foreign exchange purchases unrelated to imports by the Malaysian authorities (which never happened). Even before his Hong Kong speech, Mahathir had railed against George Soros (calling him a 'moron') and international speculators for weeks, even suggesting dark Western conspiracies to undermine the East Asian achievement. Thus, Mahathir's remarks continued to undermine confidence and to exacerbate the situation until he was finally reined in by regional government leaders, and perhaps even his cabinet colleagues.

The Prime Minister's partly — but not entirely — ill-founded attacks reinforced the impression of official denial, with blame for the crisis attributed abroad. The fact that there was some basis for his rantings was hardly enough to salvage his reputation in the face of an increasingly hostile Western media. Thus, until Soeharto's illness (in December 1997) and subsequent recalcitrant behaviour (in the eyes of the IMF and the international financial community) in 1998, Mahathir was demonised as the regional 'bad boy'. Meanwhile, some other governments in the region had little choice but to go 'cap in hand' to the IMF and the US and Japanese governments, in desperate efforts to restore confidence and to secure funds to service the fast-growing 'non-performing' foreign debt liabilities, although they were mainly privately-held.

Other official Malaysian policy responses did not help. In late August 1997, the authorities *designated* the top one hundred indexed KLCI share counters. Designation required actual presentation of scrip at the moment of transaction (rather than later, as was the normal practice), ostensibly to check 'short-selling', which was exacerbating the stock market collapse. This ill-conceived measure also adversely affected liquidity, causing the stock market to fall further. The government's threat to use repressive measures against commentators making unfavourable reports about the Malaysian economy strengthened the impression that the government had a lot to hide from public scrutiny. The mid-October 1997 announcement of the 1998 Malaysian Budget was seen by 'the market', i.e. mainly foreign financial interests, as only the latest in a series of Malaysian government policy measures tantamount to 'denial' of the gravity of the crisis and its possible causes.

A post-Cabinet meeting announcement on 3 September 1997 of the creation of a special RM60 billion fund for selected Malaysians was understandably seen as a bail-out facility designed to save 'cronies' from disaster. Although the fund was never properly institutionalised, and many government officials deny its existence, government-controlled public funds, mainly from the Employees Provident Fund (EPF) and Petronas, have been deployed to bail out some of the most politically well-connected and influential, including Mahathir's eldest son, the publicly-listed corporation set up by his party co-operative (KUB) and the country's largest conglomerate (Renong), previously controlled by his party and now believed to be ultimately controlled by him and his confidante, second-time Finance Minister Daim. The protracted UEM-Renong saga from mid-November 1997 was probably most damaging. The nature of this 'bail-out' — to the tune of RM2.34 billion — gravely undermined public confidence in the Malaysian investment environment as stock market rules were bent at the expense of minority shareholders.

The situation was initially worsened by the perception that Mahathir and Daim had taken over economic policy making from Anwar, who had endeared himself over the years to the international financial community. Daim's return to the frontline of policy-making caused ambiguity about who was really in charge from early to mid-1998, and about what to expect. Some of the measures introduced by the Finance Ministry and the central bank since early December 1997 and in late March 1998 were also perceived as preempting the likely role and impact of the National Economic Action Council (NEAC). The establishment of the NEAC had been announced in late 1997 to be chaired by the Prime Minister, although Daim was clearly in charge as executive director. Daim was later appointed Minister with Special Functions, operating from the Prime Minister's Department, in late June 1998 — right after the annual UMNO general assembly. He was subsequently made First Finance Minister in late 1998, with his protégé Mustapha Mohamad functioning as Second Finance Minister while retaining the Ministry of Entrepreneurial Development portfolio.

The question of IMF intervention in Malaysia has become the subject of some mythology, as various groups have rather different perceptions of the IMF's actual record and motives. For many of those critical of Malaysian government policy (not just in response to the crisis), IMF intervention was expected to put an end to all, or at least much, which they considered wrong or wished to be rid off. In the wake of the protracted wrangling between the IMF and Soeharto's government in Indonesia, this pro-IMF lobby in Malaysia saw the IMF as the only force capable of bringing about desired reforms which domestic forces could not bring about on their own. Ironically, many of them failed to recognise that the measures[3] introduced from December 1997 were akin to what the IMF would have liked to see. These measures (*White Paper*, Box 1, pp. 25-26) included:

- Bank Negara raising its three-month intervention rate from 8.7 per cent at the end of 1997 to 11.0 per cent in early February 1998;
- drastic reductions in government expenditure; and
- redefining non-performing loans as loans in arrears for three months, down from the previous six months.

Such contractionary measures helped transform the financial crisis into a more general economic crisis for the country.

The currency and financial crises also contributed to new macroeconomic problems, besides undermining economic development efforts more generally:

- with the massive ringgit devaluation, imported inflation was inevitable, especially for Malaysia's very open economy, whose gross exports are equivalent to the amount it produces; it seems to import slightly less, but of course, the high import content of many manufactured exports greatly exaggerates these measures of openness;
- over-zealous efforts to check inflation in these circumstances exacerbated deflationary tendencies;
- business failures, growing unemployment and reduced incomes exacerbated contractionary tendencies;
- the stock market collapse (by more than half since its peak in the first quarter of 1997) adversely affected both consumption and investment ('wealth effect');

- credit restraint policies adopted by the government from December 1997 further dampened economic activity;
- the flight of foreign funds could not be easily replaced by domestic funds which would have had to be diverted from alternative uses;
- difficulties in recovering loans have constrained the financial system and economic activity;
- the depreciated ringgit increased the relative magnitude of the mainly privately-held foreign debt as well as the external debt-servicing burden;
- technological progress is likely to slow down with the greater costs of foreign technology acquisitions as well as the greater attraction of falling back on cheap labour and production costs, instead of making the human resource investments to achieve higher productivity.

Tighter monetary policy from late 1997 exacerbated deflationary pressures due to government spending cuts from around the same time. Thus, macroeconomic policy responses to the currency and financial crises can be said to have worsened the situation, through the adoption of contractionary policies. Given the massive currency devaluation in Malaysia's very open economy, the rise of inflation at this time was virtually unavoidable, with little to be achieved by such tight macroeconomic policy. Of course, such policies were also intended to stem the capital flight facilitated by the long-standing policy of capital account convertibility. But again, there is little evidence of success on this score, just as there was little likelihood of effectiveness in this regard in conditions of contagion and herd behaviour.

The 1998 Commonwealth Games and Asia Pacific Economic Co-operation (APEC) summit in Kuala Lumpur and various government efforts to prop up the real property market, especially its residential component, may only have served to delay its inevitable collapse. The recent and imminent completion of many more construction projects will exacerbate the glut in high class residential, office and commercial segments of the property market. The accelerated continuation of the new Putrajaya administrative capital is likely to exacerbate the over supply of office space. Given the heavy exposure of so many companies to the sector, especially among the KLCI's top one hundred counters, this could drag out the crisis in the country much longer than in neighbouring countries, where the property markets have already collapsed.

The Malaysian Government's White Paper on the *Status of the Malaysian Economy*, issued on 6 April 1999, sums up many of the factors contributing to the ongoing economic crisis as well as most of its policy responses. However, it does so by whitewashing Mahathir's and Daim's roles in worsening the crisis, and instead implies that Anwar Ibrahim was solely responsible for all domestic policy errors. Conversely, Anwar is not credited for establishing the key institutions for financial restructuring and recovery such as Danaharta, Danamodal and the Corporate Debt Restructuring Committee (CDRC). Unfortunately, the abuse of the debt workout processes has caused concern about their integrity and the overall credibility of the recovery strategy. Such a tendentious account not only contradicts the facts, but was also unlikely to inspire the investor confidence so badly needed to ensure economic recovery.

It is well known, for example, that Mahathir's KLCI 'designation' ruling drastically reduced liquidity in the stock market, precipitating a collapse from late August 1997. Similarly, the UEM reverse take-over to bail-out Renong in mid-November 1997, supported by Mahathir and Daim, resulted in a 20 per cent stock market contraction in three days! Mahathir's rhetoric about various western conspiracies against Malaysia — and the rest of the region — severely undermined international confidence and the value of the Malaysian ringgit. However, despite its current nationalist rhetoric, the White Paper shows how foreign investments have been selectively encouraged to protect and save interests the regime favours, including those who contributed to the crisis.

Boom and Bust

The suddenness of the economic contraction, in sharp contrast to the previous decade of uninterrupted economic growth averaging around eight per cent (see Tables 1.1 and 1.2), probably contributed to the marked differences in reactions. Many who saw the sustained growth and accumulated wealth of earlier years suddenly dissipate could not believe what was happening. After experiencing the severe financial shock, many expected the economic recession to be similarly catastrophic by causing massive insolvencies, unemployment and social upheaval exacerbated by hyperinflation due to the huge currency devaluations.

At the macroeconomic level, the contraction in Gross Domestic Product (GDP) was significant, especially through 1998. Tables 1.4 and 1.5 show Malaysian GDP growth rates, in total and by sector, computed annually for the 1990s, and quarterly from 1997 to 1999 (see Figure 1.1). The positive growth trend in the 1990s before 1998 is evident from Table 1.4. The quarterly data in Table 1.5 show the downward trend from the third quarter of 1997 (from decreasing, but still positive growth in late 1997) to deepening recession in 1998. The decline in 1998 was especially significant in the construction and manufacturing sectors, which contracted by 23.0 per cent

Table 1.4a

Malaysia: Annual Changes in Gross Domestic Product by Economic Activity, 1990-1999

(percentage changes based on *1987 constant prices*)

	1990	1991	1992	1993	1994	1995	1996	1997	1998	1999
Agriculture, forestry and fishing	-0.6	-0.1	6.9	-3.1	-1.9	-2.5	4.5	0.4	-4.5	3.9
Mining and quarrying	0.1	4.7	4.6	-4.0	6.0	22.9	2.9	3.0	1.8	-4.0
Manufacturing	15.3	14.0	7.0	14.6	11.4	11.4	18.2	10.4	-13.7	13.5
Construction	18.6	15.5	10.8	10.8	15.1	21.1	16.2	10.6	-23.0	-5.6
Electricity, gas and water	6.1	0.2	18.7	28.6	14.0	18.9	9.6	-5.4	3.0	4.9
Transport, storage and communications	12.2	9.2	5.9	12.1	18.7	12.1	7.4	11.6	0.9	3.8
Wholesale and retail trade, hotels and restaurants	16.3	16.1	12.3	10.9	12.0	11.5	7.9	8.0	-3.1	2.1
Finance, insurance, real estate & business services	13.3	15.4	20.3	25.3	4.2	9.7	17.0	18.9	-4.3	1.2
Government services	2.0	4.5	5.8	7.2	5.4	1.4	1.7	8.6	1.8	6.6
Other services	11.9	12.6	9.2	10.1	10.6	11.8	7.9	7.2	3.8	2.1
GDP at Purchasers' Prices	*9.0*	*9.5*	*8.9*	*9.9*	*9.2*	*9.8*	*10.0*	*7.5*	*-7.5*	*5.4*

Source: BNM, *Monthly Statistical Bulletin*, Table VI.2.

Table 1.4b
Malaysia: Annual Changes in Gross Domestic Product by Economic Activity, 1990-1999
(percentage changes based on *1978 constant prices*)

	1990	1991	1992	1993	1994	1995	1996	1997	1998	1999
Agriculture, forestry and fishing	0.2	0.2	4.7	4.3	-1.0	1.1	2.2	1.3	-4.0	4.6
Mining and quarrying	5.1	2.4	1.7	-0.5	2.5	9.0	4.5	1.0	0.8	-1.2
Manufacturing	15.7	13.9	10.5	12.9	14.9	14.2	12.3	12.5	-10.2	8.9
Construction	19.1	14.3	11.7	11.2	14.1	17.3	14.2	9.5	-24.5	-3.6
Electricity, gas and water	13.5	11.2	13.8	12.7	13.7	13.0	12.1	13.0	3.6	4.2
Transport, storage and communication	13.3	10.9	6.6	6.8	12.3	13.8	9.7	8.4	1.2	3.0
Wholesale and retail trade, hotels and restaurants	14.8	14.1	11.1	11.1	8.0	10.1	9.4	7.0	-2.0	1.5
Finance, insurance, real estate and business services	14.6	12.6	10.4	10.4	10.0	10.5	14.6	9.5	4.4	1.0
Government services	4.8	4.5	2.6	9.5	9.4	3.9	4.2	6.1	2.4	3.5
Other services	10.5	9.1	8.3	8.2	7.1	7.8	8.4	7.2	2.5	4.0
GDP at Purchasers' Prices	*9.7*	*8.7*	*7.6*	*8.3*	*9.3*	*9.4*	*8.6*	*7.7*	*-6.7*	*4.3*

Note: Figures for 1999 are in 1987 constant prices.
Sources: BNM, *Monthly Statistical Bulletin*, October 1998, Table VI.2, p. 79; April 1999, Table VI.2, p. 82. Ministry of Finance, *Economic Report 1999/2000*, Table 2.2, pp. x and xi.

Table 1.5
Malaysia: Quarterly Change in Gross Domestic Product by Economic Activity, 1997-2000
(year-on-year percentage change, at 1987 constant prices)

	1997				1998				1999				2000
	1 qtr.	2 qtr.	3 qtr.	4 qtr.	1 qtr.	2 qtr.	3 qtr.	4 qtr.	1 qtr.	2 qtr.	3 qtr.	4 qtr.	1 qtr.
Agriculture, forestry and fishing	1.8	3.9	-1.5	-2.1	-2.1	-6.9	-4.0	-4.8	-3.5	8.6	3.6	6.3	2.9
Mining and quarrying	-0.5	2.6	1.9	8.1	0.6	0.3	1.2	5.1	-2.3	-5.9	-3.0	-5.0	0.8
Manufacturing	11.8	9.6	11.3	9.2	-5.8	-10.3	-18.9	-18.6	-1.1	10.8	19.5	25.2	27.3
Construction	17.5	10.8	7.3	7.8	-14.5	-19.8	-28.0	-29.0	-16.6	-7.9	0.9	2.7	1.2
Electricity, gas and water	-4.3	-6.1	-7.1	-4.0	0.2	4.6	2.9	4.3	2.4	4.4	7.1	5.4	
Transport, storage and communication	10.5	16.8	14.6	5.2	6.4	2.9	-1.8	-3.4	1.7	0.6	3.4	9.0	
Wholesale and retail trade, hotels and restaurants	7.3	9.5	10.2	5.2	2.8	-1.9	-8.1	-4.7	-2.1	-1.5	4.0	6.8	6.3
Finance, insurance, real estate and business services	19.8	22.4	19.8	14.3	5.9	-2.6	-8.9	-10.4	-6.6	1.8	6.0	3.6	
Government services	24.3	8.7	4.8	0.1	-14.9	-12.4	4.4	5.4	14.5	1.8	2.7	9.0	
Other services	5.9	7.3	7.6	8.1	7.4	5.5	1.9	0.3	1.7	0.4	3.2	2.7	
GDP at Purchasers' Prices	8.6	8.4	7.7	5.6	-3.1	-5.2	-10.9	-10.3	-1.3	4.1	8.1	10.6	11.7

Sources: BNM, *Monthly Statistical Bulletin*, Table VI.2; Department of Statistics, *Quarterly Gross Domestic Product*, First and Second Quarter 1999; BNM, *Quarterly Economic Bulletin*, First Quarter 2000.

Figure 1.1
Malaysia: Sectoral GDP Growth by Quarter, Year-on-Year, 1997-1999

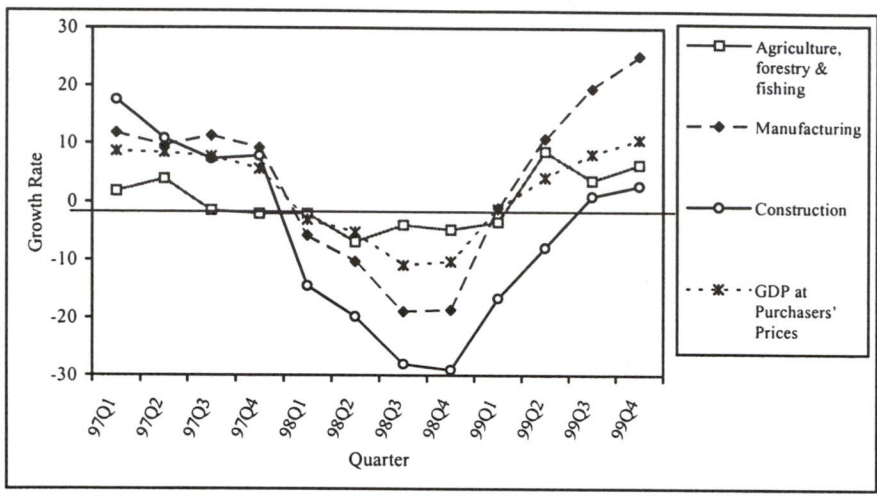

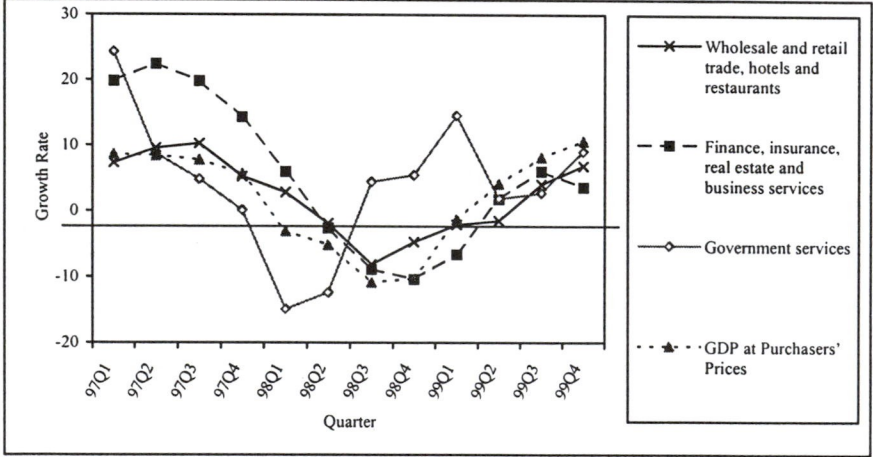

and 13.7 per cent respectively. It was less pronounced in agriculture, which declined by 4.5 per cent, partly due to the adverse impact of the El Nino drought and the agronomic impact of the substantial haze due to continuing forest fires in neighbouring Indonesia.

Figure 1.2, which traces some macroeconomic indicators from the mid-1980s to 1998, reveals important characteristics of the 1998 recession, some

Figure 1.2
Malaysia: Macroeconomic Indicators, 1984-1998

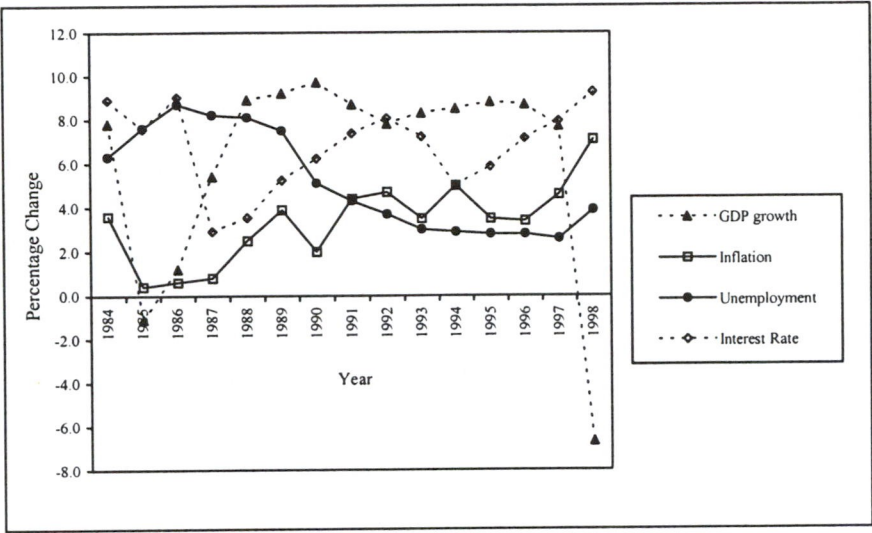

Note: The interest rate used is the three-month inter-bank rate.
Source: BNM, *Monthly Statistical Bulletin*, Tables VI.2 and VI.12.

of which have been unprecedented. It is important to note that while national output contracted sharply and inflation jumped, unemployment increased less dramatically in 1998. Of course, such statistical indicators must be used circumspectly; while numbers are crucial for analysis, their accuracy must also be considered. The inadequacy of these indicators will also be addressed later. At this stage, one should consider some stylised facts about the Malaysian economic condition from late 1997: Gross Domestic Product (GDP) shrank, unemployment and inflation rose, private investment and consumption fell, while credit growth declined as the proportion of non-performing loans (NPLs) rose. In terms of social welfare, the limited social security provisions in Malaysia have aggravated these economic impacts. The continued influence of powerful politically influential business interests over policy-making, even in response to the crisis, probably further undermined social welfare in net terms.

Manufacturing and construction had experienced high growth in the 1990s. These sectors also employ substantial numbers in the labour force. Manufacturing thrived, boosted by massive foreign direct investment and export growth. After the property slump in the late 1980s, construction boomed again in the 1990s. Wholesale and retail trade, as well as hotels and restaurants also experienced a 3.1 per cent contraction in 1998. The performance of these sectors generally reflects the vitality of consumer demand and is probably quite sensitive to the 'wealth effect'. The rapid expansion of these activities, amid buoyant consumer and investor sentiment, is evident in high annual growth rates from 1990 to 1997. Their decline in 1998 reflects decreasing private consumption expenditure. Similarly, the rapid, but somewhat erratic growth of financial, real estate and business services reflects the rise and fall of general market confidence. Growth in this sector fell from 18.9 per cent in 1997 to -4.3 per cent in 1998. Elsewhere in the economy, transport, storage and communication witnessed declining growth, from 11.6 per cent in 1997 to 0.9 per cent in 1998, while government services also fell from 8.6 per cent to 1.8 per cent growth due to fiscal cuts. On the whole, all sectors performed worse in 1998 than in the previous year, except for electricity, gas and water utilities, which had contracted earlier, during 1997. Overall economic contraction was reflected by the sharp fall in annual GDP growth, from 7.5 per cent in 1997 to -7.5 per cent in 1998, using 1987 as the base year, or from 7.7 per cent in 1997 to -6.7 per cent in 1998, using earlier data with 1978 as the base year.

Quarterly figures provide a more vivid picture of the suddenness of the recessionary impact of the financial crisis (see Table 1.5). The economy contracted in every quarter of 1998, compared to the corresponding quarters for 1997, specifically by 3.1 per cent (first quarter), 5.2 per cent (second quarter), 10.9 per cent (third quarter) and 10.3 per cent (fourth quarter) respectively. The contraction abated in the first quarter of 1999, when quarterly GDP was still 1.3 per cent less than in the first quarter of 1998.

Interestingly, as noted earlier, agricultural activities had begun to slow down from mid-1997, prior to the currency and financial crises, mainly due to El Nino weather conditions and Indonesian forest fires. Other sectors began to contract in 1998 in the aftermath of the financial crisis. Manufacturing and construction fell in 1998, most sharply in the third and fourth quarters. Manufacturing output plunged by 18.9 per cent in the third quarter of 1998 and 18.6 per cent in the fourth, while construction collapsed by 28.0 per cent and 29.0 per cent respectively. Government services were reduced by 14.9 per cent and 12.4 per cent respectively in the first two quarters of 1998, but increased in the last two quarters of 1998 by 4.4 per cent and 5.4 per cent respectively. In the first quarter of 1999, government expenditure was stepped up even more, i.e. by 14.5 per cent, becoming the fastest growing sector for that period, reflecting government efforts to boost aggregate demand while the rest of the economy was still contracting.

Quarterly GDP figures indicate recovery on almost all fronts from the second quarter of 1999, with the quarterly equivalent of an overall year on year growth of 8.1 per cent in the third quarter. These impressive positive growth numbers denote the increase from the very contractionary third and fourth quarters of 1998 when GDP dropped 9.0 per cent. Nonetheless, there are other figures to suggest that the recovery can be sustained in the medium term. Importantly, in the third and fourth quarters of 1999, the manufacturing sector produced 19.5 and 25.2 per cent more than in the third and fourth quarters of 1998. Over the same periods, the construction sector began to register positive quarterly growth, though only by modest rates of 0.9 and 2.7 per cent respectively. The utilities and service sectors (domestic trade, transport and communication, and financial and business services) also improved their performances (see Table 1.5). However, the trends for agriculture and mining have been less encouraging, with adverse implications for living standards in the countryside, especially in light of commodity price declines during this period, e.g. for palm oil (see Table 1.6).

It has been suggested that the fixed exchange rate and lower interest rates associated with the introduction of capital controls from September 1998 helped Malaysia rebound from the crisis. However, this is difficult to confirm as exchange rates became more stable and interest rates declined in the region generally from around the same time after the international responses to the Russian crisis and its aftermath on Wall Street in August 1998. Also, all the crisis-hit economies in the region recovered from the beginning of 1999, whereas Malaysian recovery dates to the second quarter. And although the Malaysian recovery since has been stronger than for Thailand and Indonesia, Korea has performed more impressively. Also, Malaysia had not been as badly affected by the crisis compared to these three other economies in the first place, so meaningful comparisons remain problematic.

Trade and Prices

Malaysia's external trade data suggest some significant changes in the composition of economic growth from the mid-1990s, as in the rest of the region. In 1998, imports declined by 18.3 per cent, while exports only fell slightly by 0.7 per cent. This contrasts with the previous sustained expansion in external trade, which grew most in 1994, when exports and imports registered 22.5 and 27.7 per cent growth respectively. Importantly, the rate

Table 1.6
Malaysia: Prices and Export Values of Selected Major Commodities, 1991-2000

Year	Petroleum* Unit Price (RM/tonne)	Petroleum* Export Value (RM mil.)	Palm Oil Export Value (RM/tonne)	Palm Oil Unit Price (RM mil.)	Sawn Timber Price (RM/m³)	Sawn Timber Export Value (RM mil.)
1991	451.2	10,195.6	906.9	5044.9	599.1	3,008.3
1992	405.0	9,146.9	974.1	5436.6	646.8	3,487.7
1993	380.0	7,996.0	985.8	5797.3	829.8	4,545.6
1994	344.0	6,548.0	1,266.7	8,365.3	911.3	4,331.1
1995	349.7	6,701.0	1,533.8	10,395.3	885.2	3,837.5
1996	412.0	7,211.8	1,296.0	9,436.0	798.9	3,120.2
1997	445.3	7,068.6	1,424.9	10,809.8	904.3	2,780.8
1998	416.9	7,509.8	2,366.4	17,779.0	941.4	2,525.7
1999	525.0	9,305.9	1,614.7	14,475.2	996.0	2,806.6
2000 (1st quarter)	745.3	n.a.	n.a.	n.a.	n.a.	n.a.

Note: * Crude and partly refined; n.a – not available.
Source: BNM, *Monthly Statistical Bulletin*, Tables VIII.6. and VIII.7.

of increase in goods trade was already slowing down before the crisis, probably due to increased investment in and production of non-tradeables during 1995 and 1996. In 1996, imports only increased 4.2 per cent, while exports increased 7.2 per cent. As in the rest of the region, Malaysian export growth was certainly lower prior to the financial meltdown, probably due to higher production costs with full employment and ringgit appreciation — together with the US dollar — from mid-1995.

Large proportions of Malaysia's agricultural and natural resource output are exported. Furthermore, export earnings are subject to fluctuations in the international demand for and prices of commodities, mostly denominated in US dollars. In the case of agriculture, climate and other conditions have also had adverse impacts on output levels, e.g. during the El Nino drought and the forest fire induced haze. Table 1.6 shows the average prices of as well as export earnings from selected commodities. Malaysia is not considered a major world producer of petroleum; it supplies substantial amounts of palm oil, rubber and tropical timber to international markets.

In 1998, oil prices declined. The weighted average price of crude petroleum dropped from US$21.1 per barrel in 1997 to US$13.8 in 1998. However, owing to the massive ringgit depreciation, the fall in refined petroleum export earnings, in ringgit per ton, was less severe, from RM445.3 in 1997 to RM416.9 in 1998. Exports of crude and partly refined petroleum substantially increased in volume, from 15.9 to 18.0 million tons, but increased only marginally in value, from 7.1 to 7.5 billion ringgit. This probably reflected official efforts to expand output to compensate for the drop in world petroleum prices. The ringgit prices of rubber and saw logs also declined from 1997 to 1998 despite the massive ringgit depreciation, slipping from 291.7 to 286.0 sen per kg, and from RM366.7 to RM344.4 per cubic metre respectively. However, not all commodity prices were adversely affected, but average sawn timber prices only increased slightly from RM904.3 to RM941.4 per cubic metre, i.e. much less than due to the ringgit depreciation.

The price of palm oil, Malaysia's largest primary commodity export after petroleum, rose from RM1,424.9 to RM2,366.4 per ton, i.e. much more than due to the ringgit's devaluation. Exports of palm oil in 1998 were lower than in 1997, slipping to 7,512.9 from 7,609.2 million tons. Despite this, the value of palm oil exports soared from RM10,809.8 million to RM17,779.0 million. By mid-1999, however, the bumper soy bean harvest began to exert tremendous downward pressure on palm oil prices, with likely impact on the fortunes of Malaysia's oil palm estates.

It is unclear to what extent the financial crisis — as opposed to other factors — impacted on the agricultural sector. Both El Nino and La Nina weather phenomena have been blamed for inflicting drought and then floods on farmland, adversely affecting the harvests of 1997 and 1998. Such perverse climatic conditions have evidently impacted on farm output and communities, although a systematic analysis has been difficult to develop.

Malaysian economic recovery may have gained from the weak ringgit although there is little evidence of an export boom due to this, perhaps because other economies with similar export profiles also suffered similar currency devaluations. The currency devaluation undoubtedly increased import — including food — costs due to the high proportion of food items in Malaysia's imports. Malaysia's food import bill amounted to RM6.3 billion in 1997 and RM6.7 billion in 1998, or 19.9 and 21.4 per cent respectively of total consumption goods imports. An estimated 73.6 per cent of exports from and 69.9 per cent of imports into Malaysia were denominated in US dollars (Haflah *et al.* 1999: 40).

Currency devaluation generally makes exports more competitive and imports more expensive; for Malaysia, considerable shares of imports are inputs into production for export, i.e. as intermediate or capital goods. In 1996, for example, the breakdown of imports was as follows: 22.4 per cent capital goods, 68.8 per cent intermediate goods, and 6.6 per cent consumption goods, with 2.9 per cent dual use goods. Hence, while the weaker exchange rate made exports more competitive, increased production costs could have offset potential gains from currency depreciation in some sectors. Thus, the currency and recession impacted on external trade, with ramifications for the rest of the economy.

Of the RM286.8 billion worth of Malaysian goods exported in 1998 (30.3 per cent increase from 1997), RM237.5 billion — or 82.8 per cent — was from the manufacturing sector. The crucial electronic and electrical sector contributed RM195.0 billion, or 68.2 per cent of the total. With this export surge, Malaysia recorded a RM58.4 billion trade surplus, reversing four previous years of trade deficits. However, export growth in 1998 was not large enough to prevent the economy from going into a slump as the expansion in export-oriented manufacturing was not enough to offset the collapse of the other economic sectors, including other manufacturing (Haflah *et al.* 1999: 5).

Producer Prices

Prices of domestically produced goods increased markedly from 1997 to 1998, with inflation rising from 2.7 to 10.7 per cent, before falling again in 1999 (see Table 1.7). A closer look at the producer price index (PPI) reveals

Table 1.7
Malaysia: Domestic Producer Price Indices, 1993-1999
(annual percentage change; 1989 base year)

	1993	*1994*	*1995*	*1996*	*1997*	*1998*	*1999*
Overall	0.7	4.0	3.9	2.3	2.7	10.7	-3.3
Components:							
Food and live animals	1.5	5.7	2.3	5.5	2.3	8.5	-2.3
Beverages and tobacco	7.6	1.9	2.2	0.5	0.1	1.5	10.2
Crude materials except fuel	0.1	10.0	7.0	-1.5	-4.9	3.0	2.7
Mineral fuels, lubricants, related materials	0.7	-4.5	-0.3	12.5	7.0	-2.6	14.2
Animal and vegetable oils and fats	3.1	20.0	25.9	-5.8	12.9	63.8	-29.4
Chemicals and related products	0.7	0.5	2.1	1.0	1.2	4.7	1.5
Manufactured goods classified by material	1.0	3.4	-0.1	0.8	0.1	6.8	-0.9
Machinery and transport equipment	2.4	0.4	-1.8	0.5	3.4	5.9	-0.5
Miscellaneous manufactured articles	0.4	5.4	2.3	3.4	-1.2	5.4	1.4

Sources: *Economic Report*, various issues; BNM, *Annual Report 1999*, Table A. 28, p. 283.

much unevenness in accounting for this trend. The aggregate rise in prices of domestically produced goods appears to have been not evenly spread, severe or sustained. Increases in one category — animal and vegetable oils and fats — by 63.8 per cent in 1998 raised the domestic PPI to 10.7 per cent. Excluding the prices of animal and vegetable oils and fats, the adjusted PPI was a much lower 3.8 per cent in 1998 (Haflah *et al.* 1999: 13). Since most refined palm oil was exported, the higher palm oil prices probably did not contribute much to higher consumer prices as the higher imported food producer price index in 1998 (14.5 per cent) was much higher than the food consumer price index (8.9 per cent). In 1999, the producer price index for domestic goods fell by 3.3 per cent, mainly due to poorer palm oil prices.

Prices of imports also significantly increased in 1998. As shown in Table 1.8, the annualised PPI for imported goods rose by 9.2 per cent in 1998 as compared to a 2.8 per cent rise in 1997. Importantly, the largest increases

Table 1.8
Malaysia: Producer Price Indices for Imports, 1993-1999
(annual percentage change; 1989 base year)

	1993	1994	1995	1996	1997	1998	1999*
Overall	-0.2	0.2	0.7	0.1	2.8	9.2	-0.9
Components:							
Food and live animals	4.0	-1.2	5.6	3.1	1.2	14.5	-0.7
Beverages and tobacco	-0.2	3.5	0.2	0.7	1.9	-0.6	1.8
Crude materials except fuel	-2.0	7.0	2.7	1.1	1.6	6.2	-1.3
Mineral fuels, lubricants, related materials	1.1	1.7	0.7	1.0	4.0	0.0	-2.4
Animal and vegetable oils and fats	-3.8	-5.8	0.1	-0.1	-0.1	1.9	0.3
Chemicals and related products	1.3	1.6	3.4	2.0	0.8	5.7	0.6
Manufactured goods classified by material	1.8	1.0	1.6	0.0	-0.3	7.3	-0.9
Machinery and transport equipment	2.0	-0.6	-2.7	-2.0	5.3	13.4	-1.1
Miscellaneous manufactured articles	5.6	3.4	1.7	-0.5	-1.1	5.4	0.2

Note: * January-August 1999.
Sources: *Economic Report*, various issues.

were for food and live animals (14.5 per cent) and machinery and transport equipment (13.4 per cent). The former must have exerted some upward pressure on food prices and the latter on industrial product prices. In the first eight months of 1999, the PPI for imported goods declined by almost one per cent, with all components of the index only registering small changes. This import price stability probably reflects the regional currency stability since the last quarter of 1998 and the impact of the ringgit peg from September 1998.

Recovery

While the worst seems to be over in Malaysia, the same can also be said of the other crisis-hit economies of East Asia (see Figure 1.3). It is therefore almost impossible to honestly claim the Malaysian recovery has been either due to or despite the September 1998 measures as proponents and opponents

Figure 1.3
ASEAN Four: GDP Growth Rates, 1982-1999

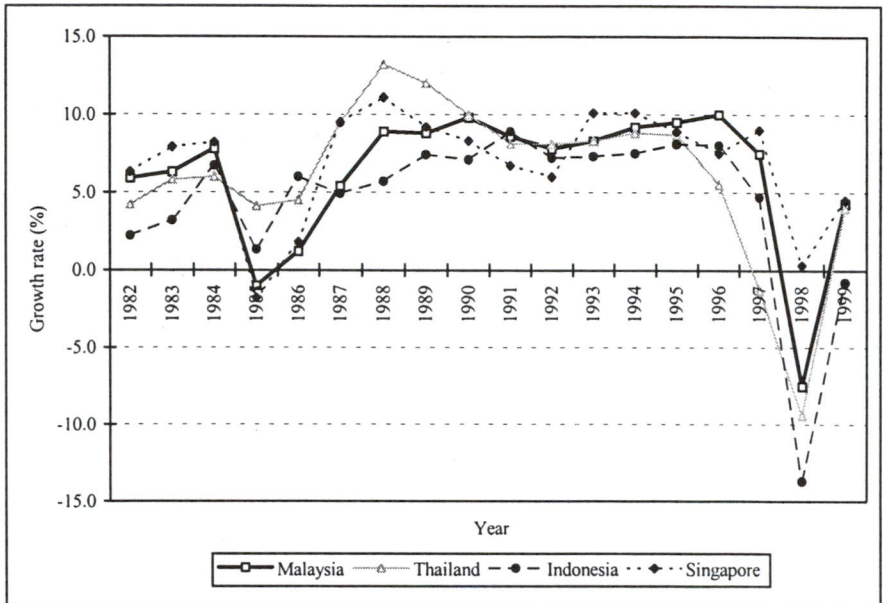

of the Malaysian controls have been keen to claim. The economic situation throughout the region has improved since late 1998; the worst period was the second half of 1998, especially the third quarter, with the Russian meltdown and then sovereign debt default. During the first quarter of 1999, South Korea grew by 4.6 per cent, Indonesia by 1.7 per cent, and Thailand by 0.9 per cent. Malaysia was the only East Asian crisis-hit economy still in recession, with the Malaysian economy contracting by -1.6 per cent. The Malaysian economy should be growing again year on year by the second quarter compared to the second quarter of 1998's -6.8 per cent. The tide has risen throughout the region, but Malaysia seems to be lagging behind, with the recovery in Malaysia in 1999 more modest than South Korea's despite the far more severe banking crises in South Korea, Thailand and Indonesia.

There is an ongoing, but unresolved debate over why the turnaround has occurred. Of course, those supporting the IMF point to Korea's impressive recovery and even to the Thai and Indonesian turnarounds from early 1999 to say that their policies have worked. Meanwhile, the Mahathir regime and its enthusiasts insist that its capital controls paved the way for recovery, not only in Malaysia, but even in the rest of the region! Mahathir can rightfully claim credit for being willing to take bold measures, but they were probably too late to check outflows and currency depreciation, except in the short-term, after Anwar's sacking, but have nonetheless incurred the costs of undermining market confidence.

While the currency controls succeeded in killing the offshore ringgit market, thus restoring control over monetary policy, no one can prove that the controls were necessary for Malaysia's subsequent recovery. At the same time, opponents of such controls cannot really show that the experiment failed. The evidence is simply not clear cut. Clearly, the Malaysian recovery lagged behind the rest of the region, and this may well have been due to the measures introduced by Mahathir in September 1998. However, for the time being, the evidence does not unambiguously support either claim as both sides can invoke statistics to support their respective claims. Bank Negara had gradually lowered its intervention rate from 11 per cent in early February 1998 to 9.5 per cent on 27 August 1998, and then to 7 per cent on 9 November 1998.

However, not all monetary measures to stimulate the economy or raise investor confidence were necessarily contingent on the imposition of capital controls, with the introduction of some such measures actually preceding the imposition of controls in September 1998. Such measures included:

* reduction of statutory reserve requirements (from 13.5 per cent on 16 February 1998 to 4.0 per cent on 16 September 1998, mainly to finance Danaharta and Danamodal);
* extending the grace period for reclassification of non-performing loans from three to six months of unpaid interest (*White Paper*, Box 2, pp. 28-29); and
* efforts to restore liquidity and to re-capitalise the banking system through institutions such as Danaharta and Danamodal.

While the later Malaysian recovery seemed to undermine Mahathirist claims, by itself, it does not prove the case for capital controls' opponents. In any case, regardless of whether the Malaysian capital controls have been successful, everyone recognises that it has had serious costs in terms of undermining previous confidence and goodwill among the investment community that the government has long cultivated rather successfully.

While the recovery has clearly begun, the prospects for returning to the sustained rapid growth of the decade before 1998 are more dubious. GDP per capita data suggest that while Malaysia has lagged further behind Singapore in the region, both Thailand and Indonesia had been catching up on Malaysia (see Figure 1.3 and Table 1.9). The Malaysian savings rate remains high, but much of Malaysia's export-led growth has relied heavily on foreign direct investment (FDI) in the past. It is going to be increasingly difficult to compete with China, India and other alternative sites for such FDI. Also, the uncertain prospects for sustaining the boom in the US and for sustained recovery in Japan raise doubts about Malaysian prospects for an export-led recovery. Not surprisingly then, the NEAC has been banking on a domestic-led recovery, though its policy package (e.g. the currently undervalued ringgit) is not fully consistent with this. More importantly, domestic-led growth requires significant redistribution of wealth and income within the country, which the government has not demonstrated any inclination to undertake.

The recent crisis suggests that Malaysia's economic boom of the previous decade had been built on some shaky and unsustainable foundations. Earlier growth had become increasingly heavily reliant on foreign resources, both capital and labour. It was becoming quite clear that Malaysia's future economic progress could no longer be secured by continued reliance on its previous economic strategy emphasising cheap labour and other production costs. Limited and inappropriate investments in human resources continued to hold back the development of greater industrial and technological capabilities in the country, as elsewhere in the region (Jomo and Felker 1999; Jomo, Felker and Rasiah 1999).

In Malaysia, the gravity of the crisis and the difficulties of recovery were exacerbated by injudicious policy responses, compromised by nepotism and other types of cronyism, though there is little persuasive evidence that cronyism in itself led to or precipitated the crisis. All this transformed the inevitable 'correction' of the overvalued ringgit into a collapse of both the ringgit and the Kuala Lumpur stock market as panic set in, amplified by 'herd' behaviour and 'contagion'. Government efforts to 'bail-out' politically influential business interests and to otherwise protect or advance such interests — usually at the expense of the public (the public purse, workers forced savings, taxpayers or minority shareholders) — exacerbated the crisis in Malaysia by undermining public and foreign confidence.

Fortunately, Malaysian central bank regulation and managed consolidation of the banking sector helped ensure its greater robustness compared to its neighbours, though the forced mergers in the wake of the crisis are less well-conceived and less likely to achieve their ostensible ends. The authorities' push for the very rapid merger of banks and financial companies has been made particularly difficult by the uncertainties due to the turbulent

Table 1.9
ASEAN Four: Comparative Per Capita Gross Domestic Product Growth, 1982-1999

Year	Annual GDP Growth Rate (%)				Per Capita GDP (current US$)				Per Capita GDP Ratios		
	Malay-sia	Thai-land	Indo-nesia	Singa-pore	Malay-sia	Thai-land	Indo-nesia	Singa-pore	Malaysia/Singapore	Malaysia/Thailand	Malaysia/Indonesia
1982	5.9	4.2	2.2	6.3							
1983	6.3	5.8	3.2	7.9							
1984	7.8	6.0	6.7	8.2	2,152	769	520	6,842	0.31	2.80	4.14
1985	-1.0	4.1	1.3	-1.8							
1986	1.2	4.5	6.0	1.8	1,595	810	490	7,410	0.22	1.97	3.26
1987	5.4	9.5	4.9	9.5							
1988	8.9	13.2	5.7	11.1							
1989	8.8	12.0	7.4	9.2							
1990	9.8	10.0	7.1	8.3	2,289						
1991	8.6	8.1	8.9	6.7	2,474	1,580	610	12,890	0.19	1.57	4.06
1992	7.8	8.1	7.2	6.0							
1993	8.3	8.3	7.3	10.1							
1994	9.2	8.8	7.5	10.1							
1995	9.5	8.7	8.1	8.9							
1996	10.0	5.5	8.0	7.5	4,543	3,025	1,146	25,150	0.18	1.50	3.96
1997	7.5	-1.3	4.7	9.0							
1998	-7.5	-9.4	-13.7	0.3							
1999	4.3	4.0	-0.8	4.5							

times and has limited chance of success, especially in light of the recent failure of a similar Thai attempt. While the consolidation of the financial sector may be desirable to achieve economies and other advantages of scale in anticipation of further financial liberalisation, the acceleration of its pace in response to the crisis seems to be less well conceived.

Regime propagandists point gleefully to the Kuala Lumpur Stock Exchange (KLSE) Composite Index (KLCI) recovery. There are many factors behind this apparently anomalous situation of delayed economic recovery and a booming stock market, and the propaganda may lull us into a fool's paradise. Unfortunately, although the nature of official denial has changed, the key economic policymakers seem to be more concerned with winning elections, saving cronies, public relations and the stock market than in sustainable real economic recovery. Instead of uniting the nation to overcome the ongoing economic crisis, leading government propagandists continue to deceive Malaysians about the actual nature of the economy. While recovery in the rest of the region has involved political change, Malaysia's failure to reform politically could well block the new dispensation the economy desperately needs.

There has also been a history of government efforts to bolster the stock market, which many blame for the EPF's loss of over RM10 billion in 1998. The National Economic Action Council's ongoing efforts to revise the 1 September 1998 measures — thus undermining their main original intent (to deter panic-driven capital flight) — have undoubtedly begun to reverse foreign investor sentiment. Foreigners and Malaysians were buying, partly in anticipation of a fillip from re-listing of the KL bourse by the Morgan Stanley index, initially in February 2000, but later postponed to May 2000. Hence, the impressive stock market recovery in Malaysia since September 1998 can be attributed to several factors:

- The greater depth of the KLCI fall, from a peak of almost 1,300 in February 1997 to 262 in early September 1998, has meant a greater potential for a stock market rebound from the trough (measuring the recovery from the exceptional fall of the index from around 300 in late August 1998 — as the Malaysian government has done — further exaggerates the magnitude of the upturn).
- The greater efforts of the Malaysian authorities to promote the Kuala Lumpur stock market, as has been the case since the mid-eighties, is truly exceptional, even by the standards of newly emerging markets.
- After announcing a domestic-led economic recovery strategy, efforts to revive the stock market have been justified in terms of their expected

'positive wealth effect', besides reversing the adverse effects of the asset price deflation for the viability of the financial system.

- Capital controls have allowed the Malaysian authorities to pursue an expansionist monetary policy with limited adverse effects for the time being. The controls helped them to lower interest rates and to increase money supply (M1) in order to increase liquidity, stimulate consumption and fuel the KLSE upturn, but for Shostak (2000: 12), this cannot go on indefinitely as it is likely to raise domestic inflation and external pressure on the ringgit peg. He argues that M1 has led the KLSE share price index by about two months on average during the nineties (this is elaborated in the chapter on capital controls). Hence, the inevitable tightening of monetary policy would probably reverse the current stock market boom.
- It is suspected that the EPF and other Malaysian government controlled institutions bought about RM2 billion of Malaysian stock through Singapore and Hong Kong based brokers to give the impression of renewed foreign investor interest in the Malaysian market.
- Meanwhile, foreigners locked in until 1 September 1999 have withdrawn their funds from the banks, offering low interest rates, to take advantage of the stock market upturn.
- A deliberate pre-polls effort to raise funds through stock market operations for the ruling Barisan Nasional coalition's electoral war chest was also widely suspected.
- With political support from the middle and propertied classes desperately needed by the regime, with its credibility significantly eroded by the political crisis since mid-1998, efforts to boost the stock market are considered crucial for electoral success.

There is considerable evidence from all over the world, including past Malaysian experience, for what have been called electoral or 'political business cycles', with incumbent governments spending more before polls to ensure electoral support. In May 1999, the First Finance Minister urged government officers to spend government allocations more speedily while the Second Finance Minister announced the suspension of tender procedures, ostensibly to accelerate government spending, but effectively also reducing transparency and facilitating politically-influenced tender awards. It is also necessary to reiterate the obvious, i.e. that stock market behaviour is only tenuously linked to economic performance. How else could the authorities explain the Malaysian market's collapse in 1997 while the economy continued to grow by almost eight per cent? Conversely, they cannot now convincingly insist that the stock market revival since September 1998 has been solely due to imminent economic recovery.

Prospects

Though economic recovery is underway, its extent and sustainability are debatable. In 1999, the economy recovered from a smaller contraction of 1.3 per cent in the first quarter to (year-on-year) expansion of 4.1 per cent in the second quarter and 8.1 per cent in the third quarter of 1999, from -8.3 per cent in the fourth quarter of 1998. Improved external conditions (especially higher demand for electronics) and increased government expenditures accounted considerably for the much smaller contraction in the first quarter of 1999. Without the increase in government expenditure, the growth rate would still be negative. When government expenditure growth slowed down in the second and third quarters of 1999, manufacturing picked up considerably, thanks mainly to the electronics boom.

Easier and cheaper credit terms eventually helped stimulate increased private consumption, which rose by 3.0 per cent from mid-1998 to mid-1999. Sales of commercial vehicles grew again from January 1999, after a decline of 76.1 per cent in 1998. Passenger car sales climbed from 23,135 in the third quarter of 1998 to 51,087 (fourth quarter 1998), 55,835 (first quarter 1999) and 59,780 (second quarter 1999). Sales tax in March 1999 recorded 3.8 per cent growth, the first positive growth in over a year (BNM, *Monthly Statistical Bulletin*, Table VI.8). Private investment indicators, however, have not been as promising. Capital formation in Malaysia shrank 31.6 per cent, year-on-year, in the first quarter of 1999 and by 49.0 per cent in the second quarter of 1999. Among other indicators, loans extended to manufacturing (-7.7 per cent annual decline from May 1998 to May 1999) as well as applications and approvals of new investments by MITI (-70.1 per cent annual drop from May 1998 to May 1999) were still negative (BNM, *Monthly Statistical Bulletin*, Table VI.10). The foreign contribution to manufacturing investment averaged a remarkably high 53.7 per cent in the 1990s.

In the second quarter of 1999, the manufacturing sector grew by 10.4 per cent from a year before. Export-oriented manufacturing gained some competitive price advantage with the depreciation of the ringgit. Exports of manufactures surged throughout 1998, especially in key sub-sectors such as semiconductors (33.3 per cent annual growth in ringgit receipts) and electronics (49.6 per cent), which contributed significantly to the total export growth of 32.8 per cent (BNM, *Monthly Statistical Bulletin*, Table VIII.5).

With imports more expensive, Malaysia gained a hefty RM36.8 billion current surplus in 1998.

Despite the massive ringgit devaluation, there has not been a commensurate export boom for many reasons, including:

- greater uncertainty and reduced confidence in the Malaysian investment environment;
- limited price competitive effect due to other devaluations in the region;
- reduced foreign demand, especially from the East Asian region;
- reduced commodity (especially petroleum and rubber) prices;
- reduced agricultural output in 1997 due to climatic (El Nino drought) and environmental (haze) factors;
- reduced investments in the region due to international economic uncertainties;
- the lag time needed for new investments to begin production.

Export earnings have nonetheless benefited from renewed demand for electronics as well as processed raw materials, mainly palm oil. The Malaysian authorities cannot really claim credit for either of these developments, though its easy credit policy has helped to revive demand for homes as well as cars, which have figured prominently in the economic turnaround since late 1998. Ominously, however, primary commodity prices have been leading the international deflationary trend in recent years, with palm oil prices likely to come under severe pressure from the recent collapse of soya bean and other vegetable oil prices.

In the long term, policies should seek to restore confidence as well as reduce volatility and short-termism. The recession has also revealed the insufficiency of many government social programs. To its credit, the government has continued support for education, health and housing by maintaining budgetary allocations to these purposes despite shrinking tax revenue (Table 1.10). Federal government counter-cyclical spending has been a positive development for recovery. Deficit spending raises concerns about the future repayment of public debt, and its possible repercussions for the economy and society (see Table 1.11). The conventional wisdom of running a surplus in good times and a deficit in lean times would apply, but not without a caveat warning against the implications of the future social debt servicing burden. Overall, the lack of a comprehensive social safety net, and the inadequacy of immediate crisis-response programs, has subjected many individuals and households to hardships that could have been better avoided or alleviated.

Table 1.10
Malaysia: Federal Government Revenue, 1995-2000 (selected components)
(RM million; percentage annual changes in parentheses)

	1995	1996	1997	1998	1999	2000[a]
Direct taxes:	22,699 (+44.5)	25,851 (+13.9)	30,432 (+17.7)	30,016 (-1.4)	26,910 (-10.3)	29,096 (+8.1)
Income[b]	20,095 (+15.9)	22,541 (+12.2)	26,978 (+19.7)	28,240 (+4.7)	25,137 (-11.0)	27,101 (+7.6)
Indirect taxes:	18,972 (+9.5)	21,421 (+12.9)	23,195 (+8.3)	15,320 (-33.9)	17,481 (+14.1)	18,483 (+5.7)
Export duties	853 (-26.3)	1,041 (+22.0)	1,053 (+1.2)	623 (-40.8)	598 (-4.0)	623 (+4.2)
Import duties	5,622 (+0.1)	6,132 (+9.1)	6,524 (+6.4)	3,868 (-40.7)	4,578 (+18.4)	4,653 (+1.6)
Excise	5,280 (+22.9)	5,790 (+9.7)	6,054 (+4.6)	3,586 (-40.8)	4,500 (+25.5)	4,754 (+5.6)
Sales tax	4,869 (+17.9)	5,473 (+12.4)	6,167 (+12.7)	3,845 (-37.7)	4,285 (+11.4)	4,622 (+7.9)

Notes: [a] Federal Budget allocations.
   [b] Including corporate, individual and petroleum.
Sources: *Economic Report, 1998/1999*, Table 4.3, pp. xxxvi-xxxvii; *Economic Report, 1999/2000*, Table 4.3, p. xxxi.

Table 1.11
Malaysia: Federal Government Revenue and Expenditure, 1993-2000
(RM million; percentage annual changes in parentheses)

	1993	1994	1995	1996	1997	1998	1999	2000*
Revenue	41,691	49,446	50,954	58,280	65,736	56,710	56,690	59,897
	(6.2)	(18.6)	(13.0)	(14.4)	(12.8)	(-13.7)	(-0.04)	(5.7)
Operating expenditure	32,217	35,064	36,573	43,865	44,665	44,585	48,927	52,351
	(0.4)	(8.9)	(4.3)	(19.9)	(1.8)	(-0.2)	(9.7)	(7.0)
Development expenditure and lending:								
Development fund	10,124	11,277	14,051	14,628	15,750	18,103	25,009	23,674
	(4.5)	(11.4)	(24.6)	(4.1)	(7.7)	(14.9)	(38.1)	(-5.3)
Direct expenditure	8,992	9,950	12,458	11,970	13,670	15,787	24,005	22,328
	(4.1)	(10.7)	(11.9)	(-3.9)	(14.2)	(15.5)	(52.0)	(-7.0)
Loan recoveries	1,004	1,303	1,531	2,028	1,305	975	1,000	1,000
Net lending	128	24	62	630	775	1,341	4	346
Total expenditure	41,337	45,038	49,099	56,465	59,110	61,713	72,936	75,025
	(2.1)	(9.0)	(9.0)	(15.0)	(4.7)	(4.4)	(18.2)	(2.9)
Overall deficit/surplus	354	4,408	1,861	1,815	6,626	-5,003	-13,745	-12,969
% of GNP	0.2	2.5	0.9	0.8	2.5	-1.8	-4.9	-4.4
Sources of finance:								
Net external borrowing	-3,134	-4,757	-1,635	-2,177	-1,681	1,784	3,160	801
Net domestic borrowing	375	1,751	-	1,291	-2,048	11,040	16,819	13,168
Change in assets	2,405	-1,402	-225	-929	-2,897	-7,821	-6,234	-1,000

Note: * Federal Budget allocations.

Sources: *Economic Report,1998/1999*, Table 4.2. p. xxxv; *Economic Report, 1999/2000*, Table 4.2, p. xxx.

Concluding Remarks

It has been difficult to accurately assess the actual economic impact of the currency and financial crises because of other contemporaneous developments. Before the crisis began in mid-1997, there was already considerable evidence of significant commodity price deflation, involving not only primary products, but also generic manufactures not enjoying monopolistic rents due to exclusive intellectual property rights held by transnational corporations (TNCs). In 1997 and 1998, agricultural output, especially in insular Southeast Asia, was adversely affected by the El Nino and then La Nina weather phenomena of drought followed by floods. Forest fires due to land clearance activity by plantation interests in Sumatra and Kalimantan resulted in tall palls of smoke in neighbouring Malaysia for several months, also adversely affecting agricultural output as well as public health and labour productivity.

Analysis of the economic impact of the crisis in Malaysia must take into account several key differences of the Malaysian experience. Unlike the three worst affected economies, namely Thailand, South Korea and Indonesia, it is generally agreed that the Malaysian financial system has been less bank-based, with a far greater role for the capital market. After the Malaysian banking crisis of the late 1980s, when the share of non-performing loans in the system rose to almost 30 per cent, the authorities significantly strengthened prudential regulation, e.g. through the Banking and Financial Institutions Act (BAFIA), 1989. Although this regulation was subsequently undermined by various liberalisation measures, it nevertheless served to protect Malaysia to a greater degree than in the more crisis-hit countries.

Most importantly, although foreign bank borrowings rose rapidly during 1996 and the first half of 1997, exposure to foreign loans was still relatively lower in Malaysia. Critically, unlike the other three, Malaysian external liabilities did not exceed its foreign exchange reserves. Also, it seems that three quarters of the corporate foreign borrowings were accounted for by three partially-privatised state-owned enterprises. Hence, Malaysia was not obliged to seek IMF emergency credit or to accept IMF policy conditionalities.

This overview chapter has argued that the economic crisis began as a currency crisis due to strong pressure on the dollar-pegged ringgit after the reversal of the yen-dollar relationship from mid-1995 and the Thai baht float under currency attack from 2 July 1997. The initial ringgit devaluation after an abortive and expensive defence of the currency accelerated the asset price deflation after the stock market reached a peak in February 1997. This asset price collapse quickly threatened the banking system with Malaysia's high level of indebtedness, including heavy exposure to property and share purchase loans.

Early official responses seemed to smack of 'denial' and 'bailing-out' politically connected corporate interests, which inadvertently served to exacerbate the growing problem, including declining confidence in official policy. While the policy reversal from late 1997 may have served to signal some checks on 'cronyism', they also exacerbated the deflationary consequences of declining domestic and regional demand. Thus, what began as a currency crisis soon generated a financial crisis, which in turn led to recession. Hence, these different aspects of the 1997-8 economic crisis were distinguished in order to be able to more carefully consider their respective social impacts.

The currency crisis from July 1997 put considerable pressure on the ringgit. After an aborted defence, which is believed to have cost over RM9 billion (then over US\$3.5 billion), the ringgit was also floated, following the Thai baht, Indonesian rupiah and Filipino peso. The ringgit devaluation lowered the foreign exchange value of Malaysian assets, especially share prices. This, in turn, triggered a vicious cycle of asset price deflation involving flight of foreign as well as domestic portfolio capital. Lower asset prices also caused lending institutions to make margin calls, requiring additional collateral. Foreign lenders became more reluctant to 'roll over' their short-term loans. Interest rates also tended to rise for a variety of reasons, exacerbating the effects of reduced liquidity in the financial system.

Of course, the ringgit devaluation also raised the prices of consumer as well as producer imports, particularly during 1998. Food prices seem to have been especially adversely affected, reflecting the high import content in the national food bill. The effects of higher producer prices due to currency devaluation are difficult to generalise about. For example, although electronic exports are reputed to have a very high import content, the ringgit devaluation would actually have the effect of reducing the cost of value added in Malaysia. And in so far as internal transfer pricing is the norm within transnational production chains, it is actually quite possible that currency devaluation would encourage increased output. But there are a variety of other arrangements that would have different outcomes and effects from higher producer import prices due to currency devaluation.

The exchange rate instability that followed the July 1997 currency floats must have made planning especially difficult for enterprises with various types of international exposure. Instability in the region unpredictably subsided from around September 1998 after the Russian crisis, LTCM collapse and Wall

Street scare of the previous month caused the US Treasury to agree to a strengthening and stabilisation of the yen and other East Asian currencies. In Malaysia, however, the imposition of selective capital controls and the pegging of the ringgit to the US dollar at RM3.8/US$ from 2 September 1998 had a similar effect, though with the benefit of hindsight, the Malaysian initiative now appears somewhat redundant and somewhat unnecessary.

As noted earlier, the banking crisis of the late 1980s in Malaysia led to stricter prudential regulation that limited the vulnerability of the banking system to the latest economic crisis. Thus, stricter prudential regulation probably limited the extent of Malaysia's banking crisis. Hence, unlike Thailand, Korea and Indonesia, Malaysia did not need to seek emergency IMF credit facilities, and thus did not have to accept accompanying conditionalities. Thus, Malaysia avoided the forced closure of banks and financial institutions that occurred in the other three economies, which exacerbated panic and undermined confidence in the domestic financial systems.

Some commercial banks in Malaysia were particularly hard hit by the currency crisis. Although private sector lending from abroad grew tremendously in the year and a half before July 1997, private corporations were largely constrained from borrowing heavily overseas. Hence, it is likely that financial institutions accounted for much of the foreign credit to private borrowers in Malaysia. In so far as they sought to profit from arbitrage and related opportunities, it is likely that they were also hurt by the currency and term mismatches suffered by their counterparts in the rest of the region.

Malaysia did briefly adopt tighter fiscal and monetary policies — desired by market sentiment as much as by the IMF — from late 1997 until early 1998. However, the depth of the recession in 1998 was probably due to other factors as well, most notably the negative wealth effect of the stock market collapse.

After reaching a peak of around 1,300 in February 1997, the decline of the Malaysian stock market index was greatly exacerbated by the currency crisis as well as its repercussions for the banking system. It had fallen by about four-fifths, or 80 per cent, to reach its nadir of 262 on 2 September 1998, on the day after the announcement of capital controls. With the relatively much higher stake of foreign portfolio investors in the Malaysian capital market, especially on the first or main board of the Kuala Lumpur Stock Exchange (KLSE), came its greater collapse. The proportionately very high capitalisation of Malaysia's share market meant that the adverse wealth effect of this collapse was probably greater than elsewhere in the region. Likewise, the recovery of the stock market since September 1998 has also probably had a significant positive wealth effect, reflected in increased domestic consumer demand.

Besides the stock market, the property sector has also been adversely affected by the asset price deflation, with significant consequences for the banking sector, e.g. with the declining value of collateral, etc. The reversal of the sector's fortunes has also adversely impacted on the construction sector, as well as supplier industries. The casualties have included employment by as well as the very survival of construction and supplier firms.

The political fall-out from the 1997-8 crisis has greatly politicised subsequent analysis and interpretation of the crisis as well as its consequences and implications. On 2 September 1998, then Finance Minister, Deputy Prime Minister and heir apparent Anwar Ibrahim was sacked from the cabinet and then from the ruling party for ostensible sexual misbehaviour by Prime Minister Mahathir. However, Anwar was soon accused of having instituted IMF-type policy measures in Malaysia from late 1997 and blamed for causing the 1998 recession and exacerbating its consequences for the Malaysian economy through such policy measures. Several major public policy pronouncements since then (e.g. the 1999 official *White Paper*) have been skewed to support this kind of interpretation of the causes and consequences of the crisis.

It appears that Anwar probably approved of the spending cuts and tighter monetary policy from late 1997, in response to market pressures as much as IMF recommendations. However, he also began to reverse himself, at least from the second quarter of 1998, when government spending started to rise and monetary policy began to be relaxed. In any case, interest rates in Malaysia were well below Thailand's before September 1998, after which Thai rates fell below Malaysia's without the aid of controls. Anwar was also in charge when temporary capital controls were introduced in early 1995, so there is little reason to believe that he was dogmatically committed to full capital account convertibility.

Although Malaysia recovered more strongly than Thailand and Indonesia during 1999, its recovery only began in the second quarter. Available evidence does not allow either proponents or opponents of the Malaysian capital control measures to conclusively prove that they enhanced or undermined recovery. However, it is generally agreed that the Malaysian approach has probably limited the reforms and restructuring which might otherwise have proven necessary if recovery was far more subject to international pressures and expectations.

Danaharta was established in mid-1998 to take out large non-performing loans from the worst-affected banks and financial institutions. This — together with recapitalisation of decapitalised banks by a companion agency, Danamodal — served to restore liquidity to the banking system. Although banks became more careful about lending for property purchases, raised lending quotas for share purchases helped boost the stock market, with positive wealth effects contributing to renewed domestic demand, helped along by expansionary fiscal policies. Similarly, consumer credit has been officially encouraged, particularly for vehicle sales (to revive the automotive industry) and residential property purchases.

The quasi-dollarisation of the ringgit since September 1998 may have helped enterprises with international exposure to plan better. Looser monetary policy from mid-1998 as well as central bank directives to increase lending — by eight per cent per annum from September 1998 and then for 1999 — sought to increase liquidity in the system.

Despite the recession through 1998 and into the first quarter of 1999, it is remarkable that the national savings rate was barely affected, remaining above 40 per cent despite the worst recession in post-war history. The government's adoption of a counter-cyclical deficit budgetary strategy from 1998 meant the substitution of government dis-savings for previous government savings, implying the increase in private savings. And since we can presume household savings to have been adversely affected by the recession as well as lower wages and property incomes due to the negative wealth effect, one can only presume an increase in corporate savings. This is not contradicted by the lower investment rate, owing to the reversal of earlier foreign savings inflows for investment in Malaysia as well as the much slower credit growth, especially for productive investments.

Opponents of the capital controls introduced in September 1998 have tended to exaggerate its likely adverse effects, which have not really been as manifest as they were wont to claim. On the other hand, proponents of the control measures are not able to demonstrate that the controls were responsible for either a speedy or a strong recovery. The three worst-affected economies all registered positive growth from early 1999, whereas Malaysia only came out of the recession from the second quarter. And while the recovery in Malaysia has been stronger than in Thailand and Indonesia, South Korea has performed better thus far. And even if Malaysia were to perform better than South Korea, it still has to be demonstrated that this was due to the capital controls, which have largely been amended and dropped except for the dollar peg and related currency controls since September 1999.

Notes

1. Some commentators claim that the resultant property price bubble has its roots in Japanese-type or more generically East Asian culture, norms and arrangements which compromise relations between the state and the private sector as well as among businesses, invariably involving welfare-reducing, if not downright debilitating rent-seeking behaviour. In so far as such relations are believed to exclude outsiders, their elimination is believed to contribute to leveling the playing field and bringing about an inevitable convergence towards supposedly Anglo-American style arms-length market relations.

2. For example, the yen fell from less than 80¥ to the US$ in mid-1995 to over 120¥ by mid-1997, while the Deutschemark had floated against the US dollar before mid-1997.

3. After tightening bank credit from December 1997, the funding of special funds for investment in food production and for small and medium industries (SMIs) as well as for car purchases (especially for the 'national cars') were increased. Nevertheless, the severe contractionary consequences of tighter liquidity have continued to slow down the economy fairly indiscriminately.

2

011 047
016 019
F21
053

PRE-CRISIS ECONOMIC
WEAKNESSES AND VULNERABILITIES

Rajah Rasiah

(Malaysia)

Malaysia suffered an economic slump when its stock and currency markets crashed following a sequence of regional downturns involving the Philippines, Malaysia, Indonesia and South Korea that started with the bursting of the Thai bubble in mid-1997. Against the US dollar, the ringgit fell by almost 50 per cent over the period September 1997 to January 1998. It was only in 1993 that the World Bank (1993) celebrated the miraculous growth of eight high performing Asian economies (HPAEs). Indonesia, Malaysia and Thailand were considered better examples for emulation due to their relatively more liberal economic policies. Their initial conditions were also seen as more typical, dominated by resource-based growth agriculture involving mining. For many commentators, the financial crisis now seems to have exposed the one time miracle for what it really was.

This chapter attempts to evaluate the causes of the financial slowdown and bust. However, to understand the crisis better the factors that helped shape the boom of 1987-97 are examined first. This involves more than a mere assessment of static macroeconomic fundamentals, which can be maintained in the short and medium turn but at the expense of real costs to the economy in the long run. The causes of the crash are examined last.

The Pre-Crisis Boom

Malaysia underwent substantial deregulation from the mid-1980s, lowering tariffs and loosening ownership conditions for both manufacturing and financial sectors. It increased export-promoting policy biases from 1986. While Japanese and first-tier East Asian NIC currencies (except for the Hong Kong dollar) appreciated after the Plaza accord of 1985, as with the others second-tier Southeast Asian NIEs, the ringgit depreciated in the mid-1980s, which helped improve the balance of payments as import prices fell. Also, aggregate wages grew far less than GDP in this period, as high labour reserves that emerged following the mid-1980s recession as well as foreign labour imports applied downward pressure. The rapid build-up of export-oriented investments soon overcame the mid-1980s' slowdown, thereby stimulating rapid growth.

FDI Upsurge

Malaysia's boom was significantly boosted by the massive redeployment of investment and production from Japan and the first-tier East Asian NIEs. The Plaza accord of 1985 led to the appreciation of the latter's currencies, which raised relative production costs, forcing many labour-intensive operations to move abroad. The withdrawal of Generalised System of Preferences (GSP) privileges from the first-tier East Asian NIEs in February 1988 further encouraged this trend. Rising protectionist pressures in developed countries' markets against exports from Japan and the East Asian NIEs encouraged the relocation of investments in Southeast Asia and China. Hence, the share of FDI in gross domestic investment in Malaysia rose from 10.7 per cent in 1980-90 to 24.6 per cent in 1991-93 (UNCTAD 1996). Taiwan emerged as a major new investor from the second half of the 1980s as a consequence. The electronics industry, where the foreign ownership share reached 91 per cent in 1993, became Malaysia's leading export-earner from 1987, accounting for 67.5 per cent of manufactured exports in 1995 (see Rasiah 1995: chapter 5; 1998).

Exchange Rates and Export Incentives

Malaysia's ringgit depreciated in the second half of the 1980s until the early 1990s, cheapening exports and making imports more expensive (see Figures 2.1 and 2.2). Malaysia's ringgit had appreciated in the early 1980s due to its quasi-peg basket of currencies, especially against the US dollar. Hence, though primary commodity prices fell in the first half of the 1980s, falling export prices and consequent increases in balance of payments deficits did not lower the real effective exchange rates of these currencies. A rise in heavy industry and infrastructure projects in Malaysia also increased demand for

Figure 2.1
Malaysia: Exchange Rate Fluctuations, 1983-1996

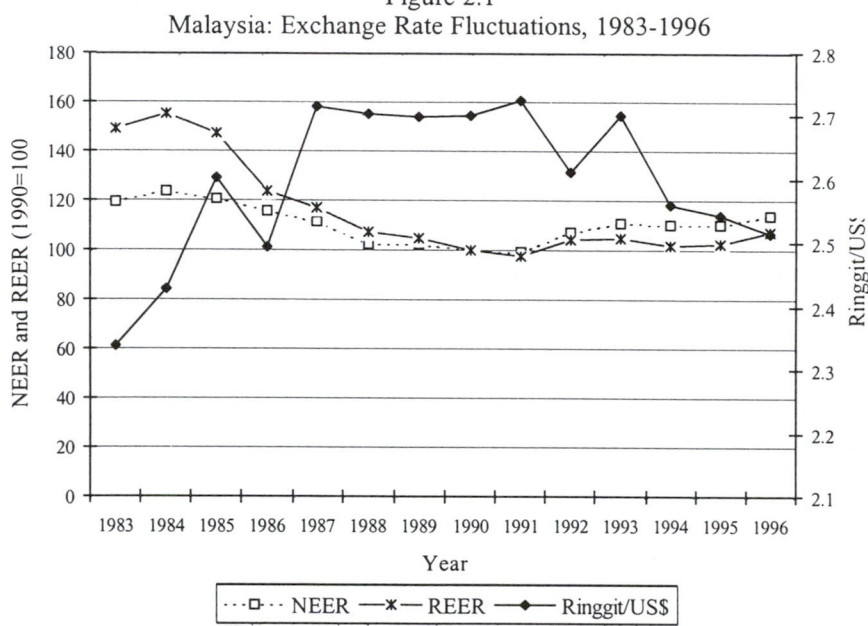

Source: Computed from IMF, *International Financial Statistics, 1998.*

Figure 2.2
Malaysia: BOP and GFCF as Percentage of GDP, 1990-1998

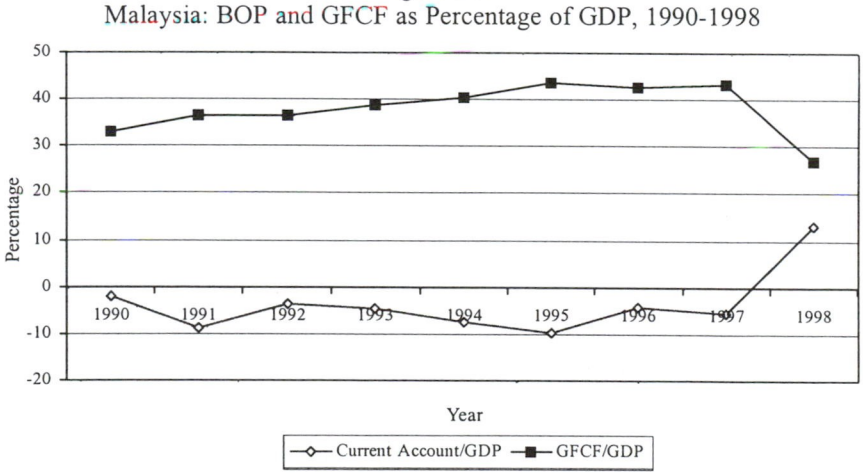

Source: Computed from Bank Negara Malaysia, *Quarterly Economic Bulletin*, 1996 and 1999.

the ringgit. Unlike Thailand and Indonesia, Malaysia did not devalue the ringgit until 1985. The early years of the 1980s were also characterised by high oil prices from the second oil price hike of 1978-79, which benefited Malaysia, a net petroleum exporter.

The value of the ringgit fell in 1986, following the strengthen of the yen and first-tier East Asian NIE currencies after the September 1985 Plaza Accord put pressure on Malaysia's nominal and real effective exchange rates (NEER and REER). The depreciating ringgit cheapened production costs in Malaysia. The massive currency depreciations as well as domestic promotional efforts encouraged the relocation of producers from Japan and the first-tier NIEs. Singapore faced a relative increase in costs, which switched production emphasis to higher value added activities, offering itself as the regional hub for production and marketing activities for the whole of Southeast Asia. Indonesia and Malaysia in particular have since successfully integrated themselves into Singapore's Singapore-Johore-Riau (SIJORI) regional production complex.

The falling REER helped reduce the adverse effects of tariff deregulation in the Malaysian economy from the mid-1980s. Tariffs shielding import-substituting (IS) industries began to fall, especially in the 1990s. Also, export producers enjoyed subsidies from double tax deductions, export credit re-financing and export-abatement allowances. Thus, the proportion of imports in final domestic demand did not soar in this period despite falling tariffs, and in industries such as machine tools, some new domestic production efforts made progress (see Rasiah, 1994a).

Generous incentives to stimulate export-oriented manufacturing increasingly characterised investment promotion. Malaysia began offering financial incentives to attract export-oriented firms with the opening of free trade zones (FTZs) from 1972. The Investment Incentives Act of 1968 initially gave export-oriented firms access to tax holidays for periods of 5 to 10 years, with pioneer status incentives, and subsequently for 5 to 10 years under investment tax allowances. FTZs and licensed manufacturing warehouses (LMWs) also offered firms tariff free movement of goods and services. However, emphasis on foreign attracting direct investment fell in the first half of the 1980s, when the government began to promote heavy industries. Initial losses and the mid-1980s' recession changed the state's emphasis again, as export incentives were re-introduced through the Promotion of Investment Act of 1986 to attract foreign direct investment. Equity regulations under the Industrial Co-ordination Act of 1975 were amended to no longer require registration when involving companies with paid up capital of less than RM2.5 million. Foreign ownership conditions were also more clearly defined as firms exporting 80 per cent or more of output were allowed to own 100 per cent of equity. Exports were also stimulated through the use of export refinancing schemes, export abatement allowances and double deduction tax exemptions.

Several industries began to experience export surges, primarily due to rising global demand and FDI redeployment. Electronics, textiles and garments production expanded manifold in Malaysia. Since the early 1970s, Singapore and Malaysia had become among the world's biggest production platforms for electronics. Local subcontractors expanded strongly into textiles and garments export markets from the late 1980s as low wages and MFA (Multi-Fibre Arrangement) quota provisions increased production operations in Southeast Asia. Resource-based exports also grew as palm oil processing and wood products from Malaysia increased in importance. Growing domestic demand also stimulated domestic manufacturing, e.g. automobile assembly, cement, steel and garments.

Crony Ventures

While early efforts to create a Malaysian Bumiputera bourgeoisie failed due to lack of effective support, the second half of the 1980s promised new opportunities for growth. Rapid growth in the export-oriented sector, coupled with resource rents, especially from petroleum, helped the state finance mega projects involving favoured Bumiputera and other Malaysian businessmen. Aggressive promotion of stock markets, using both direct state guarantees and implicit assurances, boosted confidence in projects linked to plantation agriculture, infrastructure projects, manufacturing and telecommunication sectors. The result has been a dramatic rise in shareholder capital, including foreign portfolio equity purchasers. From negligible levels in 1980, foreign portfolio equity investment reached 6.1 per cent of gross fixed capital formation (GFCF) in 1993 (see Table 2.1). Commercial banks began to disburse loans, often generously using shares as collateral. Hence, although the expansion of stock markets took place without enough regulatory mechanisms to avoid abuse, its growth initially stimulated massive investment expansion.

Protected domestic markets — which grew substantially with growth (in export manufacturing and resource-based industries) — generated demand for often monopolistic crony products and services in the country. Thus, Proton and later Perodua, Kedah Cement, Perak Hanjoong, UEM, Renong, Sime Darby and PNB reaped enormous rents. A significant share of these rents were mere transfers from domestic consumers whose options were

Table 2.1
Malaysia: Selected Financial Indicators, 1980-1996 (%)

	1980	*1992*	*1993*	*1996*
Savings in GNP	33	35	38	37
Savings-investment gap	3.0	1.0	5.0	-5.0
Portfolio Investment in GFCF	0.0	0.7	6.1	n.a.
Net FDI in GFCF	3.9	7.3	7.2	n.a.

Note: n.a. – not available.
Sources: Computed from World Bank, *World Development Report*, various issues;
         IMF, *International Financial Statistics*, various issues.

restricted by tariffs, regulations and government procurement. Domestic demand grew so much that even export-oriented interests (e.g. textile firms) began to move into real estate speculation and property development.[1] With the exception of a few obvious failures such as Perwaja, microeconomic losses in consumer welfare were not apparent during the boom of 1987-95 as strong macroeconomic fundamentals masked pure transfers of dead-weight losses. Hence, domestic grew with export manufacturing growth without adversely affecting the bubble.

In short, Malaysia experienced massive increase growth and structural change from 1986 due to a combination of external forces and local initiatives. The macroeconomic environment improved as FDI and local investors expanded export-oriented operations. Cronyism piggy-backed this rapid growth without immediate debilitating consequences.

Slowdown and Bust

Most of Malaysia's macroeconomic fundamentals were generally sound at the time of the crash. Low inflation and falling unemployment had characterised the economy over the preceding decade (see Figure 2.3). Savings rates continued to rise to become one of the highest in the world. However, three major variables began to suggest serious problems by the mid-1990s. The current account of the balance of payments and the savings-investment gap were recording worsening imbalances. Yet, short-term foreign debt and current account deficits as proportions of international reserves in Malaysia were better than in South Korea, Thailand, the Philippines and Indonesia,

Figure 2.3
Malaysia: Unemployment and Inflation Rates, 1990-1998

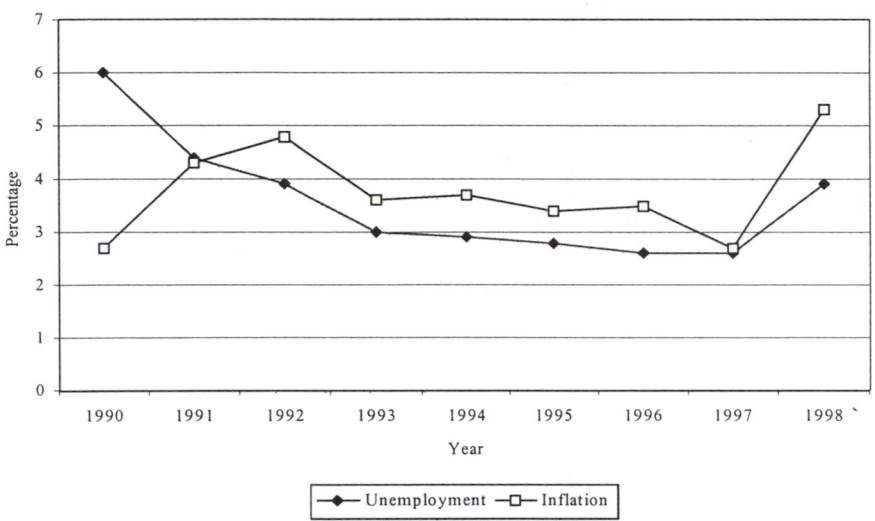

Source: Computed from Bank Negara Malaysia, *Quarterly Economic Bulletin*, 1996 and
1999.

thereby averting the need for an international bailout (see Table 2.2). However, domestic credit expansion had soared by the mid-1990s. In addition,
nominal and real exchange rates appreciated in the first half of the 1990s
(see Figure 2.1).

Fundamental weaknesses in the real economy more generally also slowed
down growth in the mid-1990s. The growing shift to knowledge- and skill-
intensive production and the emergence of China and India as major low
wage production sites also threatened export-oriented manufacturing in the
country. Unlike the Northeast Asian economies, Malaysia has not sufficiently
strengthened the institutions needed to generate rapid technical change and
firm progress towards the technology frontiers.

Exchange Rate Appreciation and Growing Imports

If falling exchange rates assisted export-competitiveness between 1986 and
the early 1990s, the mid-1990s' reversed brought about the opposite effect
after that (see Figure 2.1). The appreciation, especially since mid-1995, and

Table 2.2

ASEAN 4: Debt Service and Short-term Debt, 1980-1996

	Debt Service as a Proportion of Exports (%)			Short-term Debt (US$ billion)[a]				Current Account Deficit Plus Short-term Debt as Share of International Reserves (%)[b]			
	1980	*1992*	*1995*	*1992*	*1994*	*1995*	*1996*	*1992*	*1994*	*1995*	*1996*
Indonesia	13.9	32.1	30.9	18.2	14.0	16.2	17.9	191	139	169	138
Malaysia	6.3	6.6	7.8	3.6	7.6	7.5	8.5	29	46	60	55
Philippines	26.6	27.7	16.0	4.4	9.7	11.0	12.0	100	212	203	149
Thailand	18.9	14.1	10.2	14.7	29.2	41.1	44.0	101	127	152	153

Notes: [a] Year end figures.
  [b] As a percentage of reserves, measured by dividing the current account deficit plus short-term debt by international reserves (1992 figures computed from World Bank data).

Sources: UNCTAD (1997: Table 14); World Bank (1994: Tables 20, 23; 1997: Table 17).

the decline of the yen from mid-1995, was substantial. With the renminbi devaluations of 1990 and 1994, the appreciation of the ringgit had a negative impact on the balance of payments' current account and on FDI inflows. The rising ringgit as well as declining tariffs and other trade controls pushed up imports (see Figure 2.2). There were no efforts to adjust exchange rates to neutralise the impact of import liberalisation.[2] Also, Malaysia's manufacturing export structure had become somewhat rigid and was not sufficiently exchange rate elastic. Unlike agricultural and final goods, which have competitors and substitutes, intra-firm trade (especially transnationals directly exporting assembled and processed items abroad) has accounted for much of the trade in manufacturing. The largely transnational-dominated manufacturing trade — where demand is primarily determined in major markets abroad — meant that import demand continued to be strong. The cheaper ringgit has brought little change in investment demand in 1997. Unlike long-run gradual currency depreciation, which can attract production from abroad especially when accompanied by strong macroeconomic fundamentals, volatile currency movements tend to discourage such inflows. Otherwise, strong macroeconomic fundamentals tend to strengthen currency values in the absence of government devaluation efforts.

In electronics, for example, foreign subsidiaries in Malaysia mainly assemble and test manufactures mainly produced in developed economies. The 1997-98 currency crash has lowered production costs in Southeast Asia vis-à-vis North America and Europe, but less so against Japan, Taiwan and South Korea. Besides, because most major electronics firms have most of their low value added production stages in Southeast Asia, the crisis has neither lowered import demand nor expanded export demand significantly. The recovery in the industry from 1998 has increased intermediate imports even though the ringgit and regional demand has fallen. Since electronics is Malaysia's main manufactured export, sticky wage rates is likely to reduce the amount of additional foreign exchange earnings that can be gained from the devalued ringgit.[3] The industry's recovery, can nevertheless, help reduce the scale of the unemployment problem.

Over-expansion in construction and services before achieving industrial maturity has also dented Malaysia's capacity to finance manufacturing growth. Unlike other successful industrialisers, services grew after extensive industrial deepening and productivity increments, their accelerated expansion in Malaysia has come while its manufacturing sector is still dominated by low value added OEM activities. To make matters worse, its limited capacity to export services and construction materials have aggravated the trade imbalance. Instead construction and services have been responsible for massive increases in imports in the 1990s. Unlike recovery after the mid-1980s recession largely due to the massive relocation of East Asian investments, FDI inflows on a similar scale of are unlikely.

Meanwhile, Malaysia neglected — rather than modernised — its agriculture so that a growing share of its food consumption has been imported. Food imports in 1996 alone came to around RM10 billion. Presuming that manufacturing value added will always be significantly higher than agriculture, the government even promoted relocation of food production to neighbouring Indonesia, Thailand and the Philippines. The typical structuralist argument posited a circular price relationship between agriculture and with agriculture supporting manufacturing initially, but subsequent support by the latter for the former's modernisation would lead to some equalisation of the terms of exchange between the two. Despite sharply rising prices of a number of basic consumption items, demand for such items, remains fairly inelastic, and declines of demand in the short-run will be limited.

Short-termist Debt-driven Investment

Although the Malaysian foreign debt situation was more favourable than in South Korea, Thailand, the Philippines and Indonesia (see Table 2.2), investment in Malaysia expanded far more than savings in the 1990s (see Table 2.1). As a proportion of GDP, gross fixed capital formation (GFCF) has shown a trend increase (see Figure 2.2), which has inevitably caused falling capital productivity. Given the faster rise in investment over GDP, incremental capital output ratios (ICOR) for these economies would have risen.[4] Large injections of capital during early industrialisation also require stable financing, which has traditionally been supported in Malaysia by natural resource endowments, but has also come with FDI, particularly since the mid-1980s. Gross FDI as a proportion of GDP reached 22 per cent for Malaysia in 1995 (UNCTAD 1997: Figure II.19). Without repayment pressures, FDI can clearly complement limited domestic capital to enhance growth. Although FDI can generate problems, it is clearly less footloose than portfolio investment and can help meet both capital and technology needs. FDI to Indonesia, Malaysia, the Philippines and Thailand together rose by 43 per cent in 1996 over 1995 (UNCTAD 1997: 81). Its share of GFCF fell in 1996, however. The Southeast Asian share of total FDI going to South, East and Southeast Asia also fell from 61 per cent in 1990-91 to 30 per cent in 1994-96. China and India have become major rivals, for labour-intensive FDI.

Investment volatility in the country rose sharply following aggressive promotion of stock markets from the late 1980s. Portfolio investment's share of GFCF has risen, especially since 1993. Malaysia's net foreign portfolio investment rose from negligible levels in 1980 to 0.7 per cent in 1992 and 6.1 per cent in 1993 (see Table 2.1). Investors can thus subject firm capitalisation to substantial fluctuation as sentiments can change swiftly. The recent crisis brought stock markets crumbling down as investors, both local and foreign, began selling their shares. Yet, until the crash, investment levels in Malaysia continued to rise substantially, though, arguably, beyond its capacity to absorb capital effectively, causing overheating in the mid-1990s. Though Malaysian government was thus clearly warned of overheating, it chose to ignore, rather than to try to ameliorate the situation.

Better access to bank loans due to crony relationship eventually brought firms supported privileged by the government to the brink. The easy expansion of credit, especially in the 1990s, raised the loans-equity ratios to extremely high levels. Collapses further in share prices aggravated such imbalances. Loans and advances as a share of GNP at purchasers' values rose from 133 per cent in 1992 to 185 per cent in 1995 (computed from Bank Negara, 1997).

FDI Slowdown

Malaysia also faced a slowdown in FDI inflows from 1996. Declining FDI and a world semiconductor glut depressed manufacturing growth in Malaysia. The decline in FDI and exports growth reduced domestic demand for services and construction since the latter are both functions of growth. The fall in FDI to Southeast Asia from late 1996 was a consequence of a number of factors. Firstly, the mid-1990s did not see a further massive exodus of Northeast Asian capital seeking new investment sites elsewhere. The upsurges in earlier episodes has been neither sustained nor replaced. The falling yen from the mid-1990s also reduced the significance of the already decline Japanese FDI inflows.

Secondly, the exhaustion of labour reserves in Malaysia — the most attractive of the second-tier Southeast Asian NIEs for FDI — had already started to discourage prospective labour-intensive investors. Malaysia had a foreign labour force exceeding two million in 1996, which accounted for 20-30 per cent of the country's labour force. The incentive structure in Malaysia had also changed in the early 1990s so that labour-intensive firms faced pressure to relocate to less developed locations within the country, or even abroad (see Rasiah 1998b). The crisis is likely to discourage FDI flows for months, if not years.

Cronyism

The 1990s were also characterised by increased liberalisation, including cronyistic privatisation. The private sector's role in allocation and co-ordination, either through opaque crony alliances or via banking or the stock market became more dominant (see Polanyi 1957; Kornai 1962). Powerful interests dominating the markets — enjoying either political or economic clout captured much of the rents associated privatisation. The abuses did not seem overly debilitating due to rapid growth. As in the early 1980s, unsustainable expenditures (involving mega-projects) began undermining both the current account as well as the treasury. The number of public institutions privatised rose from two in 1983 to 72 in 1993 (Rugayah 1995; Rasiah 1997). Private interests, working hand in hand with the politically powerful, began dominating financially profitable rentier activities. In the absence of risk taking — as several such ventures enjoyed state guarantees of domestic market monopolies — significant numbers of the newly created managerial class hardly had entrepreneurship.

External liberalisation pressures forced the removal of a number of incentives and tariffs, pushing private interests into other rentier activities. The World Trade Organisation's formation in 1995 and other regional trade deregulation efforts, such as AFTA and APEC, accelerated the liberalisation process. Incentives used to promote exports (e.g. the export abatement allowance) and tariffs that sheltered domestic producers began to fall sharply by the mid-1990s. Rentier activity shifted to other sectors.

Unproductive investment ventures, including property and share purchases, attracted financing from banks and other financial institutions. The government launched uneconomic projects, often at unnecessarily high expense. The Petronas KLCC twin towers and the Bakun dam are examples of uneconomic mega-projects. Private banks and finance companies facing liberal regulations began to extend loans for quick returns, based on collateral and links with powerful politicians. Hence, the share of loans to the property sector rose from 18.1 per cent in 1990 to 32.0 per cent in 1992 before falling slightly to 30.3 per cent in 1996. In contrast, the share of loans to manufacturing declined slightly from 23.2 per cent in 1990 to 21.0 per cent in 1996. General commerce and agriculture also experienced relative declines (see Table 2.3). Construction and real estate thus grew significantly faster than GDP.

Table 2.3
Malaysia: Loans and Advances by Commercial Banks, 1990-1996 (%)

	1990	*1991*	*1992*	*1993*	*1994*	*1995*	*1996*
Manufacturing	23.2	23.8	23.4	22.5	23.0	23.3	21.0
Agriculture	5.2	4.5	4.3	3.4	2.5	2.1	2.0
General Commerce	14.4	12.6	11.9	11.4	10.8	10.5	9.8
Broad Property[a]	18.1	28.8	32.0	31.6	29.3	29.3	30.3

Note: [a] Comprises construction, real estate and housing.
Sources: Bank Negara Malaysia, 1992, 1997.

Slow Technological Progress

While industrial policy in the first-tier Asian NIEs ensured strong institutional support driving technical change, it has generally failed to do so in Malaysia. Singapore has successfully developed and maintained institutions necessary to sustain its leading role as the Southeast Asian regional hub for medium to high technology-intensive production and services. Japan, South Korea and Taiwan have successfully developed the necessary institutions to not only speed up the absorption and development of technologies, but also to strengthen their capacities to support new product development. Excessive credit expansion and the inadequate supervision sowed the seeds for the financial crisis in 1997, but slow technological deepening in the real sector slowed the country's growth potential. With the exception of resource based industries, such as palm oil processing, Malaysia has yet to go beyond original equipment manufacturing (OEM) capabilities, and does not have the institutions to adequately generate the required human and other technological capabilities to support rapid technical change. Institutional deficiencies in Malaysia could be seen in four major areas — viz., one, instruments supporting technological deepening, two, human resource gaps, three, technology diffusion mechanisms, four, complementary disciplinary mechanisms.

Ambitious and increasingly expensive technology deepening institutions and mechanisms were also introduced from the late 1980s without much concern for ensuring competitiveness. High technology activities were promoted strongly from 1988, and especially from 1990, when the Action Plan for Industrial Technology Development (APITD) was launched. Tax deduction incentives for high technology firms, double deduction benefits for approved R&D, aggressive promotional efforts, technology prospecting and specially developed and subsidised infrastructure for high tech firms have developed in Malaysia. Substantial investments were directed to industrial and technological initiatives in the 1990s, e.g. MIMOS' wafer fabrication plants, Malaysian Industry-Government High Technology (MIGHT), the Malaysian Technology Development Corporation (MTDC), the Second Industrial Master Plan (IMP2) and Multi-media Super-Corridor (MSC) activities. While such initiatives had important technological deepening objectives serious co-ordination failures have restricted their viability. For example, the government has started several wafer fabrication plants in the country when the scope for market access for the sale of fabricated wafers and micro-chips appears limited. One wafer plant may be justified to enhance learning in a technological frontier industry. The four plants emerging suggest a lack of understanding of markets and of scale economies (see Rasiah 1998c; 1998d).

Rising production costs and tough external competition forced Malaysia to review its export strategies and domestic capabilities. Growth in foreign — dominated export-processing activities have largely involved expansion of relatively low value-added production. With labour reserves exhausted, especially in the West Coast industrial corridor of Peninsular Malaysia, firms began facing serious capacity expansion limits. In industries where changing production technologies have required more high technology process tasks, as in microelectronic assembly and testing, demand for skilled workers grew even before labour shortages gripped the Malaysian economy (see Rasiah 1996). The premium for skilled workers has thus gone up in Malaysia, thereby accentuating a dual or segmented labour market. Especially cheap labour imports into Malaysia from neighbouring countries has held down unskilled workers' wages and slowed down labour-intensive firm initiatives to upgrade their process technologies (see World Bank 1995; Rasiah 1995; Edwards 1996). As a consequence, a dual regime of multi-skilled and casualised workforces co-exist within and among firms (see Rasiah and Osman-Rani 1997).

Structural transformation towards achieving higher productivity inevitably requires complementary developments in human resource capabilities. Given imperfections associated with labour markets — especially training and education involving long gestation periods — and information asymmetries that typify underdeveloped markets, there is a strong need to stimulate state-business collaboration in creating and co-ordinating institutions to generate human resources for technological upgrading. In Japan, Taiwan and South Korea, the share of engineers and R&D scientists and technicians rose quickly with the strong incentives offered for increasing their number. Malaysia lacked such human resource support to facilitate a rapid transition to higher technology manufacturing. The share of technology-related human resources in Malaysia has been substantially lower than in the first-tier East Asian NIEs and developed economies. Malaysia had four R&D scientists and technologists per thousand people in the period 1986-90 (see Table 2.4). Aggressive efforts in the 1990s to ameliorate the situation came up against serious co-ordination problems (Malaysia 1990; 1994; Rasiah 1998d).

By all measures, official technology transfer mechanisms have increased in Malaysia. The number of technology transfer agreements in the manu-facturing sector rose from 144 in 1975-77 to 2,224 in 1993 (Rasiah 1996a: Table 7). Institution building to facilitate local technology absorption and development has, however, been weak. The country does not have effective

Table 2.4
Selected Human Capital Indicators, Selected Economies

Countries	Scientists and Technologists per 1,000 People (1986-90)	R&D Scientists and Technologists per 10,000 People (1986-89)	R&D Expenditure as % of GNP (1987-92)
Japan	110	60	2.8
United States	55	n.a.	2.9
Sweden	262	62	2.8
Germany	86	47	2.9
France	83	51	2.3
Canada	174	34	1.4
United Kingdom	90	n.a.	2.3
South Korea	46	22	2.1
Turkey	26	4	n.a.
Brazil	30	n.a.	0.6
Malaysia	n.a.	4	0.4
Thailand	1	2	0.2
Indonesia	12	n.a.	n.a.
Jamaica	6	0	n.a.
Kenya	1	n.a.	n.a.
Bangladesh	1	n.a.	n.a.

Note: n.a. – not available.
Sources: UNDP (1995); MASTIC (1994).

mechanisms to govern technology transfer. In Japan, South Korea and Taiwan, governments established institutions to vet *ex ante* agreements in order to assist local licensees to strike more favourable bargains with foreign licensors and to rigorously monitor and appraise *ex post* in order to speed up absorption and development of promoted local technological capabilities (Johnson 1982; Amsden 1989; Fransman 1985; Wade 1990). The Malaysian authorities began monitoring technology transfer agreements in 1975. Without proficient technocrats from the private sector and a coherent and viable plan, the screening process has so far failed to integrate technology transfer agreements with local capability building (Rasiah 1996a; 1997; Rasiah and Anuwar 1996).

Weak monitoring and enforcement mechanisms have restricted the extent of technology transfer and competitive gains in international markets. Until liberalisation, governments intervened to support firm participation in activities not favoured by the market mechanism in Japan, South Korea and Taiwan (such as catching-up and frontier R&D activities). Conditions imposed by governments ensured that unsuccessful firms did waste rents for too long. The use of performance standards effectively eliminated under-performers from continuing activities without prospect of success for too long. Given the significance of the scale economies and learning involved (that, *inter alia,* helped move the long-run average cost curve left), subsidies have been critical for the emergence of many latecomers, e.g. Hitachi, Mitsubishi, Posco and Hyundai (see Freeman 1987; Fukasaku 1992; Scherer 1992; Wade 1990; Amsden 1989; Chang 1994). Northeast Asian economies have created institutions to promote desired investments, while minimising rent abuses.

In Malaysia, few performance standards exist, let alone effective institutions to manage and enforce them. Malaysia has qualifying standards to access rents or incentives specified, e.g. investment and employment levels and industrial classifications to qualify for tax breaks, and minimal export shares (of output) to access export credits and refinancing loans at subsidised rates. Export targets for local firms — so important in South Korea (Amsden 1989) — have been absent. As a consequence, the heavy industries of Malaysia have not been exposed to external competition to benefit from the 'gales of creative destruction' (see Schumpeter 1934). The Malaysian steel maker, Perwaja Steel, has continued to operate for more than 10 years under different managements despite generating huge losses. Proton, which has been recording profits since 1989, has received high levels of protection (see Rasiah 1998a). Exposing local firms to the discipline of the external market, which would reduce much of the rents enjoyed, should raise competitiveness.

Cronyism has thus successfully insulated many such ventures from competition. The involvement of the politically-connected in such unproductive rent-sapping activities has drained substantial resources in the country.

The limited development of domestic capabilities has resulted in substantial leakages, with a significant share of value added extended to foreign economies, so that imports and profit repatriation have reduced domestic spin-offs. While transnationals have been reluctant to source more inputs locally, local firms have also not adequately developed productive capabilities to increase their participation in foreign firms' value-added chains (Rasiah 1992). Industrial policies have not done much to cultivate and strengthen the capacity of local firms to take greater advantage of domestic content stipulations. A few notable exceptions — e.g. Penang's machine tool firms — have resulted in relatively strong development of local supply capacities (Rasiah 1994a). Yet, the initial progress achieved by these firms has enjoyed little industrial policy support apart from the indirect effects of attracting transnationals. Meanwhile, the share of imports in domestic Malaysian demand rose from 40.7 per cent in 1973 to 61.1 per cent in 1992 while the merchandise trade imbalance worsened in the 1990s before the crisis (Rasiah 1996: Table 3).

It can be seen that a number of economic fundamentals had become weak before the crisis. Inadequate deepening of innovative and productive capabilities pushed Malaysian to an impasse as labour reserves evaporated and cheaper sites for labour-intensive operations emerged elsewhere. Malaysia faced serious skill and other labour shortages in the mid-1990s. With manufacturing becoming increasingly technically-oriented and knowledge-intensive, job generation has become difficult without adequate education and training programmes. Malaysia introduced some measures to address these weaknesses, but generally with ineffective co-ordination and disciplinary mechanisms.

Speculation and Contagion

While overheating and weak second order economic fundamentals had already began to slow down Malaysia's growth, the scale and suddenness of the contraction the currency and financial crises were severely magnified by speculation and regional contagion. The country could be viewed as a small leaking boat caught by violent winds, which aggravated and deepened the crash. The extent of speculation in currency and capital markets magnified in the 1990s. The rise in foreign exchange dealings can be compared with the 1977 figures, when global official foreign exchange reserves were US$266 billion and daily turnover was US$18 billion. Global exports in 1977 were US$1.3 trillion, while foreign exchange transactions that year amounted to US$4.6 trillion. By 1995, the daily foreign exchange turnover had reached US$1,300 billion, which exceeded official global foreign exchange reserves by US$1,202 billion (Khor 1997: 14). World exports reached US$4.8 trillion while foreign exchange transactions skyrocketed to US$325 trillion. Trade transactions as a share of total foreign exchange transactions in 1995 had thus fallen to 1.5 per cent from 29 per cent in 1977.

Hedge funds — which are unregulated funds contributed by firms, institutions and wealthy individuals, some of which generate returns of over 50 per cent, have the capacity to deploy 10 to 100 times more capital than they have (Korten, cited in Khor 1997: 15). Sometimes, even central banks, including Malaysia's Bank Negara, participate in speculation. Big speculators could, then, easily access funds bigger than the GDPs of small economies. Malaysia's liberal financial environment has exposed it to speculative attacks. As noted earlier, Malaysia's short-term debt problem at the time of the crash was not as serious as others affected by the crisis.

Large players, with enormous market power, actually dominate markets. Unmonitored and uncontrolled financial markets allow speculators to participate at any time. Their sheer size would raise prices, the benefits of which they could then reap when exiting. With the existence of forward markets, they can also profit as prices fall. The efficient market hypothesis is only relevant when players are small, and information asymmetries and scale effects do not exist.

Large foreign exchange and share transactions may be necessary and unavoidable. It is also almost impossible to distinguish a speculative purchase of currencies from a real trade transaction. A small open economy such as Malaysia is thus seriously disadvantaged and thus becomes vulnerable to powerful speculators.

Confidence Undermining

The Malaysian government exacerbated the crisis by announcing conflicting statements and attempting some of the deflationary reforms recommended by the IMF for Thailand, Indonesia, South Korea and the Philippines. As sentiments matter, news of bank closures, required by the IMF as part of its bailout arrangements, in Thailand, South Korea and Indonesia, further undermined confidence in the country, sending panic signals about the banking sector and causing a massive credit squeeze. The market capitalisation of firms in Malaysia dwindled sharply as a consequence. The lower value of bank collateral as a consequence also adversely affected credit.

Malaysians transferred their deposits to foreign banks operating locally or converted them into foreign currencies, contributing to the capital flight. Also, the credit squeeze debilitated most firms, irrespective of performance levels. Recent efforts to review such plans have hit other problems. One, performance measures used have linked loans to collateral and repayment records rather than to development potential and microeconomic performance criteria. New manufacturing firms with insufficient collateral have thus come under serious pressure as a consequence.

Conclusions

Weak economic fundamentals and poorly conceived liberalisation contributed to the financial crisis in Malaysia. Although first order macroeconomic fundamentals had improved substantially before the crisis, and a number have been very favourable, growth and deficits had already become unsustainable by the time the crisis struck. To varying extents, chronic current account imbalances, worsening savings-investment gaps and soaring indebtedness adversely affected it. Malaysia had been facing continuous current account deficits and savings-investment gaps in the mid-1990s. Domestic loans and advances as a proportion of GNP had risen beyond sustainable levels by the mid-1990s.

Malaysia's deeper economic fundamentals have generally been weak. The requisite mechanisms for effective technology development to improve competitiveness have been inadequate. Despite efforts to ameliorate the situation, various limitations have restricted its capacity to improve and sustain competitiveness in international markets. Hence, at the time of crash, the country was already handicap by serious institutional drawbacks restricting industrial upgrading. Efforts to strengthen its second order fundamentals cannot be effectively led by crony rentiers.

Cronies enjoying privileged access to credit undoubtedly undertook huge investments in unnecessary and often unviable ventures. Privileged access to and control of rent creation and distribution have led to much rent dissipation continue without developmental gains. With liberalisation, greater market power has also been responsible for strengthening such rentiers, e.g. in real estate and property development.

Financial liberalisation has checked some government abuses as well as instruments aimed at promoting development zone restricting speculation.

Confidence destroying statements by political leaders and the International Monetary Fund (IMF) further undermined sentiments. There have been no serious efforts to check unproductive rent seeking, and news of bail-outs by the government added fuel to fire. Restricting credit worsened the situation.

Notes

1. Open auctions may not be the best allocative mechanism to maximise efficiency *ex post* (Amsden 1989; Chang 1994; Rasiah 1998). Export quotas were among the disciplinary mechanisms used to force firms to achieve efficiency gains in South Korea. Few such mechanisms were used in Malaysia.
2. See Amadeo (1996) for a lucid account of exchange rate management to restrict potential import explosion due to trade liberalisation.
3. Domestic demand for final electronics goods has fallen due to the increased costs of imported items. Final domestic demand, however, constitutes a small share of overall electronics output in Malaysia and Thailand.
4. Nevertheless, considering the early stage of growth and rapid structural change, capital and total factor productivity measures should not be a major source of alarm as they are generally associated with large initial outlays of lumpy investments.

3

FINANCIAL REGULATION, CRISIS AND POLICY RESPONSE

Jomo K. S. and Natasha Hamilton-Hart

The recent debate on the East Asian region's currency and financial crises has raised a number of questions about the wisdom and nature of the financial reforms carried out in the 1980s as well as in early and mid-1990s. The defining characteristics of the Malaysian financial system in the years leading up to the crisis are not easily assessed. In some analyses, Malaysia had a substantively liberalised financial system. In other accounts, the same financial system was substantively controlled. Some commentators have sought refuge in the assessment that financial reform in the region was 'incomplete'. This formulation usually suggests the desirability of further financial liberalisation, rather than liberalisation without adequate prudential regulation — which may better explain much of the financial system's vulnerability to crisis.

Banking system fragility remains a serious problem, with high levels of non-performing loans. Malaysia was confronting a large problem loan situation in the banking system as of 1998. A full-scale financial crisis has, however, been avoided: there was no serious foreign currency debt problem, and intervention by the regulatory authorities ensured that credit to productive sectors of the economy, especially the export-oriented manufacturing sector, did not entirely dry up. The effects of the crisis have not been confined to the financial sector. It has had spill-over effects on the real economies of most countries in the region. From the first quarter of 1998, Malaysia was in recession for five quarters until the second quarter of 1999. Unemployment levels rose sharply during 1998 not only in finance and construction, but also in other industries.

So what went wrong? At this stage, it is sufficient to point out that different interpretations reflect fundamental differences in opinion as to how financial markets operate and, consequently, the implications of different financial policies. If financial markets are seen as inherently imperfect, the origins of financial crisis are more likely to be traced to the inadequacy of public or private mechanisms to overcome market failure. In this view, the crisis and its severity may be attributed to factors such as inadequate prudential regulation, uneven development of financial markets, and poor policy responses.

Financial markets tend to allocate resources imperfectly, even in the best of circumstances. Such problems are more serious in developing countries, which are more prone to serious financial instability, particularly following substantial liberalisation. Managing financial markets is thus a demanding task for government, regardless of whether the policy regime is committed to more market-based allocation. Largely bank-based financial systems, in which competition is limited, may in fact be appropriate for developing countries — given the risks associated with more dynamic, but unstable liberalised systems.

Developing and maintaining appropriate financial governance is a crucial factor determining policy outcomes, since the main cause of failure is often in the implementation — rather than the design — of financial policy. Significantly, the scope for abuse by politically influential interests may not diminish, but may actually increase with financial sector deregulation. Indeed, the consequences of inadequate regulatory capacity to control such interests are likely to become more costly as the financial sector develops under liberalised policy regimes. The international openness of financial markets also increases the risk of instability associated with financial liberalisation, creating additional demands on national — and international — governance systems.

The first section below reviews pre-reform financial policies, structures and outcomes in Malaysia. The next section discusses the Malaysian financial reform experience. The penultimate section draws on the information to assess contending explanations of the 1997-98 financial crisis in Southeast Asia, particularly Malaysia. Some conclusions are offered in the final section.

Pre-Reform Financial Regime

This section looks at banking and financial policy in Malaysia in the years before the major reforms in the financial sector. First, the major features of financial policy and financial system organisation are described. The degree of government activism in the financial system is assessed and, more specifically, the nature of government intervention. Second, monetary and foreign exchange policies are reviewed with the aim of summarising the major policy goals, mechanisms and outcomes. Third, we examine the underlying conditions that enabled or compromised national policy in these areas.

Until the 1990s, Malaysia's financial system remained bank dominated, with most industrial and development financing sourced from the commercial banks. At Independence in 1957, foreign banks were the most significant actors in the financial system. Over time, their role has steadily decreased, with government-controlled banks playing an increasingly important role from the late 1960s, when the two banks that were to emerge as the country's largest, Bank Bumiputra and Malayan Banking (known today as Maybank), were established or put under effective government control. Domestic private sector banking interests up to the 1970s were primarily ethnic Chinese entrepreneurs who had ventured into banking. Government influence in the financial sector in the pre-reform period (which, by most counts, extended to the end of the 1970s) through financial policy was significant. Significant constraints on banks included the requirements to lend to the government and to direct loans to certain priority sectors and categories of borrowers. Interest rates were set by Bank Negara (the central bank), but were generally positive, set in relation to market rates in London. Controls on entry and restricted competition provided Malaysian banks with a relatively high degree of protection.

With the establishment of Bank Negara in 1959, the government moved to influence market structure and development. The change in the position of foreign and local banks was brought about through restrictions on the establishment and operations of foreign banks from the late 1960s. Regulations have limited foreign bank branches, their freedom to set interest rates, and their use of expatriate bank personnel. Foreign banks have also faced more stringent capital requirements than local banks, and since the introduction of the Banking and Financial Institutions Act (BAFIA), 1989, they were required to incorporate locally by 1994, causing one foreign bank to relinquish its license. Foreign investors have also been required to use Malaysian banks for at least a specified portion of funds raised in Malaysia.

Bank Negara placed early priority on the development of the banking system and the mobilisation of domestic savings. This included initiatives to upgrade the national payments system, and to encourage the spread of banking facilities nation-wide (Lee 1981, 1987; Singh 1984). The government was influential in generating confidence in the banking system since the banking sector was, for the first time, subject to some Bank Negara prudential regulation and disclosure requirements. The central bank has since been able to act as lender of last resort and performed this role effectively during episodes of financial crisis, e.g. in the second half of the 1980s.

The government has also attempted to influence the spread of local commercial bank branches. Until the late 1960s, this was done by exhortation and with some use of incentives (Singh 1984; BNM 1989: 18). The early 1960s was a period of rapid bank branch expansion, with the number of banking offices more than doubling between 1959 and 1963 (BNM 1994: 518). Much of the later spread of banking facilities into smaller towns was led by government banks. The result was to change the distribution of bank branches in the 1960s and 1970s, reducing the previous concentration in the major urban centres (Lee 1981: 38-41) to spread the banking habit, and encourage monetisation of the rural sector.

The mobilisation of savings was further encouraged through the state-run National Savings Bank (Bank Simpanan Nasional), originally the Post Office Savings Bank. This bank has since declined in importance, but provided deposit services across the country at a time when much of the population did not have access to commercial bank offices. The government has also operated a compulsory savings fund, the EPF (Employees Provident Fund), to which all employees and employers are required by law to contribute.

Rather than extensive disbursal of 'policy loans' through the banks, the government has financed its industrial policy by budget appropriations, borrowing by state enterprises and direct loans to the private sector. Until the 1990s, commercial banks generally accounted for around 75 per cent of credit to industry. While only making limited and generally indirect interventions in the credit decisions of commercial banks, Bank Negara has, at times, urged banks to limit lending for property development and shares, and to increase lending to the indigenous ethnic groups, known as Bumiputeras, low-cost housing, small-scale enterprises, manufacturing (until 1984) and agriculture. In 1975, lending directives were formally introduced by the central bank, stipulating minimum lending levels to different categories of borrowers. The most significant directive mandated a minimum proportion of bank credit to Bumiputeras. Although the sectoral distribution of bank credit shifted over time, this was probably not a result of government banking policy or central bank 'moral suasion', which were said to be ineffective, thus justifying directives to increase loans to Bumiputeras. Manufacturing's share of bank credit rose through the 1970s, but agriculture's share declined.

Table 3.1
Malaysia: Distribution of Bank Credit, 1966-1996 (%)

	Manufacturing	*Property*	*Shares*	*Agriculture*
1966-70	2.6	8.8	–	9.2
1971-75	8.5	17.0	–	8.6
1976-80	18.8	22.5	1.8[*]	7.1
1981-85	21.1	32.0	1.8	6.5
1986-90	20.1	33.5	2.4	5.6
1992-96	22.6	30.5	3.8	2.9

Notes: [*] 1979-80. Property includes loans for building, construction, real estate and housing.

Sources: BNM (1994: 506), BNM, *Quarterly Economic Bulletin*, BNM, *Annual Report*, various issues.

Interest rate controls were not a major policy instrument. All interest rates were set by the central bank until 1972, when rates on three-year fixed deposits were freed. In 1978, all interest rates were freed except for interest rates on loans to priority sectors. The interest rates for deposits were maximum rates intended to prevent 'excess competition' among banks — mainly to prevent foreign banks outbidding local banks (Lee 1981: 67). Lending rates set by the central bank until 1978 were mostly minimum rates, also aimed at limiting competition from foreign banks (Emery 1970: 279; Abang 1986: 306). The central bank also set a marginally cheaper rate for government borrowings (0.5 per cent less than the prime rate).

One reason for maintaining near-market interest rates was the relatively open capital account in Malaysia. After independence, capital was free to move within the Sterling Area, with the Sterling Area limit lifted in 1973. Malaysia, Singapore and Brunei had a common currency that was issued by the Currency Board and pegged to sterling until 1967, after which their currencies were exchangeable at face value until 1973. For foreign investors, profits and capital could always have been freely repatriated. The need to roughly maintain parity with rates in London is frequently referred to in early central bank reports. The desire for greater monetary autonomy was one reason why Malaysia ended the currency board system shared with Singapore and Brunei in 1967, and then moved towards more flexible exchange rates in 1973 (Lee 1981; Lee 1990). But the openness of the economy meant that

Malaysia was always subject to international inflation and interest rate trends. Foreigners seeking relatively liquid investment opportunities could, and did, invest on the stock exchange, which was active from the 1960s, and then amalgamated with the Singapore exchange until 1973. However, the foreign exchange market was quite small until the 1980s. The greater part of foreign exchange transactions was trade-related throughout the 1960s and 1970s.[1]

Financial policy outcomes in Malaysia in the pre-reform period were generally positive. In terms of savings mobilisation, Malaysia has always performed well despite elements of financial restraint, including mandatory reserve ratios and moderate interest rate controls. Although at independence, Malaysia had a more developed financial system than, say, Indonesia, the formal financial sector was restricted to major towns and larger businesses. The general population relied on the post office savings bank system and the EPF much more than the banking system. Two decades later, with total financial assets at 139 per cent of GDP in 1980, Malaysia's financial system could no longer be called undeveloped. Meanwhile, the M2 to GDP ratio had increased from 0.28 in 1965 to 0.48 in 1978 (Skully and Viksnins 1987: 141).

Economic growth in Malaysia was high throughout the pre-reform period, averaging nearly 6 per cent per annum in the 1960s and 8 per cent in the 1970s (BNM 1994: Table 1.1). Inflation was low — on average less than 1 per cent per annum in the 1960s and 5.5 per cent in the 1970s. Government debt increased significantly as a result of increased state activism from the early 1970s — from RM2.7 billion in 1965 to RM23.4 billion in 1980. However, around 80 per cent of government debt in this period was financed domestically, primarily through the issue of securities to captive institutions, mainly banks and the EPF (BNM 1994: Table A.37). Export growth was strong, with exports, which had always been significant, increasing in value from 47 per cent of GNP during 1965-67 to 55 per cent of GNP in 1975-79 (BNM 1994: Table A.38).

The impressive record of macroeconomic stability then was associated with conservative fiscal and monetary policies, and not for the most part, due to the government's financial policy. In the first place, the government's industrial finance policy and targeted credit initiatives were very limited. Even the specialised industrial finance organisations accounted for a very small share of lending to industry. Most industrial development in the 1970s was due to foreign investment, often in export processing zones, with few linkages to the domestic economy. Secondly, although the increase in economic growth rates in the 1970s coincided with an increased fiscal policy role for the government, it also coincided with an increase in natural resource revenues. The government became more actively involved in the economy through state-owned enterprises. In the early 1980s, although growing more slowly than the manufacturing sector, the primary sector, especially petroleum, remained the single largest part of the economy (Jomo 1990: 42).

Macroeconomic stability cannot be taken for granted or simply attributed to fiscal conservatism. The government maintained stability in circumstances of greatly increased government spending and new initiatives in a variety of sectors, including finance, in the 1970s. These initiatives were taken as a result of increased political demands for the state to play a greater redistributive and growth-enhancing role. They were introduced as a result of heightened ethnic tension and began when parliamentary government was suspended after race riots in May 1969. Taken together, this would have been a recipe for severe monetary instability in most developing countries. That Malaysia avoided this outcome can be attributed to the capacities of its government.

Malaysia's administrative system in the 1970s remained highly bureaucratic, a legacy of the role that leading civil servants had played in the country's transition to Independence. Partly as a result of traditions inherited from the colonial period, the civil service was relatively less corrupt and more efficient, maintaining fairly strong internal norms that constrained behaviour, such as private money-making ventures or personal indebtedness (Federation of Malaya 1956; Tilman 1964). An orderly system of advancement by seniority was maintained through the 1970s and, although loyalty to the ruling party was taken for granted, in the context of a high degree of elite consensus, this did not translate into competing factional loyalties being played out in the ranks of the bureaucracy.[2] The civil service was, in contrast to the Philippines, a career service with few overt political appointees and very limited lateral entry. Bureaucrats seemed imbued with the norms of rational decision-making and empirical observation (Tilman 1964: 132). Through the 1970s, the civil service was still able to recruit many of the country's 'best and brightest', although a shortfall in technical specialists was also becoming apparent. However, rapid expansion of the economy meant that many who were mediocre also entered government service. Nonetheless, the calibre of the country's officials meant that they still provided the 'indispensable steel frame which has held this precarious state together even when the political processes failed' (Esman 1972: v).

In the financial sector, the principal government regulator, and monetary policy maker was the central bank, Bank Negara Malaysia (BNM). Bank

Negara was first established in 1959. Unlike Bank Indonesia, it did not have the legacy of growing out of a colonial-era commercial bank. It had a planned and carefully structured birth, and assumed responsibilities gradually.[3] Currency issue was left to the currency board until 1967; fixed exchange rates and the maintenance of exchangeability at par with the Singapore currency until 1973 meant that active monetary policy was not attempted until the 1970s. The central bank's leadership was then primarily concerned with establishing acceptable banking standards as well as confidence in the ringgit.

This meant that for more than a decade after its establishment, Bank Negara concentrated on its internal organisation as well as the regulation and development of the banking system. Bank Negara has developed as a strong institution, internally meritocratic, and externally, authoritative and largely insulated. The external authority and internal discipline maintained by Bank Negara in the pre-reform era had much to do with the efforts of its first Malaysian Governor, Ismail Ali (1962-1980). His competence, attention to detail, discipline over staff and demands for high professional standards were legendary. He was held in high respect, if not fear, by most banks. His friendship with the Finance Minister, Tun Tan Siew Sin in the 1960s and close connections with other members of Malaysia's political elite added to the central bank's influence, as did the fact that many of its officers were among the best-trained economists and administrators the country could field. The position of private bankers *vis-à-vis* the central bank — that emerges from the bank's history (Singh 1984) — was the polar opposite of the relationship between regulators and bankers in the Philippines (Hutchcroft 1998). It was generally reverent, distant and correct.

Malaysia's system was well suited to its financial policies until the 1980s, providing good regulation and stability, but failing on more developmental goals.[4] The conservative, disciplined and bureaucratic element in government was oriented to maintaining macroeconomic stability. It was able to continue this even when early fiscal conservatism gave way to significant government borrowing in the 1970s, largely because captive institutions — the banks and the EPF — could be pressed into holding large amounts of government debt. To make this system work, increases in spending were strictly controlled, financial stability maintained, and the use of government-controlled EPF forced savings kept prudent. In maintaining this discipline, more ambitious industrial finance and targeted credit schemes were also avoided. Malaysia's most interventionist industrialisation and redistributive policies deliberately went outside the core of the civil service and Bank Negara, which were perceived as too cautious and insufficiently entrepreneurial.

A final feature of the Malaysian administrative system that has greatly influenced economic policy is the ethnic dimension of almost all initiatives. After the ethnic riots in 1969, the period of greater government activism that was ushered in had an explicitly redistributive agenda. The New Economic Policy (NEP), officially embarked on from 1971, aimed to reduce poverty in general, but also to reduce interethnic economic disparities. Many government policies were aimed at raising the business strength of Bumiputeras relative to the ubiquitous ethnic Chinese business community and the dominant foreign-owned sector. Thus, from the start of its developmental phase, the government's economic goals were infused with strong ethno-political considerations. From the point of view of this political agenda, industrial policy worked well (Jesudason 1989). In economic terms, however, Malaysia did not have an industrial finance system that even approached activist systems such as Korea's, in either design or execution. The goals and mechanisms employed in Korea were simply not in line with Malaysia's political economy or administrative system.

Financial Reform

This section briefly reviews the financial reform experience in Malaysia. The reforms were initiated in the 1980s and continued in the 1990s. The major domestic policy changes and outcomes are summarised. The effects, both intended and unintended, of these changes on pre-reform governance systems are analysed, along with other changes to financial governance that have occurred. Finally, an attempt is made to weigh the relative importance of structural and systemic economic imperatives for reform against the political forces influencing the reform agenda with redistributive or rentier motives.

Financial reform in Malaysia was incremental, starting with interest rate decontrol in 1978, followed by increased prudential standards from 1989.[5] Deregulation and active promotion of the financial sector was accompanied by significant growth (Lin 1993). Credit through the banking system increased rapidly. There was a stock market boom in the early 1980s, and even more rapid growth in stock exchange turnover and inter-bank assets occurred in the late 1980s and early 1990s. The government also led the effort to establish and promote an offshore banking facility located in Labuan Island, off Sabah in East Malaysia from 1991. Malaysian companies began to source greater amounts of capital from the equity market in the 1990s. Specialised industrial finance and development banks became even less important from the 1980s, as the assets of development finance institutions declined from an already low 2.9 per cent of total financial assets in 1983 to 1.6 per cent in 1995.

Certain forms of intervention continued. Besides compulsory EPF contributions, voluntary savings institutions were set up and encouraged, including rural co-operatives and the national and state unit trust schemes.[6] Special credit funds established in the 1970s for particular borrowers or activities were maintained in the post-reform period, with some new funds — especially bank-backed unit trusts — set up in this period.[7] The special credit directives brought in during the 1970s continued to operate but, while significant at the time, they were of little significance by the 1990s. The most significant directive in 1975 mandated 20 per cent of bank credit to Bumiputeras when such lending was low, but by the 1990s, it was well over the stipulated 20 per cent. The amounts required for other designated sectors were negligible. Some control of interest rates was re-instituted during the 1980s, when banks were required to publish their 'base lending rates', determined in relation to the cost of funds, and specified types of loans were not to be charged more than a set amount from the base rate. This system continued until 1991 (Zainal *et al.* 1994).

Government influence over the sectoral distribution of credit remained minimal. Property loans did not moderate in the 1980s despite being frequently cited as problematic. Bank Negara often stated that lending for property and share purchases was too high in the first half of the 1980s, but such lending increased in the second half of the decade, both in absolute and relative terms. Directives on the direction of lending were largely irrelevant. For example, the 1989 banking law limits exposure to property and shares, but lending to these sectors in the 1990s was similar to what it was in the early 1980s, later judged to be too high. Considering the string of troubled banks in the mid-1980s, mainly due to over-exposure to property and shares, more stringent limits might have been expected.

Government transfers and lending to the private and state enterprise sectors have been significant (Zainal *et al.* 1994: 287; Kanapathy and Ismail 1994: 107), but in line with the policy to reduce the state's role in the economy, such transfers became less significant from the mid-1980s. However, one of the largest state-owned banks, Bank Bumiputra, required two bailouts during the 1980s (and another two after 1997). Other banks required extensive liquidity support in the late-1980s. An undisclosed amount of public money was spent overcoming the banking crisis of the late 1980s, when RM25 billion in non-performing loans (NPLs) were acknowledged. This episode was considered well managed and, with the exception of the Bank Bumiputra bailouts, not an excessive burden on public finances.

Foreign borrowing by Malaysian companies was not high. Permission was required for loans above a certain size, but this was readily given (Abang 1986: 307). However, the availability of domestic credit meant that incentives to borrow offshore were not great. In the 1990s, the most significant Malaysian issuers of foreign debt were some large public enterprises. Restrictions on foreign currency debt acquisition by Malaysian companies have recently received more emphasis (BNM *Annual Report*, 1997: 192-93). The current account remained generally open, with no controls on short-term outflows, although reporting requirements were significant. The major control that continued until the period of strong capital inflows in the 1990s was that trade-related foreign currency earnings were to be repatriated within six months of receipt. Until the reversals from mid-1997, the 1990s saw an absolute and relative increase in the size of portfolio flows, largely due to mutual funds from developed countries turning their attention to emerging markets in Asia (Khan and Reinhart 1995). In 1993 in particular, capital inflows were very high. In early 1994, temporary controls aimed at limiting portfolio inflows were put in place, but were removed by the end of the year.

Efforts to maintain monetary autonomy with exchange rate stability continued in the 1990s. Over the period 1990-93, the currency hardly moved at all against the US dollar, despite the extremely large capital inflows.[8] The currency strengthened slightly over 1994-96, before dropping precipitously in the regional currency crisis of 1997-98. Given the large inflows of capital and rapid growth in the economy, keeping the currency undervalued contributed to excess domestic liquidity and inflationary pressures. Bank Negara attempted to deal with these pressures by targeting interest rates, a monetary policy lever that only began to be employed seriously from 1990 (BNM 1994). The massive sterilisation efforts by Bank Negara saw official external reserves increase by 55 per cent in 1992 and by 62 per cent in 1993. The costs of these efforts remain undisclosed, but were probably high (Kahn and Reinhart eds. 1995). Further, the expectation of eventual appreciation further enhanced capital inflows, compounding the effect of continued high interest rates due to sterilisation. The ringgit appreciated against the US dollar in 1994 and 1995, but remained lower than what many market analysts saw as realistic or consistent with fundamentals.[9] And in mid-1997, it was considered only slightly overvalued (Tan 1998).

Reforms in Malaysia were driven by political considerations more than by systemic imperatives. The moderately high levels of state debt run up in the early 1980s were certainly not sustainable, and some measures, such as the more permissive foreign direct investment regime, were probably necessary to pull Malaysia out of recession in the mid-1980s. However, many of the measures to deregulate the financial system and disengage the state from the economy occurred either before the slowdown in the early 1980s (e.g. interest rate decontrol) or in the context of high growth, with little fiscal pressure on the government from the late 1980s (e.g. promotion of the offshore capital and equity markets, and extensive privatisations).

Clear political favouritism can be seen in the implementation of many of the economic reforms of the 1980s and 1990s. Privatisation has been associated with significant favours to politically-connected private interests (Jomo ed. 1995). Many changes in the ownership structure of the banking sector corresponded with the rise of Bumiputera interests in general and politically-connected groups in particular (Gomez and Jomo 1999). Certainly, vested interests linked to or supportive of the ruling party have benefited extensively from banking sector developments and from the robust growth of the equity market. Favoured individuals have made huge windfall profits from preferential allocation of new stock market issues (*AWSJ*, 19 June 1995), while political party fundraising efforts were probably behind stock market manipulation in 1993 (Gomez 1996). This may explain the strong official promotion of the stock market in a country that does not have an optimal banking system (Chin and Jomo 1996).

An increasingly close identity of political and business interests emerged from the mid-1980s. Although not unknown earlier, the high proportion of politicians and ruling party officials with extensive business involvement is a development from the 1980s (Doh 1985: 109-15; Leigh 1992; Bowie 1994). There has also been the growth of money politics within UMNO, the dominant partner in the ruling coalition and the divestment of party assets to trusted individuals (Gomez and Jomo 1999). Mahathir had an explicit policy of reducing the role of the state, especially the size of the bureaucracy, and implementing reforms to make the civil service more efficient and responsive to the private sector (Root 1996: 65-89). Downsizing the public sector through privatisation combined with extensive new opportunities in the private sector, resulted unfortunately in some reduced administrative capacity in government, as talented and capable personnel moved to the private sector. Some regulatory agencies became less effective due to reduced powers, demoralisation, personnel changes and other factors. The Capital Issues Committee (CIC) was taken from the relatively efficient and effective central bank in the mid-1980s to the Treasury only to be reconstituted later within the Securities Commission (SC) in 1993.

However, it would be an exaggeration to conclude that politics and favouritism have dominated financial policy to the exclusion of other considerations. Corruption and the manipulation of government policy for private purposes were a long way from levels seen in Indonesia in the 1990s or in the Philippines under Marcos in the 1980s. In comparative surveys of corruption, Malaysia was consistently in the middle ranks, among countries such as Japan and South Korea (Root 1996: xv). Also, allegations of corruption and influence mostly involve politicians, not civil servants — which may be an indication of where the centre of decision-making is, but this also means that when political interest is not high, the interests motivating bureaucratic action can be reasonably independent, making for a moderately regularised and coherent administration.

Bank Negara was not untainted by scandal, but was considered to be one of the more competent, more meritocratic and independent government bodies. It was, at various times, tasked with cleaning up private and state sector institutions not under central bank supervision at the time. This includes involvement in the aftermath of a corruption and mismanagement scandal of a state development bank in 1978, and failures of deposit-taking co-operatives and problem banks from 1986 and the insurance industry in the late 1980s. Most accounts of the central bank's resolution of these problems concur that the bank did reasonably well in these instances. Doubts about whether some private shareholders were sufficiently punished have been voiced, but it is significant that the financial problems of the institutions under Bank Negara supervision were mostly resolved, which stands in contrast to Bank Indonesia's record of ongoing deterioration of the banks under its supervision and control. On the other hand, political constraints may have deterred Bank Negara from taking tougher disciplinary action against favoured interests.[10]

Currency and Banking Crises, 1997-98

The recent decade-long economic boom came unstuck owing to the economic consequences of and policy reactions to the massive asset price deflation — due to panic ('irrationally' pessimistic herd behaviour) greatly exaggerating the impact of successful currency speculation against untenable virtual currency pegs against the US dollar. Such market behaviour sought to gain advantage or minimise losses from some unintended consequences of the region's currency appreciations. The overvalued regional currencies had emerged from partial financial liberalisation, which had also created the conditions for the asset price inflationary bubbles that burst in mid-1997 with such devastating consequences. Such problems were further exacerbated by injudicious official policy responses along lines advocated by the IMF. Failure to recognise the true nature of the processes of accumulation and growth in Malaysia had generally prevented the implementation of appropriate and adequate proactive strategies of well-designed and sequenced deregulation in the face of growing WTO and other pressures for financial liberalisation.

There is now little serious disagreement that the Malaysian economic turmoil since mid-1997 began as currency and liquidity crises. It is also increasingly agreed that the crisis was principally due to the undermining of the previous system of financial governance due to deregulation and other developments associated with globalisation, and the growing influence of financial interests at both international and national levels as well as other pressures for financial liberalisation. Such developments have included the subversion of effective financial governance at both international and national levels, which has created conditions increasingly vulnerable to financial crisis. It is now also widely acknowledged that the currency and liquidity crises became a crisis of the 'real economy', mainly due to ill-conceived and IMF inspired government policy responses as problems emerged (e.g. Jomo 1998b).

High growth rates and high rates of return on capital (high interest rates as well as high returns to portfolio investments) plus predictable exchange rates (with currencies in the region pegged to the US dollar) as well as the absence of regulations on capital flows attracted enormous short term capital flows of two types. On the one hand, international banks were especially keen to lend to both banks as well as corporations in the region. To minimise risks and cut costs, they tended to lend short, but borrowers in the region were quite happy to deploy such borrowed funds for long-term purposes. Fortunately, Malaysian central bank regulation limited such borrowings within the country, ostensibly only to companies able to demonstrate foreign exchange earning capacity. However, of the three main corporate borrowers from abroad, only MAS, the national air carrier, really qualified under this criterion; neither the privatised electricity giant Tenaga Nasional nor the main telecommunications provider Telekom Malaysia, the other two big borrowers from abroad, have much foreign earnings to speak of.

On the other hand, foreign portfolio investments increased markedly. Inflows were actively promoted by the Malaysian government, particularly after the Kuala Lumpur Stock Exchange (KLSE) parted ways with the Stock Exchange of Singapore (SES) at the beginning of the 1990s. The government organised frequent 'road shows' — involving no less than the Prime Minister himself — to the major international financial centres of the East Asian region, Europe and the United States. These efforts were in line with the promotion of newly emerging securities markets by the International Finance Corporation, an affiliate of the World Bank. Buoyant conditions in the region and implicit government guarantees of easy repatriation of capital and profits further encouraged portfolio inflows.

In Malaysia, the rapid growth of equity finance involved some relative, if not absolute financial disintermediation. In terms of overall financial development, Malaysia had high levels of domestic bank borrowings and consequently, relatively high debt-equity ratios. Its stock market capitalisation was exceptionally high by any standards. Table 3.2 summarises some pre-crisis indicators for Malaysia and its neighbours.

Table 3.2

Pre-Crisis Financial Development and Internationalisation
(billions of U.S. dollars and as a percentage of GDP)[11]

	Credit[a]		Money[b]		Stocks[c]		Capital Inflows[d]	
	$bn	%	$bn	%	$bn	%	$bn	%
Indonesia	123.9	55.0	94.9	42	43.5	19	10.8	4.8
Philippines	40.5	49.0	36.1	43	31.3	38	7.7	9.3
Malaysia	92.2	93.5	67.1	68	223.5	227	9.5	9.6
Thailand	185.0	100.0	130.3	70	142.0	77	19.5	10.5

Notes: [a] Claims on private sector held by deposit money banks, end 1996 (Source: IMF, *International Financial Statistics*, November 1998).

[b] Quasi-money (Source: IMF, *International Financial Statistics*, November 1998).

[c] Stock market capitalisation, December 1995 (Source: Crosby Research figures cited in *Euromoney*, 1996: 84).

[d] Net inflows of capital: financial and capital account of the balance of payments, 1996.

Sources: IMF, *International Financial Statistics* (November 1998) except Philippines: preliminary figures from *Philippine Statistical Yearbook 1997*.

Malaysia's large current account deficits were being financed by short-term capital inflows into the fast-growing domestic securities markets and, to a lesser extent, by borrowings from abroad. The current account deficits were partly due to short-term capital which were used for the production of 'non-tradables', much of which was related to accelerated construction activity in response to real property booms as well as the government's often grandiose 'mega-projects'. These inflows were 'sterilised' to minimise consumer price inflation, as desired by the financial community, but also fuelled asset price inflation, mainly involving real estate and share prices.

Despite official claims that the region's currencies were determined by the market based on representative baskets of currencies of their major trading partners, for all intents and purposes, they had been pegged — within narrow bands — to the US dollar for many years. Such quasi-pegging had offered certain advantages, including the semblance of exchange rate stability against the US dollar. The 1994 devaluation of China's renminbi put greater competitive pressure on the Southeast Asian economies (especially Thailand), which had been producing for similar export markets. Then, as the US dollar strengthened against the Japanese yen from mid-1995, the dollar-pegged ringgit appreciated in tandem, adversely affecting Malaysia's export competitiveness.

This was exacerbated by Malaysia's failure to progress more rapidly to higher value-added production, mainly due to inadequate public investments in education and training as well as limited indigenous industrial capabilities. This state of affairs also reflected the political weakness of export manufacturer interests — compared to the financial community in terms of influencing economic policymaking — since most internationally competitive industrial capability outside of resource-based manufacturing is still foreign-owned, while state-promoted Bumiputera ownership of the banking sector advanced most rapidly in the seventies. The high investment rates may also have led to some over-capacity as well as declining 'investment quality and productivity'.[12]

The establishment and expansion of various new international financial facilities in the region to ease access to foreign funds also undermined financial governance, especially prudential banking regulation, at the national level. The Malaysian authorities set up Labuan as an international off-shore financial centre (IOFC) from 1993, while Malaysian borrowers also had relatively easy access to other financial facilities in Singapore, Hong Kong and elsewhere. Such reforms and the growth of 'private banking' and 'relationship banking' in the region as well as intensified competition among 'debt-pushing' and balance sheet expanding banks also weakened the scope and effectiveness of national financial governance. Other domestic as well as international financial sector reforms — such as the Uruguay Round's General Agreement on Trade in Services (GATS) — also considerably reduced the powers and jurisdiction of the region's central banks and other financial authorities. Ironically, this has been further undermined in the aftermath of the outbreak of the crisis with amendments to the IMF's Articles of Agreement to extend its jurisdiction to the capital account, and the late 1997 World Trade Organisation's Financial Services Agreement. International co-operation aimed at different purposes will be necessary if governments are to deal with the effects of global capital flows.

In the immediate aftermath of the outbreak of the crisis in mid-1997, many economic observers immediately assumed that the crises in the Southeast Asian region were due to poor macroeconomic management, as suggested by the second generation of currency crisis theories. However, it soon became clear that all the affected Southeast Asian economies had been maintaining decent macroeconomic balances except for Malaysia's and Thailand's large balance of payments' current account deficits which had been financed by massive, mainly short-term capital inflows. With the debt — especially foreign borrowings — mainly involving the private sector, and with continued high savings and growth rates, apparent fiscal surpluses as well as low consumer price inflation, national monetary and financial authorities had been encouraged by the international financial community and persuaded by the IMF, World Bank and WTO to accelerate —rather than reduce — international financial liberalisation.

The recent currency and financial crises seem to suggest that Malaysia's economic boom of the 1990s had been built on some vulnerable and unsustainable foundations. Much of the retained wealth generated had been captured by vested interests associated with those in power, who in turn contributed to growth by mainly re-investing much of their captured rents in the 'protected' domestic economy, e.g. in import-substituting industries, commerce, services and privatised utilities and infrastructure. Despite various weaknesses, this Malaysian brand of ersatz capitalism — involving changing forms of *crony rentierism* — had sustained rapid growth for four decades.

Once it became clear that Malaysia's macroeconomic indicators were not seriously awry, and in the wake of the recent debates on Asian values and other cultural, institutional and behavioural differences, many commentators increasingly invoked cronyism, associated rent-seeking and their alleged consequences as new explanations for the crises. Most such critics condemned some caricatured images of cronyism and rent-seeking — as reflected in various alleged departures from some 'market fundamentalist' ideal — to explain the crises, usually ignoring all the subtlety and nuance of extant analyses of rent-seeking in the country (Gomez and Jomo 1999). Thus, Malaysia's financial turmoil came to be portrayed as having been induced mainly by crony capitalism and rent seeking.

Business organisations, networks, practices and norms — that had previously been credited with the Malaysian 'miracle' — have since been condemned as the sources of the debacle. It also became fashionable in some quarters to suggest that such practices and developments had their roots in Japanese-type or more generically East Asian culture, norms and relationships. These are said to have compromised relations between the state and the private sector, generating moral hazard and involving welfare-reducing, if not debilitating rent-seeking behaviour. In so far as such relations are believed to exclude outsiders, their elimination is expected to contribute to levelling the playing field and to bringing about an inevitable convergence towards supposedly Anglo-American style arms-length market relations.

Such arrangements and institutions — previously celebrated as part of the basis for the region's phenomenally rapid growth — are now derogatorily referred to as elements of crony capitalism and rent seeking. While popular with the neo-liberal international media and not without moral appeal, it cannot be conclusively proven that they actually directly precipitated the crisis, nor even that they satisfactorily explain its bases and origins. However, cronyism (and nepotism) have certainly influenced — and compromised — official policy responses to the crises in Malaysia (Jomo 1998b). More importantly, such influences may well have exacerbated the crises and are likely to continue to undermine confidence in government efforts, and further delay recovery.

The first generation of currency crisis theories — which had focused on public sector foreign debt related to fiscal deficits — had quickly been recognised as irrelevant to Malaysia, where the government had consistently maintained budgetary surpluses in recent years. Apparently, however, this did not deter other international analysts — perhaps more familiar with Latin American or Eastern European problems — from prescribing the deflationary government spending cuts which characterised early IMF prescriptions to the Southeast Asian governments seeking its credit assistance. The prestige and influence of the IMF ensured that many — from within and without the region — were quick to echo and push the Fund's policy recommendations, even to governments such as Malaysia's, which did not require emergency credit facilities from the IMF.

With the benefit of hindsight, it is now widely agreed that IMF policy responses exacerbated — rather than ameliorated — the crises in the region (Sachs and Radelet 1998). It appears that the Fund initially saw the currency crises as similar to earlier ones in Latin America and elsewhere (Kregel 1998). Even though the Malaysian government had not run fiscal deficits for some time (mainly due to 'one-off' revenue from the sale of public assets through privatisation), IMF and financial markets' influenced international public opinion insisted on fiscal spending cuts, which exacerbated the deflationary effects of the sudden massive currency devaluations. Given Malaysia's fiscal position, temporary counter-cyclical budget deficits would have helped to counter the deflationary impact of the crises. At the end of 1997, the government cut public spending on several controversial 'mega-projects' to reduce the anticipated budget deficit, only to increase social spending, mainly on subsidised housing, from June 1998.

The Fund also urged raising domestic interest rates, ostensibly to try to immediately reverse capital outflows, even though there was little immediate prospect of success while there was a crisis of confidence. The high interest rates in Malaysia from late 1997 did little to stem capital flight, but instead created further debt servicing burdens on borrowers, and consequently exacerbated the banks' bad debt problems. It should be noted, however, that the Malaysian authorities then did not simply allow interest rates to rise as dictated by the market and advised by the IMF, but instead tried to moderate interest rates. With the huge off-shore ringgit market emerging, mainly in Singapore, it would have been almost impossible to keep interest rates down while protecting the ringgit exchange rate from deteriorating further in early and mid-1998 without drastic measures such as those adopted in September 1998. Since the vast majority of growing businesses were already heavily in debt (this being a common feature of corporate expansion in Malaysia), high interest rates rendered the private sector — already beleaguered by the adverse consequences of the ringgit collapse — more vulnerable to collapse. To make matters worse, the credit ratings of both Malaysia and Malaysian corporations were downgraded, further raising the cost of badly needed external funds.

The IMF also exacerbated the situation by insisting on immediate drastic actions against problematic financial institutions in the region, thereby transforming a temporary liquidity problem into an insolvency crisis, which has been compared to 'shouting fire in a crowded darkened theatre'. While structural reforms are undoubtedly necessary — in the medium term — to rebuild stronger financial systems, the timing of these actions further undermined the fragile confidence in domestic financial institutions, causing runs on many of them, thus worsening the viability of these financial systems. Almost inevitable government actions — as lenders of last resort to save these systems in the absence of viable alternatives — have since been denounced as evidence of government policy interventions contributing to moral hazard, although there is little real evidence of explicit government guarantees which can be construed as the bases for such claims. In other words, the fact of subsequent government interventions to save distressed financial institutions does not, in itself, prove that the governments had contributed to moral hazard by explicitly making such guarantees before the crises.

Other IMF demands for immediate structural adjustments and systemic reforms — previously prescribed elsewhere over the medium term (e.g. accompanying the short-term stabilisation measures introduced in the wake of the 1980s' debt crises) — only worsened the situation by overloading the reform agenda at a time of chaos and uncertainty as well as reduced capacity and resources. In some cases, the conditionalities imposed were not even relevant to solving the immediate problems at hand, but instead reflected particular 'market fundamentalist' views of how Southeast Asian economies should be reorganised. For example, the Malaysian authorities redefined 'non-performing loans' more stringently, reducing the grace period from six months to the international norm of three months, thus causing systemic stress to worsen at a time when the effects of the worsening financial crisis were reverberating through the economy.

In the third quarter of 1997, the Japanese Government offered to contribute generously to the US$100 billion suggested for the establishment of some kind of Asian monetary facility to address the region's rapidly unfolding crisis. This initiative was blocked by opposition from the Clinton administration, China and the IMF, which may have felt that its authority would have been undermined by alternative sources of emergency credit accessible on less onerous terms. The slow US response to the East Asian regional crisis contrasted with its earlier intervention to save Mexico from going belly up in 1995 as well as its almost unconditional support for the Yeltsin regime in August 1998. In the aftermath of the Russian and Long-Term Credit Management (LTCM) crises and ensuing Wall Street panic of August 1998, however, the Clinton administration did not openly oppose the Miyazawa Initiative to provide US$30 billion towards East Asian credit needs, but instead tried to gain some credit at the Asia Pacific Economic Co-operation (APEC) Forum in Kuala Lumpur in early November by offering to top up the Japanese offer with a much more modest financial aid offer of its own. In the meantime, however, the US Federal Reserve brought down interest rates in September 1998 causing the yen and other East Asian currencies to strengthen until September 1999. Thus, fixing the Malaysian ringgit at RM3.80 to the US dollar, which was intended to prop up the value of the currency, inadvertently depreciated it, with mixed, but generally positive consequences for export recovery.

The Malaysian currency controls since September 1998 provided a critical window of opportunity by restoring government control over monetary policy, enabling the authorities to lower interest rates (previously subject to offshore currency trading) and to peg the exchange rate (ironically, against the US dollar again). By moving briskly to take over non-performing loans and to re-capitalise the banks through Danaharta and Danamodal respectively, the Malaysian authorities succeeded in salvaging the banking system and restoring financial confidence. However, there is also evidence of considerable abuse of this window of opportunity to bail out and even extend vested interests, especially in the financial sector, e.g. through forced bank mergers, even involving healthy banks and those which have not sought government assistance. Also, the failure to draw meaningful policy reform lessons from the banking crisis of the late 1980s for subsequent prudential regulation — or perhaps the failure to sustain the greater prudence which initially emerged after that episode — casts doubt as to whether the financial system is able to effectively internalise lessons from past experiences, including previous crises.

Conclusion

This study has argued that the institutional foundations of the financial policy regime matter, though this does not mean that financial policy design is unimportant (e.g. Chin and Jomo 1996). Particular strengths and weaknesses stem from particular organisational and political settings. The institutional foundations of governance that work relatively well in sheltered systems, may fail when the policy regime favours greater financial liberalisation. Poor governance is likely to produce policy failures no matter what particular policies are attempted. In other words, financial governance is important, and good policy design, in itself, cannot alone guarantee good outcomes. Good policy can fail because of poor implementation or enforcement and the lack of political will.

This study has also highlighted the particular pitfalls of financial liberalisation, internationalisation and unregulated capital mobility in the absence of robust regulatory regimes. In contrast, the consequences of regulatory failure appear to be much less serious in more protected financial systems. Some degree of international openness may be a salutary source of discipline, but this discipline tends to be ambiguous, post-hoc and counterproductive since international financial markets often respond to market sentiment, rather than economic fundamentals.

Malaysia's governance capacities were well suited to relatively conservative bank-based financial development. The breakdown from the mid-

1980s of its previously strong regulatory record and exceptional financial stability (by developing country standards) corresponded with the changed orientation of the country's financial policy (e.g. official stock market promotion resulting in some relative financial disintermediation), increased political subversion of regulation and a rise in private sector influence over policy ('Malaysia Incorporated'). The problem of mania or over-exuberance followed by panic — that seems to be a common feature of financial market behaviour — has been exacerbated by the growing internationalisation of financial market activity.

The study also shows that undue influence exerted by special interests often distorts policy and its implementation. The inherent imperfections of financial markets mean that there is a strong case for some government role, both for prudential regulation and to take a more proactive role in better allocating financial resources to ensure desirable, sustained and equitable development. In both cases, more attention needs to be directed to building the necessary governance capacity. In some cases, this may be achieved by private sector mechanisms for controlling financial transactions, but the broader policy and regulatory framework, together with a country's political and administrative conditions, must be conducive to effective private sector governance. Hence, it is unlikely that relatively efficient financial markets can be created and sustained in the absence of uncompromised and consistent government authority. It is not simply a matter of making the right prudential and financial development policies, but also of ensuring that they are effectively implemented or enforced.

Notes

1. Figures on foreign exchange transactions were not available until the 1980s. Comments in the annual reports of the central bank suggest that before then, transactions were mainly trade-related.
2. The major studies of the bureaucracy, on which this account is based, are Tilman (1964), Esman (1972), Puthucheary (1978) and Khasnor (1984).
3. A World Bank mission in 1954 recommended establishing a central bank, more detailed plans for which were put forward in the Watson-Caine report of 1956 (Sherwood 1966). The primary study of central banking in Malaysia is Lee (1987).
4. This argument is elaborated further in Hamilton-Hart (1999, Ch. 4).
5. A concise overview of financial policies over time is given by Zainal *et al.* (1994).
6. Savings through the ASN and ASB schemes amounted to over RM12 billion between 1981 and 1992 (Khalid, in Al Alim 1994: 171).
7. These funds are described in BNM (1994: 164-83).

8. The end-year rates are slightly deceptive. From December 1992 to September 1993, the currency did appreciate 2 per cent but dropped nearly 6 per cent in the last quarter of 1993, due to heavy selling by the central bank to reduce the Malaysian-currency value of its foreign exchange losses.
9. The assessment that the currency was undervalued was made by the IMF Managing Director in July 1996. A Morgan Stanley report predicted in 1994 that the ringgit should trade at RM2.00 to the dollar by 1996. See Ong (1996: 10) and Zeti (forthcoming).
10. Details are given in Hamilton-Hart (1999: Ch. 4).
11. Calculated according to the following exchange rates and GDP values:

	1996 GDP *(billions, local currency)*	*Exchange rate* *per US$, end 1996*
Indonesia	532,631	2383
Philippines	2171.9	26.288
Malaysia	249.503	2.529
Thailand	4689.6	25.343

Source: IMF, *International Financial Statistics* (November 1998).

12. These notions are somewhat nebulous and may refer to the increasing share of 'non-productive' investments, e.g. in real estate, and sometimes to financial losses after the bubble burst as asset values and actual rates of return turn out to be well below expected capital gains and rates of return to investments.

4

FINANCIAL LIBERALISATION AND SYSTEM VULNERABILITY

Chin Kok Fay and Jomo K. S.

To trace the roots of the currency and financial crises in Malaysia, we begin with a discussion of financial developments in the country prior to the crisis before considering the broader macroeconomic situation.[1] Given the dominance of the banking system and the growing importance of the stock market, our discussion will concentrate mainly on banking and stock-market developments to give insights into the structure of Malaysia's financial system. Analysis of the characteristics of financial developments and reforms in the years leading to the crisis will shed light on how financial interests and liberalisation have undermined effective financial governance, both at the international and national levels, causing greater vulnerability of the system to crisis. In this chapter, we show how financial interests favoured certain policies, including selective financial liberalisation, which led to increased lending for unproductive purposes, asset price inflation, massive reversible short-term capital inflows and an overvalued currency.

Development of the Financial System

Although Malaysia's financial system was relatively developed during the British colonial era and in the early post-independence period compared to other developing countries, it played a limited role in financial intermediation, the main function of banking services being that of facilitating trade. Banks mainly provided funds for the agency houses, which dominated the exports of the country's primary commodities (tin and rubber) as well as the imports of consumer and capital goods.[2] Financing was thus essentially short-term and self-liquidating as it was mostly in the form of bills of exchange, letters of credit, overdrafts and trust receipt facilities, which normally did not exceed 180 days in maturity. And it was repaid as soon as the goods concerned were received or exported (Hing 1987: 421).

Conscious efforts to develop the financial system only began after the setting up of the Central Bank of Malaya, which was renamed Bank Negara Malaysia (BNM) after the formation of Malaysia in September 1963. Since then, the financial system has been restructured, reorganised and reshaped to meet the increasing investment needs of the growing economy. It has certainly become much deeper, broader and more diverse, with a host of institutional developments taking place over the decades.

The banking system in Malaysia, which has always been the core of the financial system, not only consists of monetary institutions[3] (comprising BNM and commercial banks including Bank Islam), but also non-monetary institutions[4] (including finance companies and merchant banks). The turn of the decade also saw aggressive promotion and rapid growth of the capital market. The turn of the last decade saw two important developments with enormous implications for the future development of Malaysia's financial system. In 1989, the Banking and Financial Institutions Act (BAFIA) was passed by Parliament, with vast implications for governance of the financial system. Soon after, the Kuala Lumpur Stock Exchange (KLSE) broke off from its Siamese twin, the Stock Exchange of Singapore (SES), paving the way for its subsequent rapid growth. In recent years, the government has adopted several measures to promote a venture capital market in order to facilitate the mobilisation of financial resources for technology development in the manufacturing sector.[5]

Table 4.1 and Figure 4.1 reflect growing monetisation and financial deepening in Malaysia. Table 4.1 shows that the M2/GNP ratio increased from 0.46 in 1975 to 0.70 in 1985, and subsequently to 1.11 in 1997, reflecting rapid monetisation in the country. This is also reflected in a sharp increase of the M2/M1 ratio, from 2.3 in 1975 to 3.71 in 1985 and to 4.61 in 1997. The increasing monetisation of the economy has been accompanied by further deepening of Malaysia's financial system. As shown in Figure 4.1, the M3/GDP ratio in 1997 was more than double its value in 1980, although the transaction demand for M1 relative to GDP remained fairly stable over the period.

Table 4.1
Malaysia: Monetisation and Financial Deepening, 1975-1997

	1975	*1980*	*1985*	*1990*	*1991*	*1992*	*1993*	*1994*	*1995*	*1996*	*1997*[*]
M1/GNP	0.20	0.19	0.19	0.22	0.22	0.22	0.27	0.26	0.25	0.25	0.24
M2/GNP	0.46	0.54	0.70	0.76	0.78	0.81	0.89	0.89	0.96	0.98	1.11
M2/M1	2.30	2.87	3.71	3.46	3.57	3.77	3.35	3.45	3.83	3.85	4.61
Currency/M1	0.51	0.49	0.46	0.41	0.41	0.40	0.32	0.34	0.34	0.31	0.34

Notes: [*] Bank Negara Malaysia estimates.
   M1 = Currency and demand deposits.
   M2 = M1 plus savings deposits.
Source: Bank Negara Malaysia, *Quarterly Economic Bulletin*, various issues.

Figure 4.1
Malaysia: Deepening of Financial System, 1980-1997

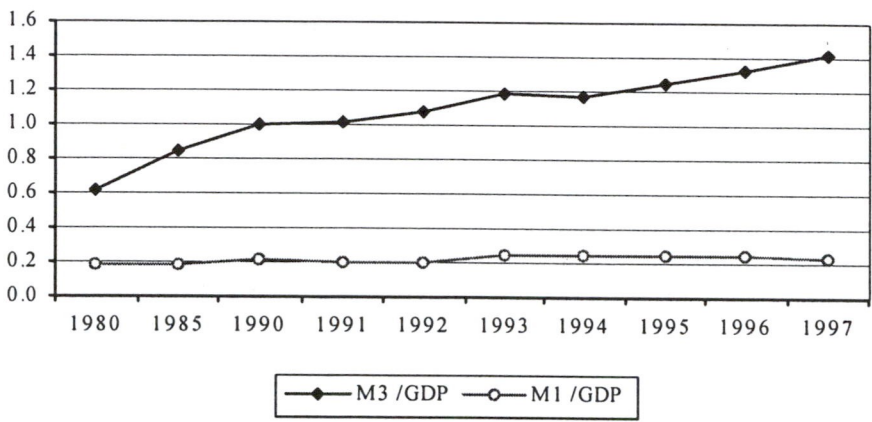

Source: Bank Negara Malaysia, *Quarterly Economic Bulletin*, various issues.

The Banking System

Generally, the differences between financial systems have been the result of interactions of a number of factors that have exerted influence over a long period of time (Rybczynski 1984: 280-2). The evolution of different financial systems can be traced back to the political, social and economic history of the countries concerned. Being a former British colony and being greatly influenced by trends in the United Kingdom and the United States since independence, the Malaysian financial system has exhibited many features of the Anglo-American model, which restricts banking activities to accepting deposits, granting loans and other specified activities.

During the early post-colonial period, loans advanced for general commerce remained high, reaching 42 per cent of total loans of the commercial banking system while those advanced to agriculture and manufacturing were low, amounting to less than 20 per cent. Even in 1960, loans for general commerce constituted about 25 per cent of all loans of the financial system while those for manufacturing and agriculture were less than 15 per cent (Table 4.2). As Ho (1990: 2) commented: 'Banks concentrated on discounting of trade bills, providing the letters of credit and checking the credit-worthiness of traders and merchants. In this sense, they were nothing more than foreign outfits to process trade papers and to act as insurers for merchants.'

Table 4.2

Malaysia: Direction of Loans and Advances by Sector, 1960-1992 (% share)

Sector	1960	1970	1980	1988	1990	1992
Manufacturing	7.9	15.5	19.9	16.5	19.0	18.4
Agriculture	5.6	23.0	8.4	5.8	4.9	4.1
General Commerce	24.7	13.7	18.0	12.5	10.1	8.2
Broad Property*	15.7	13.1	27.6	34.5	27.9	28.3

Note: * Comprises construction, real estate and housing.
Sources: For 1960-70, Bank Negara Malaysia (1989b); for 1980-92, Bank Negara
Malaysia (1994).

Despite the relatively recent rapid growth of the securities market in Malaysia (first established in the early 1960s by the Malaysian Industrial Development Finance), the banking system had long remained the main source of funds for the private sector in both absolute and relative terms. But, being fashioned after the 'Anglo-American model', banks in Malaysia are kept at arm's length from corporate governance and management. They also tend to be conservative, mainly extending loans on the basis of collateral, rather than project viability. 'These policies... impose on industry a similarly cautious and short-term view of investment, profitability and profit allocation, and inhibit long-term or high-risk industrial investment' (Hing 1987: 422).

Under the Banking (Control of Acquisition and Holding of Shares) Regulations of 1968,[6] a bank could only invest up to 10 per cent of the bank's paid-up capital and reserves (or 10 per cent of the net working funds in the case of a foreign bank) in trustee shares. A domestic bank was not permitted to hold shares of companies exceeding 25 per cent of the bank's paid-up capital and reserves, while a foreign bank was not permitted to invest more than 25 per cent of its net working funds in such shares (BNM 1989: 101). Also, it was not permitted to own shares worth more than 10 per cent of its paid-up capital and reserves (5 per cent of net working funds in the case of a foreign bank), whichever is lower. The value of these shares was not to exceed 25 per cent of a domestic bank's paid-up capital and reserves, or 25 per cent of a foreign bank's allowed net working funds.

Apart from historical accidents, many institutional arrangements and developments in the financial system have been due to the regulatory framework, which has evolved over the decades. Commercial banks — the oldest established financial intermediaries — have remained the largest institutions within the banking system, with total assets worth RM362 billion or 57.5 per cent of the total assets of the banking system in 1996 (BNM 1997a: 85). Their significance has been due to their roles as retail deposit takers as well as providers of current accounts. They provide financing in the forms of overdrafts, trade bills and term loans. This traditional pattern of lending has, however, changed significantly over time, as reflected by the declining share of general commerce in total loans and advances since independence (Table 4.3). Another positive development in the evolution of commercial bank lending has been increased term lending, lengthening the average maturity period for credit. There was a decline in the use of overdrafts for short-term financing — from 37.2 per cent of total loans and advances in 1978 to 29.7 per cent by the end of 1990 (Zainal *et al.* 1994: 307). This can partly be attributed to the BNM urging commercial banks to emphasise term lending in view of the rising demand for long-term credit with rapid industrialisation and economic growth.

The 1965 establishment of Bank Bumiputra, the first state-owned commercial bank in Malaysia, marked the beginning of active direct government intervention in finance. Following a resolution of the First Bumiputera Economic Congress in 1965, the state-owned bank was set up in 1966 to provide commercial loans to Malay entrepreneurs. The government became a major shareholder of Malayan Banking in 1969 after a run on the bank in 1966. By 1976, when the then United Malayan Banking Corporation (UMBC)[7] came under government control, the government dominated the banking system, owning the three largest commercial banks in the country.

These state-owned banks were used to facilitate implementation of the New Economic Policy (NEP), introduced in 1970, especially for redistribution as well as the heavy industrialisation program that the government launched in 1981. The state-controlled joint venture with foreign capital began to invest in heavy industries such as Perwaja Steel and Proton (Perusahaan Otomobil Nasional Berhad). These state-sponsored corporations have received loans at subsidised interest rates.

The first half of the 1980s saw many abuses by the directors and staff of banks and finance companies in lending operations. Some major Bumiputera-controlled conglomerates emerged then, mostly under the patronage of powerful politicians, with soft loans from state-owned banks and the award of major projects and lucrative licenses as well as other business opportunities including privatisation (Gomez 1994: 9). The ownership of financial institutions as well as top corporations by the government and by state-owned

Table 4.3
Malaysia: Commercial Bank Lending and Advances to Selected Sectors, 1960-1996 (% share)

Sector	1960	1965	1970	1975	1980	1985	1990	1991	1992	1993	1994	1995	1996
Manufacturing	10.4	15.3	19.8	19.6	22.3	17.5	23.2	23.8	23.4	22.5	23.0	23.3	21.0
Agriculture	7.2	8.5	10.2	7.5	7.9	6.0	5.2	4.5	4.3	3.4	2.5	2.1	2.0
General Commerce	42.2	37.1	32.1	26.6	22.1	17.9	14.4	12.6	11.9	11.4	10.8	10.5	9.8
Broad Property*	3.7	7.3	8.8	18.9	25.4	34.7	18.1	28.8	32.0	31.6	29.3	29.3	30.3

Note: * Comprises construction, real estate and housing.
Sources: For 1960-85, Lee (1987: 312-3); for 1990-91, BNM, *Annual Report, 1992*; for 1992-96, BNM, *Annual Report, 1997*.

enterprises, and later, the privatisation of some of them, served to encourage such developments. Huge loans could be obtained without going through proper procedures, and were often given for speculative get-rich-quick schemes, rather than for productive investments. As such, other national developmentalist priorities, e.g. industrial policy, have been neglected.

Meanwhile, many major corporate groups controlled by non-Bumiputeras[8] have also grown due to political patronage, arising from close ties with powerful, often, Malay politicians (Gomez and Jomo 1997). During the height of implementation of the ethnic redistributive New Economic Policy, many Chinese capitalists minimised their vulnerability to long-term risks by moving capital abroad, mainly from the mid-1970s until the late 1980s (Jomo 1990). Within the country, many preferred short-term investments in construction, commercial property and residential housing at the expense of longer-term investments, as in manufacturing.

The 1980s saw the mushrooming of poorly regulated deposit-taking co-operatives (DTCs) with weak capital bases engaging in speculative and unproductive investments as well as connected lending to or investments in subsidiaries and related companies. Taking advantage of the more liberal interest rate regime and lax regulation, most of these DTCs, which were already insolvent due to hidden losses from heavy investments in shares and property, offered higher deposit rates and attractive commission for their staff to attract deposits. This created the illusion of high liquidity and disguised the rapid deterioration of their actual asset position (BNM 1987: 129). By the mid-eighties, 24 ailing DTCs have collapsed, involving over 522,000 depositors and total deposits of RM1.5 billion (Sheng 1989: 22). As pointed out by Hino (1998: 7), 'the presence of small institutions came to pose systemic risks, not only because of the large number of such institutions that failed, but also because these weaker institutions had attracted larger shares of banking system deposits.'

After the DTC scandal as well as stock and property market crashes from the mid-1980s, the Banking and Financial Institutions Act (BAFIA) was passed by Parliament in 1989, with vast implications for governance of the financial system. For example, since September 1989, the scope of per-missible investments by commercial banks has been broadened.[9] They were then allowed to invest in Malaysia Airline System Berhad (MAS), the Malaysian International Shipping Corporation (MISC), and other approved 'blue chip' shares as well as the shares of manufacturing companies and property trusts, subject to prescribed limits (for details, see BNM 1989: 101; Lee 1992: 281).

Malaysia has had restrictions on the entry and branching by foreign banks, but on October 1, 1990 the government created on the island of Labuan an international offshore financial centre (IOFC). To attract customers by making it comparable to some of the 'best' IOFCs around the world, a relatively liberal regulatory environment was established on the island (Awang Adek 1997). Exchange rate control regulations pertaining to offshore business activities were made very liberal. Preferential tax treatment for income, profits, dividends and interest earned from offshore business activities has been offered.[10] By the end of December 1993, 21 banks held Ministry of Finance licenses to conduct offshore banking activities in Labuan (BNM 1994: 46).

Some earlier efforts to deregulate the Malaysian financial system had encouraged the proliferation of unproductive investments in, for example, the property sector. Following the liberalisation of interest rates in October 1978,[11] there was a property boom, reflecting the banking sector's preference for making collateralised loans with high rates of return rather than for productive long-term investments. In fact, as shown in Table 3.1, the share of bank credit to the property sector rose from 8.8 per cent in 1966-70 to 33.5 per cent in 1986-90, before declining slightly to 30.5 per cent in 1992-96.

This huge increase in property-related lending, which reflected the greater profitability of real estate investments, contrasts with the relatively modest importance of building and construction in GDP. Loans by the banking system for consumption credit also rose, together with loans for purchases of stocks and shares. Bank lending to the stock market only began in the late seventies and averaged 3.8 per cent during 1992-96. As a result, the share of bank credit to the manufacturing sector only rose modestly, while the proportion of lending to agriculture actually declined during the same period despite a sharp increase in the manufacturing sector's share of GDP and agriculture's continued, albeit more modest, growth.

Malaysian banks tend to be conservative, mainly extending loans on the basis of collateral rather than project viability (Hing 1987). Such emphasis on loan security has favoured loans to the real property sector and for share purchases and consumption (rather than production) when the property and stock markets have been bullish. Only about a quarter of Malaysian commercial bank lending went to manufacturing, agriculture and other productive activities (Tables 3.1 and 4.3). This modest share for productive investments is likely to be even smaller for foreign borrowings, most of which has been collateralised with assets such as real property and stocks. The lack of incentives for Malaysian bankers to favour long-term lending for productive investments is one reason for the limited development of Malaysian manufacturing capabilities, especially in non-resource-based export-oriented industries, which are dominated by foreign investors instead. Export-oriented manufacturing only accounts for a very small percentage of total outstanding loans extended by commercial banks. With the exception of export credit and some relatively minor financial institutions, there is little evidence that the government has used financial policy as an instrument for promoting industry (Chin and Jomo 2000; Chin 2000).

A BNM Survey of Private Investment in Malaysia found that the lack of bank credit to the manufacturing sector caused firms to increasingly rely on internally generated funds. On average, the surveyed firms financed 52 to 66 per cent of their capital expenditure from internally generated funds during 1986-90 while bank financing accounted for only about 10 to 14 per cent. Although banks still provided a larger share of external finance than the capital market (ranging from 1 to 8 per cent), this probably reflected the less developed state of the capital market relative to the banking system then. Company size was also found to be an important determinant of access to credit, larger companies enjoying, on average, lower credit costs. This could be due to the fact that financial institutions imposed less stringent requirements for loans to larger companies since they had better track records and reputations than smaller companies (Zainal *et al.* 1994: 313). Such 'discrimination' was more pronounced during the recession of 1985-86, when the average cost of credit for large companies was almost 11 per cent lower than for small and medium-sized enterprises.

With relative — but not absolute — financial disintermediation in Malaysia — due to the rapid growth of the stock market, especially in the early and mid-nineties — more and more corporate borrowers have resorted to tapping funds directly from the capital market. Thus, banks became less assured of easy and stable sources of income from large loans given to well-established corporations. Due to the shrinking customer base for lending following growing competition from the capital market, banks have had to give more attention to servicing small and medium enterprises (SMEs) and households, which generally do not have direct access to the capital market. However, Malaysian banks' typical emphasis on loan security — rather than project viability — has discouraged loans, even to viable SMEs, due to lack of collateral.[12] They thus became more interested in giving direct loans for purchase of residential property and consumer durables (particularly cars), especially with the steady increase in incomes due to rapid growth and rising household wealth due to the appreciation of property and stock market prices from the late 1980s.

In the mid-nineties, well before the crisis, the BNM began trying to consolidate Malaysian banks in anticipation of further financial liberalisation. A new two-tier regulatory system, which sought to provide incentives for smaller banks to re-capitalise and merge, was introduced in December 1994. Tier-one status allows a bank the privilege to handle certain lucrative types of transactions (such as opening foreign currency accounts) denied to other banks without such status. To qualify for tier-one status, banks had to have an equity base of at least RM500 million.

Banks in Malaysia have been heavily used by the state with the New Economic Policy (NEP). With increasing Bumiputera dominance of the Malaysian banking system from the 1970s, financial restraint has been used primarily to ensure bank profitability. As Bumiputeras advanced their interests in the financial sector, competition was limited in some areas, especially from foreign banks, in order to enhance rents for bank owners. However, other policies encouraged wasteful competition in the banking sector that eroded some of these rents. For example, lucrative banking margins have fostered too many bank branches competing for limited business in many areas, resulting in socially wasteful duplication and limiting scale economies in the provision of banking services (Chin and Jomo 2000).

The almost singular pre-occupation with interethnic economic redistribution has compromised the purpose, nature and quality of state intervention generally and of financial policy in particular. In other words, financial policy in Malaysia has been used more as an instrument for interethnic economic redistribution and other related public policies and less as an instrument for promoting long-term productive investments, especially in non-resource-based export-oriented manufacturing. It should be emphasised, however, that it was not the New Economic Policy — with all its consequences for banking — that caused the recent financial problems culminating in the crisis. Rather, the roots of the crisis can be traced to inappropriate and improperly sequenced liberalisation of the Malaysian banking system. Malaysia should have been much more prudent in deregulating the domestic financial sector. With appropriate deregulation as well as continued prudential regulation (e.g. of capital flows to constrain their exit), Malaysia might have been able to mitigate some of the worst excesses that contributed to the recent crisis.

Stock Market Development[13]

Since the late 1980s, promotion of stock markets all over the world by the International Finance Corporation (IFC) of the World Bank has resulted in the growing significance of equity finance and stock markets in the Southeast

Asian region, especially in Malaysia with its British colonial heritage. The split between the Kuala Lumpur Stock Exchange and the Stock Exchange of Singapore at the end of the 1980s gave momentum to the growth of the stock market in Malaysia. The 1992 passage of the Securities Act and the subsequent establishment of the Securities Commission (SC) gave further impetus to stock market growth in Malaysia.

Share trading in Malaysia began as early as the 1870s involving British companies dealing primarily in rubber, tin and international trade. Public trading of stocks and shares was not undertaken until May 1960 when the Malayan Stock Exchange was established (Drake 1969: 210; Zeti 1989: 90-1). The Exchange was renamed the Stock Exchange of Malaysia in 1964 after the formation of Malaysia on 14 September 1963. It was renamed again the Stock Exchange of Malaysia and Singapore after the separation of Singapore from Malaysia in 1965, but it continued to operate as a unified stock exchange with separate trading rooms in Kuala Lumpur and Singapore (Zeti 1989: 92). In 1990, the one in Kuala Lumpur broke off from its Siamese twin, paving the way for its subsequent rapid expansion.

As noted by Singh (1995: 27), contemporary stock market development in many developing countries has not been a spontaneous response to market forces; governments have played a major role in the expansion of these markets. This is particularly true of Malaysia. Between September 1961 and June 1964, the embryonic stock market enjoyed a boom (Drake 1975), but in 1965, it turned bearish,[14] plagued by the existence of counterfeit shares. From 1968, however, under the supervision of the Capital Issues Committee (CIC) and with the government requirement that companies granted pioneer status tax relief go public, there was marked growth in new market issues (Zeti 1989: 97).

With the promulgation of the NEP in 1970, redistribution, especially along interethnic lines, became the most important government public policy priority. Since 1976, firms issuing shares to the public have had to offer 30 per cent of their equity to Bumiputeras.[15] The Foreign Investment Committee (FIC) has become an important government body to monitor and influence non-Bumiputera and foreign-owned corporations to restructure their equity to comply with the NEP's ownership regulations. Together with the FIC, the CIC set the prices of shares issued by local Chinese and foreign firms to Malay interests, including special government-financed trust agencies and investment funds for Bumiputeras.

The prices were usually set below market prices[16] to ensure positive returns for these special investment funds to accelerate capital accumulation

Table 4.4
Malaysia: Over-subscription of New Listings, 1989-1996

Year	Main Board	Second Board
1989	56.3	14.6
1990	52.5	20.1
1991	33.6	25.2
1992	15.9	13.7
1993	41.2	34.5
1994	46.7	32.5
1995	60.8	46.3
1996*	76.8	56.7

Note: * First quarter.
Source: Securities Commission (1996).

and speed up acquisition of corporate assets on behalf of Bumiputeras. Mohamed Ariff *et al.* (1993) argued that excessive under-pricing of Malaysia's initial public offerings (IPOs) was mainly due to government intervention in price setting, and not merely the consequence of asymmetric information, winner's curse or *ex ante* uncertainty or seasoning.[17] Excessive under-pricing of new issues has meant good prospects for capital gains through immediate sale in the market after successful subscription allocation, resulting in the over-subscription of new issues (Table 4.4). As a result of the significant under-pricing of IPOs, particularly in the case of the KLSE Second Board[18] new listings (Securities Commission 1996: 73), the over-subscription of Second Board IPOs grew rapidly, almost catching up with those of the Main Board, which generally have been hovering around 50 times. In addition, the possibility of making quick tax-exempt capital gains, encouraged even more to subscribe to new shares (Ng 1989: 44).

The stock market has grown with considerable support from the government and those who have sought to use the stock market and publicly-listed firms to capture various types of rents and to secure better access to relatively cheap funds (Chin and Jomo 2000). In August 1985, the Finance Minister allowed banks to give up to 100 per cent loan support for share purchases, despite persistent warnings from Bank Negara Malaysia against giving out loans for share speculation (Khor 1987: 101). The increased availability of such credit must have boosted share trading and stock prices as well as increased bank vulnerability to asset price deflations, e.g. in the mid-1970s, mid-

1980s, 1994 and 1997-8. The minister also directed government-controlled investment institutions, such as the Employees Provident Fund, to invest in stocks. The privatisation of state-owned enterprises boosted stock market growth, especially in the early and mid-1990s. The substantial funds raised by the capital market since 1990 can be partly attributed to the government's privatisation program, which has undoubtedly deepened Malaysian's stock market considerably.

The Malaysian stock market increased in relative significance as a source of corporate finance, particularly at the expense of domestic and foreign bank loans, and emerged as a more important source of funds than the commercial banks from the early 1990s. Table 4.5 shows that the early 1990s saw some financial disintermediation with commercial bank deposits' share of savings declining from 23 per cent in 1990 to 16 per cent in 1994, and the KLSE's share rising from 48 per cent to 62 per cent over the same period. Table 4.6 shows that the stock market became more important as a source of funds,

Table 4.5

Malaysia: Classification of Deposits by
Financial Institutions, 1990-1996 (% share)[a]

	1990	*1991*	*1992*	*1993*	*1994*	*1995*	*1996*
Commercial Banks[b]	22.8	23.1	20.1	13.4	16.1	17.3	16.1
Finance Companies[b]	10.4	10.6	8.5	5.3	6.2	6.3	5.7
National Savings Bank[c]	1.0	0.9	0.8	0.5	0.6	0.5	0.5
Employees Provident Fund	16.9	16.0	13.4	8.1	10.3	10.5	9.2
Life Insurance Companies	0.6	0.6	0.5	0.3	0.4	0.5	0.4
Unit Trust Funds	n.a.	n.a.	3.4	3.1	4.4	4.7	4.7
K.L. Stock Exchange	48.2	48.8	53.3	69.4	62.1	60.2	63.4

Notes: [a] Allow for +/- 3% variation.
[b] Figures do not include Negotiable Certificates of Deposits (NCDs) issued and Repurchase Agreements (Repos).
[c] Figures consist of 'amount standing to credit of depositors' plus 'Premium Savings Certificates depositors.'
n.a. — not available.

Sources: Asian Banker, cited by *Banker's Journal Malaysia* (1995: 33); BNM, *Annual Report, 1997*; Ministry of Finance (1996 and 1997); and Kuala Lumpur Stock Exchange (1997).

Table 4.6
Malaysia: Funds Raised by the Private Sector, 1980-1996 (% shares)[a]

	1980-85	*1990-96*
Bank Loans	67	51
Private Debt Securities	1	13
Equity	9	19
EPF[b]	–	3
Foreign Borrowing	23	14

Notes: [a] Excluding loans to individuals and CAGAMAS (National Mortgage Corporation) papers.
[b] Direct equity financing.
Source: Compiled from BNM, *Annual Report, 1997* (Chart IX.2).

while the share of bank loans as a proportion of total funds raised by the private sector declined correspondingly. Specifically, the share of equity market financing of total funds raised by the private sector rose significantly from 9 per cent during 1980-85 to 19 per cent during 1990-96, while the bank loans' share dropped correspondingly from 67 per cent to 51 per cent. During the same period, the additional funds raised through share issues since 1993 are reflected in increased stock market capitalisation, especially in terms of share volume.

Although the Malaysian stock market has emerged as a more important source of funds than commercial banks since 1990, funds thus mobilised during the stock market boom did not necessarily go to productive investments. More than 50 per cent of the total funds raised in the equity market through initial public offerings (IPOs) in 1990-96 went to privatised projects (BNM 1997: 149). In other words, with privatisation, capital resources that might otherwise have been invested into expanding productive capacity have been diverted into acquiring or transferring existing public sector assets (Jomo 1995: 51). Adam and Cavendish (1995: 37-39) suggest that such privatisation issues may well have crowded out other private investment issues, unless total foreign portfolio capital inflows were very high.

By 1993, the Malaysian stock market had gained a reputation as a kind of casino, with active trading fuelled by heady optimism, sudden interest from foreign institutional investors, and a frenzy of speculation about corporate take-overs (*Asian Wall Street Journal*, 26 March 1996). The KLSE Composite Index (KLCI) almost doubled to 1,275 points before crashing to 971 points

Table 4.7

Kuala Lumpur Stock Exchange: Selected Indicators, 1990-1996

	1990	*1991*	*1992*	*1993*	*1994*	*1995*	*1996*
Price Indices							
Composite	506	556	644	1275	971	995	1238
EMAS*	131	141	162	384	284	279	348
Second Board	–	127	140	352	261	299	576
Total Turnover							
Volume (billion units)	13.1	12.4	19.3	107.8	60.2	40.0	66.5
Value (RM billion)	29.5	30.1	51.5	387.0	328.1	178.9	463.3
Market capitalisation (RM billion)	132	161	246	620	504	566	807
Market liquidity: Turnover value/market capitalisation (%)	22.3	18.7	20.9	62.4	65.1	31.6	57.4

Note: * The Exchange Main Board All-Share Index incorporating all stocks listed on the Main Board.
Source: Bank Negara Malaysia, *Annual Report*, various issues.

in the following year, while market capitalisation as a proportion of GDP rose more than twofold from the year before. The volume of shares traded jumped by more than 450 per cent and rose by more than 650 per cent in value terms to reach RM387 billion (Table 4.7).

Since 1993, the increased funds raised through rights issues were reflected in the expansion of existing stocks or capitalisation. Table 4.8 shows that much of the funds raised from the equity market in 1996 was from rights issues, which mobilised 43 per cent of the total funds raised during 1993-7, while initial public offers only accounted for 31 per cent.

The growth of the Malaysian stock market was extraordinary by regional standards, with KLSE capitalisation more than triple the annual GNP by 1996 (Table 3.2). While total capital inflows into Malaysia were not extra-ordinarily high in comparison with those into Thailand and Indonesia, a much higher proportion of its inflows went into the stock market rather than being intermediated through the banking system.

The swelling equity flows were partly due to the gradual liberalisation of financial markets and regulations. The government announced an 18-point financial market liberalisation program to enhance Malaysia's position as a

Table 4.8

Kuala Lumpur Stock Exchange: New Share Issues, 1992-1997[a] (RM million; % of shares)

	1992	%	1993	%	1994	%	1995	%	1996	%	1997	%
Initial Public Offers	5,415.8	59	912.7	26.6	2,972.9	35	4,175.0	36	4,099.2	26	4,781.0	26
Rights Issues	3,437.8	37	1,176.9	34.3	3,436.7	41	5,240.2	46	5,268.5	33	8,524.9	46
Special Issues[b]	300.4	3.3	684.2	19.9	1,249.4	15	875.5	7.7	2,002.3	13	1,818.8	10
Private Placements[c]	27.5	0.3	658.8	19.2	798.9	9.4	1,146.9	10	4,554.4	29	3,233.6	18
Preference Shares	–	–	–	–	–	–	–	–	–	–	–	–
Total	9,181.5	100	3,432.6	100	8,457.9	100	11,437.6	100	15,924.4	100	18,358.3	100

Notes: [a] Excluding funds raised by the exercise of Employee Share Options Schemes, Transferable Subscription Rights, Warrants and Irredeemable Convertible Unsecured Loans Stocks.

[b] Issues to Bumiputera investors and selected investors.

[c] Including Restricted-Offer-For-Sale.

Source: Adapted from Bank Negara Malaysia, *Annual Report*, *1997* (p. 249) and *1998* (p. 290).

Table 4.9
IFC: Barriers to Portfolio Investments in Selected Asian Stock Markets, 1996

| Country | *Withholding Taxes* | | *Foreign Investment Ceiling for Listed Stocks* |
	Dividends (%)	*Long-term Capital Gains (%)*	
Malaysia	0.0	0.0	100% in general[a]
Indonesia	20.0	0.1	49% in general; 85% for securities companies
Philippines[b]	15.0	0.5	40% in general; 30% for banks
Thailand	10.0	0.0	10%-49% depending on company by-laws
India	20.0	10.0	24% in general
Korea[c]	16.5	0.0	20% in general; 15% for KEPCO and POSCO
Taiwan	35.0	0.0	25% in general

Notes: [a] Actually 30% under the Industrial Coordination Act, 1975.
[b] Transactions tax in lieu of a capital gains tax.
[c] Rates are for funds in which US investments total more than 25%. Tax rates shown include 10% resident tax applied to base rates.
Source: IFC, *Emerging Stock Market Factbook, 1997*.

major international financial centre. One strategy was to attract more foreign institutional investors by allowing fund managers to buy more equity in Malaysian corporations and by reducing the tax rate on their profits to 10 per cent. Table 4.9 reports the withholding tax rates for dividends and long-term capital gains that selected emerging markets offered to US-based institutional investors, as well as restrictions on foreign ownership of listed stocks in 1996. Malaysia clearly seemed to be the most liberalised market according to the IFC. With greater access to the Malaysian stock market as well as reduction or removal of capital gains and dividends withholding taxes, the interest of international investors in the Malaysian stock market grew rapidly, inducing enormous foreign portfolio investment inflows.

According to some stock market analysts, by early 1997, over one quarter of the stock in the Kuala Lumpur Stock Exchange was in foreign hands with another quarter held by Malaysian institutions and the rest constituting 'retail trade' by individuals. While most Malaysian shareholders only operate within the Malaysian stock market, foreign institutional investors see the Malaysian market as only one of many different types of financial markets in a global financial system including many national markets; i.e. the global financial system is hardly a market of equals. Although always in the minority, foreign investment institutions 'made' the stock markets in the region, shifting their assets among securities markets as well as among different types of financial investment options all over the world. In the face of limited transparency, the regional nature of their presence, the nature of fund managers' incentives and remuneration and the short-term investment horizons, foreign financial institutions were much more prone to herd behaviour and contributed most to the regional spread of contagion. To quote Mansor (1995: 10): 'Although only about 20 per cent of daily market activity has been attributed to foreign funds, the influence of foreign funds is more than their share of the volume of activity, as they are generally considered market leaders. Their presence is crucial to lending credibility and international standing, which are important elements in raising future capital, locally and overseas.'

Origins of the Currency Crisis

The Malaysian economic boom from the late 1980s was helped by the significant depreciation of the ringgit against the US dollar from late 1985. Meanwhile, the Japanese yen, and then the Korean won, the new Taiwanese dollar and the Singapore dollar all appreciated against the US dollar, and hence, even more against the ringgit. High growth was sustained for almost a decade, during most of which fiscal balances were in order, monetary expansion was not excessive and inflation was generally under control. Nevertheless, there were some potential problems.

Despite the claim by the central bank that the ringgit had been pegged to a basket of the currencies of Malaysia's major trading partners, for all intents and purposes, it had in effect been pegged to the US dollar at least since the 1980s. This unofficial peg offered certain advantages, especially the semblance of stability — including low inflation — so much desired by financial interests. With the depreciation of the US dollar against the yen and other East Asian currencies between 1985 and 1995, the Southeast Asian currencies depreciated as well, effectively reducing production costs in the region. In this context, the 1990 and then the 1994 devaluations of China's renminbi put greater competitive pressure on the emerging second-tier or second-generation Southeast Asian newly industrialising countries (NICs), including Malaysia. But the reversal of this decade-long currency depreciation from mid-1995, when the US dollar began to appreciate against the yen again, then implied the declining cost competitiveness of the region. Renewed capital inflows continued to be sterilised with complicated consequences.

There was widespread consensus that the ringgit had become overvalued by being pegged to the US dollar as the greenback strengthened significantly from mid-1995.[19] Hence, the ringgit was expected to depreciate to around RM2.7–2.8 against the dollar (Tan Eu Chye, personal communication), the supposed equilibrium exchange rate based on calculations taking account of purchasing power parity, etc. However, from mid-July 1997, the Malaysian ringgit fell far more precipitously, reaching RM4.88 to the US dollar in early January 1998, its lowest level ever; this represented a collapse by almost half within less than half a year from a high of RM2.47 in July 1997. The stock market fell more severely, with the main Kuala Lumpur Stock Exchange Composite Index (KLCI) dropping to 262 in early September 1998 from almost 1,300 in February 1997.

This sudden and massive collapse of the ringgit — politely referred to in the financial community as 'overshooting' — by much more than the anticipated 'correction' of RM2.7-2.8, raises serious questions about the very nature of the international monetary system. Other international, regional and domestic speculators also contributed to the collapse by reacting in their own self-interest to perceived and anticipated market trends — rather than as part of some conspiracy as claimed by Malaysian Prime Minister Mahathir. As investors scrambled to get out of positions in the ringgit and other regional currencies, the currencies fell further and, with them, the stock and other markets. With financial liberalisation, fund managers had an almost infinite variety of investment options to choose from, and can move their funds much more easily than ever before, especially with the capital account convertibility Malaysia and other crisis-affected countries in the region prided themselves on. The operations and magnitude of hedge fund operations and other currency speculation undoubtedly exacerbated these phenomena, with disastrous cumulative consequences.

Financial Fragility and Crisis

The Malaysian currency and financial crises since mid-1997 can be traced to financial liberalisation and its consequent undermining of national monetary and financial regulation. The ringgit's virtual peg to the US dollar encouraged huge foreign capital inflows, which served to finance the persistent current account deficit. Thus, foreign savings supplemented the already high domestic savings rate (40 per cent in 1996) to raise the investment rate to

45 per cent, which contributed to an asset price bubble involving shares and real property.

As elsewhere in the Southeast Asian region, besides encouraging portfolio investments as well as bank borrowings from abroad, the unofficial peg also became a target for currency speculators as regional currencies appreciated with the US dollar despite adverse consequences for export competitiveness and growth. Meanwhile, financial liberalisation had also opened up lucrative opportunities for taking advantage of anticipated changes in foreign exchange rates, thus accelerating and exacerbating the collapse of the region's currencies and share markets. All this, together with ill-considered official Malaysian responses, transformed the inevitable 'correction' of the overvalued ringgit into massive collapses of both the ringgit and the KLCI as panic set in, exacerbated by 'herd' behaviour and 'contagion'.

Earlier, we showed how increased liberalisation of the financial sector reduced the franchise value of the banking sector, crucial for inducing the banks to effectively monitor and manage the risk in their loan portfolios (Hellmann, Murdock and Stiglitz 1997).[20] Although banking licenses were not granted to foreign banks after 1974 and various restrictions have been imposed on them, the franchise value of large Malaysian banks has declined. The share of deposits in the ten largest banks declined from about 84 per cent of the total in 1975 to 77 per cent in 1990, while their share of total assets fell from 80 per cent to 72 per cent over the same period (Zainal *et al.* 303-5).[21] Thus, banks experienced disintermediation on both sides of their balance sheets. In the absence of strong institutional arrangements for effective prudential regulation and supervision to realign incentives, the erosion of franchise value further distorted the banks' risk-taking behaviour, exacerbating moral hazard problems and hence the fragility of the banking system.[22]

High Loan Exposure Fuelled Asset Price Inflation

Notwithstanding its efforts to improve the regulatory and supervisory systems, the BNM was rather ineffective in checking the growing fragility of the financial sector, particularly due to trends in bank lending. Despite several warnings by the BNM and the growth in non-performing loans after the property market collapse of 1986, banks continued to lend to the property sector. In 1986, such loans accounted for 55 per cent of all new loans, compared to 32 per cent in 1980 (Zainal *et al.* 1994: 309). When the property and stock markets collapsed following the recession in the mid-1980s, many banks were in serious trouble, as a large percentage of property-based loans became non-performing. Such a big overhang of non-performing loans in the banking system — reaching almost thirty per cent at its apex — required substantial provisions for interest in suspense and bad debts. The banking crisis in the late-1980s had been short-lived due to rapidly improving external conditions and manufacturing expansion following selective deregulation and other new incentives attracting foreign direct investment from the late eighties, which contributed to the revival of the stock and property markets. Despite adopting the Banking and Financial Institutions Act (BAFIA) in 1989, Malaysian policymakers did not seem to insist on more prudent lending practices, perhaps due to the speed of the late 1980s' recovery. Moreover, in the face of greater competition to lend in the more liberalised and competitive market, banks preferred financing real estate and share purchases, as long as such loans were collateralised. Thus, exposure to property and share purchases grew quickly in the early and mid-1990s as in the preceding decade, with property and stock prices rising rapidly. The easy availability of such credit encouraged over-investment in non-tradeables, in turn aggravating current account deficits (with greater imports but no corresponding exports) and fuelling asset price bubbles.

Thus, the economic boom from the late 1980s was increasingly being built on some shaky and unsustainable foundations. Meanwhile, growth in Malaysia became increasingly heavily reliant on foreign resources, both capital and labour. Foreign direct investment significantly supplemented domestic investment, accounting for 19 per cent[23] of gross fixed capital formation on average during 1990-6.[24] With more intense competition from lower-cost exporters, especially China,[25] as well as rising production costs, Malaysia's future economic progress could no longer be secured by continued reliance on its strategy of offering cheap labour and lowering other production costs through 'competitive' currency devaluation. Inappropriate investments in human resources and infrastructure continued to limit the development of greater industrial and technological capabilities in the country. Inappropriate financial policy also continued to limit commitment[26] on the part of financial institutions to provide long-term resources for manufacturing, let alone for more innovative and higher technology-based activities requiring longer gestation periods (Chin, 2000).

Build-up of Private External Debt

Foreign savings supplemented the already high domestic savings rates in the region to further accelerate the rate of capital accumulation, albeit in increasingly 'unproductive' activities, owing to the foreign domination of most internationally competitive industries in the region. Malaysia's savings-investment gap, which was 5 per cent of GNP in 1997, lay behind the current account deficit, which had exceeded RM12 billion since 1994.

Before the 1990s, the savings-investment gap had mainly been bridged by foreign direct investment (FDI), though high FDI and foreign debt have, in turn, caused growing investment income outflows abroad. In the early and mid-1990s, however, the current account deficit was increasingly covered by short-term capital inflows. Much portfolio investment went into the stock market in 1992-3, and again, from 1995 until early 1997, with adverse consequences following their sudden and hasty exit each time. Many post-crisis confidence restoration measures actually seek to induce such short-term inflows once again, and, when successful, will be expected to finance current account deficits once again.

Some companies and banks in Malaysia also borrowed heavily from abroad, thus supplementing investment inflows (Tables 4.10 and 4.11). According to Bank Negara,[27] commercial banks' net foreign liabilities increased by almost 150 per cent in 18 months from RM10.3bn at the end of 1995 to RM25.2bn in June 1997, while their net external reserves position deteriorated from -RM5.3bn to -RM17.7bn over the same 18 month period! Thanks to stricter central bank supervision, a smaller proportion of such

Table 4.10

Malaysia: Outstanding External Short-term Debt of the
Banking and Non-Bank Private Sector, 1988-1997 (RM million)

	Banking Sector	Non-bank Private Sector
1988	2,464	n.a.
1989	3,343	n.a.
1990	4,415	n.a.
1991	7,171	n.a.
1992	13,157	n.a.
1993	17,320	n.a.
1994	9,840	4,404
1995	11,293	4,911
1996	17,648	8,098
1997	32,665	11,322

Note: Short-term debt refers to debt with tenure one year and below.
Source: BNM Quarterly Economic Bulletin, various issues.

Table 4.11
Lending by BIS Reporting Banks to Selected Asian Economies by
Sector, as of end-June 1997 (US$ billion)

	South Korea	Thailand	Indonesia	Malaysia
Total Borrowings	103.4	69.4	58.7	28.8
Banks	67.3	26.1	12.4	10.5
(%)	(65.1)	(37.6)	(21.1)	(36.5)
Private Non-bank	31.7	41.3	39.7	16.5
(%)	(30.6)	(59.5)	(67.6)	(57.3)
Government	4.4	12.0	6.5	1.9
(%)	(4.3)	(17.3)	(11.1)	(6.6)

Source: Bank for International Settlements (BIS) as cited by Jomo (1998a: 32).

Malaysian foreign borrowings were of a short-term nature[28] compared to Thailand and Indonesia, and a greater proportion was hedged, owing to the' lower costs of hedging for Malaysian borrowers.

Ironically, stock exchange listing in Malaysia has been an important means to access more bank borrowings on better terms, rather than to raise funds on the stock market itself. The establishment of the Labuan International Offshore Financial Centre (IOFC) also facilitated greater Malaysian access to international funds on less transparent terms. According to the Cash Balance of Payments Reporting System of the BNM, net international funds sourced from the Labuan IOFC increased from RM69 million in 1991 to RM7,441 million in 1996. On the supply side, intense competition among 'debt-pushing' Japanese and continental European banks (attracted by the comparatively higher interest rates available for dollarised loans to the region) further eased access to foreign funds. These and other financial liberalisation reforms as well as the growth of 'private banking' and 'relationship banking' in the region also weakened the scope and efficacy of national-level prudential regulation. On the demand side, more Malaysian corporations seeking lower financing costs began to tap funds from abroad.

As a result, in recent years, there was a surge of private sector borrowings from abroad (Table 4.10). The non-bank private sector in Malaysia was the major recipient of international bank loans, accounting for more than half of all foreign borrowings by the end of June 1997. Nevertheless, Malaysian private sector external debt exposure was both absolutely and relatively less than in Thailand, Indonesia and South Korea (Table 4.11). Foreign borrowings of almost 90 of Malaysia's largest listed and KLCI-indexed companies have been estimated at around RM35 billion, with the three largest borrowers — Malaysian Airline System Berhad, Tenaga Nasional Berhad and Telekom Malaysia Berhad — alone accounting for three-quarters of this foreign corporate debt.

Thus, Malaysia's medium and long-term debt as a percentage of net external reserves rose dramatically over two and a half years from 102 per cent at the end of 1994 to 176 per cent in June 1997, after declining after the mid-1980s crisis (Jomo 1990). These capital inflows, both equity investments and bank borrowings, helped finance the current account deficits due to the growing proportion of non-tradeables being produced in Malaysia, much of which involved (infrastructure as well as property) construction activity. These capital inflows were 'sterilised' to minimise currency appreciation as well as consumer price inflation, but instead fuelled asset price inflation, mainly involving real estate and share prices.[29]

In so far as such investments did not contribute directly to export earnings, they aggravated the current account deficit, and contributed to the problem of currency mismatch. Term mismatch also became a serious problem as a high proportion of foreign borrowings was of short-term maturity (Table 4.12), but were often deployed on medium to long-term bases.

Surge of Portfolio Investment Inflows

More than other emerging markets in the region, Malaysia experienced an unprecedented surge in portfolio investment inflows in the early and mid-1990s, attributable to various push and pull factors.[30] Active government encouragement of such foreign portfolio investments succeeded in attracting massive inflows seeking to maximise the capital gains in the bullish Malaysian stock market (Table 5.1). During 1991-95, when net foreign portfolio investment averaged 5.1 per cent of GDP, portfolio investments accounted for 88 per cent of identified gross capital inflows (Ong 1998: 222-223). In 1993 and 1994, the portfolio investment inflows alone surpassed GDP in current market prices, reaching US$67 billion and US$87 billion respectively.

Encouraging foreign financial institutions to invest in the Malaysian stock market inevitably made the national economy much more vulnerable to international macroeconomic fluctuations as well as capital flight, and rendered the tasks of exchange rate management and controlling inflation much more difficult. The huge short-term capital inflows proved to be destabilising as they involved closer links between two inherently unstable markets — the

Table 4.12
Maturity Distribution of Lending by BIS Reporting Banks to
Selected Asian Economies, 1996 (US$ million)

	All Loans			Under 1 Year			1-2 Years		
	June 1996	Dec. 1996	June 1997	June 1996	Dec. 1996	June 1997	June 1996	Dec. 1996	June 1997
South Korea	88,027	99,953	103,432	62,332	67,506	70,182	3,438	4,107	4,139
Thailand	69,409	70,147	69,382	47,834	45,702	45,567	4,083	4,829	4,592
Indonesia	49,306	55,523	58,726	29,587	34,248	34,661	3,473	3,589	3,541
Malaysia	20,100	22,234	28,820	9,991	11,178	16,268	834	721	615

Source: Bank for International Settlements (BIS) as cited by Jomo (1998a: xvi).

stock and currency markets. The central bank was reported to have incurred high costs in trying to maintain tight monetary policy by neutralising the potentially destabilising inflows of foreign speculative funds.[31] After a sudden exodus of such money in early 1994, temporary controls aimed at limiting portfolio inflows were put in place, but these were removed from mid-year once speculative pressures on the ringgit declined.

Speculation and Contagion

It did not take very long for contagion from the Asian financial crisis, which is usually dated from the floating of the Thai baht on 2 July 1997, to spread to Malaysia. With the baht down, currency speculators turned their sights on other economies in the region that had similarly vulnerable quasi-pegs to the US dollar. A glut in the property market was expected due to rapid over-expansion in recent years. The decline of the KLCI after February 1997, the reversal of portfolio investment funds and the economy's recently enhanced exposure to short-term foreign borrowings (albeit relatively less than its crisis-hit neighbours in the region) did not inspire confidence. Speculative attacks on the pegged ringgit increased as net portfolio capital outflows began to accelerate. The BNM, which initially put up a spirited defence of the ringgit, finally gave up currency support operations after hefty losses of several billion US dollars. The ringgit fell since mid-July 1997, eventually reaching RM4.88 to the US dollar in early January 1998 — collapsing by almost half in six months from a high of RM2.47 in July 1997. The stock market fell more severely, with the KLCI dropping to 262 on 1 September 1998 from almost 1,300 in the first quarter of 1997.

Nevertheless, Malaysia was relatively better off than its neighbours devastated by the crisis. Although weakened in recent years, especially due to financial liberalisation, prudential regulation remained better than in most other countries in the region besides Singapore, thus saving Malaysia from some of the worst excesses witnessed elsewhere in the region. Lower domestic interest rates had also limited the extent of foreign borrowings, most of which were hedged, owing to the relatively lower costs of hedging in Malaysia.

Banking System Distress

At least three other developments after the currency crisis began in July 1997 probably made things worse for the banking system. First, the authorities adopted a tighter definition of non-performing loans in late 1997, reducing the grace period from six to three months, thus increasing the number of NPLs by redefinition in the midst of the crisis. Greater monitoring, reporting and transparency were also required. Second, banks were obliged to meet higher statutory reserve requirements, which raised the cost of funds. Third, credit growth slowed down and did not rise after September 1998 despite central bank directives to increase credit growth to eight per cent in both 1998 and 1999.

Hence, tighter monetary policy from late 1997 must have exacerbated contractionary pressures due to government spending cuts from the same time. Thus, the adoption of deflationary macroeconomic policies in response to the currency and financial crises can be said to have worsened the situation. Such policies were intended to stem the capital flight facilitated by Malaysian capital account liberalisation, though there is little real evidence of success on this score. Official policy as well as market pressures served to push up interest rates, though the rise in the nominal rate was higher than the real increase, owing to contemporaneous inflationary pressures.

Table 4.13 shows that the one-year fixed deposit interest rates rose from 7.25 per cent in February 1997 to a peak of 10.28 per cent in July 1998, before declining even before the September 1998 measures were introduced. Thus, even before the capital controls were introduced, interest rates rose by around 300 basis points, much less than in the neighbouring economies obliged to hike interest rates to attract foreign funds, stem capital flight or pursue policies dictated by creditors, especially the IMF.

Table 4.14, Table 4.15 as well as Figures 4.2a and 4.2b show the base lending rate for commercial banks rising from a January low of 9.19 per cent for 1997 to a peak of 12.27 per cent in June 1998 before declining, again before the September 1998 measures were introduced. They also show a corresponding increase for finance companies from 10.66 per cent to 14.70 per cent over the same period. The increase in base lending rates for both commercial banks and finance companies thus also rose little more than three percentage points. While such an increase over a year and a half must have been onerous for borrowers, the increases were much less than in the worse affected economies in the region with their bank-based financial systems.

The private sector was badly affected by the financial crisis. Private investment collapsed by 57.8 per cent between 1997 and 1998 (*White Paper*, Table 1, p. 5), concurrently with declines in various other macroeconomic measures: private consumption fell by 12.4 per cent, public consumption by 3.5 per cent and public investment by 10.0 per cent. In the wake of the currency crisis, interest rates rose, reflecting tighter liquidity as money supply contracted due to domestic capital flight in response to the currency crisis,

Table 4.13

Malaysia: Yearly and Monthly Average Twelve-Month Fixed Deposit Interest Rates, 1984-1999 (%)

Year	Fixed Deposit Interest Rate (for 12 months)	Month	Inflation (CPI)	Fixed Deposit Interest Rate (for 12 months)	Month	Inflation (CPI)	Fixed Deposit Interest Rate (for 12 months)
1984	10.50	Jan-97	3.2	7.26	Jul-98	5.8	10.28
1985	7.30	Feb-97	3.1	7.25	Aug-98	5.6	9.45
1986	6.30	Mar-97	3.2	7.25	Sep-98	5.5	6.12
1987	2.50	Apr-97	2.6	7.26	Oct-98	5.2	6.02
1988	3.30	May-97	2.5	7.30	Nov-98	5.6	5.79
1989	5.00	Jun-97	2.2	7.38	Dec-98	5.3	5.74
1990	7.00	Jul-97	2.1	7.52	Jan-99	5.2	5.66
1991	8.00	Aug-97	2.4	7.56	Feb-99	3.8	5.54
1992	7.90	Sep-97	2.3	7.63	Mar-99	3.0	5.40
1993	6.50	Oct-97	2.7	8.54	Apr-99	2.9	4.06
1994	5.30	Nov-97	2.6	9.11	May-99	2.9	3.80
1995	6.60	Dec-97	2.9	9.31	Jun-99	2.1	3.80
1996	7.18	Jan-98	3.4	9.34	Jul-99	2.5	3.79
1997	9.30	Feb-98	4.4	9.55	Aug-99	2.3	3.79
1998	5.74	Mar-98	5.1	9.81	Sep-99	2.1	3.79
1999	3.90	Apr-98	5.6	10.03	Oct-99	2.1	3.93
		May-98	5.4	10.10	Nov-99	1.6	3.93
		Jun-98	6.2	10.24	Dec-99	na.	3.93

Sources: Bank Negara Malaysia, *Quarterly Economic Bulletin*, Table V.6, Table VI.1 and Table VI.13.

Table 4.14
Malaysia: Annual Base Lending Interest Rates, 1985-1999

	Commercial Banks	*Finance Companies*
1985	10.75	12.00
1986	10.00	11.50
1987	7.50	9.25
1988	7.00	9.00
1989	6.99	8.74
1990	7.49	9.20
1991	8.68	10.01
1992	9.29	10.58
1993	8.22	9.97
1994	6.83	8.40
1995	8.03	9.38
1996	9.18	10.65
1997	9.53	11.09
1998	9.61	12.65
1999	7.29	8.56

Note: Average rates at end of period.
Source: BNM, *Monthly Statistical Bulletin*, Table V.1.

the reversal of capital inflows (foreign bank lending), and tighter central bank monetary policy (as demanded by financial markets and the IMF). Commercial banks' base lending rates climbed from a monthly pre-crisis average of 9.50 per cent in June 1997 to 12.27 per cent in June 1998 (Table 4.15 and Figure 4.2a), as finance companies raised their rates from 10.85 per cent to 14.70 per cent. These increases were gradual and substantial, but not sudden and astronomical. Nevertheless, the higher interest rates increased loan defaults, slowed credit growth and exacerbated economic contraction.

Loan defaults and foreclosures increased as the financial crisis undermined the real economy, gathering momentum through 1998 until the radical change in monetary policy from September. As shown in Table 4.16, the size of commercial banks' non-performing loans (NPLs) rose from RM9.3 billion in June 1997 to RM42.2 billion in August 1998 before dropping to RM35.3 billion in September 1998. Banks' and finance companies' non-performing loans (NPLs) as shares of total loans increased. For commercial banks, this ratio soared from 3.5 per cent in June 1997 to a high of 9.4 per cent in August 1998, after which the definition of NPLs was loosened. Finance companies were worst hit, with their non-performing loans increasing from 4.3 per cent in June 1997 to 17.3 per cent in August 1998. These numbers had risen suddenly with the tighter redefinition of NPLs from November 1997 to include

Table 4.15
Malaysia: Monthly Base Lending Interest Rates, 1997-2000

	Commercial Banks	*Finance Companies*
Jan 1997	9.19	10.66
Feb	9.20	10.66
Mar	9.24	10.67
Apr	9.25	10.67
May	9.27	10.71
Jun	9.50	10.85
Jul	9.58	11.01
Aug	9.61	11.22
Sep	9.61	11.28
Oct	9.53	11.20
Nov	10.07	11.88
Dec	10.33	12.22
Jan 1998	10.44	12.33
Feb	11.08	13.16
Mar	11.96	14.23
Apr	12.16	14.56
May	12.21	14.65
Jun	12.27	14.70
Jul	12.07	14.49
Aug	11.70	14.17
Sep	8.89	10.54
Oct	8.49	10.00
Nov	8.04	9.50
Dec	8.04	9.50
Jan 1999	8.04	9.50
Feb	8.04	9.50
Mar	8.04	9.48
Apr	7.64	9.00
May	7.24	8.50
Jun	7.24	8.50
Jul	7.24	8.50
Aug	6.79	7.95
Sep	6.79	7.95
Oct	6.79	7.95
Nov	6.79	7.95
Dec	6.79	7.95
Jan 2000	6.79	7.95
Feb	6.79	7.95
March	6.79	7.95

Source: BNM, *Monthly Statistical Bulletin*, Table V.1.

Figure 4.2a
Malaysia: Commercial Banks' Monthly Base Lending Rates and Non-performing Loans, 1997-1999

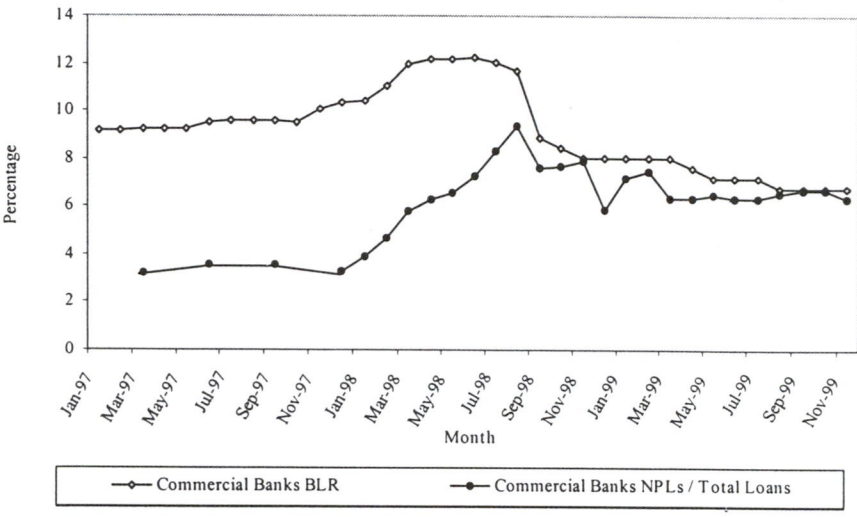

Figure 4.2b
Malaysia: Finance Companies' Monthly Base Lending Rates and Non-performing Loans, 1997-1999

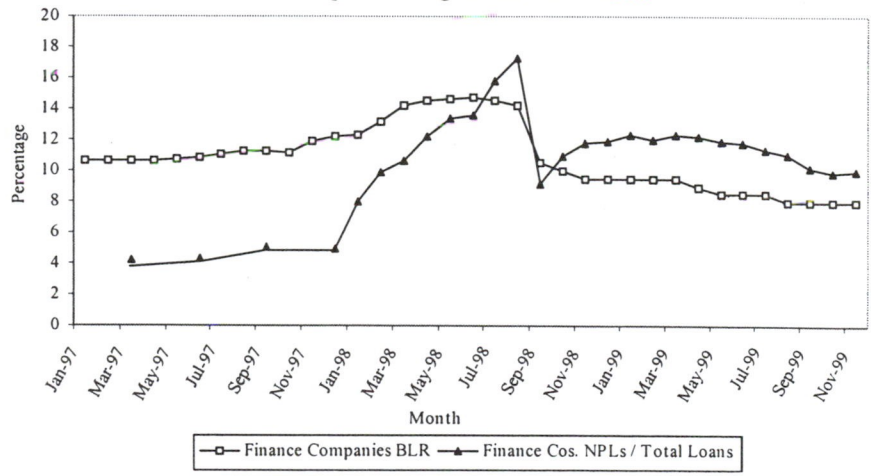

Note: Non-performing loans were defined more tightly (3 months grace) from November 1997 and then more loosely again (6 months grace) from September 1998.

Table 4.16
Malaysia: Non-Performing Loans, 1988-2000

End of Period	Non-performing Loans (RM million)			Non-performing Loans/Total Loans (%)		
	Commercial Banks	Finance Companies	Merchant Banks	Commercial Banks	Finance Companies	Merchant Banks
1988	16,935	5,413	1,203	29.6	33.7	24.8
1989	16,554	5,713	989	24.3	28.3	17.9
1990	16,562	5,858	792	20.1	21.3	12.6
1991	15,518	5,473	647	15.7	15.8	8.7
1992	15,992	6,109	583	14.7	15.6	6.9
1993	15,171	5,832	490	12.6	13.0	5.0
1994	9,643	5,130	1,107	6.9	9.9	9.5
1995	8,932	4,285	1,103	4.9	6.6	7.8
1996	8,163	4,002	315	3.6	4.7	1.7
1997 Mar	7,978	3,842	348	3.2	4.2	1.7
Jun	9,287	4,243	433	3.5	4.3	2.0
Sep	9,141	5,401	458	3.4	5.1	2.0
Dec	14,159	9,974	1,096	3.3	5.0	3.6
1998 Jan	16,746	11,088	1,563	3.9	8.0	5.3
Feb	19,206	13,448	1,898	4.7	9.9	6.2
Mar	22,278	14,282	1,821	5.8	10.6	5.0
Apr	26,131	15,862	2,266	6.3	12.2	7.1
May	28,585	17,194	2,634	6.6	13.4	8.5
Jun	32,378	17,474	3,019	7.3	13.6	9.1
Jul	36,864	19,238	3,800	8.3	15.8	12.0
Aug	42,154	20,819	4,426	9.4	17.2	14.0
Sep	35,324	13,292	3,137	7.6	9.2	8.8
Oct	37,012	14,894	3,441	7.7	10.9	9.4
Nov	39,202	16,092	4,059	7.9	11.8	11.5
Dec	32,086	16,092	3,888	5.9	11.9	10.9
1999 Jan	35,093	16,545	4,348	7.2	12.3	12.0
Feb	35,807	15,699	4,470	7.5	12.0	13.3
Mar	32,145	15,772	4,141	6.4	12.3	11.2
Apr	32,362	15,227	4,334	6.4	12.2	11.5
May	33,829	14,679	4,634	6.5	11.9	12.8
Jun	33,970	14,422	4,775	6.4	11.8	13.8
Jul	34,018	14,538	4,242	6.4	11.4	15.1
Aug	34,402	14,308	4,115	6.6	11.1	14.2
Sep	34,838	13,584	3,955	6.7	10.2	13.3
Oct	34,346	13,411	3,958	6.7	9.9	12.8
Nov	33,649	13,675	4,021	6.4	10.0	12.8
Dec	30,402	13,571	3,487	5.7	8.6	12.3
2000 Jan	30,779	13,837	3,504	5.7	8.8	12.7
Feb	30,903	13,893	3,458	5.8	8.7	12.3

Note: A loan was considered non-performing if it was not serviced for six months until November 1997, when the period was reduced to three months before reverting to six months in September 1998.

Source: BNM, *Monthly Statistical Bulletin*, Tables III.16, III.17 and III.18.

loans in arrears for only three months as compared to the previous definition period of six months before the government reverted to the six month definition in September 1998. Consequently, the ratio of NPLs to total loans fell slightly to 7.3 per cent for commercial banks and 14.0 per cent for finance companies in December 1998. In the aftermath of the mid-1980s' recession, NPLs had reached even higher levels, e.g. 29.6 per cent of commercial banks' total loans in 1988 (see Table 4.16). The highest proportion of NPLs in the economy during 1998 was therefore much less than in 1988.

The breakdown of non-performing loans by sector reflects the uneven impacts of the recession on the economy. Tables 4.17 and 4.18 corroborate earlier diagnoses about the differential impact of the recession on different sectors. Commercial banks' NPLs in manufacturing, the sector with the largest share of NPLs, swelled from RM2.12 billion in September 1997 to RM7.56 billion in September 1998, i.e. by 256.6 per cent. Meanwhile, manufacturing's share of total loans fell from 23.2 to 17.2 per cent. Every sector recorded dramatic increases in their shares of NPLs, with construction, purchase of securities, purchase of (residential and non-residential) property, real estate, business services and consumption credit heavily mired in loan default. Total NPLs are still sizeable, and in fact increased in manufacturing, construction and business services in the first quarter of 1999. Debt servicing only improved in mid-1999, months after the lowering of interest rates from September 1998. For commercial banks, loans for the 'purchase of securities' experienced the most marked improvement among the different categories of NPLs between September 1998 and March 1999 as the stock market recovered (see Table 4.17).

In the early months of the financial crisis, rumours led to runs on several Malaysian-incorporated banks. As a consequence, there were substantial transfers of funds from such banks to foreign-incorporated as well as larger or better domestic banks with good branch networks in the country. The central bank intervened to allay fears and concerns, thus preventing more widespread depositor panic in the aftermath of bank and finance company closures in neighbouring Thailand and Indonesia.

By the second quarter of 1998, the Malaysian authorities had set up key institutions to save the banking system from greater distress. By early 2000, Danaharta had expended RM47 billion to take over non-performing loans from financial institutions, at a (substantial) discount, thus providing them with the means to restore badly needed liquidity to the system. Meanwhile, Danamodal had spent another RM7 billion to re-capitalise the banks in the aftermath of the havoc wreaked by the financial crisis.[32]

Table 4.17
Malaysia: Commercial Banks' Non-Performing Loans by Sector, 1997-1999 (RM million at end of month)

Sector	Mar 97	Jun 97	Sep 97	Dec 97	Mar 98	Jun 98	Sep 98	Dec 98	Mar 99	Jun 99	Sep 99	Dec 99
Agriculture, hunting, forestry and fishing	235.3	229.8	226.5	246.8	259.5	380.9	454.1	568.0	573.4	609.4	609.4	635.0
Mining and quarrying	40.5	22.4	73.1	81.2	31.2	93.8	128.4	166.4	201.1	282.4	282.4	199.1
Manufacturing	1,823.9	2,324.7	2,121.1	2,734.0	3,801.1	5,395.0	7,561.6	7,220.3	7,532.1	7,761.6	7,761.6	7,365.0
Electricity, gas and water	18.0	5.5	7.5	23.7	122.4	403.5	236.6	38.9	32.5	58.3	58.3	39.7
Wholesale, retail, restaurants and hotels	827.3	855.6	1,007.3	1,338.6	1,969.6	2,514.5	3,293.4	3,138.0	3,442.0	3,464.1	3,464.1	4,060.6
Wholesale trade	377.9	395.2	499.0	687.1	1,083.1	1,512.7	1,884.7	1,753.0	1,859.9	1,872.2	1,872.2	2,002.2
Retail trade	341.1	355.1	370.9	471.6	612.6	762.9	941.9	878.6	904.1	962.9	962.9	1,118.7
Restaurants and hotels	108.4	105.3	137.4	179.9	273.9	238.8	466.8	506.4	678.0	629.0	629.0	939.7
Construction	966.3	1,069.2	901.2	1,349.6	3,002.1	4,127.4	5,558.4	5,220.7	5,661.4	6,558.0	6,558.0	6,054.7
Purchase of residential property	1,125.0	1,138.5	1,119.1	1,632.0	2,454.7	2,731.8	3,058.3	3,001.9	3,189.1	3,440.9	3,440.9	3,580.4
Purchase of non-residential property	508.5	589.2	574.7	907.0	1,328.9	1,825.2	2,631.5	2,398.5	2,410.4	2,263.7	2,263.7	2,540.4
Real estate	626.5	981.2	857.7	934.3	1,437.5	2,126.7	2,456.0	2,594.8	2,176.2	2,469.5	2,469.5	2,392.6
Transport, storage and communications	109.0	115.3	139.2	242.3	575.3	733.0	1,479.5	1,501.1	1,341.6	1,318.5	1,318.5	1,354.1
Finance, insurance and business services	292.6	368.5	400.7	886.6	1,157.6	2,227.7	2,929.6	3,092.0	3,546.1	3,391.8	3,391.8	3,375.9
Financial services	104.3	103.8	107.8	587.2	651.5	1,322.3	1,811.3	2,006.7	2,257.2	2,284.1	2,284.1	2,197.7
Insurance	5.8	3.6	2.4	4.2	8.0	113.2	108.2	138.2	142.5	144.3	144.3	156.7
Business services	182.6	261.1	290.5	295.2	498.1	792.2	1,010.2	947.1	1,146.4	963.4	963.4	1,021.4
Consumption credit:	881.2	1,041.4	805.2	1,144.8	1,851.6	2,161.3	2,492.5	2,392.2	2,347.2	2,300.3	2,300.3	2,246.5
Credit card loans	270.9	316.5	286.7	344.7	423.7	510.5	544.7	554.0	566.3	430.9	430.9	366.3
Personal use	563.0	677.3	430.9	715.4	1,310.9	1,485.0	1,811.5	1,766.3	1,670.7	1,779.3	1,779.3	1,794.7
Purchase of consumer durables	47.3	47.5	87.6	84.7	117.0	165.7	136.3	71.9	902.0	90.2	90.2	85.4
Purchase of securities	153.8	224.6	436.2	1,411.5	3,011.8	6,187.3	8,273.0	4,130.3	3,019.6	2,988.3	2,988.3	2,743.0
Purchase of transport vehicles	9.5	4.7	15.4	15.0	8.3	6.1	119.8	188.6	218.2	381.3	381.3	462.5
Others	360.5	316.1	456.3	1,212.0	1,266.1	1,464.2	1,741.8	1,602.0	1,386.2	1,572.2	1,527.2	1,582.5
Total non-performing loans	7,977.8	9,286.7	9,141.1	14,159.0	22,277.7	32,378.3	42,414.3	37,253.5	37,077.1	38,815.2	38,815.2	38,361.9

Source: BNM, *Monthly Statistical Bulletin*, Table III.18, p. 43.

Table 4.18
Malaysia: Finance Companies' Non-Performing Loans by Sector, 1997-1999 (RM million at end of month)

Sector	Mar 97	Jun 97	Sep 97	Dec 97	Mar 98	Jun 98	Sep 98	Dec 98	Mar 99	Jun 99	Sep 99	Dec 99
Agriculture, hunting, forestry and fishing	70.1	74.1	79.4	133.4	207.2	289.8	222.5	172.1	145.3	130.9	120.4	117.2
Mining and quarrying	23.9	15.5	15.5	38.3	62.1	102.4	85.7	57.3	77.4	79.6	71.4	70.0
Manufacturing	239.8	283.9	318.3	783.2	877.8	1,423.0	1,355.2	1,242.2	1,213.7	1,141.5	1,117.9	1,031.5
Electricity, gas and water	1.0	1.5	3.0	4.3	22.4	19.9	18.3	12.9	18.5	18.3	17.8	16.8
Wholesale, retail, restaurants and hotels	91.7	88.7	99.5	164.4	313.4	620.9	538.6	621.0	796.7	578.9	597.4	546.4
Wholesale trade	25.9	24.9	33.9	62.7	130.7	234.5	239.7	238.1	350.4	271.4	282.6	255.1
Retail trade	48.9	44.3	45.8	66.0	122.2	307.5	228.9	205.1	219.5	179.8	180.5	174.8
Restaurants and hotels	16.8	19.5	19.9	35.7	60.4	78.8	70.0	177.8	226.8	127.7	134.3	116.5
Construction	722.4	563.6	447.2	972.8	1,492.1	1,861.0	2,028.8	1,721.9	1,978.4	2,360.3	1,804.8	1,989.4
Purchase of residential property	470.2	505.4	536.1	922.8	1,117.1	1,351.4	1,556.6	1,099.4	1,270.1	1,194.1	1,277.5	1,211.9
Purchase of non-residential property	153.4	202.0	359.9	772.7	1,009.4	1,445.9	1,755.9	1,435.3	1,560.9	1,433.6	1,240.4	1,227.8
Real estate	656.6	842.6	1,116.5	1,127.8	1,347.4	1,554.4	2,031.6	1,903.9	844.4	508.3	505.7	550.3
Transport, storage and communications	101.3	115.8	134.6	375.2	502.7	946.3	1,076.3	996.4	813.9	795.6	560.7	564.0
Financing, insurance and business services	49.6	54.2	295.4	402.0	560.8	774.9	937.3	757.3	801.1	697.3	672.1	643.8
Financial services	8.9	8.4	259.1	304.4	333.1	303.9	355.6	320.1	289.6	308.3	269.6	243.9
Insurance	0.8	0.9	0.4	1.5	2.5	11.0	2.9	2.2	1.9	2.3	2.3	2.1
Business services	39.9	45.0	35.9	96.2	225.1	460.0	578.8	435.0	509.6	386.7	400.2	397.9
Consumption credit:	306.0	334.0	292.4	449.5	565.5	557.6	619.1	511.1	437.6	277.8	265.0	268.0
Credit card loans	70.4	67.8	73.0	116.7	114.1	109.5	174.1	196.1	95.8	40.9	47.7	62.7
Personal use	172.9	175.1	133.9	188.5	276.7	340.1	356.8	236.8	269.9	209.8	188.2	178.8
Purchase of consumer durables	62.7	91.1	85.5	144.3	174.7	108.0	88.3	78.1	71.9	27.2	29.2	26.5
Purchase of securities	60.7	79.2	407.9	865.2	1,502.5	1,515.6	2,268.3	2,419.4	2,098.5	1,753.4	1,885.8	1,729.6
Purchase of transport vehicles	748.5	992.7	1,164.2	2,812.5	4,438.0	4,554.9	5,100.7	4,415.5	4,200.6	3,951.7	3,919.4	3,973.5
Others	147.3	90.2	130.7	150.3	263.5	445.4	362.3	535.7	578.7	568.8	568.9	474.9
Total non-performing loans	3,842.4	4,243.3	5,400.6	9,974.3	14,281.8	17,463.6	19,957.2	17,901.3	16,835.8	15,489.9	14,625.2	14,415.2

Source: BNM, *Monthly Statistical Bulletin*, Table III.19, p. 44.

Financial Liberalisation and System Vulnerability

125

However, the major beneficiaries of these measures may have been few and privileged, while some rescued sectors and enterprises can hardly be considered socially productive. The activities of Danaharta, in particular, have given cause for concern (*Annual Report 1998,* p. 27; *Annual Report 1999,* p. 30). At the end of 1998, after its first half-year of operations, 22 per cent of the NPLs acquired by Danaharta were from offshore bank operations, where the transparency of operations is limited. This was followed by an abrupt drop in the proportion of Danaharta-acquired NPLs from offshore operations in 1999 to 0.03 per cent. Two banking groups accounted for 58.0 per cent of the total NPLs absorbed by Danaharta by the end of 1999.

Reflecting the nature of the crisis and the major victims of the resultant liquidity squeeze, Danaharta has tended to take over NPLs associated with speculative or high risk activity. At the end of 1998, 16.9 per cent of Danaharta's NPL portfolio comprised loans for the purchase of securities, although such loans constituted only 11.1 per cent of total commercial bank NPLs. The corresponding figures at the end of 1999 were 17.5 per cent and 7.2 per cent respectively, suggesting an exacerbation of this trend. The property sector has also been favoured. At the end of 1998, the proportion of construction and real estate NPLs in the Danaharta portfolio were 16.8 per cent and 8.3 per cent respectively. A year later, 'broad property', combining these two sectors, comprised 29.7 per cent of Danaharta-acquired NPLs. Also at the end of 1999, 13.6 per cent of Danaharta's portfolio consisted of financing, insurance and business services, although the fraction of this sector's NPLs to total commercial bank NPLs was significantly less, at 3.5 per cent. Amid such efforts to rescue floundering businesses, there have also been efforts by the politically best connected and those who came through the crisis relatively unscathed to consolidate and extend their business interests.

Despite the abuses, such prompt and transparent action by the Malaysian authorities contained the possibility of Thai or Indonesian style panics, in which the decline in depositor confidence in the aftermath of closures of financial institutions caused bank runs. These pre-emptive Malaysian institutional initiatives and policy measures limited the damage caused by the financial crisis to the national banking system, restoring liquidity, lowering the costs of funds, rehabilitating the banking system and reducing the growth of NPLs, saving businesses and jobs in the process.

However, the authorities have also taken the opportunity to attempt consolidation of the banking sector through directed mergers and acquisitions. The number of finance companies had already been reduced by more than half and was to be reduced further. In mid-1999, the government announced a controversial scheme, very much associated with Finance Minister Daim, to merge all commercial banks, merchant banks and finance companies into six groups decided upon by the authorities. Widespread unhappiness about the scheme, particularly among the ethnic Chinese community, obliged the government to suspend the scheme before the November 1999 general election. In early 2000, however, the government announced an amended scheme involving ten — instead of six — groups. The four additional anchor groups are all led by bankers with personal connections to the Prime Minister, three of whom were previously thought to have fallen from grace.

Several consequences of the financial crisis — including loss of investor confidence, sudden and massive capital outflows, credit crunch — had various adverse effects on the real economy. The impact on growth was lagged, dropping from 7.7 per cent growth in 1997, including 6.0 per cent in the last quarter. The Malaysian economy contracted by -6.7 per cent in 1998 — or by -2.8 per cent, -6.8 per cent, -9.0 per cent and -8.1 per cent in the four quarters of 1998 — and by -1.5 per cent in the first quarter of 1999, before recovering from the second quarter onwards. Thus, the currency and financial crises, triggered by the collapse of the baht in July 1997, thrust Malaysia and its Southeast Asian neighbours towards economic recession.

Like the early debate on the origins of the financial crisis itself, initial discussion on the impact of the financial crisis on the real economy tended toward either denial or alarm. The suddenness of the financial contraction, amplified by the contrast with the previous seven years of uninterrupted economic growth averaging around eight per cent, probably contributed to the marked divergence in reaction. Many who saw the accumulated wealth of many years suddenly dissipate refused to believe what was happening. After experiencing the financial system shock, others expected the economic recession to be similarly catastrophic by causing hyperinflation, massive unemployment and social upheaval.

Conclusions and Policy Implications

Much contemporary economic thinking about the appropriate role of finance in promoting economic development had been profoundly influenced by the 1973 McKinnon-Shaw critique of so-called 'financial repression'. This critique contrasted with earlier work by Gurley and Shaw, which seemed to support a proactive role for government in promoting bank intermediation to allocate savings for developmental purposes. The critique of financial repression was soon translated into policy, especially with the resurgence of 'neo-liberal' 'free market' conservatism in the Anglophone world, boosted by the political ascendance of Margaret Thatcher in Britain (1979) and Ronald Reagan in the United States (1980). Foreign and domestic advocates of financial liberalisation promised increased savings and investments, net capital inflows from abroad and higher economic growth. With the debt crisis of the early and mid-1980s, debt-strapped governments in Latin America, Africa, Eastern Europe and elsewhere were soon obliged to accept and implement various conditionalities accompanying debt relief packages. Thus, international financial institutions were able to promote, if not impose, policies advancing both domestic as well as international financial liberalisation.

Although the resolution of the debt crisis generally protected the interests of the international banks, the protracted negotiations and losses incurred served to discourage international bank lending to the developing country governments. Instead, such banks found new customers in the burgeoning private sectors of the developing world, especially in East Asia. The new economic policy orthodoxy favoured lending to the private sector, ostensibly to avoid a recurrence of the 1980s' international debt crisis. Meanwhile, the Bank of International Settlements (BIS) imposed more onerous lending conditions, which served to discourage such long-term lending, and resulted instead in greater short-term lending (for periods of less than a year), rendering such loan flows much more easily reversible. The willingness of international banks to seemingly indefinitely 'roll over' such loans in good times encouraged a false sense of confidence in the continued availability of such lending, encouraging many borrowers to invest or lend long term with these seemingly perpetually available funds.

From the late 1980s, the Bretton Woods financial institutions began actively promoting the internationalisation of capital markets in a big way. In particular, the International Finance Corporation (IFC), a World Bank subsidiary, encouraged investment in the 'newly emerging markets' of the developing countries and transitional economies. Mutual funds, hedge funds and other institutional and even individual investors were keen to invest in the rapidly growing economies of East Asia, where growth performances contrasted favourably with the prolonged slow growth, if not recessions of the advanced industrial economies of Europe and elsewhere.

New conditions in Southeast Asia also contributed to financial liberalisation in the region. Unlike Japan, South Korea and Taiwan, where indigenous entrepreneurs and technological capabilities had developed, transnational corporations from the North controlled much of the internationally competitive export-oriented industries in Southeast Asia. This was especially true of Malaysia, which was second only to Singapore in terms of the contribution of foreign direct investment to gross domestic capital formation, especially in the manufacturing sector. Consequently, domestic capital tended to dominate the non-industrial sectors, including finance. While domestic financial interests were generally opposed to full-blown international financial liberalisation for obvious reasons, they were keen to profit from the availability of cheaper funds from external sources as well as inflation of the value of financial and other assets due to foreign portfolio investment inflows.

Despite some erosion of financial governance in Malaysia from the mid-1980s, the tighter regulation of the financial sector in Malaysia, compared to its neighbours, rendered it less vulnerable to the reversal of short-term bank lending. However, earlier Malaysian success in attracting foreign portfolio capital inflows to its stock market rendered it more vulnerable on a different front. Hence, unlike Thailand, Indonesia and South Korea, the crisis in Malaysia was not primarily exacerbated by vulnerability to short-term foreign bank borrowings. Instead, the greater vulnerability of its relatively much larger stock market to international investor sentiment proved to be its Achilles' heel. The 1996 bull-run had already been reversed after February 1997 as international portfolio investor sentiment toward Malaysia began to sour. This change in sentiments was further reinforced by contemporary regional developments, especially after the mid-July 1997 collapse of the Malaysian ringgit's unsustainable dollar peg. Investor sentiment was further undermined by inappropriate policy responses as well as the Malaysian Prime Minister's contrarian rhetoric. But ill-informed negative international perceptions of the region as a whole probably wreaked the most havoc by causing investor herd panic, resulting in sudden and massive capital flights, and thus serving as the principal vectors of regional contagion.

The recent financial crisis points to the importance of prudentially managing risk in the financial system: failing to do so had enhanced the vulnerability of the financial system. While financial restraint can promote banks' commitment to act as long-run agents as well as enhance their capability to cope with risks, this has not been the case in Malaysia. Financial restraint in Malaysia has primarily sought to ensure bank profitability, especially with increasing ethnic Bumiputera dominance of the Malaysian banking system from the 1970s. In other words, financial restraint has been used to advance interethnic economic redistribution and other related public policies, rather than to favour long-term productive investments, especially in non-resource-based export-oriented manufacturing, with financial liberalisation exacerbating most of these trends.

An important lesson from the East Asian crisis is that prudential regulation by the government is necessary to manage the trade-off between the competitive efficiency of markets and the security of the banking system (Park 1994: 21; Chowdhury and Islam 1993: 144). As Stiglitz (1999) pointed out, developing countries should be encouraged to find the appropriate regulatory structures or governance systems to manage the incentives and constraints which affect financial institutions' exposure to and ability to cope with risk to engage in rapid financial market liberalisation, especially massive cross-border capital flows.[33] Furthermore, he makes the point that the requirements of good risk management in developing countries may differ markedly from those for developed countries since the former generally face larger risks, lacking well developed information system flows, and typically having weaker risk management capacities than the latter. Building such financial infrastructures in developing countries should be a precondition for appropriate and properly sequenced financial liberalisation.

Careful analysis of pre-crisis financial reforms and developments suggests that the crisis can be traced to financial liberalisation and the consequent undermining of effective financial regulation both at international and national levels. Liberalisation of the domestic financial system — (eliminating interest rate controls and credit allocation and thus allowing more market forces to work) before putting in place the strong institutions needed for effective prudential regulation and supervision — led to moral hazard problems. Promoting securities markets before an effective and mature banking system was well-established, diminished the franchise value of the banking system, resulting in increased risk-taking and aggravating banking system fragility.

Official promotion of the stock market from the late 1980s encouraged foreign financial institutions to invest in the stock market. The high proportion of foreign portfolio investments in the stock market made the Malaysian economy much more vulnerable to external shocks, especially capital flight, and rendered the tasks of exchange rate management and inflation control much more difficult. Unlike the banking crisis of the late 1980s, brought on by a prolonged world recession that began in the West in the early 1980s, the crisis of 1997-98 was precipitated in the turbulent financial market, with the massive withdrawal of funds. In its enthusiasm to establish the country as yet another key financial centre in Southeast Asia, Malaysia did not develop any well-conceived prudential regulatory instruments to manage the much more volatile and greater portfolio investment inflows, notwithstanding some temporary controls aimed at discouraging portfolio flows in 1994. Malaysia was thus ill equipped to deal with the currency and financial crises and, with injudicious policy responses to the crises, had turned them into a crisis of the real economy (Jomo 1998b).

Notes

1. For a critical review of how the currency and financial crises in Malaysia became a crisis of the real economy, see Jomo (1998b).
2. For a brief historical review of the development of commercial banks in Malaya and later Malaysia, see Lee (1990: Chapter 4).
3. Those institutions whose principal liabilities are generally accepted as money.
4. Those institutions which are closely linked to monetary institutions and whose liabilities are generally accepted as near money.
5. For details, see Chin (2000).
6. Initially, these regulations were imposed on commercial banks, but were later extended to merchant banks from 1979.
7. Known as the Sime Bank after the takeover by the Sime Darby group, it was subsequently acquired by the RHB Bank.
8. Non-Bumiputeras refer to those not considered indigenous to Malaysia, referring mainly to ethnic Chinese and Indians.
9. The extension of limits allows banks to invest in Malaysia Airline System Berhad (MAS), the Malaysian International Shipping Corporation (MISC), and other approved 'blue chip' shares, as well as the shares of manufacturing companies and property trusts, subject to prescribed limits (for details, see BNM 1989: 101, Lee 1992: 281). As for investments in the shares of manufacturing companies, the shares held by a commercial bank should not exceed 10 per cent of its paid-up capital and reserves (or 5 per cent of a foreign bank's net working funds), whichever is lower. The sum of these shares should not exceed 25 per cent of a domestic bank's paid-up capital and reserves, or 25 per cent of a foreign bank's net working funds.
10. For details, see BNM (1994: 46-47).
11. Except for interest rates on loans to priority sectors.
12. In a televised interview with a local TV station, Looi Teong Chye, the President of the Small and Medium Industries Association of Malaysia, mentioned that some bankers requested collateral of double the value of loans applied for by small-scale entrepreneurs.
13. Part of this section draws from Chin (1999).
14. There was only one public issue in 1965 (Drake 1975).
15. Bumiputera refers to the 'indigenous' population of Malaysia, mainly comprising the Malays of Peninsular Malaysia.
16. Some examples are provided by Jesudason (1989: 126, endnote 31).

17. One may disagree by arguing that shares which are issued at their intrinsic values, can be bid up by an overly optimistic market, leading us to wrongly interpret demand pressures as under-pricing. However, demand pressure at or after listing may push up prices above their intrinsic values in the short-run, as prices of new issues decline in the longer run after demand pressure subsidies.

18. As the minimum paid-up capital for companies to be listed on the KLSE Main Board is RM50 million, the KLSE Second Board was launched in 1988 to enable smaller companies (with minimum paid-up capital of at least RM10 million, but less than RM50 million) to tap additional funds through public listings.

19. For example, the yen fell from less than 80¥ to the US$ in mid-1995 to over 120¥ by mid-1997, while the Deutschemark had floated against the US dollar before mid-1997.

20. As discussed in Hellmann, Murdock and Stiglitz (1997), an important aspect of the franchise value is that it creates long run equity that cannot be appropriated in the short run since banks have an ongoing interest to stay in business. Thus, franchise value creates incentive and commitment for the banks to act as long-run agents, to effectively monitor firms they finance and to manage the risk of their portfolio of loans.

21. A similar declining trend over the same period was also observed for the three and five largest banks (Zainal *et al.* 305).

22. In examining the empirical relationship between banking crisis and financial liberalisation, Demirgüç-Kunt and Detragiache (1998) show that the adverse impact of financial liberalisation on banking sector fragility is stronger where the institutions needed for the correct functioning of financial markets are not well-established.

23. Computed from Table 2 in UNCTAD and ICC (1998).

24. The share of foreign direct investment in gross capital formation in Malaysia was exceptionally high, not only rising above 10 per cent during the period 1980-90 (Rasiah 1998), but also much higher than the other Asian countries affected by the crisis (i.e. South Korea, Thailand, Indonesia and the Philippines), where the ratio never surpassed 10 per cent (see Table 2 in UNCTAD and ICC, 1998). Foreign direct investment also accounts for very significant export shares, particularly in electrical and electronic industries, reaching more than half of manufacturing exports and more than 40 per cent of total exports (UNCTAD and ICC 1998).

25. Bhattacharya, Ghosh and Jansen present evidence that recent growth of China's market shares of its top 10 manufactured exports was associated with small declines in the Malaysian market shares for these products as well as Thailand (see World Bank 1998: 23).

26. Commitment here refers to the financial institutions' willingness to assume a major role in industrial finance, promoting longer time horizons, rather than mainly lending short-term working capital.

27. With financial liberalisation, it is likely that official measures of such flows underestimate the actual extent of these borrowings.

28. According to the Bank of International Settlements (BIS) (*Asian Wall Street Journal*, 6 January 1998), 56 per cent of Malaysian foreign borrowings from commercial banks were short-term in nature. According to the Malaysian central bank, however, only 30 per cent of all foreign borrowings were short-term in nature, with another nine per cent due in the next year, i.e. 39 per cent in all.
29. Some commentators claim that the resultant property price bubble has its roots in Japanese-type or more generically East Asian culture, norms and relationships which compromise relations between the state and the private sector as well as among businesses, invariably involving welfare-reducing, if not downright debilitating rent-seeking behavior. In so far as such relations are believed to exclude outsiders, their elimination is believed to contribute to leveling the playing field and bringing about an inevitable convergence towards supposedly Anglo-American style arms-length market relations.
30. See Akyuz (1995) and Griffith-Jones (1997).
31. For further details, see BNM (1993). For instance the BNM had to absorb large interest payments for issuing bonds to mop up extra liquidity in the financial system.
32. Danamodal had injected RM7.1bn into 10 financial institutions, of which RM1.9bn has since been repaid. Banks jockeying for 'anchor bank' status after the mid-1999 announcement of accelerated bank consolidation preferred to pay Danamodal back rather than heed the central bank's call for increased lending. So, as of late March 2000, the net amount injected by Danamodal was RM5.2bn, with little new Danamodal activity since then.

    By 31 December 1999, total NPLs acquired were worth RM47bn. As much of this was accounted for by Bank Bumiputra and Sime Bank, the balance was about RM20bn. The average discount for these NPLs acquired (i.e. for the RM20bn) was 55 per cent, and about 45 per cent if one also excludes the controversial 'national service' loans to Hottick for it to acquire National Steel Corporation of the Philippines from Joseph Chong's Westmont group. There seems to have been very little change in the first half of the year to 30 June 2000, with the discount averaging 47-48 per cent (presumably sans Hottick) (Leslie Lopez, 'Steelmaker's Demise Roils Malaysian Banks, Taxpayers', *Asian Wall Street Journal*, 19 September 2000).
33. Stiglitz calls this approach to effective financial regulation, from the perspective of risk management, the Dynamic Portfolio Approach.

5

CAPITAL FLOWS

Jomo K. S.[*]

There has been growing attention given to the role of reversible capital flows into the East Asian region as the principal cause of the 1997-98 crisis. It is increasingly widely accepted that the national financial systems in the region did not adapt well to international financial liberalisation (e.g. Jomo 1998). The bank-based financial systems of most of crisis-hit East Asia were especially vulnerable to the sudden drop in the availability of short-term loans as international confidence in the region dropped suddenly during 1997. Available foreign exchange reserves were exposed as inadequate to meet financial obligations abroad, requiring the governments to seek temporary credit facilities to meet such obligations mainly incurred by their private sectors.

Malaysia's recent experience with regards to capital flows differs in important ways from the problems faced by the other East Asian crisis-hit economies in several respects. First, Malaysian banks and corporations had far less access to international borrowing than their counterparts in the other crisis-affected economies. Second, unlike the others, foreign bank loans did not figure as significantly in the Malaysian crisis. Instead, capital market flows, especially into and out of the stock market, figured more prominently. Third, due to its lower exposure to private bank borrowings from abroad, Malaysia did not have to seek emergency international credit facilities. For most of the second half of 1997, and again from mid-1998, the Malaysian authorities deliberately pursued unconventional measures in response to the deteriorating situation, with rather mixed results. Some of these are discussed in other chapters in this volume.

This chapter focuses on capital flows into and out of the Malaysian economy. Foreign capital inflows have long been important for the Malaysian economy, with mixed consequences. Before the nineties, foreign direct investment was especially important, while official development assistance declined in relative significance with economic growth. Foreign portfolio investment flows became very significant in the nineties. (In the following chapter, such flows will be shown to have been very volatile and often short-term in nature.) While public sector borrowing from abroad declined rapidly from the mid-eighties, the private sector began to borrow heavily in the nineties. However, foreign borrowings were less significant in Malaysia compared to the other crisis-affected economies, and a smaller proportion of such loans was short-term in nature. Instead, as the next chapter shows, portfolio capital inflows, mainly into Malaysia's relatively huge stock market, proved to be even more easily reversible than short-term borrowings, with disastrous consequences for the stock market as well as the real economy.

Foreign Capital Inflows

According to orthodox economic theory, foreign capital inflows (FCI) contribute to economic growth by raising investment levels, usually by simultaneously closing the classical two (foreign exchange as well as savings-investment) gaps. While Rosenstein-Rodan (1961) and Chenery and Strout (1966) argued that foreign capital inflows contribute to economic growth, Griffin and Enos (1970) and Weisskoff (1972) have dissented. The former regard foreign capital inflows as supplementary to domestic savings, while the latter claim that foreign capital inflows replaces domestic savings, and thus do not necessarily enhance growth and development since foreign capital inflows may also adversely affect the domestic savings rate. Foreign capital inflows would also increase investment payments abroad — which would detract from its positive contributions.

Empirical assessment of the role of foreign capital inflows in Malaysian economic development between 1966 and 1996 has sought to evaluate its impact on output growth (Wong with Jomo 1999). The analysis considers both direct and indirect effects of foreign capital inflows discussed in the conventional as well as the critical economic literature, paying particular emphasis to foreign capital inflows' impact on investments and on savings. The composition and magnitude of foreign capital inflows in Malaysia has undergone various shifts over the last three decades. Foreign direct investment (FDI) has been important since the sixties. Official development assistance from the sixties grew in the seventies and early eighties. Portfolio investments and private borrowings from abroad grew rapidly in the early and mid-nineties.

Much of the early FDI in Malaysia was attracted by the various incentives offered to promote import-substituting industrialisation from the late fifties and the export-oriented manufacturing from the late sixties. A sizeable portion of the funds for the large public expenditures from the seventies until the mid-eighties was obtained through foreign borrowings. Hence, public foreign debt increased from the 1970s until the mid-1980s, ballooning when the ringgit depreciated against the Japanese yen during the mid-1980s (Jomo 1990). While government foreign debt has declined since the late eighties, private debt has grown, especially in the nineties, though the central bank has continued to limit corporate borrowing from abroad. The growing share of private — as opposed to public — debt has also meant a higher proportion of short-term debt from commercial sources. This trend must have contributed to the rising proportion of short-term inflows — relative to medium and long term capital inflows — in the nineties. Unlike other East Asian economies that experienced tremendous inflows of short-term bank borrowings, however, the main reason for the more volatile nature of foreign capital inflows in Malaysia in the last decade was the growing share of (easily reversible) foreign portfolio investments.

Analysis by Wong with Jomo (1999) of the impact of long-term foreign capital inflows (FCI) into Malaysia over three decades from 1966 until 1996 (see Appendix 5.1 for the regression results) found that:

- foreign capital inflows have augmented domestic savings for investment, and has generally served as a supplement to, and not substitute for domestic savings.
- however, foreign capital inflows seem to have adversely affected the domestic savings rate, albeit only indirectly.
- foreign capital inflows have augmented foreign exchange reserves, e.g. thus financing additional imports and encouraging current account deficits.
- foreign capital inflows have adversely affected factor payment outflows, export and import propensities, the terms of trade and capital flight, worsening the balance of payments.

While there are cumulative long-term effects of foreign capital inflows, in the short term, the financial system has also become more vulnerable to greater volatility. The sudden massive outflow of funds from the latter part of 1997 shocked Malaysia's financial system. These outflows formed a vicious cycle with the depreciation of the Malaysian ringgit, as contagion from the Thai baht crisis spread to similarly vulnerable neighbouring economies. Stock prices also plummeted, with the collapse of investor confidence, exacerbated by herd behaviour and perceptions of inappropriate government policy responses. The combined effects of currency depreciation, asset price deflation, higher interest rates, economic recession and lost in investor confidence saddled many Malaysian companies with heavy (mainly domestic) debt and collapsed asset values.

This chapter will attempt to develop a more detailed understanding of the pattern of foreign capital flows. It examines the changing nature and role of capital flows into and out of Malaysia, particularly with a view to understanding and explaining the recent crisis. A longer view of such flows is taken in order to highlight how such flows have changed in character, magnitude and significance in the nineties. Particular attention will be given to the changing relationship of such capital flows to the rest of the Malaysian financial system and real economy. The following chapter shows how the sudden massive reversal of such flows contributed to the crisis from mid-1997. Yet another chapter looks at Malaysia's unique response to the crisis, by introducing selective capital controls.

Magnitude of Foreign Capital Flows

The Malaysian government has made efforts to attract foreign capital to supplement domestic savings since Malayan independence in 1957. From the late fifties until the eighties, this mainly consisted of foreign direct investment (usually in line with industrialisation policy priorities) as well as foreign aid. Foreign investors initially dominated the new import-substituting industries for over a decade from the late fifties, and later, non-resource-based export-oriented industries from the seventies. With rapid development, Malaysia's eligibility for foreign aid declined, but there was a spate of official borrowings — mainly from Japan — in the first half of the eighties to finance the then new Mahathir government-sponsored heavy industries. Investments from Japan had become significant in the seventies, but accelerated with other investments from the first-tier East Asian newly industrialising economies from the second half of the eighties.

As with many other newly 'emerging markets', foreign portfolio inflows into Malaysia only rapidly grew in significance from the late eighties. The de-linking of the Kuala Lumpur Stock Exchange (KLSE) from the Stock Exchange of Singapore (SES) at the turn of the decade gave an added boost to the Malaysian bourse. The Malaysian authorities opened the gates more widely to foreign capital in the 1990s. Like other emerging markets in the region, Malaysia experienced an unprecedented surge of foreign investment inflows, especially from portfolio management funds, attributable to various factors.[1] Liberalisation of the financial market provided the impetus for the massive portfolio inflows seeking to maximise capital gains in the generally bullish Malaysian stock market. As Tables 5.1 to 5.4 show, net portfolio capital inflows have proved to be very volatile, rising from -1.5 per cent of GDP in 1991 to 14.5 per cent in 1993, before dropping off to 1.2 per cent in 1995. Bank loan flows have also been almost as volatile, while foreign direct investment and official development assistance have been far less volatile.

Table 5.1

Malaysia: Net Capital Inflows by Major Category, 1989-1995 (% of GDP)

	1989	*1990*	*1991*	*1992*	*1993*	*1994*	*1995*
Net Capital Inflows	3.5	4.2	11.9	15.2	16.8	1.6	8.5
Official Development Finance	-2.4	-2.4	-0.5	-1.4	0.6	0.3	2.7
Foreign Direct Investment	4.4	5.4	8.5	9.0	7.8	6.0	4.7
Commercial Bank Funds	1.1	2.0	2.8	6.3	6.6	-7.0	0.1
Portfolio Equity	n.a.	n.a.	-1.5	5.6	14.5	5.7	1.2

Source: BNM's Cash BOP Reporting System, as cited by Ong (1998: 222).

Table 5.2a

Malaysia: Annual Foreign Investment Inflows, 1991-1998 (RM million)

Period	Total Portfolio Investment		External Equity Investment (FDI)		External Investment	
	Receipts	Net Inflows	Receipts	Net Inflows	Receipts	Net Inflows
1991	19,346	-1,928	4,482	3,944	8,776	7,694
1992	60,935	7,892	3,766	2,991	14,195	12,713
1993	187,782	25,654	3,413	1,355	17,474	13,691
1994	238,454	14,029	7,769	4,477	28,873	22,047
1995	106,414	5,360	5,850	456	26,874	18,938
1996	144,933	8,766	8,261	516	31,081	20,366
1997	156,156	-28,430	5,949	-1,210	35,964	25,506
1998	75,524	-2,065	5,943	467	27,757	19,344

Table 5.2b
Malaysia: Quarterly Foreign Investment Inflows, 1991-1998 (RM million)

Period	Total Portfolio Investment		External Equity Investment (FDI)		External Investment	
	Receipts	Net Inflows	Receipts	Net Inflows	Receipts	Net Inflows
1991 Q1	4,316	242	747	680	1,364	1,223
1991 Q2	5,822	143	1,187	1,079	2,597	2,386
1991 Q3	5,454	-1,663	1,256	1,052	2,236	1,796
1991 Q4	3,754	-650	1,292	1,133	2,579	2,289
1992 Q1	13,849	1,254	905	756	3,475	3,190
1992 Q2	12,168	2,746	894	813	3,140	2,931
1992 Q3	16,201	1,753	881	672	3,594	3,201
1992 Q4	18,717	2,139	1,086	750	3,986	3,391
1993 Q1	23,572	4,477	764	511	3,484	3,082
1993 Q2	41,872	6,649	937	178	5,019	3,918
1993 Q3	51,777	6,255	890	584	3,969	3,113
1993 Q4	70,558	8,270	822	82	5,002	3,578
1994 Q1	61,255	6,812	2,089	1,657	7,951	6,966
1994 Q2	46,986	-1,346	2,220	1,583	6,939	5,133
1994 Q3	69,322	7,442	2,246	1,490	7,568	5,994
1994 Q4	60,891	1,121	1,214	-253	6,415	3,954
1995 Q1	32,243	-2,460	1,372	113	4,851	2,953
1995 Q2	28,111	6,046	1,493	482	5,695	4,102
1995 Q3	26,909	2,261	1,618	569	8,812	7,066
1995 Q4	19,151	-487	1,367	-708	7,516	4,817
1996 Q1	32,131	4,078	1,563	-21	6,508	4,228
1996 Q2	32,671	2,257	1,366	-365	6,601	4,177
1996 Q3	34,215	-66	2,462	-220	5,871	2,709
1996 Q4	45,916	2,497	2,870	1,122	12,101	9,252
1997 Q1	47,431	5,647	1,180	-750	7,025	4,404
1997 Q2	41,793	-8,584	1,674	-185	11,909	9,373
1997 Q3	39,614	-16,000	1,355	-30	9,055	6,252
1997 Q4	27,317	-5,492	1,739	-246	7,975	5,476
1998 Q1	27,005	5,596	978	-166	6,484	4,663
1998 Q2	12,284	-3,275	1,106	-287	6,083	4,237
1998 Q3	8,918	-3,669	913	-876	5,333	2,754
1998 Q4	5,652	-717	2,946	1,797	9,858	7,691

Source: Bank Negara Malaysia, *Quarterly Economic Bulletin*, various issues.

Table 5.3
Malaysia: Annual Capital Inflows by Type, 1991-1998
(US$ million, % GDP)

Year	*Inflows*		*Outflows*		*Net Inflows*	
	% GDP	*US$ mil.*	*% GDP*	*US$ mil.*	*% GDP*	*US$ mil.*
Foreign Portfolio Investment						
1991	16.7	7,035	18.3	7,736	-1.7	-701
1992	48.2	23,896	42.0	20,801	6.2	3,095
1993	135.2	73,067	116.7	63,085	18.5	9,982
1994	157.2	91,013	147.9	85,658	9.2	5,355
1995	63.9	42,396	60.6	40,261	3.2	2,135
1996	79.1	57,513	74.3	54,035	4.8	3,479
1997	79.2	55,572	93.6	65,689	-14.4	-10,117
1998	41.4	19,266	42.6	19,793	-1.1	-527
Foreign Direct Investment						
1991	3.9	1,630	0.5	196	3.4	1,434
1992	3.0	1,477	0.6	304	2.4	1,173
1993	2.5	1,328	1.5	801	1.0	527
1994	5.1	2,965	2.2	1,256	3.0	1,709
1995	3.5	2,331	3.2	2,149	0.3	182
1996	4.5	3,278	4.2	3,073	0.3	205
1997	3.0	2,117	3.6	2,548	-0.6	-431
1998	3.3	1,516	3.0	1,397	0.3	119
External Loans						
1991	3.0	1,263	0.4	175	-2.5	-1,088
1992	7.5	3,611	0.5	248	-7	-3,363
1993	2.9	4,784	0.3	571	-2.6	-4,213
1994	13.0	7,722	2.1	1,263	-10.9	-6,458
1995	11.6	7,643	1.3	830	-10.4	-6,813
1996	11.9	8,654	1.3	951	-10.6	-7,703
1997	14.8	7,495	1.5	760	-13.3	-6,735
1998	11.7	5,625	1.6	744	-10.2	-4,881

Source: Bank Negara Malaysia, *Quarterly Economic Bulletin*, various issues.

Table 5.4
Malaysia: Quarterly Capital Inflows by Type, 1991-1998 (US$ million)

Quarter	Foreign Portfolio Investment			Foreign Direct Investment			External Loans		
	In-flows	*Out-flows*	*Net Inflows*	*In-flows*	*Out-flows*	*Net Inflows*	*In-flows*	*Out-flows*	*Net Inflows*
91 Q1	1,569	1,481	88	272	24	247	152.9	21.5	131.3
91 Q2	2,117	2,065	52	432	39	392	441.4	30.1	411.3
91 Q3	1,983	2,588	-605	457	74	383	261.4	80.4	181.0
91 Q4	1,365	1,601	-236	470	58	412	391.5	41.5	350.0
92 Q1	5,431	4,939	492	355	58	296	907.7	48.1	859.6
92 Q2	4,772	3,695	1,077	351	32	319	797.7	45.2	752.5
92 Q3	6,353	5,666	687	345	82	264	993.6	67.8	925.8
92 Q4	7,340	6,501	839	426	132	294	1,005.7	92.6	913.2
93 Q1	9,172	7,430	1,742	297	98	199	966.8	51.4	915.4
93 Q2	16,293	13,705	2,587	365	295	69	1,460.5	121.2	1,339.3
93 Q3	20,147	17,713	2,434	346	119	227	1,083.3	187.9	895.4
93 Q4	27,454	24,237	3,218	320	288	32	1,429.4	227.6	1,201.9
94 Q1	23,380	20,780	2,600	797	165	632	2,064.2	180.6	1,883.6
94 Q2	17,934	18,447	-514	847	243	604	1,711.2	432.3	1,278.8
94 Q3	26,459	23,618	2,840	857	289	569	1,915.2	292.6	1,622.7
94 Q4	23,241	22,813	428	463	560	-97	1,896.3	340.9	1,555.4
95 Q1	12,846	13,826	-980	547	502	45	1,210.5	223.6	986.9
95 Q2	11,200	8,791	2,409	595	403	192	1,574.5	201.6	1,372.9
95 Q3	10,721	9,820	901	645	418	227	2,700.3	231.0	2,469.3
95 Q4	7,630	7,824	-194	545	827	-282	2,262.8	186.3	2,076.5
96 Q1	12,750	11,132	1,618	620	629	-8	1,844.2	231.4	1,612.8
96 Q2	12,965	12,069	896	542	687	-145	2,010.3	213.2	1,797.1
96 Q3	13,577	13,604	-26	977	1,064	-87	1,274.3	123.3	1,151.0
96 Q4	18,221	17,230	991	1,139	694	445	3,556.9	386.9	3,170.1
97 Q1	19,049	16,781	2,268	474	775	-301	2,267.6	236.4	2,031.2
97 Q2	16,585	19,991	-3,406	664	738	-73	3,959.6	223.1	3,736.5
97 Q3	13,161	18,476	-5,316	450	460	-10	2,309.0	412.8	1,896.3
97 Q4	7,246	8,703	-1,457	461	527	-65	1,559.4	121.3	1,438.2
98 Q1	7,221	5,724	1,496	261	306	-44	1,477.5	175.0	1,302.5
98 Q2	3,071	3,890	-819	277	348	-72	1,171.3	103.0	1,068.4
98 Q3	2,347	3,312	-966	240	471	-231	1,142.9	197.9	945.0
98 Q4	1,487	1,676	-189	775	302	473	1,788.4	266.6	1,521.8

Source: Bank Negara Malaysia, *Quarterly Economic Bulletin*, various issues.

Foreign Portfolio Investment

With the lure of fast and lucrative returns, and encouragement to diversify internationally, portfolio funds have made inroads into developing countries. Thus, the role and influence of portfolio management funds, including pension, mutual and hedge funds, expanded dramatically in the 1990s. Stock markets in developing and transitional economies, both packaged as 'emerging markets', welcomed the rising tide of portfolio inflows, which seemed to contribute to general prosperity through asset price inflation.

With the growing ease of moving portfolio funds into and out of Malaysia, both inflows and outflows accelerated intermittently, generating net inflows most of the time. Annual foreign portfolio investment (FPI) inflows rose from RM19.3 (US$7.0) billion in 1991 to RM238.5 (US$91.0) billion in 1994 (Table 5.5). Annual inflows fluctuated significantly after 1994, growing more slowly to RM106.4 (US$42.4) billion in 1995, and then soaring once again to RM144.9 (US$57.5) billion in 1996. Annual FPI outflows were also sizeable in the 1990s, rising from US$7.7 billion in 1991 to a peak of US$85.7 billion in 1994. Outflows were generally smaller than inflows, resulting in positive net annual inflows from 1992 to 1996. However, focussing on such annual figures as well as net flows tends to obscure often short-term fluctuations. Official figures for quarterly flows, shown in Table 5.6, reflect the tremendous fluctuations in net inflows. Net FPI inflows were sometimes paralleled by other movements of funds, including bank loans, foreign direct investment and other investments, with some cumulative consequences.

Malaysia was more successful than any other economy in capturing capital flows to newly emerging markets. In 1996, Malaysia obtained 14 per cent of such flows worth US$2.162 billion to the 44 markets covered by the International Finance Corporation's Emerging Market Data Bank, compared to 13 per cent for South Korea, 7 per cent for Thailand, 6 per cent for Indonesia and 5 per cent for Thailand (IFC 1997).

Net inflows of portfolio investments were substantial up to the first quarter of 1997. In fact, for all of 1997, inflows totalled RM156.2 (US$55.5) billion, even higher than 1996 inflows in ringgit terms, and only slightly lower than 1995's US$57.5 billion of inflows. This swell of FPI was eventually reversed by even more massive outflows, which amounted to RM184.6 (US$65.7) billion in 1997 (Table 5.5). Interestingly, although there was net capital flight of RM28.4 billion in 1997, inflows remained reasonably high, possibly reflecting short-selling activity from abroad to gain from the falling bear market.

Malaysia experienced net FPI outflows from the second quarter of 1997 (Table 5.6). In other words, the reversal began prior to the devaluation of

Table 5.5
Malaysia: Annual Net Foreign Portfolio Investments by Type, 1991-1998 (RM million)

	Shares and Corporate Securities	Malaysian Government Securities	Foreign Government Securities	Private Debt Securities	Money Market Instruments	Financial Derivatives	Total Portfolio Investments	
							Receipts	Net Inflows
1991	-1,879	17	-66	–	–	–	19,346	-1,928
1992	6,843	890	159	–	–	–	60,935	7,892
1993	24,659	1,944	-949	–	–	–	187,782	25,654
1994	14,432	-894	491	–	–	–	238,454	14,029
1995	5,345	-1,024	1,039	–	–	–	106,414	5,360
1996	6,681	-26	292	-234	2,038	15	144,933	8,766
1997	-22,004	16	-1,243	1,970	-7,247	78	156,156	-28,430
1998	-2,220	-650	81	-497	-2,906	-648	75,524	-6,840

Source: Bank Negara Malaysia, *Monthly Statistical Bulletin*, Table III.15.

Table 5.6
Malaysia: Quarterly Net Portfolio Investment Inflows by Type, 1991-1998 (RM million)

	Shares and Corporate Securities	Malaysian Government Securities	Foreign Government Securities	Private Debt Securities	Money Market Instruments	Financial Derivatives	Total Portfolio Investments	
							Receipts	Net Inflows
1991Q1	229	16	-3	–	–	–	4316	242
1991Q2	77	-10	76	–	–	–	5822	143
1991Q3	-1,374	11	-300	–	–	–	5454	-1,663
1991Q4	-811	0	161	–	–	–	3754	-650
1992Q1	964	0	290	–	–	–	13,849	1,254
1992Q2	1,982	57	707	–	–	–	12,168	2,746
1992Q3	1,155	457	141	–	–	–	16,201	1,753
1992Q4	2,742	376	-979	–	–	–	18,717	2,139
1993Q1	4,100	392	-15	–	–	–	23,572	4,477
1993Q2	5,827	471	351	–	–	–	41,872	6,649
1993Q3	7,020	866	-1,631	–	–	–	51,777	6,255
1993Q4	7,709	215	346	–	–	–	70,558	8,270
1994Q1	6,973	-189	28	–	–	–	61,255	6,812
1994Q2	-1,805	-842	1,301	–	–	–	46,986	-1,346
1994Q3	7,641	369	-568	–	–	–	69,322	7,442
1994Q4	1,623	-232	-270	–	–	–	60,891	1,121

(continued…)

Table 5.6 (continued)
Malaysia: Quarterly Net Portfolio Investment Inflows by Type, 1991-1998 (RM million)

	Shares and Corporate Securities	Malaysian Government Securities	Foreign Government Securities	Private Debt Securities	Money Market Instruments	Financial Derivatives	Total Portfolio Investments	
							Receipts	Net Inflows
1995Q1	-2,378	-651	569	–	–	–	32,243	-2,460
1995Q2	6,361	-315	0	–	–	–	28,111	6,046
1995Q3	2,292	-91	60	–	–	–	26,909	2,261
1995Q4	-930	33	410	–	–	–	19,151	-487
1996Q1	3,813	-15	280	n.a.	n.a.	n.a.	32,131	4,078
1996Q2	2,246	-1	12	n.a.	n.a.	n.a.	32,671	2,257
1996Q3	-1,950	-41	0	142	1,779	4	34,215	-66
1996Q4	2,572	31	0	-376	259	11	45,916	2,497
1997Q1	3,625	5	-82	546	1,540	13	47,431	5,647
1997Q2	-7,427	-1	-516	164	-821	17	41,793	-8,584
1997Q3	-11,781	-4	-679	1,121	-4,715	58	39,614	-16,000
1997Q4	-2,422	16	35	139	-3,250	-10	27,317	-5,492
1998Q1	4,224	94	-36	196	1,325	-207	27,005	5,596
1998Q2	-1,693	0	70	-124	-1,290	-238	12,284	-3,275
1998Q3	-2,329	-760	12	-708	309	-193	8,918	-3,669
1998Q4	-2,186	0	-19	1,156	343	-11	5,652	-717

Source: Bank Negara Malaysia, *Monthly Statistical Bulletin*, Table VIII.15.

Table 5.7
Malaysia: Quarterly Net Portfolio Investment Inflows by
Major Source Economies, 1991-1998 (RM million)

Period	US	Belgium	Hong Kong	Japan	Germany	Singapore	UK
1991Q1	21	-1	-135	-20	0	332	44
1991Q2	42	-121	403	13	1	-320	79
1991Q3	21	-196	-342	3	181	-1,069	-242
1991Q4	219	0	-531	14	24	-306	-65
1992Q1	89	2	618	21	-91	755	-48
1992Q2	628	3	650	-68	72	1,077	284
1992Q3	284	5	703	11	32	1,049	-404
1992Q4	-808	28	1,090	20	-127	1,706	31
1993Q1	354	-21	1,368	-9	14	2,625	54
1993Q2	1,023	-6	1,027	18	319	4,733	-624
1993Q3	1,325	3	2,994	-19	-63	3,351	-1,230
1993Q4	-3	246	1,370	1,483	-1	3,601	1,368
1994Q1	1,054	473	68	274	-71	2,380	2,663
1994Q2	991	-451	-4,799	132	532	306	1,958
1994Q3	704	6	795	356	-809	6,371	-838
1994Q4	703	4	-3,196	-169	-431	3,152	1,176
1995Q1	1,922	-95	-1,690	-318	-46	-2,107	16
1995Q2	675	46	1,410	104	-10	2,801	764
1995Q3	2,906	34	-547	-138	-14	-727	450
1995Q4	792	-7	-1,681	48	0	108	341
1996Q1	1,343	179	1,439	-274	-8	449	656
1996Q2	883	191	89	48	43	555	380
1996Q3	402	488	-895	-75	90	-693	693
1996Q4	410	250	-320	-140	9	2,296	-77
1997Q1	1,123	808	-3,535	-226	17	2,313	1,302
1997Q2	1,281	-223	-6,830	50	-10	-2,553	-260
1997Q3	-1,434	-106	-8,044	-363	-123	-4,969	-166
1997Q4	-1,311	16	-3,517	8	16	270	-770
1998Q1	717	108	1,938	79	34	1,485	832
1998Q2	-42	56	-1,473	-61	-47	-1,560	-281
1998Q3	-801	-30	-893	19	-25	-1,724	242
1998Q4	663	-13	-837	-19	-2	-400	121

Source: Bank Negara Malaysia, *Monthly Statistical Bulletin*, Table VIII.16.

the Thai baht in early July 1997. Clearly, anxiety among investors over the over-heating of Southeast Asian economies, especially Thailand, was already mounting before the currencies began to fall in July 1997. After the baht was floated on 2 July 1997 and the ringgit fell in mid-July (after an expensive, but futile ringgit defence effort), FPI inflows fell drastically, and continued to dwindle throughout 1998. FPI inflows fell from US$16.6 billion in the second quarter of 1997 to US$7.2 billion in the fourth quarter of 1997, and to US$1.5 billion in the fourth quarter of 1998. Table 5.7 also shows considerable variation over time among net foreign portfolio investment flows by source, suggesting an additional element of imported volatility.

The massive collapse of the stock market also reflected the leading role that foreign investors had come to play. While remaining a minority (accounting for perhaps a quarter of total stock market capitalisation by mid-1997), their behaviour had a disproportionate impact on the bourse, owing to their greater activity (compared to domestic institutional investors) and their greater magnitude (compared to 'retail players'). Hence, their rapid withdrawal of capital from Malaysia contributed greatly to the massive (four fifths) market decapitalisation, from a KLSE Composite Index (KLCI) February 1997 high close of 1,300 to the 2 September 1998 low of 262.

Table 5.6's quarterly data on inflows and outflows, reflected in Figure 5.1, reflect the ebb and flow of foreign funds. For example, net portfolio inflows fell from late-1993 to mid-1994, and again, from late-1994 through most of 1995. However, during this period, net inflows fluctuated tremendously, falling to minus RM2 billion from a positive RM8 billion. Inflows started to decline again from early 1997, but net inflows fell most as contagion spread in the third quarter of 1997 and the fall of the ringgit precipitated capital flight, mainly from the stock market. This time, outflows overwhelmed inflows. Besides showing the rapid reversal in the wake of the crisis, the chart also reflects the volatile behaviour of portfolio capital flows.

Most portfolio investment into Malaysia has been channelled into the stock market. Hence, the trends for aggregate portfolio inflows parallel those for the purchase of shares and corporate securities. In 1991, RM13.6 billion worth of shares and corporate securities, equivalent to 8.5 per cent of market capitalisation, was held by foreigners. By 1994, this figure had ballooned to RM130.0 billion, or 25.5 per cent of market capitalisation (also see Table 5.8). In contrast, Malaysian government securities have not been very attractive to foreign fund managers. After their introduction in 1996, private debt securities have attracted quite sizeable inflows, while advanced money

Figure 5.1
Malaysia: Foreign Portfolio Investment, by Quarter, 1991-1998

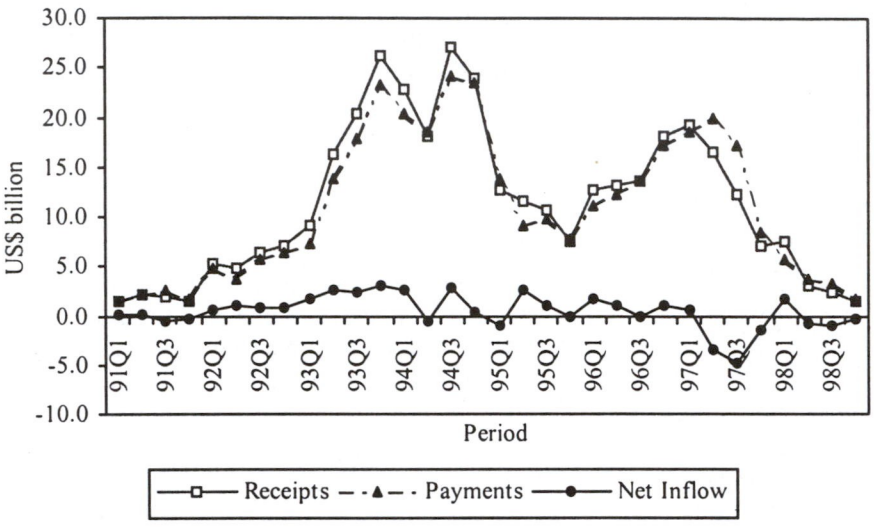

Table 5.8
Malaysia: Foreign Portfolio Investment as
Share of Market Capitalisation, 1991-1998 (%)

Year	Shares and Corporate Securities			Total Portfolio Investment		
	Inflow	*Outflow*	*Net Inflow*	*Inflow*	*Outflow*	*Net Inflow*
1991	8.5	9.6	-1.2	12.0	13.2	-1.2
1992	13.6	10.8	2.8	24.8	21.6	3.2
1993	18.8	14.9	4.0	30.3	26.2	4.1
1994	25.5	22.7	2.8	46.9	44.1	2.8
1995	16.1	15.1	0.9	18.8	17.9	0.9
1996	15.8	15.0	0.8	18.0	16.9	1.1
1997	32.7	38.6	-5.9	41.6	49.1	-7.6
1998	16.1	16.6	-0.5	20.2	20.7	-0.6

Source: BNM, *Quarterly Economic Bulletin*, various issues.

market instruments and financial derivatives have expanded more cautiously. As shown in Figure 5.2, the stock market towers over the other categories of foreign portfolio investments, while its short-termist and volatile propensities parallel those of portfolio flows more generally. Comparison with Figure 5.3 underscores the relative volatility of net inflows of portfolio funds, reflecting the ease with which such investments can take flight.

The dominance of the stock market has probably been inevitable due to the limited range of investment instruments that foreign investors can choose from. During the period 1991-95, portfolio investment funds accounted for 88 per cent of all identified gross capital inflows, while net foreign portfolio investment averaged 5.1 per cent of GDP (Ong 1998: 222-223). In 1993 and 1994, portfolio inflows alone surpassed annual GDP in current market prices, reaching US$67 billion and US$87 billion respectively. Figures 5.2 and 5.3 show that FPI inflows into private debt securities, money market instruments, and financial derivatives only began in 1995, and have remained modest in comparison to the total funds flowing in and out of Malaysia. Although non-stock market flows — especially money market instruments, which recorded an inflow of RM15.8 billion and outflow of RM23.1 billion in 1997 — were of increasing importance, such flows remained less significant in the domestic

Figure 5.2
Malaysia: Foreign Portfolio Investment Inflows, by Type, 1991-1998

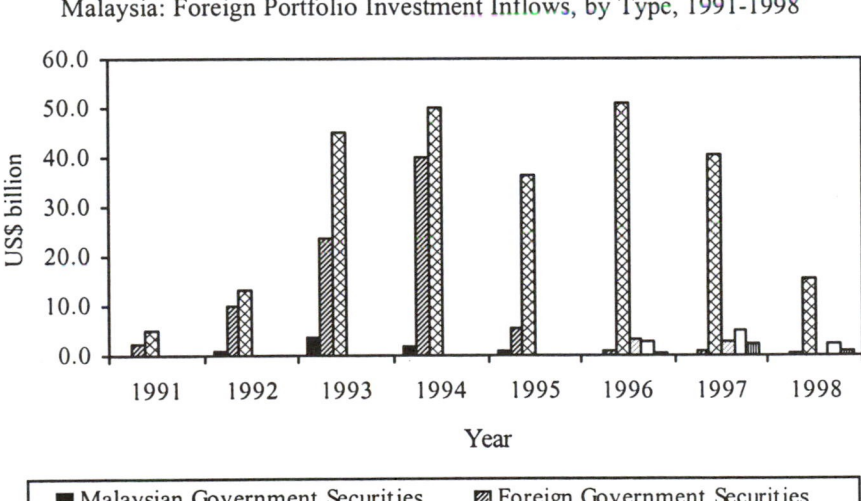

Figure 5.3

Malaysia: Foreign Portfolio Investment Net Inflow, by Type, 1991-1998

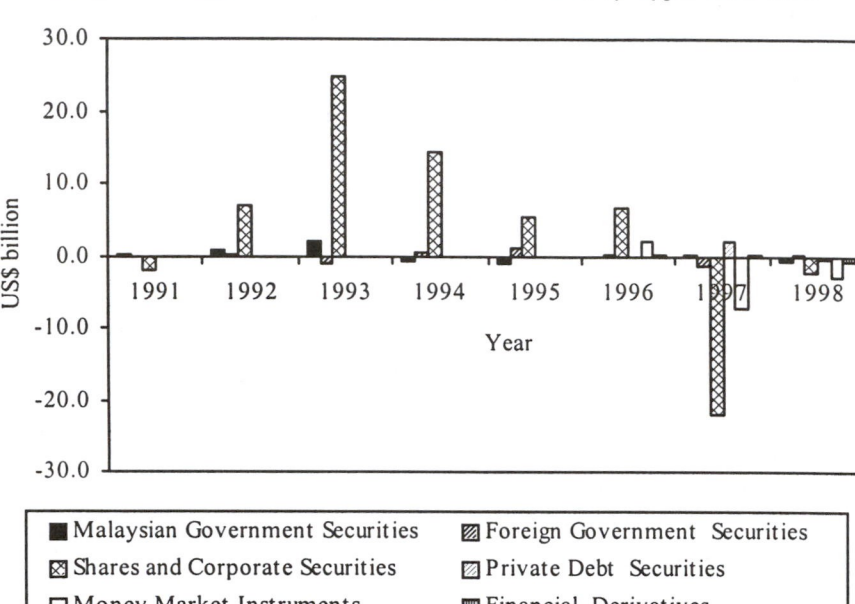

capital market. Some nonetheless served as additional vectors of contagion, while the development of the markets for these instruments has undoubtedly been set back by the financial crisis.

As noted earlier, the increased foreign capital flows into and out of Malaysia, with the growing share of portfolio investment funds involved, allowed foreign institutional investors to develop disproportionately greater influence on the Malaysian stock market. The growing presence of foreign funds also subjected the Kuala Lumpur bourse much more to international vicissitudes of various types. Inevitably, the national economy became much more vulnerable to international macroeconomic fluctuations as well as capital flight, rendering the tasks of exchange rate management, controlling inflation and capital account management much more difficult. The huge short-term capital inflows proved to be especially destabilising as they linked two inherently unstable markets, i.e. the stock and currency markets. The central bank was reportedly incurring high costs in maintaining a tight monetary policy to sterilise the potentially destabilising speculative inflows of foreign portfolio funds.[2] After a sudden exodus of such funds in early 1994, temporary controls aimed at limiting portfolio inflows were put in place, but these were removed once speculative pressures on the ringgit declined by the end of the year.

It has been noted earlier that stock market analysts estimate that by mid-1997, about a quarter of the stock in the Kuala Lumpur Stock Exchange was in foreign hands, with another quarter held by Malaysian institutions, and the remaining half by 'retail investors'. While most petty Malaysian shareholders only operate within the Malaysian stock market or financial system, foreign institutional investors see the Malaysian stock market as only one of many different investment options in a global financial system including many national markets for different types of investment instruments. Unlike the typical Malaysian retail investor who reputedly chooses between the fixed deposit interest rate on offer and the stock market, foreign investment institutions can shift their funds among various securities markets as well as among other types of financial investment options all over the world. Of course, the specialisation among investors which has emerged over the years circumscribes the actual range of investment options available to particular types of investment institutions, e.g. mutual funds, hedge funds or more specialised investment funds such as fixed income investment funds.

Facing poor information, exacerbated by limited transparency, and the short-termism of their investment horizons, many stock market players are prone to herd behaviour, especially in response to panic. The nature of foreign fund managers' incentives as well as their much more varied operations and options mean that foreign financial institutions are also more liable to cause such herd behaviour to be transformed into the trans-border spread of contagion. Although their proportion of share ownership has remained in the minority, the influence of foreign funds has grown disproportionately as they became market leaders, with their greater turnover compared to domestic institutions and their far greater clout compared to local 'retail players'.

Foreign Direct Investment

Foreign direct investment (FDI),[3] as conventionally understood, is associated with investors with longer-term investment commitments. FDI, or DFI, refers to the establishment or expansion of businesses, including joint ventures, in which the foreign investor has effective voice in the management of the business. Besides new 'green-field' investments, FDI may also refer to the reinvestment of profits for business expansion or development as well as to mergers and acquisitions by foreign owners of investments or businesses. Hence, it is generally assumed that FDI is more committed to developing the productive capacity and technological capabilities of the firm. The potential for capturing market share and reducing costs, as well as prospects for product development and production efficiency, among other managerial concerns, are therefore more likely to be investment criteria. Foreign participation in equity investment, or FDI, is often desired for achieving long-term development goals, especially in sectors that benefit from foreign expertise and technological hardware not sufficiently available domestically.

With the earlier decline of the relative role of overseas development assistance, FDI gained in relative significance. But with the more recent growth of foreign portfolio investment, foreign direct investment has come to account for a much smaller share of total capital inflows or total foreign investment in Malaysia. Annual inflows of FDI into Malaysia rose from US$1.6 billion in 1991 to peak at US$3.6 billion in 1996, before declining to US$2.1 billion in 1997 and US$1.5 billion in 1998 (also see Figure 5.4).

FDI outflows have also increased over the 1990s; with considerable government encouragement, Malaysian direct investment abroad rose from

Figure 5.4
Malaysia: Foreign Direct Investment, by Year, 1991-1998

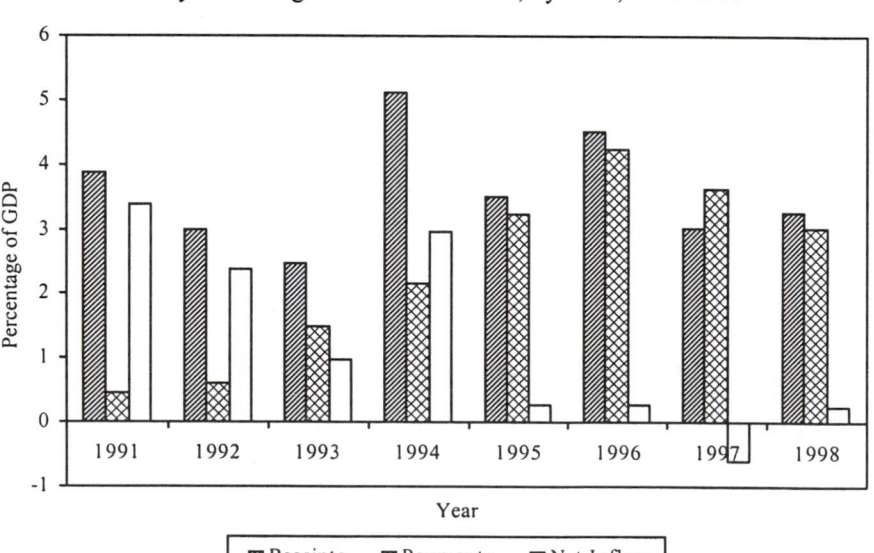

US$196 million in 1991 to US$3.1 billion in 1996. Malaysia remained a net importer of FDI until 1997, when there was an unprecedented net outflow of FDI amounting to US$431 million. This can be attributed to the decline of FDI as the crisis set in; uncertainties attributable to the crisis were probably exacerbated by the unorthodox and apparently compromised nature of government policy responses as the crisis unfolded. Direct investment inflows have experienced significant fluctuations, e.g. between 1996 and 1997, when inflows dropped from US$3.3 billion to US$2.1 billion, i.e. by 36.0 per cent. On balance then, while net FDI inflows have fluctuated considerably in recent years, these fluctuations have not been of the same magnitude and volatility as FPI. Table 5.9 suggests that anomalous increases in FDI can be attributed to major, often 'lumpy' investments from one or two source countries, e.g. large FDI inflows from Singapore in mid-1994, Germany in late 1996 and the UK in late 1998.

External Borrowings[4]

External borrowing has been another source of foreign capital. Malaysian resident individuals and corporations have borrowed increasingly heavily from abroad in the last decade. The quasi-pegs of the ringgit and most other Southeast Asian currencies to the US dollar facilitated these flows. Most borrowings, regardless of source (i.e. including those from Japanese or European banks), tended to be US dollar-denominated. Meanwhile, the long-standing pegs — despite official claims that the currency's value was based on a basket of currencies of the country's major trading partners — served to enhance export competitiveness as the US dollar declined against the Japanese yen between 1985 and mid-1995. However, the strengthening of the US dollar (especially against the yen) from mid-1995 effectively appreciated the Southeast Asian currencies, adversely affecting export competitiveness and growth, as well as industrial growth and industrial investments more generally.

On the supply side, intense competition among 'debt-pushing' Japanese and continental European banks (who appreciated the higher interest rates available for dollarised short-term loans to the region) further eased access to foreign funds. These and other financial reforms as well as the growth of 'private banking' and 'relationship banking' in the region also weakened the scope and efficacy of national-level prudential regulation. On the demand side, Malaysian corporates sought to lower their financing costs by tapping

Table 5.9
Malaysia: Net External Equity Investment by Major Source Country, 1991-1998 (RM million)

Period	US	Singa-pore	Thai-land	China	Hong Kong	Japan	Taiwan	Ger-many	Hol-land	Switzer-land	UK	Aus-tralia	Labuan IOFC
1991Q1	30	106	-1	–	44	232	109	13	5	11	86	8	-11
1991Q2	44	104	-1	-5	69	572	155	15	12	-2	19	32	–
1991Q3	64	39	7	–	105	466	170	15	2	2	118	36	–
1991Q4	96	139	2	–	125	361	132	7	33	3	133	4	–
1991	234	388	7	-5	343	1631	566	50	52	14	356	80	-11
1992Q1	32	162	2	1	43	193	81	25	-3	26	103	-3	-10
1992Q2	115	175	-6	–	146	184	77	40	15	19	46	8	-1
1992Q3	35	205	8	1	87	214	115	27	1	-41	37	-43	–
1992Q4	127	205	-10	-10	63	112	155	43	9	14	-3	2	–
1992	309	747	-6	-8	339	703	428	135	22	18	183	-36	-11
1993Q1	111	31	–	5	23	150	75	13	32	3	1	8	–
1993Q2	-15	-21	12	-29	-28	163	171	23	-6	-7	3	-5	–
1993Q3	50	94	6	-12	-6	147	88	11	36	11	88	-12	-13
1993Q4	-202	95	4	-43	-2	107	101	-1	77	7	-47	-45	–
1993	-56	199	22	-79	-13	567	435	46	139	14	45	-54	-13
1994Q1	282	356	-23	-29	776	263	54	7	6	3	56	-59	–
1994Q2	39	1014	2	-26	-28	427	61	2	1	–	317	-186	–
1994Q3	164	438	49	-25	-45	164	127	152	84	10	515	-9	–
1994Q4	184	-42	2	-56	-281	142	131	53	-84	-36	-71	-130	–
1994	669	1766	30	-136	422	996	373	214	7	-23	817	-384	–

(continued...)

Table 5.9 (continued)
Malaysia: Net External Equity Investment by Major Source Country, 1991-1998 (RM million)

Period	US	Singa-pore	Thai-land	China	Hong Kong	Japan	Taiwan	Ger-many	Hol-land	Switzer-land	UK	Aus-tralia	Labuan IOFC
1995Q1	124	42	–	-27	28	370	121	32	-30	-8	-7	-236	-9
1995Q2	193	270	-5	-117	-23	219	137	8	58	-40	41	-46	-25
1995Q3	427	44	-45	-72	-96	238	109	34	57	2	-4	-16	14
1995Q4	164	-701	-20	-64	61	429	55	11	43	-10	-176	-91	-76
1995	908	-345	-70	-280	-30	1256	422	85	128	-56	-146	-389	-96
1996Q1	32	98	-7	-100	45	180	99	5	23	26	-136	-23	–
1996Q2	-91	-150	-28	-148	-42	85	76	18	49	-7	-114	-32	199
1996Q3	-153	278	-36	-51	-37	-114	39	7	144	563	90	-3	352
1996Q4	122	-119	-16	-139	-25	84	42	1472	-2	-30	-22	-60	74
1996	-90	107	-87	-438	-59	235	256	1502	214	552	-182	-118	625
1997Q1	-26	154	-19	-105	-24	182	2	47	-1	-57	-126	-85	-47
1997Q2	-264	175	-22	-92	-34	253	30	1	-1	-9	-23	-37	-53
1997Q3	137	216	-17	-45	-55	113	13	-8	5	-11	-41	-45	-17
1997Q4	206	183	-34	29	108	434	31	7	26	16	-1107	2	-5
1997	53	728	-92	-213	-5	982	76	47	29	-61	-1297	-165	-122
1998Q1	138	8	-240	-1	7	231	45	16	20	5	-366	-24	-12
1998Q2	-253	-98	–	-25	72	266	90	42	67	44	32	19	-152
1998Q3	-832	-42	-205	-4	16	270	18	-4	14	12	2	5	19
1998Q4	347	12	-14	-15	49	258	-4	35	48	3	1676	1	-102
1998	-600	-120	-459	-45	144	1025	149	89	149	64	1344	1	-247

Source: Bank Negara Malaysia, *Monthly Statistical Bulletin*, Table VIII.13.

funds from abroad. Stock exchange listing has become an important means to access more bank borrowings on better terms. The establishment of the Labuan International Offshore Financial Centre (IOFC) also facilitated easier and greater Malaysian access on better terms to international funds. According to the Cash Balance of Payments Reporting System of the BNM, net international funds sourced from the Labuan IOFC increased from RM69 million in 1991 to RM7,441 million in 1996.

Table 5.10 shows the rapid growth of private foreign debt. Inflows of loans amounted to a mere US$1.2 billion in 1991, a small fraction of the US$10.4 billion of debt amassed by 1997. Figure 5.5 shows foreign borrowings into and out of Malaysia as shares of GDP. While Malaysia's net external debt exposure undoubtedly grew quickly during the early and mid-nineties, mainly due to the rapid build-up of private debt as the government accelerated pre-payment of public foreign debt, such liabilities were still much smaller than in other crisis-affected economies in East Asia. Also, the relatively negligible amount of loans extended to foreigners contrasts starkly with the amounts received.

Most of these foreign loans were borrowed by Malaysian banks that wished to profit from international interest rate differentials. For instance, in January 1997, US and Japan discount rates (5.0 per cent and 0.5 per cent respectively), the UK base lending rate (6.0 per cent), and Singapore three-month inter-bank lending rate (2.6 per cent) were all substantially lower than Malaysia's commercial bank base lending rate of 9.2 per cent (Bank Negara

Table 5.10a
Malaysia: Annual External Loans, 1991-1998 (RM million)

Year	Loans Received	Loans Extended	Net Debt Inflow
1991	3,436	477	2,959
1992	9,440	648	8,792
1993	12,845	1,533	11,312
1994	19,729	3,228	16,501
1995	19,405	2,108	17,297
1996	21,856	2,403	19,453
1997	29,172	2,958	26,214
1998	21,375	2,829	18,546

Table 5.10b
Malaysia: Quarterly External Loans, 1991-1998 (RM million)

Quarter	Loans Received	Loans Extended	Net Debt Inflow
1991Q1	426	60	366
1991Q2	1,230	84	1,146
1991Q3	715	220	495
1991Q4	1,065	113	952
1992Q1	2,340	124	2,216
1992Q2	1,995	113	1,882
1992Q3	2,476	169	2,307
1992Q4	2,629	242	2,387
1993Q1	2,502	133	2,369
1993Q2	3,749	311	3,438
1993Q3	2,756	478	2,278
1993Q4	3,838	611	3,227
1994Q1	5,532	484	5,048
1994Q2	4,449	1,124	3,325
1994Q3	4,903	749	4,154
1994Q4	4,845	871	3,974
1995Q1	3,059	565	2,494
1995Q2	3,834	491	3,343
1995Q3	6,767	579	6,188
1995Q4	5,745	473	5,272
1996Q1	4,663	585	4,078
1996Q2	5,016	532	4,484
1996Q3	3,194	309	2,885
1996Q4	8,983	977	8,006
1997Q1	5,622	586	5,036
1997Q2	9,994	563	9,431
1997Q3	7,485	1,338	6,147
1997Q4	6,070	472	5,598
1998Q1	5,378	637	4,741
1998Q2	4,858	427	4,431
1998Q3	4,343	752	3,591
1998Q4	6,796	1,013	5,783

Source: Bank Negara Malaysia, *Monthly Statistical Bulletin*, Table VIII.14.

Figure 5.5
Malaysia: External Loans, by Year, 1991-1998

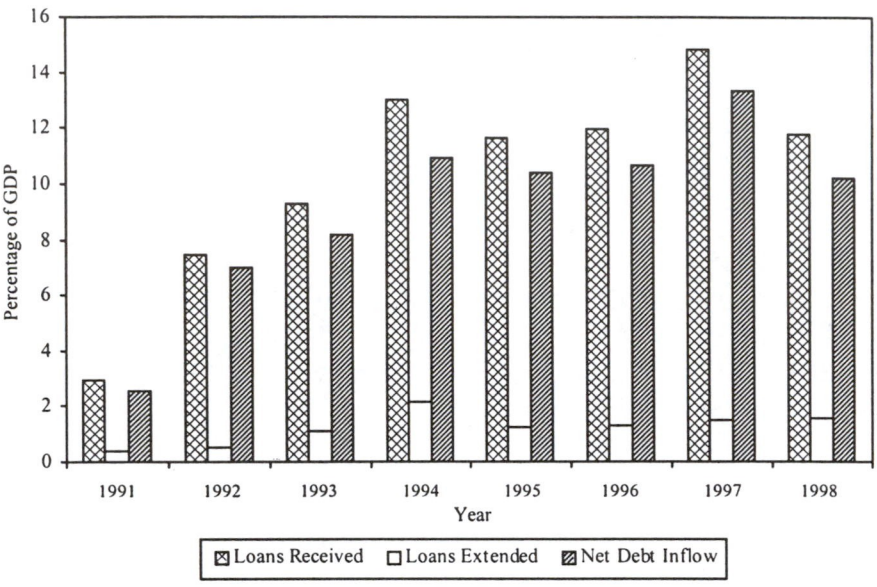

Malaysia, *Monthly Statistical Bulletin*, Table IX.2). Some of these loans were then re-lent to domestic borrowers, willing to pay relatively higher interest rates, with considerable opportunities for arbitrage. However, strict central bank supervision limited such arbitrage activities in Malaysia compared to other crisis-affected economies. Table 5.11 shows the major sources of such external borrowings.

Figures 5.6 and 5.7 show the growth and distribution of short-, medium- and long-term foreign debt from 1988 to 1998 (also see Tables 5.12 and 5.13). The absolute amount of short-term debt grew at great speed, rising from RM2.4 billion in 1988 to RM43.3 billion in 1997, while the share of short-term debt in the total debt increased from 5.0 per cent to 25.7 per cent over the same period as well. Medium- and long-term debt also increased from RM47.0 billion to RM127.5 billion, although their share of the total debt declined from 95.0 per cent to 74.3 per cent. After the massive exit of capital in early 1994, the Malaysian authorities introduced temporary capital control measures, which reduced the inflow of short-term borrowings during 1994-95.

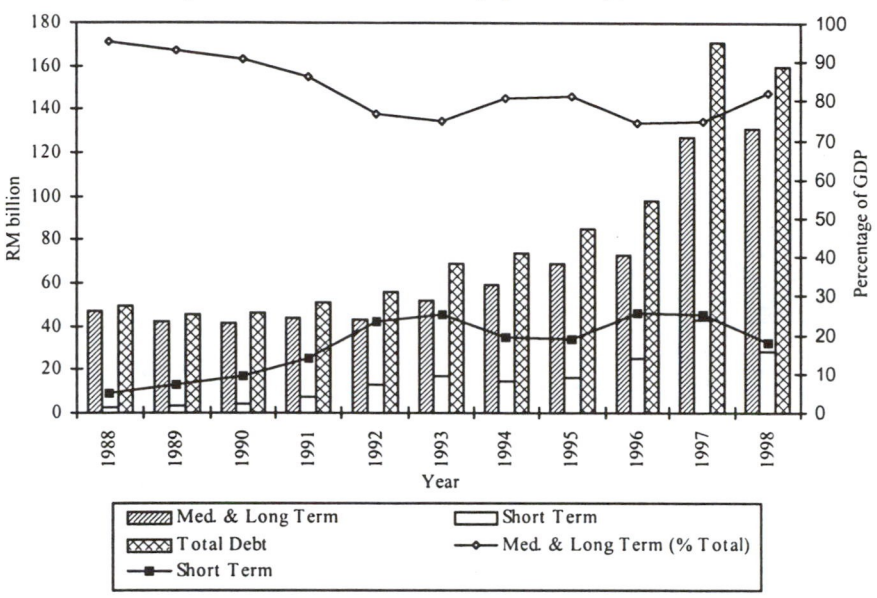

Figure 5.6
Malaysia: Annual External Debt, by Maturity, 1988-1998

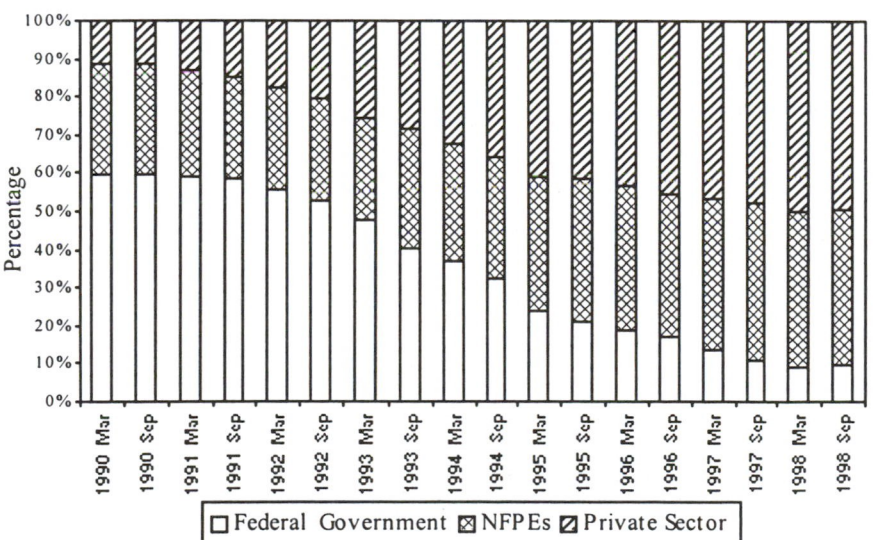

Figure 5.7
Malaysia: Percentage Distribution of External Debt, 1990-1998

Table 5.11
Malaysia: Net External Loan Inflows by Major Source, 1991-1998 (RM million)

Period	US	Bermuda	Singapore	Japan	Germany	UK	Labuan IOFC
1991Q1	110	0	62	141	0	-11	0
1991Q2	245	0	45	184	4	520	0
1991Q3	173	21	75	128	4	29	46
1991Q4	409	55	108	244	0	59	23
1991	937	76	290	697	8	597	69
1992Q1	381	90	735	423	5	295	175
1992Q2	566	24	213	302	4	244	145
1992Q3	1,061	0	238	370	57	85	88
1992Q4	438	31	281	874	4	447	148
1992	2,446	145	1,466	1,969	70	1,071	556
1993Q1	309	11	558	1,044	7	146	175
1993Q2	808	91	307	541	-95	680	427
1993Q3	454	86	186	424	385	63	625
1993Q4	1,081	175	168	271	3	170	877
1993	2,652	363	1,219	2,280	300	1,059	2,104
1994Q1	1,138	233	187	1,811	-7	34	1,251
1994Q2	1,714	471	89	94	12	313	946
1994Q3	889	212	146	867	3	178	918
1994Q4	2,175	269	53	146	93	582	687
1994	5,916	1,185	475	2,918	101	1,107	3,802

(continued…)

Table 5.11 (continued)
Malaysia: Net External Loan Inflows by Major Source, 1991-1998 (RM million)

Period	US	Bermuda	Singapore	Japan	Germany	UK	Labuan IOFC
1995Q1	335	64	-5	520	54	106	1,380
1995Q2	475	410	195	237	82	234	1,449
1995Q3	2,644	187	130	210	94	67	2,577
1995Q4	2,382	245	252	308	184	-109	1,979
1995	5,836	906	572	1,275	414	298	7,385
1996Q1	1,381	116	181	381	116	-122	1,966
1996Q2	839	94	246	1,089	65	–	2,013
1996Q3	738	137	136	175	82	-22	1,586
1996Q4	5,840	8	32	172	370	-277	1,876
1996	8,798	355	595	1,817	633	-421	7,441
1997Q1	82	1,654	300	1,010	105	-21	2,100
1997Q2	423	4,602	214	242	123	-26	4,048
1997Q3	99	1,806	352	842	220	-67	3,081
1997Q4	22	1,469	529	366	339	1,179	1,664
1997	626	9,531	1,395	2,460	787	1,065	10,893
1998Q1	329	923	503	788	235	-102	2,134
1998Q2	125	1,389	236	538	175	4	1,786
1998Q3	147	1,071	-187	705	408	65	1,247
1998Q4	114	1,241	317	2,514	204	-146	1,265
1998	715	4,624	869	4,545	1,022	-179	6,432

Source: Bank Negara Malaysia, *Monthly Statistical Bulletin*, Table VIII.14.

Table 5.12
Malaysia: External Debt as Share of GDP, 1991-1998 (%)

	External Loans Received	*Short Term Debt*	*Medium and Long Term Debt*	*Total Debt*
1991	3.0	6.2	37.7	43.9
1992	7.5	10.4	33.9	44.3
1993	2.9	3.9	11.8	15.8
1994	13.0	9.4	39.1	48.5
1995	11.6	9.7	41.3	51.0
1996	11.9	13.7	39.7	53.4
1997	14.8	21.9	64.7	86.6
1998	11.7	15.6	72.0	87.6

Source: Calculated from BNM, *Monthly Statistical Bulletin*, Tables VIII.10 and VIII.15.

Table 5.13
Malaysia: External Debt as Share of Foreign Reserves, 1991-1998 (%)

	External Loans Received	*Short Term Debt*	*Medium and Long Term Debt*	*Total Debt*
1991	11.2	23.5	143.4	166.9
1992	20.0	27.8	90.5	118.3
1993	16.8	22.6	67.8	90.4
1994	28.9	20.9	87.0	107.9
1995	30.4	25.4	107.8	133.1
1996	31.2	35.9	103.7	139.6
1997	51.0	75.6	222.7	298.2
1998	21.5	28.6	131.9	160.5

Source: Calculated from BNM, *Monthly Statistical Bulletin*, Tables VIII.10 and VIII.15.

As shown in Table 4.10 (Chapter Four) banks were responsible for much of this short term debt, though of course, some of this debt consisted of trade credit and other short-term debt deemed essential to ensuring liquidity in an economy. However, the very rapid growth of short-term bank debt during 1992-3 sug-gests that much of it was due to factors other than trade credit expansion. The temporary capital controls introduced in early 1994 clearly dampened the growth of such debt, but by 1996 and early 1997, a new short-term bor-rowing frenzy was quite evident, involving not only the banks, but also other private corporations.

As in Thailand and Indonesia, the non-bank private sector in Malaysia was the major recipient of international bank loans, accounting for more than 50 per cent of total foreign borrowings by the end of June 1997 (see Table 4.11 in Chapter Four). Tables 4.10 and 4.11 also show that Malaysian banks were borrowing extensively from abroad. According to BNM, commercial banks' net foreign liabilities increased from RM10.3 billion at the end of 1995 to RM25.2 billion in June 1997 (i.e. by almost 150 per cent in 18 months). Meanwhile, their net external reserves position deteriorated dramatically from -RM5.3 billion to -RM17.7 billion over the same 18-month period.

From the beginning of the decade, Malaysia sustained a current account deficit. Over-investment of investible funds in 'non-tradeables' only made things worse. In so far as such investments-e.g. in power generations and telecommunications-did not contribute to export earnings, they aggravated the problem of currency mismatch, with foreign borrowings invested in activities not generating foreign exchange. An additional problem of 'term mismatch' also arose as a high proportion of these foreign borrowings were short-term in nature (see Tables 4.10 and 4.12), but were deployed to finance medium to long-term projects.

Tables 5.10 and 5.11 break down the Malaysian external debt by maturity period. The tables suggest a smaller proportion of short-term debt compared to the BIS data. Short-term debt is shown to be a principally private sector phenomenon, emerging in significance only from the late eighties. The tables also show that most short-term debt was incurred by the banking sector, and grew rapidly in the nineties from RM4.4 billion in 1990 to RM32.3 billion in 1997 before coming down. Non-bank private external debt also grew rapidly in the mid-1990s from RM4.9 billion in 1995 to RM11.0 billion in 1997, but had gone up to RM11.2 billion in the first half of 1999 after dipping in 1998.

While the federal government's external debt ceased climbing after 1986, it began to come down rapidly after 1991 until after the crisis broke in 1997. In contrast non-financial public enterprise external debt ballooned in the 1990s from RM11.4 billion in 1992 to RM29.2 billion in 1996 and RM52.5 billion in 1997 (partly due to currency depreciation in the second half of 1997 as can be seen from comparing the two tables), before levelling off. Private sector medium to long-term external debt also ballooned in the 1990s from RM4.9 billion in 1990 to RM33.0 billion in 1996 and RM62.1 billion in 1997.

The direction of this external debt by category of debtor is shown in Figure 5.7. From 1990 to 1998, the federal government's share of total foreign debt steadily decreased, while the private sector's share increased. Non-financial public enterprises (NFPEs) also raised their share of total debt, but more slowly than the private sector. Since greater shares of government and quasi-government (NFPE) debt were accounted for by medium and long-term borrowings, the proportion of short-term loans in total private debt must have been much higher. For conventional economic wisdom, the build-up of private debt was considered less onerous than public debt. It was also generally assumed that private sector agents would make better use of such funds. Due to such beliefs, the rapid accumulation of private debt by the fast developing East Asian countries was not treated with much concern, although a much higher proportion of such debt was short-term in nature.

The increase in foreign borrowings and other foreign capital inflows financed Malaysia's persistent pre-crisis current account deficit during the nineties (see Tables 5.14 and 5.15) until 1998: the lowest and highest deficits were RM5.6 billion in 1992 and RM21.3 billion in 1995 respectively. These current account deficits were covered by surpluses on the capital account during the early and mid-nineties. The latter were mainly due to growing foreign direct and portfolio investments as well as net external borrowings. While the current account comprises transactions in goods and services, the growing significance of foreign portfolio investment flows in the nineties

Table 5.14
Malaysia: Current Account and Balance of Payments, 1991-1998

Year	Current Account		Balance of Payments	
	US$ mil.	*% of GDP*	*US$ mil.*	*% of GDP*
1991	-4,234	-10.0	1,246	3.0
1992	-2,205	-4.4	6,566	13.2
1993	-3,084	-5.7	11,377	21.0
1994	-5,606	-9.7	-3,123	-5.4
1995	-8,495	-12.8	-1,625	-2.4
1996	-4,455	-6.1	2,478	3.4
1997	-5,630	-8.0	-3,876	-5.5
1998	9,386	20.2	10,281	22.1

Source: Bank Negara Malaysia, *Monthly Statistical Bulletin.*

Table 5.15
Malaysia: Annual Balance of Payments, 1991-1998 (RM million)

	1991	1992	1993	1994	1995	1996	1997	1998
Current Account	-11,644	-5,622	-7,926	-14,689	-21,323	-11,226	-15,820	36,794
Official Long-term Capital	-665	-2,876	979	861	6,147	748	4,645	2,137
Corporate Investment	10,996	13,204	12,885	10,798	10,464	12,777	14,450	8,490
Balance of Long-term Capital	10,331	10,328	13,864	11,659	16,611	13,525	19,095	10,627
Basic Balance	-1,313	4,706	5,938	-3,030	-4,712	2,299	3,275	47,421
Private Capital (net)	5,135	11,957	13,931	-8,485	2,529	10,317	-12,913	-20,633
Errors and Omissions	-395	81	9,370	3,333	-1,896	-6,371	-1,254	13,513
Overall Balance	3,427	16,744	29,239	-8,182	-4,079	6,245	-10,892	40,301

Source: Bank Negara Malaysia, *Monthly Statistical Bulletin*, Table VIII.1.

meant that the capital account was becoming much more vulnerable to speculation and volatility. Thus, the Malaysian economy became even more vulnerable to shifting capital market sentiments, including contagion from other economies. To add to this vulnerability, Malaysia's total external debt to foreign exchange reserves ratio was becoming dangerously high before the crisis, reaching 139.6 per cent in 1996 before jumping to 298.2 per cent in 1997 (Table 5.13).

As the economic recession deepened in 1998, foreign borrowings decreased to 1996 levels, after peaking at RM29.2 billion in 1997. With a lower proportion of short-term loans compared to the other East Asian economies hit by the crisis, fluctuations in foreign bank borrowings in Malaysia have been less severe. It is noteworthy that borrowing from offshore financial centres, namely Labuan IOFC and Bermuda, rose in the aftermath of the financial crisis.

The Bank for International Settlements (BIS) and other banking regulations as well as other banking practices inadvertently encouraged short-term debt — compared to medium- or long-term debt — in the exposure of OECD countries-based banks, especially to emerging markets or developing countries. Loans for less than a year only required 20 per cent capital backing compared to full (100 per cent) capital backing for loans for a year or more. Further, the degree of Malaysian exposure to such short-term debt was partly mitigated by more prudent central bank regulations, supervision and enforcement, as well as limiting foreign borrowings by Malaysian banks as well as corporations.

Thus, Malaysia actually fared relatively better than most other crisis-hit countries in this regard, because it had accumulated relatively less foreign borrowings, with a smaller proportion of debt of short-term maturity. For instance, in June 1997, short-term debt as a share of total reserves for Malaysia was approximately 60 per cent, significantly lower than South Korea (more than 200 per cent), Indonesia (about 170 per cent) and Thailand (just under 150 per cent), and slightly lower than Brazil (80 per cent). Countries with lower ratios included Chile (45 per cent) and China (25 per cent) (Ishak Shari *et al.* 1999).

Also, financial market observers note that the costs of hedging foreign loans in Malaysia were relatively lower compared to its neighbours besides Singapore, though there are some anecdotal claims that the central bank actually discouraged Malaysian external borrowers from hedging their debt. Also, the majority of loan funds disbursed through the Labuan international off-shore financial centre (IOFC), which grew rapidly in the 1990s, were secured by residents of Malaysia. For example, before the crisis, of all loans sourced through the Labuan IOFC, approximately 80 per cent in 1995 and 70 per cent in 1996 were obtained by Malaysians (Awang Adek 1997: 7). There is also anecdotal evidence of Malaysian individuals and companies borrowing off-shore, especially in Singapore and Hong Kong, but again, systematic evidence is not available.

Figure 5.8 shows how the Malaysian ringgit vacillated around RM2.5 against the US dollar during the first half of 1997. After the Thai baht was floated on 2 July 1997, like other currencies in the region, the ringgit was under strong pressure, especially because, like Thailand, Malaysia had maintained large current account deficits during the early and mid-nineties. The monetary authorities' efforts to defend the ringgit actually strengthened it against the greenback for a few days before the futile ringgit defence effort was given up by mid-July. The aborted ringgit defence effort is widely believed to have cost over nine billion ringgit. As Figure 5.9 shows, the ringgit — like the currencies of other crisis-hit economies — fluctuated wildly until mid-1998, weeks before the ringgit was fixed at RM3.8 against the US dollar on 2 September 1998. While much of the downward pressure on the ringgit was externally induced by regional developments as well as adverse perceptions of the regional situation, there is evidence to suggest that inappropriate political rhetoric and policy measures by the political leadership

Figure 5.8
Malaysia: Ringgit Movements Against US Dollar, January-July 1997

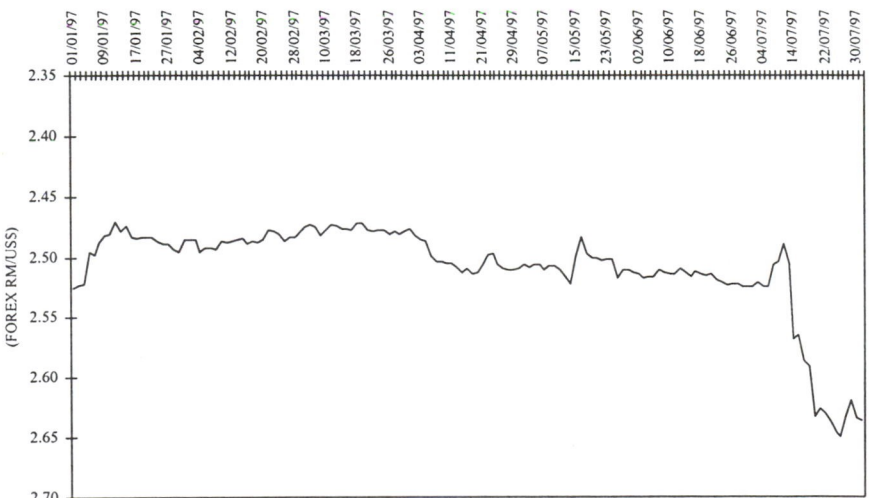

Figure 5.9
Malaysia: Ringgit Movements Against US Dollar, 1997-1999

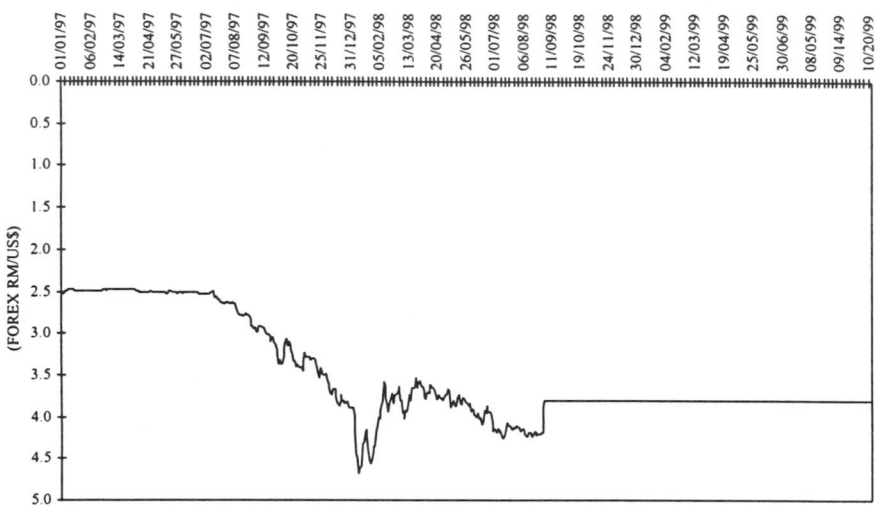

Figure 5.10
Malaysia: Foreign Exchange Reserves, January 1997 – September 1999

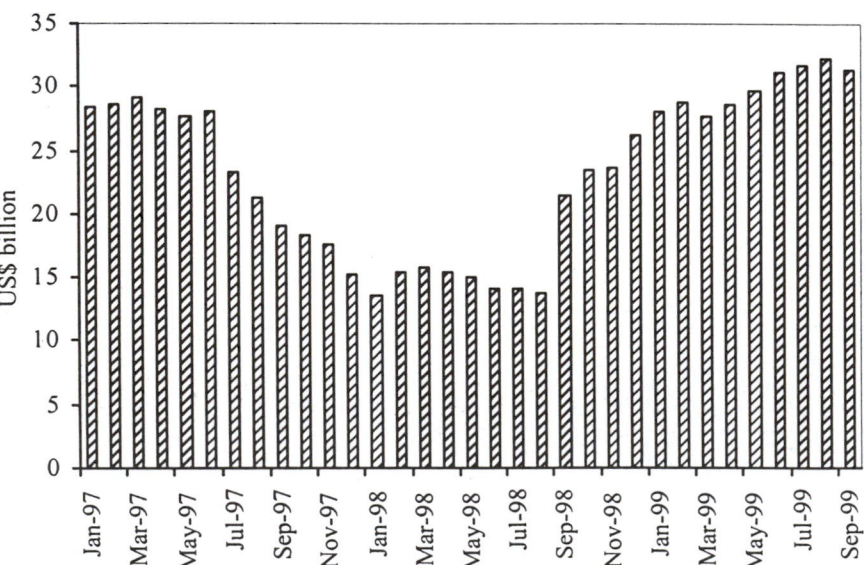

exacerbated the situation. As Figure 5.10 shows, Malaysia's foreign exchange reserves depleted rapidly from July until November 1997, before improving in December, and especially after the imposition of capital controls in September 1998.

Conclusion

Foreign capital inflows into Malaysia augmented the high domestic savings rate to raise the domestic investment rate as well as Malaysian investments abroad in the nineties. Thus, though there is some evidence that foreign capital inflows may have adversely affected the domestic savings rate indirectly, foreign capital inflows generally supplemented, rather than substituted for domestic savings. It is difficult to be conclusive on this point as the nature of foreign capital inflows has changed significantly over time. Hence, even if earlier foreign capital inflows adversely affected domestic savings, it is quite possible that the changed composition of recent foreign capital inflows may no longer adversely affect foreign capital inflows.

Increased foreign capital inflows have also reduced foreign exchange constraints, allowing the financing of additional imports, but thus, also inadvertently encouraging current account deficits. Finally, foreign capital inflows into Malaysia appear to have adversely affected factor payment outflows, export and import propensities, the terms of trade and capital flight, and thus, the balance of payments. These results suggest caution in determining the extent to which foreign capital inflows should be encouraged. Also, Malaysia's heavy dependence on foreign direct investment in gross domestic capital formation, especially manufacturing investments, has probably also limited the development of domestic entrepreneurship as well as many other indigenous economic capabilities by requiring greater reliance on foreign capabilities, often associated with some types of FDI (Jomo *et al.* 1997).

After mid-1995, the Southeast Asian currency pegs to the US dollar — which had enhanced the region's competitiveness as the dollar declined for a decade after the 1985 Plaza accord — became a growing liability as the yen began to depreciate once again. The overvalued currencies became attractive targets for speculative attacks, resulting in the futile, but costly defences of the Thai baht and Malaysian ringgit, and the rapid regional spread of herd panic called contagion. The resulting precipitous asset price collapses — as the share and property market bubbles burst — undermined Malaysia's heavily exposed banking system for the second time in little over a decade, threatening financial system liquidity, and hence, economic recession.

Undoubtedly, international financial liberalisation succeeded in generating net capital inflows into East Asia, including Malaysia, unlike other developing and transitional economies, many of which experienced net outflows. But it also exacerbated systemic instability and reduced the scope for the developmental government interventions responsible for the region's economic miracle. In Southeast Asia, especially Malaysia, FDI domination (well above the average for developing countries) of internationally competitive manufacturing had weakened domestic industrialists, inadvertently enhancing the dominance of finance capital and its influence over economic policy making.

Prior to the crisis, there had been a steady trend towards financial liberalisation in Malaysia, dating back to the mid-eighties. This had included considerable promotion of the Kuala Lumpur's 'newly emerging' stock market, growing central bank speculative activity abroad (until it lost at least sixteen billion ringgit [over US$6 billion then] after the sterling collapse of September 1992) and greater capital account convertibility. As in the rest of fast growing East Asia, Malaysia succeeded in attracting a great deal of capital inflows. However, unlike the other crisis-affected economies which succeeded in attracting considerable, mainly short-term US dollar bank loans into their more bank-based financed systems, Malaysia's vulnerability was primarily due to the volatility of international portfolio capital flows, mainly into its stock market.

As a consequence, the nature of Malaysia's external liabilities at the beginning of the crisis was quite different from that of the other crisis-stricken East Asian economies. A greater proportion consisted of equity, rather than debt. Much more of the liabilities, including the debt, were private — rather than public — compared to Malaysia's exposure in the mid-eighties. Compared to the others, much more of Malaysian debt in the late nineties was long-term — rather than short-term — in nature. Monetary policy as well as banking supervision in Malaysia had generally been much more prudent compared to the other crisis victims. Banks in Malaysia had not been allowed to borrow heavily from abroad to lend in the domestic market, as in the other economies. Such practices involved currency and term mismatches, which increased financial system vulnerability to foreign bankers' confidence as well as pressure on the exchange rate pegs.

These differences have lent support to the claim that Malaysia was an 'innocent bystander' which fell victim to the regional contagion for being in the wrong part of the world at the wrong time. Such a view takes a benign perspective on portfolio investment inflows, and does not recognise that such inflows are even more easily reversible and volatile than bank loan inflows.

The magnitude of the gross inflows and outflows reflect the much greater volatility of these flows, often obscured by focussing on net flows. But even the net flow data indicates the relative size of these flows. A net sum of over RM30 billion of portfolio investments flowed out in the last three quarters of 1997, much more than the total net inflows from 1995, and equivalent to almost a fifth of annual GNP. This exodus included RM21.6 billion of shares and corporate securities, and RM8.8 billion of money market instruments. In just one quarter, from July to September 1997, a net RM16 billion of portfolio investments left the country.

Contrary to the 'innocent bystander' hypothesis, Malaysia's experience actually suggests the greater vulnerability of its greater reliance on the capital market. As a consequence, the Malaysian economy became hostage to international portfolio investor confidence. Hence, when the government leadership engaged in rhetoric and policy initiatives that upset such investment confidence, Malaysia paid a heavy price as portfolio divestment accelerated. IMF prescriptions and conventional policy-making wisdom urged government spending cuts in the wake of the crisis. Such contractionary measures transformed what had started as a currency crisis, to become a full-blown financial crisis, into a crisis of the real economy. Thus, all the region's economies that had previously enjoyed massive capital inflows — whether in the form of short-term bank loans of portfolio investments — went into recession during 1998, following Thailand. From 7.7 per cent growth in 1997, including 6.0 per cent in the last quarter, the Malaysian economy shrank by -6.7 per cent in 1998, or by -2.8 per cent, -6.8 per cent, -9.0 per cent and -8.1 per cent in the four quarters. The stock market dropped more dramatically from almost 1,300 in February 1997 to a low of 262 in early September 1998, eighteen months later.

Notes

1. See Akyuz (1995) and Griffith-Jones (1997).
2. For further details, see BNM (1993). For instance, the BNM had to absorb large interest payments for issuing bonds to mop up extra liquidity in the financial system.
3. Foreign Direct Investment (FDI) is used here to refer to what Bank Negara Malaysia refers to as External Equity Investment, which refers specifically to the establishment or expansion of businesses, including joint ventures, in which the foreign investor has effective control of the business.

   Official BNM data understates actual FDI by omitting reinvested earnings as well as equity in the form of imported plant and equipment as the following letter on Bank Negara Malaysia data on capital flows from a BNM official dated 27 July 1999 to Jacques Cailloux makes clear (my italics):

"For your information, the data on FDI, portfolio flows and loans that you retrieved from the Bank Negara Malaysia website are sourced from the Cash BOP Reporting System of Bank Negara Malaysia and should be used as an indicator only. At present, the Malaysian Department of Statistics, the official compiler of balance of payments statistics, *does not publish data on FDI in Malaysia*. The FDI is currently reflected in the net private long-term capital account, which also includes Malaysian investment overseas and foreign borrowing by Malaysian-owned companies. The Department is, however, in the process of conducting a new survey to capture the gross flows of private capitals into and out of Malaysia.

"The Cash BOP Reporting System was implemented by Bank Negara to capture transactions, on a cash basis, between residents and non-residents effected through the domestic banking system, as well as inter-company and overseas accounts. Since the System captures data on a cash basis, it *does not capture data on reinvested earnings as well as direct equity that came into Malaysia in the form of machinery*."

4. Stiglitz calls this approach to effective financial regulation, from the perspective of risk management, the Dynamic Portfolio Approach.

Bank of International Settlements (BIS) data understates Malaysian external debt as the following clarification from a BNM official dated 27 July 1999 makes clear (my italics):

"As for the data on loans, the data that you retrieved refer to gross borrowings by the Federal Government as well as the non-bank private sector that are sourced from the Cash BOP Reporting System. This data gives an indication on the countries that extended or received loans to/from Malaysia. The official data on External Debt, which is published in Table VIII.10, are sourced from various sources, such as the Accountant General's Office, quarterly report (*sic*) from the non-bank private sector as well as from the banking institutions. Table VIII.10 refers to the *outstanding balance of external loans* (by type of borrower), which *comprise inter-company loans, bonds raised in the international capital markets as well as bank lending*. On the other hand, the *BIS data refers only to bank lending*. As such, the data reported by BIS is *much lower compared with BNM data* (as at end-1998, BNM: RM161.9 billion (US$42.6 billion); BIS: US$20.8 billion."

APPENDIX 5.1
Regression Analysis: Impact of
Foreign Capital Inflows on the Malaysian Economy

From Wong Hwa Kiong (with Jomo K.S.), "The Impact of Foreign Capital Inflows on the Malaysian Economy, 1966-1996."

Regression analysis, conducted for a 30-year time period (1966-1996) using official annual data, yielded the following results from three model specifications:

Model 1

$$\ln y = 0.98 + 0.024S/Y + 0.019FCI/Y + 0.010\Delta L/L + 0.056SC$$
$$\quad\;\; (6.65) \quad (3.76) \qquad (2.57) \qquad\quad (0.36) \qquad (9.12)$$
$$\quad\;\; R^2 = 0.962 \qquad\qquad D.W. = 1.8387$$

where: $\ln y$ = real GDP growth,

I/Y = the investment rate, i.e. gross capital formation as a proportion of GDP,

$\Delta L/L$ = growth rate of the actual numbers employed as proxies for the labour force growth rate,

SC = manufacturing value added as a proportion of GDP proxies for structural change,

Figures in parentheses are t-statistics.

Model 2

Disaggregating FCI into two — debt and FDI — this regression equation tests their relative contributions to growth:

$$\ln y = 0.91 + 0.03S/Y + 0.02DEBT/Y + 0.01FDI/Y + 0.006\Delta L/L + 0.05SC$$
$$\quad\;\; (5.56) \quad (4.53) \qquad (1.88) \qquad\quad (0.84) \qquad (0.2) \qquad (7.47)$$
$$\quad\;\; R^2 = 96.3\% \qquad\qquad D.W. = 1.538$$

Model 3

To test the impact of FCI on domestic savings:

$$X4 = -2.59 - 0.3046FCI/Y + 0.0084CX + 11.167 \ln y + 0.486\Delta L/L$$
$$\quad\;\; (-0.47) \quad (-3.78) \qquad (9.57) \qquad (4.79) \qquad\quad (2.59)$$
$$\quad\;\; R^2 = 86.3\% \qquad\qquad D.W. = 1.882$$

where: X4 = gross domestic savings as a proportion of GDP,

FCI/Y = foreign capital inflows as a proportion of GDP,

CX = change in exports as a proportion of GDP,

$\ln y$ = real GDP growth,

$\Delta L/L$ = labour force growth rate as a proxy for change in the population structure.

6

CAPITAL FLOWS VOLATILITY

Jomo K. S. with Liew San Yee and Laura Kaehler

(Malaysia)

Following on from the previous chapter showing the significant increase in easily reversibly capital flows during the nineties, this chapter will show the growing volatility of such foreign capital flows, and examine the consequences of inflow surges and sudden massive capital outflows. This study will focus on the volatility of the different types of capital flows into — and out of — Malaysia in the pre-crisis period as well as after the crisis began in July 1997. The introduction of capital controls in September 1998 has added an additional element of interest in the Malaysian case. In the Malaysian context, the desirability of free international capital flows, involving capital account convertibility, remains a particularly contentious issue. Domestic banking deregulation and official international promotion of Malaysian securities markets, coupled with rapid international financial liberalisation, helped create conditions prone to greater market volatility and contagion, thus contributing to the recent financial crisis. In the aftermath of the crisis, there is now greater concern, at least temporarily, for the potential and pitfalls of continuing unrestricted international capital flows.

Although the financial crisis in Malaysia was triggered by contagion from abroad and exacerbated by poor policy responses, changes in economic structure (e.g. increasing influence of the financial system over the real economy, including the manufacturing sector), policy biases (e.g. favouring rent-seeking) and the changing institutional context (e.g. the growing influence of the stock market) also increased the vulnerability of the Malaysian financial system in the longer term.

An important lesson of the East Asian crisis is that Malaysia should have been more prudent in liberalising its financial sector and the capital account. In Southeast Asia, there is considerable evidence that efforts to liberalise domestic financial systems were underway before strong institutions needed for effective prudential regulation, monitoring and supervision were well-established, thus exacerbating the vulnerability of these systems to the potentially disruptive effects of massive trans-border surges of capital. Prudent official regulation is necessary to help maintain a balance between the competitive efficiency of markets and the requirements of a robust and efficient banking system (Park 1994: 21; Chowdhury and Islam 1993: 144). More effective regulation of the capital account to ensure more selective entry would also have served to limit volatility associated with certain types of capital inflows. This would have avoided some of the worst excesses that contributed to the recent financial crises in Southeast Asia in general and in Malaysia in particular.

These problems were partly mitigated by Malaysia's stronger tradition of prudential management of the banking system, strengthened by the Banking and Financial Institutions Act (BAFIA), 1989, after the share of non-performing loans in the banking system rose to almost 30 per cent in the late 1980s. Furthermore, Malaysia had greater restrictions on private foreign borrowings, a relatively less bank-based financial system compared to the three other most crisis-affected economies (Thailand, Indonesia and South Korea) and stronger macroeconomic and financial conditions before the onset of the crisis. Nevertheless, analysis of prior financial reforms and developments suggests that the Malaysian financial crisis from mid-1997 can be traced to financial liberalisation and its consequent undermining of effective financial governance or regulation, both at international and national levels. High investments in non-tradeables, with private external debt and unrestricted portfolio investment inflows arising from financial liberalisation increased the vulnerability of the domestic financial system. The 1997-8 financial crisis points to the importance of prudentially managing risk in the financial system, as failing to do so enhanced the vulnerability of the financial system. Increasing financial liberalisation has exacerbated most of these trends, and further reduced the financial sector's support of productive long-term investments.

Furthermore, promotion of securities markets before an effective and mature banking system was well-established, diminished the franchise value of the banking system. This resulted in increased risk-taking, aggravating the fragility of the banking sector. This was also evident in seeming risk management by the excessive (collateralised) bank lending to the property sector observed in the years leading up to the banking crisis in 1985-88 and the recent financial crisis from mid-1997.

Such lending for property and also share purchases fuelled asset price inflation, generating wealth effects and hence, raising consumption levels with the help of easier consumer credit. But while such bubbles take months to build up, they collapse much more suddenly, usually with devastating consequences. In an increasingly liberalised and integrated international environment, capital flows, especially portfolio investments, seem to have become disproportionately important as being most susceptible to volatility and sensitive to trans-border contagion.

Instead of encouraging developing countries to engage in excessively rapid financial market liberalisation, Stiglitz (1999) argues that they should focus on finding the right regulatory structure to manage the incentives and constraints that affect financial institutions' exposure to and ability to cope with risk. (He calls this approach to effective financial regulation, from the perspective of risk management, the Dynamic Portfolio Approach.) This, he argues, is due to the fact that financial institutions are both a source of risk to and also liable to be affected by risks in the rest of the economy. According to Stiglitz (1999), "the best way to manage risk management in developing countries may differ markedly from that in developed countries, simply because they face larger risks, with poor information and typically have weaker risk management capacities."

While financial restraint can promote banks' commitments to act as long-run agents and enhance their capability to cope with risks, this has, however, not been the case in Malaysia. In so far as financial restraint has been practised in Malaysia, it has primarily sought to ensure bank profitability, especially with increasing ethnic Bumiputera dominance of the Malaysian banking system from the 1970s. Banks in Malaysia have been heavily used by the state for the wealth redistribution policies of the NEP. Though utilised to support interethnic economic redistribution and other public policies, financial restraint in Malaysia has not been used very much to favour long-term productive investments, especially in non-resource-based export-oriented manufacturing, which continues to be dominated by foreign direct investment.

Meanwhile, external financial liberalisation in the early nineties sought to encourage foreign financial institutions to invest in the Malaysian stock market by pegging the ringgit to the US dollar and allowing free international movements of capital. This made the national economy much more vulnerable to external shocks (including capital flight), rendering the tasks of exchange rate management and controlling inflation much more difficult.

Unlike the previous Malaysian banking crisis in the second half of the eighties, triggered by a prolonged world recession that began in the advanced economies in the early eighties, the recent crisis stemmed from the liberalised financial system itself, exacerbated by sudden massive withdrawals of funds. Although less of a problem in Malaysia compared to the other East Asian crisis-affected economies, foreign indebtedness in 1997 was primarily generated by the private sector, rather than by the public sector, as in the mid-eighties. Also, unlike its neighbours, the main source of volatility and the main transmission mechanism for contagion in Malaysia was through the stock market, rather than due to short-term foreign bank borrowings (and related problems of currency and term mismatches).

Ultimately, how and whether foreign capital contributes to economic development is of utmost importance. The earlier official enthusiasm for attracting foreign capital inflows (FCI), generally presumed to be beneficial, has come under more critical scrutiny since the advent of the crisis in mid-1997. In their enthusiasm to try to attract more foreign portfolio (especially institutional) investors, the Malaysian authorities did not have any effective regulatory instruments in place to deal with the surge of destabilising portfolio investment inflows and the threat of its sudden reversal.

With the commanding role of foreign portfolio investors in the Malaysian stock market, declining interest and confidence in the region after early 1997 began a reversal of net portfolio investment flows from the second quarter. The mid-July 1997 collapse of the Malaysian ringgit — after a costly, but unsuccessful defence of the currency in the face of regional contagion after the Thai baht float from 2 July 1997 — accelerated the collapse of the asset inflationary build-up. This, in turn, hastened the flight of the very same foreign portfolio capital that had contributed to the share price and property booms in the first place.

The collapse of the bubble was thus speeded up by portfolio and other capital outflows. This, in turn, undermined the banking sector which had become so vulnerable to asset price deflation and its concomitant wealth effect. While often intended to stem contagion or to restore market confidence in the face of increasingly negative investor sentiment, injudicious government policy responses by both sides of an increasingly divided government mainly served to exacerbate the crisis (Jomo 1998b). Thus, what started of as currency and then financial crises in Malaysia later became a recession, i.e. a crisis of the real economy.

With the benefit of hindsight, it is now clear that the worst in the region was over in the third quarter of 1998. Regional currencies strengthened and stabilised after the greater volatility of the preceding 14 months, as interest rates came down with US rates after the Russian, LTCM and Wall Street scares of August 1998. Soon, renewed foreign investor interest became evident, even if only to take advantage of the 'fire sales' in the region. In March 1999, the Malaysian authorities announced that they would consider foreign-led mergers and acquisitions as FDI, instead of just 'green field' investments, which actually add new economic capacity. For the first time since the sixties, Britain became the source country of the most FDI in Malaysia in 1998, with British firms acquiring controlling stakes in previously Malaysian controlled cement plants, electricity generators and telecommunications firms catering primarily for the domestic market (whereas previously, FDI had mainly been encouraged for export-oriented industries).

Broad Trends

Figure 6.1 presents quarterly movements of three types of net capital inflows — namely portfolio investment inflows (PFN), foreign direct investments (FDI) and bank loan inflows (BLI) — with the Kuala Lumpur Stock

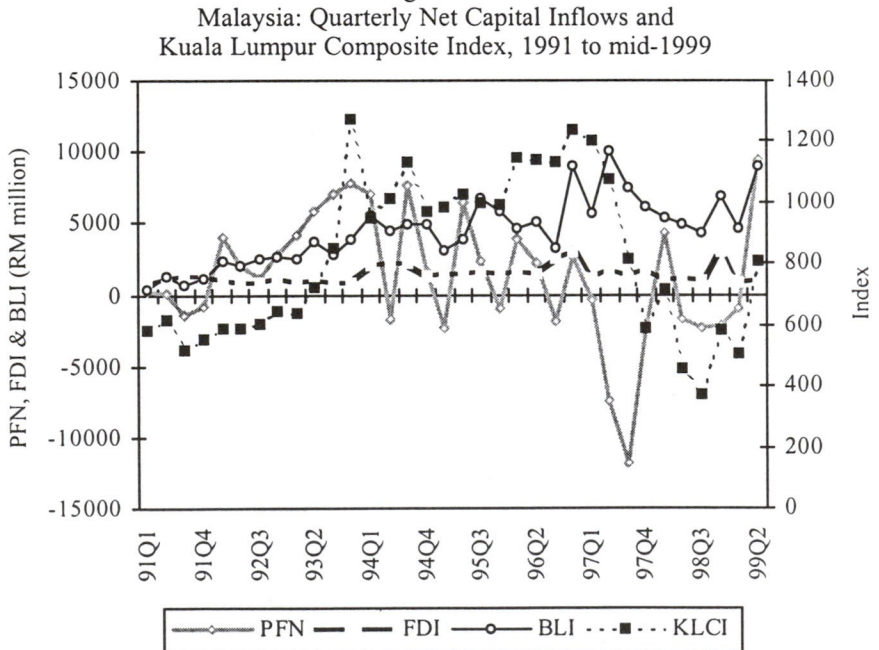

Figure 6.1
Malaysia: Quarterly Net Capital Inflows and
Kuala Lumpur Composite Index, 1991 to mid-1999

Exchange Composite Index (KLCI) during the period from 1991 until mid-1999. The graph suggests broadly parallel movements between FDI and BLI, but little else. It also underscores the tremendous volatility of PFN.

Figure 6.2a only shows the quarterly movements of net portfolio investment inflows against the Kuala Lumpur Stock Exchange Composite Index (KLCI). The graph suggests broadly parallel movements during the period from 1991 until mid-1999. This would be expected during both boom and bust periods, with portfolio investment flows moving to and strengthening a rising or bull market and fleeing from and thus undermining a declining or bear market. Figure 6.2b plots quarterly changes for these two items. While the extreme volatility of net portfolio investment inflows becomes very clear, there do not appear to be such strong parallels after all.

Figure 6.3a presents monthly movements of the Malaysian ringgit (RM)/ US dollar (US$) exchange rate against the Kuala Lumpur Stock Exchange Composite Index (KLCI). The graph suggests an indifferent relationship until the onset of the crisis in July 1997, after which one finds broadly parallel movements until the ringgit was pegged against the US dollar from September 1997. Figure 6.3b plots quarterly changes for these two trends. This time, there appears to be some correspondence, perhaps with some lag with the KLCI seeming to trail foreign exchange movements.

Figure 6.4a only shows the quarterly movements of foreign direct investments (FDI) and bank loan inflows (BLI). The graph suggests broadly parallel movements during the period from 1991 until mid-1999, with the average quantity of BLI rising much more than the average volume of FDI. This suggests some relationship between BLI and FDI. Figure 6.4b plots quarterly changes for these two items. Again, there appears to be some correspondence. Quarterly data also suggests some volatility in both inflows, but this may be due to the lumpy magnitude of some FDI as well as loans.

Volatility Measures

Interest in the volatility of capital flows has grown in recent years, with growing recognition of the increased volatility of such flows in recent years and their implications (Cailloux and Griffith-Jones 1997). There have also been attempts to establish hierarchies of such volatility, to help distinguish between relatively 'hot' and 'cold' flows. Such efforts have remained problematic and controversial. For example, the low frequency of available data reduces the range of econometric tools that can be meaningfully used to gauge the volatility of capital flows. Available data from national and international

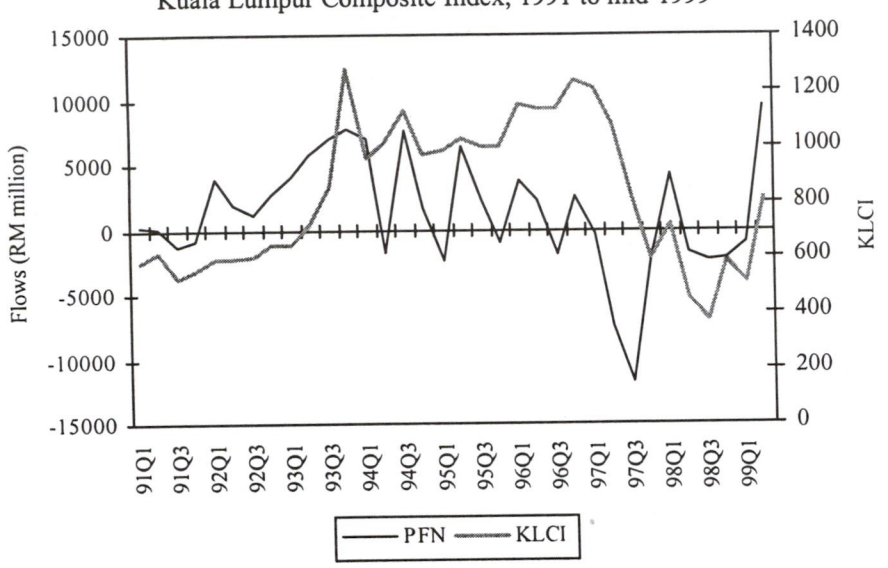

Figure 6.2a
Malaysia: Quarterly Net Portfolio Investment Inflows and
Kuala Lumpur Composite Index, 1991 to mid-1999

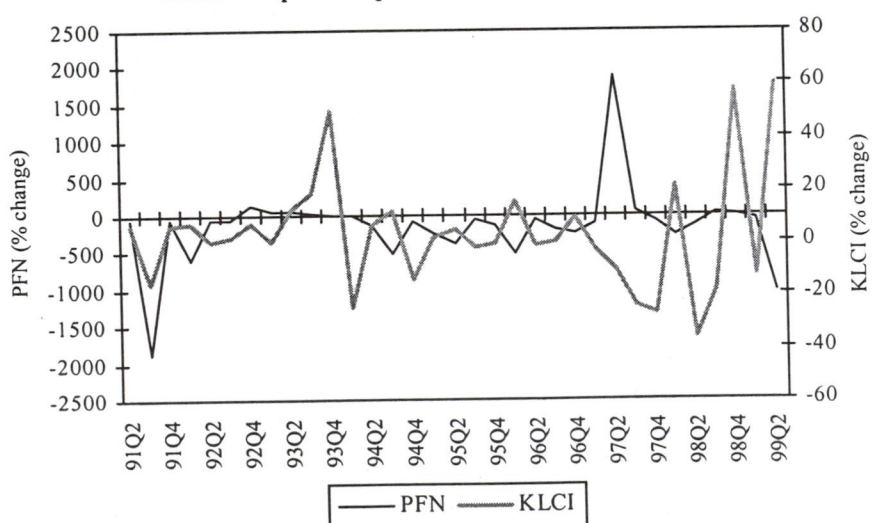

Figure 6.2b
Malaysia: Changes in Quarterly Net Portfolio Investment Inflows and
Kuala Lumpur Composite Index, 1991 to mid-1999

Figure 6.3a
Malaysia: Monthly Ringgit/US Dollar Exchange Rate and
Kuala Lumpur Composite Index, 1991 to mid-1999

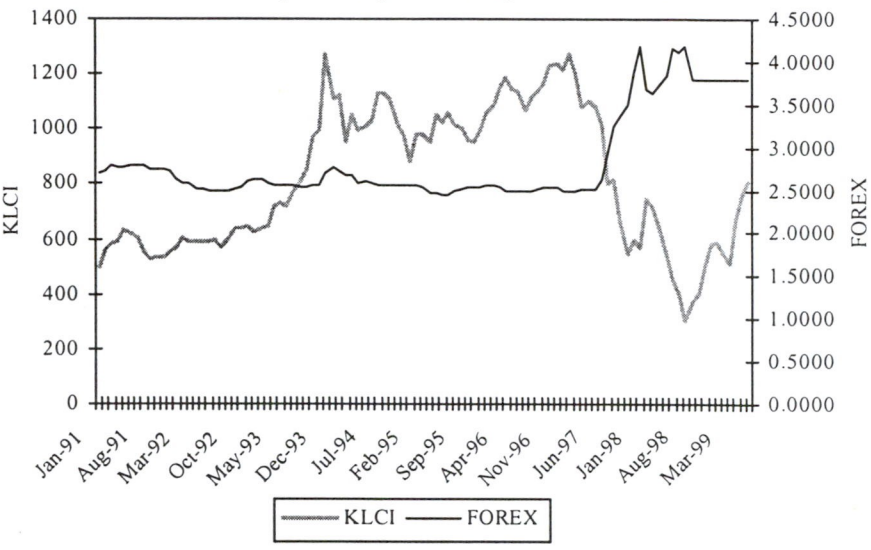

Figure 6.3b
Malaysia: Changes in Monthly Ringgit/US Dollar Exchange Rate and
Kuala Lumpur Composite Index, 1991 to mid-1999

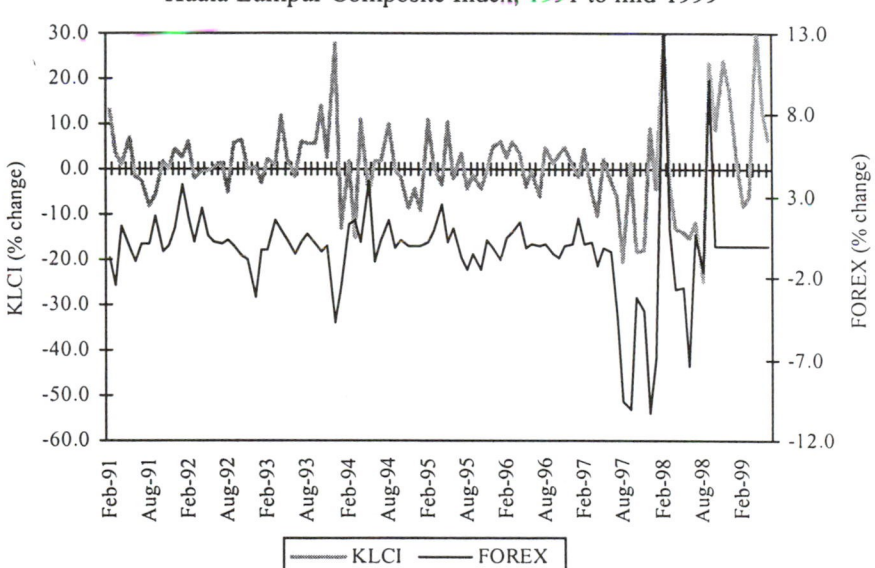

Figure 6.4a
Malaysia: Quarterly Foreign Direct Investments and
Bank Lending Inflows, 1991 to mid-1999

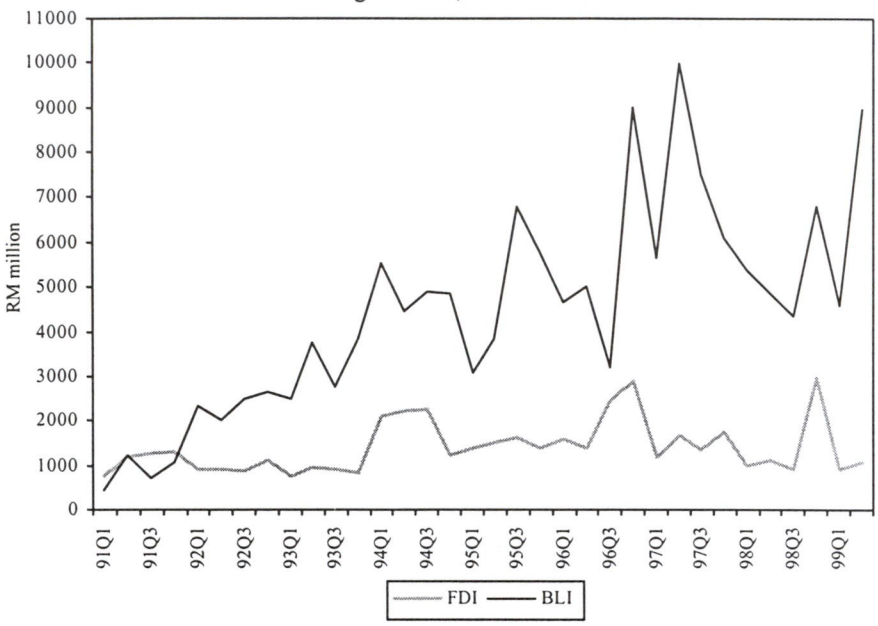

Figure 6.4b
Malaysia: Changes in Quarterly Foreign Direct Investments
and Bank Lending Inflows, 1991 to mid-1999

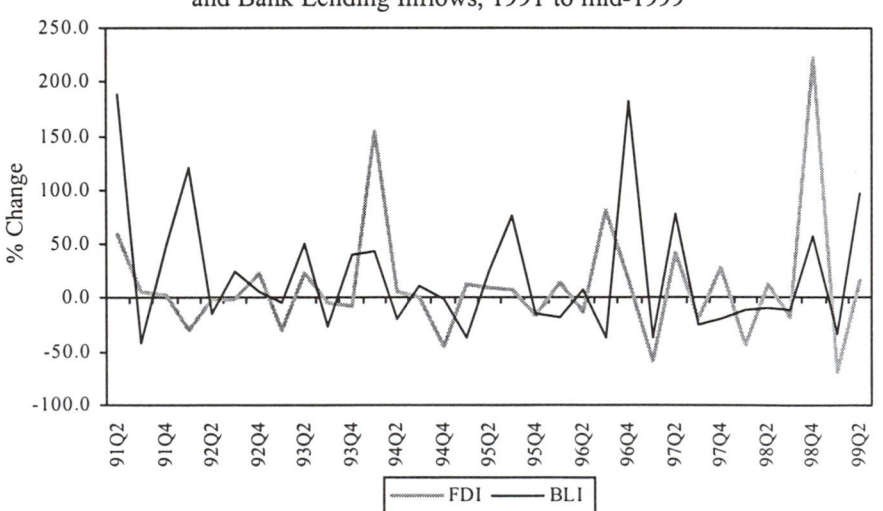

sources are often not reliable or even consistently defined. Even when available, the focus on net flows over particular periods obscures the possibly massive inflows and outflows underlying relatively modest net flows.

Cailloux and Griffith-Jones (1999: 19-21) have correctly criticised current reliance on the coefficient of variation, i.e. the ratio of the standard deviation of flows over their means. Instead, they have proposed a new indicator, namely the standard deviation of the flow of investment at time m divided by the moving average of cumulated flows. For them, the moving average — which makes the indicator less sensitive to large shocks occurring just before the new flow measured — is calculated over the four quarters preceding the inflow. When monthly data has been available, i.e. for the pre-crisis period before July 1997, we have done the same for monthly data. We have also considered both portfolio fund inflows as well as outflows. The results are presented in Tables 6.1 (for the period 1991 until the third quarter of 1999) and 6.2 (for the period January 1991 until June 1997).

Table 6.1 shows that although the five quarter moving average adjustment significantly reduces the coefficient of variation, the adjusted measures reiterate the high volatility of other investments, followed by net portfolio investment inflows, with a slightly lower measure for the subset of net in-flows of stocks and corporate securities. Foreign direct investments were the least volatile, with bank loans slightly more volatile. According to the quarterly data for the pre-crisis period (1991 until mid-1997), volatility was also greatest for other investments in this period, followed by net portfolio investment inflows, with the volatility of net inflows for stocks and securities slightly higher. Again, foreign direct investments were the least volatile, followed by bank loans.

Interestingly, when comparing volatility in the pre-crisis period (1991 until mid-1997) with the entire period under study (1991 until third quarter of 1999), volatility was greater in the pre-crisis period for other investments (probably because they only began to grow in the mid-nineties), and even slightly higher for foreign direct investment. Surprisingly, there was little difference in volatility for bank lending, contrary to expectations and the general trend in the rest of the crisis-affected East Asian region. This supports the argument in this paper that unlike Malaysia's neighbours, net foreign portfolio investment inflows (and the relatively small other investment inflows) were primarily responsible for the crisis in Malaysia and were the main vector for the spread of the regional contagion to the economy.

Analysis in Table 6.2 with the monthly data (for the pre-crisis period only) also included gross data on foreign portfolio investment inflows as well as

Table 6.1
Malaysia: Quarterly Foreign Capital Inflow Volatility, 1991-1999

	FDI	BL	SCSN	PFN	OIN
Sample: 1991Q1 to 1999Q3					
Mean	1391.9	4507.6	1191.1	1084.6	-136.1
Median	1256.0	4575.0	1155.0	1254.0	-31.0
Maximum	2946.0	9994.0	9450.0	9862.0	2020.0
Minimum	747.0	426.0	-11781.0	-16001.0	-4220.0
Standard Deviation	578.0	2349.2	4408.0	5048.1	1303.1
Coefficient of variation (%)	41.5	52.1	370.1	465.4	-957.6
Observations	35	35	35	35	35
Sample: 1991Q1 to 1997Q2 (pre-crisis)					
Mean	1399.8	3935.7	1972.2	2114.9	59.8
Median	1274.0	3791.5	2114.0	1946.0	12.0
Maximum	2870.0	9994.0	7709.0	8270.0	2020.0
Minimum	747.0	426.0	-7427.0	-8584.0	-2710.0
Standard Deviation	565.0	2330.7	3687.2	3719.3	900.3
Coefficient of variation (%)	40.4	59.2	187.0	175.9	1505.3
Observations	26	26	26	26	26
Sample: 1991Q1 to 1999Q3 (adjusted for 5-quarter moving average)					
Mean	1417.6	4483.0	1213.5	1085.3	-188.9
Median	1463.0	4681.0	1336.0	1670.0	-21.0
Maximum	2065.0	8021.0	6882.0	6997.0	960.0
Minimum	853.0	859.0	-5501.0	-7108.0	-1876.0
Standard Deviation	357.3	1821.1	3020.2	3457.7	685.6
Coefficient of variation (%)	25.2	40.6	248.9	318.6	-363.0
Observations	31	31	31	31	31
Sample: 1991Q1 to 1997Q2 (pre-crisis; adjusted for 5-quarter moving average)					
Mean	1378.1	3714.3	2650.9	2756.1	36.0
Median	1443.5	4152.0	2218.0	2484.0	14.0
Maximum	2065.0	5704.0	6882.0	6997.0	960.0
Minimum	853.0	859.0	-470.0	-482.0	-693.0
Standard Deviation	389.9	1477.3	1963.0	2002.2	385.7
Coefficient of variation (%)	28.3	39.8	74.0	72.6	1070.0
Observations	22	22	22	22	22

Key: FDI = Foreign Direct Investments   BL = Bank Loans
     PFN = Net Portfolio Investment Flows   OIN = Other Investments
     SCSN= Net Shares and Corporate Securities Flows
Source: *Quarterly Economic Bulletin* (1999Q3), Tables VIII.13, VIII.14 and VIII.15.

Table 6.2
Malaysia: Pre-crisis Monthly Foreign Capital
Inflow Volatility, 1991 until mid-1997

	PFI	*PFO*	*PFN*	*FDI*	*BL*
Sample: Jan 1991–June 1997 (pre-crisis monthly data)					
Mean	9936.2	9258.7	677.4	458.6	777.7
Median	9969.5	8683.0	604.5	380.5	664.5
Maximum	29776.0	24949.0	6351.0	2033.0	3772.0
Minimum	1055.0	979.0	-2591.0	175.0	110.0
Standard Deviation	6651.7	6053.6	1617.3	302.6	588.3
Coefficient of variation (%)	66.9	65.4	238.7	66.0	75.6
Observations	78	78	78	78	78
Sample: May 1991–June 1997 *(monthly data; adjusted for 5-month moving average)*					
Mean	10077.7	9321.4	756.3	460.9	739.0
Median	9802.2	8942.3	690.3	425.7	634.8
Maximum	24494.8	22222.0	3533.0	1016.5	1870.3
Minimum	1379.3	1504.0	-990.5	238.3	215.5
Standard Deviation	6242.8	5717.6	1027.1	172.5	372.0
Coefficient of variation (%)	61.9	61.3	135.8	37.4	50.3
Observations	74	74	74	74	74

Key: FDI = Foreign Direct Investments   BL = Bank Loans
PFI = Portfolio Investment Inflows   PFO = Portfolio Investment Outflows
PFN= Net Portfolio Investment Flows
Source: *Monthly Statistical Bulletin*, Table VIII.1 (various issues).

outflows. Interestingly, the unadjusted measures of the volatility of inflows and outflows were not significantly different than for foreign direct investment, and less volatile than for bank loans and especially for net portfolio investment flows. However, the adjusted measures suggested the following hierarchy of volatility, with foreign direct investments least volatile, followed by bank loans and then, portfolio investment inflows and outflows, with net flows most volatile.

Vector Auto-regression Analysis

The goal of Vector Auto-regression (VAR) analysis is to determine the inter-relationships among the variables (not the parameter estimates). To assess the impact of a shock on the different flows, we create an impulse response function using the VAR analysis. An impulse response function traces the response of the endogenous variables in the system to shocks in the errors. By analysing the response pattern, we may be able to see the direction of inter-relationships among variables and to determine whether or not a particular variable is volatile over time. Our equation, consisting of four variables (KLCI, PFN, BLI and FDI), is stated as follows:

$$Y_t = A_0 + A_1 Y_{t-1} + A_2 Y_{t-2} + A_3 Y_{t-3} + e_t$$

where: Y_t is a (4x1) vector containing KLCI, PFN, BLI and FDI respectively at time t,

A_0 is a (4x1) vector of intercept terms,

A_i is a (4x1) matrices of coefficients, and

e_t a (4x1) vector of error terms.

To determine the specification of the lags in the VAR equation, we use the Akaike Information Criterion (AIC) and Schwarz Criterion (SC) (see Pindyck and Rubinfeld 1997: 238-239). In our tests, the best results were obtained from VAR equations with 1 to 3 month lags, and only these are presented here. Our monthly observations are from January 1991 to June 1997, i.e. after increased capital inflows, but before the crisis began in July 1997 as BNM has ceased to publish monthly data since July 1997. The results from the analysis are reported below.

From the t-statistics obtained (see Table 6.3), KLCI appears to be highly correlated with its own past values, especially in the previous month, and to a lesser extent, with net portfolio inflows three months before. PFN appears to be highly correlated with KLCI values in the previous two months, but with little else. BLI also seems to be highly correlated with KLCI two months earlier, but little else. FDI seems little correlated with its own and other past values. The graphs in Figure 6.5 plot the impact of a one standard deviation shock involving each of the different variables on the other variables, illustrating the same trends graphically, while Figure 6.6 combines the effects of particular shocks into composite graphs.

- From the graphs, it can be seen that the impact of a one standard deviation KLCI shock caused the KLCI to respond positively and PFN to respond positively before turning negative and fluctuating around zero. The response of BLI is generally modest but positive. The impact on FDI is not very significant, converging towards zero over time.
- The strong initial response of PFN to a one standard deviation PFN shock

Table 6.3
VAR Analysis: Vector Auto-regression Estimates

	KLCI	PFN	BLI	FDI
KLCI (t–1)	0.934872	15.62586	-1.252141	1.002735
	(7.54596)	(5.41228)	(-1.28122)	(1.52530)
KLCI (t–2)	0.291978	-13.36979	4.124552	0.645276
	(1.85884)	(-3.65250)	(3.32871)	(0.77418)
KLCI (t–3)	-0.309755	-3.457074	-1.641574	-1.127562
	(-2.12889)	(-1.01957)	(-1.43022)	(-1.46043)
PFN (t–1)	-0.004454	0.240606	-0.032457	0.000227
	(-0.77872)	(1.80526)	(-0.71941)	(0.00748)
PFN (t–2)	0.005069	-0.041077	-0.060014	-0.047480
	(1.04420)	(-0.36308)	(-1.56711)	(-1.84312)
PFN (t–3)	-0.010974	-0.003747	-0.046735	-0.001984
	(-2.25489)	(-0.03304)	(-1.21730)	(-0.07684)
BLI (t–1)	-0.020010	0.005600	0.175846	0.141466
	(-1.28344)	(0.01541)	(1.42977)	(1.70995)
BLI (t–2)	0.088380	0.689203	0.262334	-0.172840
	(4.58747)	(1.53511)	(1.72616)	(-1.69071)
BLI (t–3)	-0.008687	0.136584	0.033755	-0.080243
	(-0.40192)	(0.27118)	(0.19799)	(-0.69969)
FDI (t–3)	-0.006941	0.115552	-0.263387	-0.030499
	(-0.29652)	(0.21183)	(-1.42637)	(-0.24554)
FDI (t–3)	-0.023667	-0.356872	-0.246284	0.025831
	(-1.01034)	(-0.65374)	(-1.33279)	(0.20781)
FDI (t–3)	-0.003321	0.145942	-0.214911	0.144806
	(-0.14011)	(0.26418)	(-1.14924)	(1.15116)
C	58.55301	922.9142	-204.9080	37.15128
	(2.18144)	(1.47547)	(-0.96775)	(0.26084)
Adj. R-squared	0.948099	0.414901	0.470908	0.120975
Akaike Information Criteria	57.53011			
Schwarz Criteria	59.13690			

Note: t-statistics in parentheses.

Figure 6.5
VAR Analysis: Responses to One Standard Deviation Shock

Response to One S.D. Shock ± 2 S.E.

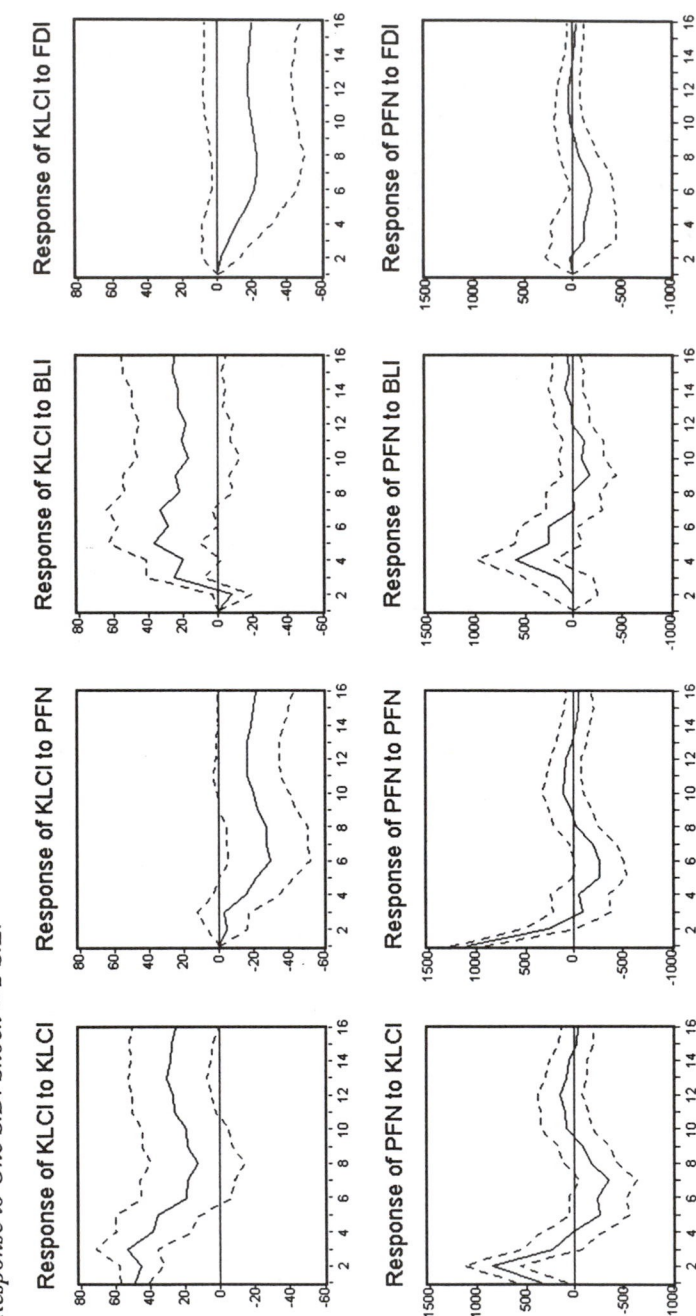

Figure 6.5 (continued)

VAR Analysis: Responses to One Standard Deviation Shock

Response to One S.D. Shock ± 2 S.E.

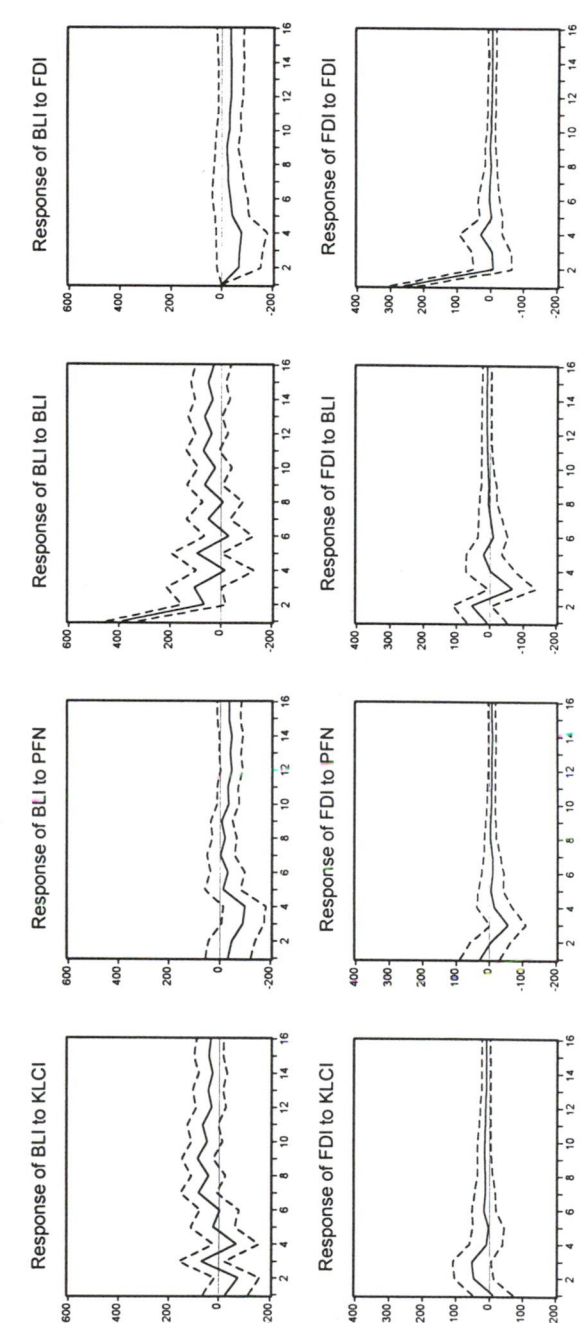

Figure 6.6
VAR Analysis — Combined Response Graphs

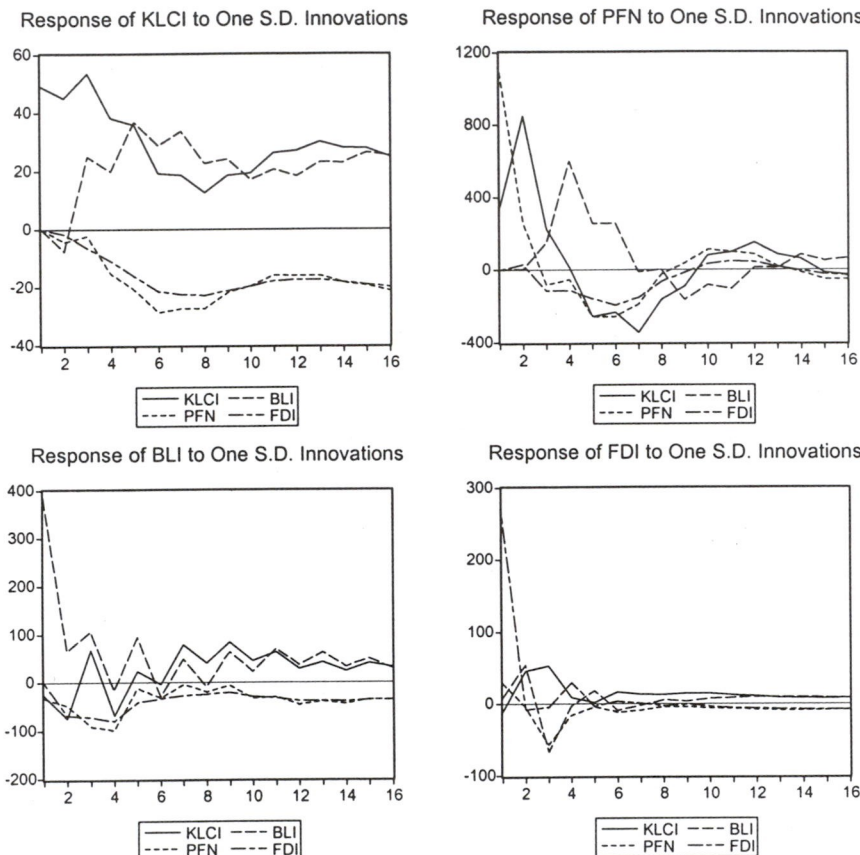

quickly petered out, whereas the KLCI responded negatively after some time to the same. Both BLI and FDI do not respond strongly to such a shock.

- After a strong initial response of BLI to a one standard deviation BLI shock, the response becomes modestly positive. However, the KLCI responds positively after some time. PFN responds positively after a short lag before petering out, whereas FDI responds both positively and then negatively before quickly petering out.
- FDI seems to initially respond positively to a one standard deviation FDI shock, before petering out. After a slow initial response of KLCI to such

a shock, the response seems to remain consistently negative! Both PFN and BLI responded modestly but negatively to such FDI shocks before petering out.

Given the nature of VAR analysis, one would expect the strong positive response of each variable to a one standard deviation shock on itself. However, only the KLCI seemed to respond positively over time, suggesting likely reinforcement of the self-perpetuating nature of virtuous as well as vicious cycles involved in share price inflation and deflation. Such a finding would not contradict the possibility of herd behaviour as well as speculative bubbles and their bursting.

Ironically, both PFN and FDI seem to have negative impacts on KLCI after an initially modest response. The negative impact of PFN on KLCI may suggest the likelihood of boom-bust cycles associated with foreign portfolio capital inflows and PFN as a vector for contagion from abroad. Conversely, KLCI seems to respond positively to BLI suggesting that foreign borrowings ` probably contribute to share price inflation.

KLCI and other inflows do not seem to affect FDI very much. This suggests that unexpected drops in the KLCI do not necessarily lead to sudden pull-outs of FDI. Whereas the strong initial responses of PFN to PFN, KLCI and BLI seem quite significant. From the above analysis, PFN appears to be much more volatile than FDI and even BLI.

Foreign Portfolio Investor Perspectives

To understand the perceptions and behaviour of foreign portfolio investors operating in the Malaysian capital market, several foreign managers and analysts were interviewed (see Appendix 6.1). These interviews were conducted to get a sense of what they perceived to be significant in making investment as well as divestment decisions. An open-ended questionnaire format was used to determine their personal and company investment frameworks and guidelines. Such information proved useful and complementary to the statistical and other analyses employed to understand foreign capital inflows into and out of Malaysia.

Before the crisis, most respondents had most of their holdings in corporate securities (most commonly around 80 per cent, if not more) with the remainder usually in money market instruments or cash. Everyone agreed that the market for financial derivatives was very small before the crisis and this was even more true by the time of the interviews in September 1999. Because money market rates were so low then, most foreign fund managers seemed to be holding cash if they were holding anything. Malaysian government securities and private debt securities were not being held by anyone interviewed. They were considered illiquid pre-crisis, and only held by local funds and insurance companies. Everyone was almost exclusively focusing on corporate securities, and the overall percentage allocated to them — as opposed to fixed income securities — did not change post-crisis, remaining instead around 20 per cent. Over the previous 18 months, there had been a significant shift from assets to cash (and then, back to assets) because the capital controls tax was imposed on the repatriation date, not on the date of sale.

All comments only addressed corporate securities, virtually 'the only game in town'. There was broad variation in average holding time. Of the five fund managers, three viewed 6 to 12 months as long term, with the other two investing on a two year time horizon before, during and after the crisis in line with standard fund practice, though they agreed that this was rare. The three fund managers in Singapore all said that they were managing long term money, 6-12 months in the one case, 2 years in another, and 3-4 years in the third. All stated that holding time was basically unchanged post-crisis.

Everyone interviewed saw hedge funds as having the shortest average holding period, ranging from weeks to 3 months. They reasoned that this is because hedge funds do not have to worry about trustees, and because they are trading on volatility, not on fundamentals. Mutual funds are seen as medium to short term, averaging from 6 to 12 months. Pension funds and Insurance Funds (especially from Japan) tend to be more long term, ranging from 1 to 3 years. These responses corroborated Maxfield's (1997: 72) findings.

Basically, everyone interviewed was in search of higher returns, but if they were covering the spread according to Morgan Stanley Capital International (MSCI), then that also entailed diversification. According to a 1990s' Credit Lyonnais survey of fund managers, 80 per cent of them operated with the MSCI benchmark. In effect, what most people were saying in September 1999 was that the main reason for investing in Malaysia was to cover the benchmark in anticipation of Malaysia being restored in February 2000 (since postponed to May 2000).

The only push factors mentioned for pre-crisis investment in Malaysia and the rest of the region were the European recession in 1992 and low interest rates in Euro-American markets in the 1990s. This response could have been affected by the interview sample consisting of local agency brokers, local brokers, local analysts, and Singapore based fund managers. The basic division of labour within global funds between 'strategists' (who focus on liquidity and push factors) and 'economists' (who focus on countries and, hence, more on pull factors) means that the sample did not include those who carefully compare emerging markets in relation to more developed markets. Everyone claimed that they or their clients were investing in East Asia as the best of the emerging markets.

Specific pull factors cited for Malaysia, as opposed to other countries in the region, were: good infrastructure, political stability, the size of the market (implying bigger industrial spread), good economic fundamentals, good corporate governance. One reason for the strong flows into Malaysia before the crisis, e.g. in 1995-96, was Malaysia's listing on both the Developed Markets' and the Emerging Markets' Morgan Stanley (MSCI) Indices. This apparent anomaly was due to the pre-1990s' Siamese twin relationship of the Kuala Lumpur Stock Exchange (KLSE) to the Stock Exchange of Singapore (SES). The absence of barriers to portfolio investment was not seen as a crucial positive factor.

Geographical Differences

American fund managers were perceived by Malaysian analysts and brokers as over-emphasising political risks and uncertainties. They also tend to cover all emerging markets, not just Asia, and so tend to pay less attention to local information. However, others saw Hong Kong fund managers as also worried about the political risk factor. Singapore fund managers seemed much more informed about the political situation in Malaysia, and were less likely to make inappropriate comparisons with Indonesia. But in general, in September 1999, everyone interviewed was focused on the (29 November 1999) elections and the (later suspended) government-announced (forced) bank mergers as key indicators.

Attractive Stocks

Nothing on the KLSE second board was recommended by those interviewed. Gaming, utilities and also consumer-oriented stocks were seen to have good potential upside. Banking was seen as a mixed bag, but everyone seemed positive about Malayan Banking, the largest bank (controlled by the government). Investors were mainly looking for secure returns, low risks and liquidity. In 1996, before the crisis, they were mainly looking at privatisation, contracted-out (implying good political connections and implicit government guarantees) projects, and small companies, including the second board.

After the crisis, in September 1999, they were looking more at banking, manufacturing, electronics, utilities and export oriented companies.

Hedge Funds

Tracking hedge fund activity and flows proved especially difficult. Anecdotally, they seemed unaffected by the controls because lots of funds were contracting with stock lenders offshore and then short-selling the stocks to domestic buyers. When the controls came in, they just worked out cancellation agreements with the stock lenders. Also anecdotally, most of the 'new' money in recent flows to the KLSE is, ironically, hedge fund money.

Capital Controls

Most of those interviewed saw the institution of capital controls as generally contributing to the economic recovery, but questioned the timing and manner of their implementation. Most people thought they would have helped more if instituted in February or even June 1998. Many argued that for local business and manufacturing, they were crucial. A few were uncertain whether the controls had net positive or negative effects, and insisted on waiting to see what the medium to long term impacts on FDI and portfolio flows would be. Two people rejected the majority's positive assessment of capital controls, arguing that controls were too late and, as instituted, simply caused a suspension of international flows. All agreed that a clear schedule for their implementation and removal would be beneficial. As they stood then, the exit tax and capital gains levy were said to be deterring inflows because foreign fund managers cannot or do not want to cope with the messy accounting required to track old and new money, and so, it was claimed, were staying out entirely. In Singapore, the fund managers saw Malaysia's recovery paralleling those of other Southeast Asian economies, and argued that the recovery was not necessarily linked to the controls. One fund manager stated that they were mainly politically — not economically — motivated. None of the Singapore fund managers interviewed were affected by the CLOB issue.

Everyone interviewed in Malaysia was either slightly or very positive about the prospects for the next five months (October 1999 to February 2000). Most were recommending increased exposure, with all fund managers planning small increases. However, no one expected a major increase of inflows until the beginning of 2000. In Singapore, everyone was much closer to neutral, looking especially at political uncertainty. All three were going to remain at current levels — i.e. 8 per cent, 6 per cent and 4 per cent of total allocations — at least until the then expected February 2000 reinstatement on the MSCI. One fund manager was looking for major political change, either in paradigm or leadership, before increasing exposure.

Conclusion

Undoubtedly, international financial liberalisation succeeded in generating net capital inflows into East Asia, including Malaysia, unlike other developing and transitional economies, many of which experienced net outflows. But it also exacerbated systemic instability and reduced the scope for the developmental government interventions responsible for the region's economic miracle.[1]

In Southeast Asia, especially Malaysia, FDI domination (well above the average for developing countries) of internationally competitive manufacturing had weakened domestic industrialists, inadvertently enhancing the dominance of finance capital and its influence over economic policy making. This resulted in a greater orientation during the nineties towards attracting foreign portfolio investments to boost the Malaysian stock market. Fortunately, borrowings from foreign banks were limited relative to Thailand, Indonesia and South Korea, with their more bank-based financial systems, especially before 1996, but ballooned in the year and a half before the regional currency and financial crises broke in mid-1997.

Note

1. Chuah (2000) has found that real exchange rate (RER) volatility has had a mildly dampening effect on exports. She found that for every percentage point change in RER volatility depressed exports by less than one percentage point. The impact was the same in both the short-run and in the long-run, suggesting that Malaysian exports seemed to adapt reasonably quickly and well to RER volatility. Despite the modest adverse impact, she argues that it is important to maintain RER stability to avoid risks arising from a long-run divergence of the RER from its equilibrium value.

APPENDIX 6.1
Interviews with Managers of Foreign Funds

Ten managers and analysts working for foreign funds based in Kuala Lumpur were interviewed to develop a better understanding of their perceptions of Malaysian capital markets. Since considerable stock investments in Malaysia are made from Singapore or upon the advice of analysts based in Singapore, three respondents from Singapore were included in the interview sample. The open ended interviews were conducted by Laura Kaehler with a questionaire prepared with the help of Chin Kok Fay. The work was strongly influenced by Maxwell's (1997) earlier work. Those interviewed were from:

Malaysia
RHB Research Institute
KAF Management Services
CMS Dresdner Asset Management
Arab-Malaysian Merchant Bank
CLSA
Smith Zain Securities
Salomon Smith Barney
Abrar Global Asset Managers
Nomura Securities

Singapore
Aberdeen Asset Management
AXA Rosenberg Investment Management
Prudential Portfolio Managers

Note: Obviously, this is not even close to a representative sample. For the future, another way to track flows is to talk to those who do custodian services. All funds must use a nominee in Malaysia and they now must detail which particular client has what. Custodian services at Chase, HSBC, Standard Chartered and Citibank would cover most of the foreign funds.

Significant Recent Local Developments

Some of the *local developments considered to be crucial* for decision-making by fund managers included:

Feb. '00 Reinstatement (staggered or full) on MSCI (emerging market) index.

Dec. '99 Y2K uncertainties.

Nov. '99 MSCI meetings will decide whether Malaysia's reinstatement on the index will be staggered or all at once.

Elections expected — speculation that controls will be lifted after the elections, but fund managers still expected/planned to wait until the new fiscal year to increase investments.

Oct. '99 Everyone wanted clear information from the central bank on the mergers, especially the criteria for the selection of anchor banks; the government was seen as waffling on the number of anchor banks; this was seen as a key indicator of future transparency and regulatory stability.

Aug. '99 Electricity consumption (viewed as the best leading indicator) highest ever.

Feb. '99 Exit tax introduced; some money seemed to be coming from American funds (however, it was unclear if this was 'new' money or simply money held as cash, but not repatriated after selling assets, i.e. it was unclear if there was a net inflow).

Sept. '98 Capital controls, removal from MSCI.

Dec. '97 Government spending cuts.

Nov. '97 Designation of stocks caused major volatility.

Mar. '97 Bank Negara restrictions on property lending and share financing per bank decreased liquidity; current account deficits became a larger worry.

Early '96 Some funds already underweighting Malaysia, saw fundamentals, especially current account balance, as poor.

During the course of the interviews, some special mention of certain stocks provided useful insights into fund manager considerations; some examples follow:

Gamuda — 2 people recommended 'overweight', 1 recommended 'under-weight' — seen as solid and well diversified, person who recommended under-weighting did not think it was liquid enough.

Genting — 5 people recommended 'overweight' — gaming, in general, was seen as a safe bet, so Resorts World was especially recommended; it was expected to benefit from recovery in consumer spending, and was seen as very liquid.

Public Bank — 4 people recommended 'overweight' — because it is large and looks likely to emerge from forced mergers in a stronger position. (One person argued that it will be the only 'real' Chinese run bank of the six anchor banks selected after consolidation and will thus benefit from this reputation.)

Malaysian International Shipping Corp. (MISC) — 'solid' and low risk.

Maybank — seen as the flagship bank, it is expected to remain the largest and best placed bank emerging from the mergers.

Sime Darby — 5 people recommended 'overweight' — because it is perceived as 'getting back to basics', one of the oldest companies, with plenty of liquidity.

Tenaga — six people recommended 'overweight' — because it is still a *de facto* monopoly and economic driving force; it will most likely get an increase of tariff rates to survive; it is also expected to move into new power generation from its distribution monopoly in order to offset high contract prices it has been forced to accept.

United Engineers Malaysia — 1 person recommended 'overweight' — seen as solid, and undervalued by the three Singapore fund managers.

After 1997, all those interviewed had consolidated their holdings in companies that looked 'solid and conservative' for the long run, such as Malaysian Oxygen, Sime UEP, Carlsberg, Public Bank. For the smaller country funds, they added: Amway, Telekom, London Pacific Insurance (2 of 3 emphasized they had been looking for companies, since before the crisis, with no government influence/political risk, thus specifically avoiding Renong and UEM, both then and now.

199 - 215

(Malaysia)

F32
516
519
G21
G28

7

CAPITAL CONTROLS

Jomo K. S.

Malaysian Prime Minister Mahathir Mohamad's 1 September 1998 announcement of capital controls was important in several regards. Whereas Thailand, South Korea and Indonesia had gone cap in hand — humiliatingly accepting conditions imposed by the International Monetary Fund (IMF) — in order to secure desperately needed credit, the Malaysian initiative reminded the world that there are alternatives to capital account liberalisation. The capital control measures were significantly revised in February 1999. As of 1 September 1999, yet another regime came into effect. These modifications recognise the negative impact of the capital controls regime, and represent attempts to mitigate it and to encourage the return of the often condemned short-term capital.

Unfortunately, there has been a tendency since for both sides in the debate over Malaysia's capital control measures to exaggerate their own cases, with little regard for what has actually happened. Market fundamentalists have loudly prophesied doom for Malaysia ever since, though the evidence does not support their often wild claims. Meanwhile, opponents of capital account liberalisation have gone to the other extreme with some wishful exaggeration about what the Malaysian measures actually imply and their consequences (one supporter has extolled its ostensibly virtuous consequences for labour with scant regard for Malaysian realities). Both sides often forget that capital controls are often necessary means to other policy objectives, rather than ends in and of themselves. One needs to be clear about these objectives. Will capital controls be used in the interests of workers, consumers or the national public interest? Or are they mainly being used to save the politically well-connected?

Capital Controls

There are many different types of capital control measures, with different consequences, often varying with circumstances as much as the nature of the instruments. Until capital account liberalisation from the eighties, most countries retained some such controls despite significant current account liberalisation in the post-war period. Most such measures can only be understood historically, in terms of their original purposes, and there are no ready-made packages available for interested governments.

Economists favouring capital account liberalisation have made three main arguments in favour of such a policy. It is argued that capital will tend to flow from capital-rich to capital-poor economies, or between economies with different savings rates, investment opportunities, risk profiles or even demographic patterns. Capital flows thus enable national economies to trade imports in the present for imports in the future, i.e. to engage in inter-temporal trade. Capital flows also allow national economies to offset pressures to reduce imports by borrowing from abroad or by selling assets to foreigners. Such imports and borrowings may be used to enhance national economic output capacity, i.e. a country's ability to increase production in the future. The foregoing arguments are similar to those for international trade liberalisation. Foreign direct investment is also expected to involve technology transfer, which should enhance industrial capabilities. Restrictions on capital flows are considered undesirable by advocates of capital account liberalisation because they prevent capital from being utilised where it is most demanded.

On the other hand, advocates of capital controls emphasise the adverse effects of free capital flows on national economic policy-making and implementation, or worse still, by undermining economic stability. Any policy intended to restrict or redirect capital account transactions can be considered a capital control. These would include taxes, price or quantity controls, including bans on trade in certain kinds of assets. Hence, there are many different kinds of capital controls, which may be introduced for various reasons. The effects of specific controls may change over time and could become quite different from what may have been intended. The major reasons advanced for the introduction of capital controls have included the following:

1. Achieve greater leeway for monetary policy, e.g. to reflate the economy.
2. Enhance macroeconomic stability by limiting potentially volatile capital inflows.
3. Secure exchange rate stability, e.g. protect a fixed exchange rate or peg.
4. Correct international payments imbalances, both deficits and surpluses.
5. Avoid inflation due to excessive inflows.
6. Avoid real currency appreciation due to monetary expansion.
7. Reduce financial instability by changing the composition of — or limiting — capital inflows.
8. Restrict foreign ownership of domestic assets, which might cause nationalistic resentment.
9. Ensure the domestic utilisation of national savings by restricting outflows.
10. Enable governments to allocate credit domestically without risking capital flight.
11. Enable domestic financial houses to attain scale economies in order to better compete internationally.
12. Facilitate revenue generation, particularly taxation of wealth and interest income; by allowing higher inflation, more revenue can be generated.

Capital controls may well be the most acceptable alternative to the destabilising effects of capital flows on inadequately regulated financial systems characteristic of developing economies. Effective regulation may be compromised by limited capabilities and experience, fewer personnel and other resources as well as politically or otherwise compromised regulatory capacity. When a country with a fixed exchange rate experiences a net capital outflow, it can either raise interest rates or devalue. But with a sudden large capital outflow, usually associated with easily reversible capital inflows, either option is likely to exert strong recessionary pressures due to higher interest rates or further capital flight. Monetary contraction may not only dampen economic activity with higher interest rates, but may also adversely affect the economy through the (invariably government-guaranteed) banking system, which may be exposed to foreign borrowings (Kaminsky and Reinhart 1999).

Capital controls may be used to limit capital flow volatility to achieve greater economic stability by checking outflows in the event of crisis or influencing the volume or composition of inflows. Sudden massive capital outflows — usually attributable to herd behaviour — are more likely to occur in developing countries for various reasons. The greater likelihood of asset price changes to cause further changes in the same direction increases the likelihood of greater volatility as well as boom-bust cycles. Discouraging capital inflows would reduce the quantity of capital that might take flight at short notice. But changing the composition of capital inflows — e.g. to favour foreign direct investments as opposed to more liquid portfolio investments — may well better reduce such instability.

Different types of capital controls may be distinguished by the types of asset transactions they affect as well as by the very nature of the control measure itself, e.g. tax, limit, or ban. Capital controls are not identical with exchange controls though the two are often closely related in practice. Exchange controls mainly involve monetary assets (currency and bank deposits), and may be used to control the current account of the balance of payments rather than the capital account. While exchange controls function as "a type of limited capital control, they are neither necessary to restrict capital movement nor are they necessarily intended to control capital account transactions" (Neely 1999: 21-2). Some of the major differences among the types of capital controls involve:

1. *Taxes versus quantitative* controls: Taxes rely on price or market mechanisms to deter certain types of flows. Such taxes may be on certain types of transactions or returns to foreign investment, or may even involve mandatory reserve requirements, which raise the cost of the flows concerned. Quantitative controls may involve quotas, authorisation requirements or even outright bans.
2. Controls on *inflows as opposed to outflows*: Limits on inflows may allow for higher interest rates, to check money supply and inflation. Checks on outflows allow lower interest rates and greater money supply than would otherwise be possible, and have often been used to postpone hard choices between devaluation and tighter monetary policy, as with Malaysia's September 1998 controls.
3. Controls on different types of inflows, especially in terms of *expected duration*: Governments may seek to encourage long-term inflows (e.g. foreign direct investment) while discouraging short-term (e.g. bank loans or money market instruments) or easily reversible (portfolio investments) inflows.

It is important to establish at the outset what particular controls seek to achieve. With the benefit of hindsight, it is crucial to determine to what extent the measures actually achieve their declared objectives as well as their other consequences, intended or otherwise. For instance, it is important to know whether specific controls are meant to avert crisis or to assist recovery. In its *1998 Trade and Development Report*, the United Nations Conference on Trade and Development (UNCTAD) recommended capital controls as means to avoid financial crises. Almost as if endorsing the Malaysian measures, MIT Professor Paul Krugman recommended capital controls in his *Fortune* magazine column in late August 1998 to create a window of opportunity to facilitate economic recovery — which is a different objective, though some of the mechanisms or processes involved may not be altogether different.

A Previous Malaysian Experience

The September 1998 capital controls were not completely unprecedented. In fact, temporary capital controls had been introduced in early 1994 after an earlier experience of massive capital flight with the sudden reversal of massive net portfolio capital inflows in 1992-3. This earlier imposition of controls — while Anwar Ibrahim was already Finance Minister (from 1991) and soon after Ahmad Don became central bank governor — suggests that the two were not as opposed to such measures as they have been made out to be after Ahmad Don's (forced) resignation in August 1998 and Anwar Ibrahim's sacking on 2 September 1998. The 1994 measures sought to deter capital inflows by taxing them, unlike the 1998 measures that restricted capital outflows. If they had not been withdrawn so soon, it is quite likely that the magnitude of capital flight from mid-1997 would have been much less, and the 1997-98 crisis would have been less catastrophic.

The controls — introduced after the sudden collapse of the Malaysian stock market in early 1994 — were soon withdrawn after about half a year, without introducing a more permanent regime of market-based controls that could be flexibly adjusted in response to policy priorities and concerns. The central bank saw the problem as one of excess liquidity due to the massive inflow of short-term funds from abroad due to higher interest rates in Malaysia, the buoyant stock market and expectations of ringgit appreciation. Several monetary measures were introduced during early 1994, which were gradually phased out during the course of the year. The following measures sought to manage excess liquidity, especially to contain speculative inflows, restore stability in financial markets and control inflationary measures; for a fuller account, see BNM's *1994 Annual Report* (especially the Foreword, Boxes A to J and pp. 42-44):

- The eligible liabilities base for computing statutory reserve and liquidity requirements was redefined to include all fund inflows from abroad, thus raising the cost of foreign funds compared to domestic funds.

- Limits on non trade-related external liabilities of banking institutions were introduced; net external liabilities of the banking system declined from a peak of RM35.4 billion in early January 1994 to RM10.3 billion at the end of 1994.
- Sale of short-term monetary instruments was limited only to Malaysian residents to prevent foreigners from using such investments as substitutes for placements of deposits (this measure was lifted on 12 August 1994).
- Commercial banks were required to place ringgit funds of foreign banks in non-interest bearing vostro accounts.
- Commercial banks were not permitted to undertake non-trade-related swaps (including overnight swaps) and outright forward transactions on the bid side with foreign customers to prevent offshore parties from establishing speculative long forward ringgit positions while the ringgit was perceived to be undervalued (this measure was lifted from 16 August 1994).
- The statutory reserve requirements of all financial institutions were raised thrice during 1994 — by one percentage point each time — to absorb excess liquidity on a more permanent basis, absorbing an estimated RM4.8 billion from the banking system.

Mahathir's September 1998 Controls

Did Malaysia's September 1998 selective capital control measures succeed? The merits and demerits of the Malaysian government's regime of capital controls to deal with the regional currency and financial crisis will continue to be debated for a long time to come as the data does not lend itself to clearly supporting any particular position. Proponents can claim that the economic decline came to a stop soon after and the stock market slide turned around, while opponents can say that such reversals have been more pro-nounced in the rest of the region. As is now generally recognised, the one year lock-in of foreign funds in the country was too late to avert the crisis, or to lock in the bulk of foreign funds which had already fled the country. Instead, the funds 'trapped' were those which had not already left in the preceding 14 months, inadvertently 'punishing' the investors who had also shown greater commitment to Malaysia. This is also evidenced by the very low volume of outflow since the end of the lock-in on 1 September 1999.

It appears that, at best, its contribution to recovery was ambiguous, while at worst, it probably slowed it down and acted to diminish the likely recovery of foreign direct investment — which may yet have an impact on Malaysia's medium term competitiveness *vis-à-vis* its neighbours. Further, the regime remains untested in checking currency speculation, as such currency speculation abated shortly after its imposition for various reasons. Also, recovery of the Malaysian share market, which had declined much more than other stock markets during the crisis, has lagged behind the other (relatively smaller) markets in the region.

Malaysia was most fortunate in the timing of the imposition of capital controls if, indeed, as stated by Mahathir in his speech to the symposium on the first anniversary of the controls, it came about almost in desperation. At the time it was introduced, the external environment was about to change significantly, while the economy had seen the outflow of the bulk of short-term capital, so that in a very real sense, the regime was never tested. If the turmoil of the preceding months had continued until the end of 1998, or longer, continued shifts and re-pegging would have been necessary, with consequent deleterious effects.

Clearly, the ringgit peg brought a welcome respite to businessmen after over a year of currency volatility. However, exchange rate volatility across the region also effectively abated shortly thereafter due to other factors, and even the later Brazilian crisis did not renew such volatility. Moreover, it is ironic that an ostensibly nationalistic attempt to defend monetary independence against currency traders should, in effect, hand over determination of the ringgit's value to the US Federal Reserve. However, should the US dollar strengthen significantly against other currencies, Malaysia will probably have to re-peg to retain export competitiveness.

While interest rates were undoubtedly brought down by government decree in Malaysia, the desired effects were limited. Interest rates have come down dramatically across the region, in some cases, even more than in Malaysia, without others having to resort to capital controls. For example, while interest rates in Thailand were much higher than in Malaysia for over a year after the crisis began, they declined below Malaysian levels during September 1998 (see Figure 7.1). Perhaps more importantly, loan and money supply growth rates actually declined in the first few months after the new measures were introduced despite central bank threats to sack bank managers who failed to achieve the 8 per cent loan growth target rate for 1998. It has become clear that credit expansion will be a consequence of factors other than capital controls. Across the region, counter-cyclical spending has also grown, again without resorting to capital controls.

The Malaysian authorities' mid-February 1999 measures have effectively abandoned the main capital control measure introduced in September 1998,

Figure 7.1
Malaysia and Thailand: Average Inter-Bank Overnight Rates,
January 1997 – June 1999

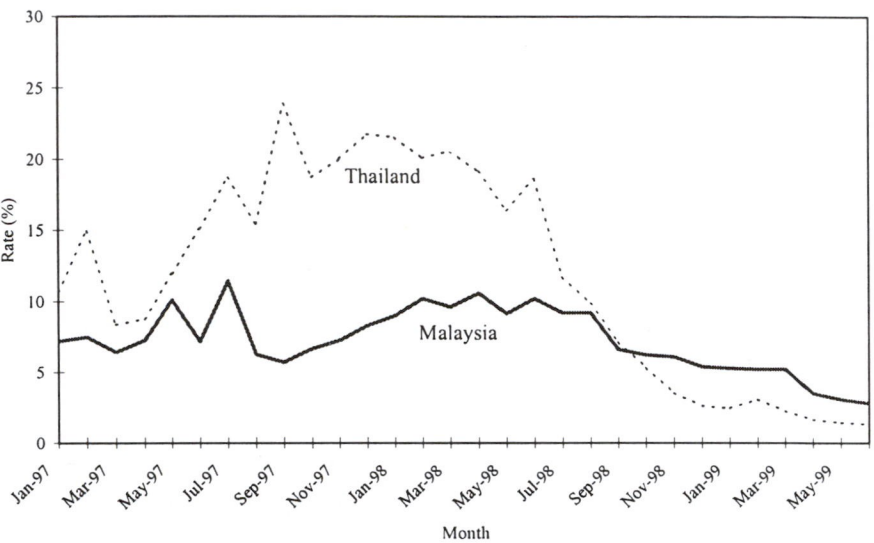

i.e. the one-year lock-in. While foreign investors were prohibited from withdrawing funds from Malaysia before September 1999, they were allowed to withdraw from mid-February 1999 after paying a scaled exit tax (pay less for keeping longer in Malaysia), in the hope that this would reduce the rush for the gates come September 1999. Meanwhile, in an attempt to attract new capital inflows, new investors would only be liable for a less onerous tax on capital gains.

The new capital gains tax will hardly deter exit in the event of a panic as investors rush to get out to cut their losses. At best, however, it could serve to discourage some short-selling from abroad owing to the much higher capital gains tax rate on withdrawals within less than a year of 30 as opposed to 10 per cent. The differential exit capital gains tax rate may have discouraged short-selling from abroad, but did nothing to address other possible sources of vulnerability and will not deter capital flight in the event of financial panic. In September 1999, the capital gains tax rate was set at a uniform rate of 10 per cent, thus eliminating the only feature that might have deterred short-selling from abroad. Effectively, Malaysia is once again almost defenceless in the face of a similar sudden exodus of capital in future, though this may not be the most urgent problem at hand for the time being.

By setting the peg at RM3.8 to the US dollar on 2 September 1998, after it had been trading in the range of RM4-4.2 per US dollar, the Malaysian authorities were then seeking to raise the value of the ringgit. Since mid-September 1998, however, the other currencies in the region strengthened after the US Federal Reserve Bank lowered interest rates in the aftermath of the Russian and LTCM crises, strengthening the yen and other regional currencies. Thus, the ringgit became undervalued for about a year thereafter instead, which — by chance rather than by design — boosted Malaysian foreign exchange reserves from the trade surplus, largely due to import compression, as well as some exchange rate-sensitive exports. As Figure 5.10 shows, Malaysia's foreign exchange reserves depleted rapidly from July until November 1997, before improving in December, and especially after the imposition of capital controls in September 1998.

Thus, the ringgit under-valuation may have helped Malaysian economic recovery, but certainly not in the way the authorities intended when pegging the ringgit in September 1998. However, the US Federal Reserve reduced interest rates soon after, with the ringgit considered under-valued. While the undervalued ringgit would favour an export-led recovery strategy, this certainly was not the intent. (Meanwhile, however, government efforts continue to be focussed on a domestic-led recovery strategy.) The under-valued ringgit is said to have had a (unintended) 'beggar-thy-neighbour' effect. Due to trade competition, the under-valued ringgit is said to have discouraged other regional currencies from strengthening earlier for fear of becoming relatively uncompetitive with regards to Malaysian production costs and exports. This may even cause China's authorities to devalue the *renminbi*, which could have the undesirable effect of triggering off another round of 'competitive devaluations', with concomitant dangers for all.

Industrial output, especially for manufacturing, declined even faster after the introduction of capital controls in Malaysia until November 1998, and continued downward in January 1999 before turning around. Except for a few sectors (notably electronics), industrial output recovery has not been spectacular since then, except in comparison with the deep recession in the year before. Meanwhile, unemployment has risen, especially affecting those employed in construction and financial services. Domestic investment proposals have almost halved, while 'green field' FDI seems to have declined by much less, though cynics claim the actual trends have been obscured by quicker processing of applications (see Figure 7.2).

Figure 7.2
Malaysia: Manufacturing Investment Applications and Approvals, 1991-1999

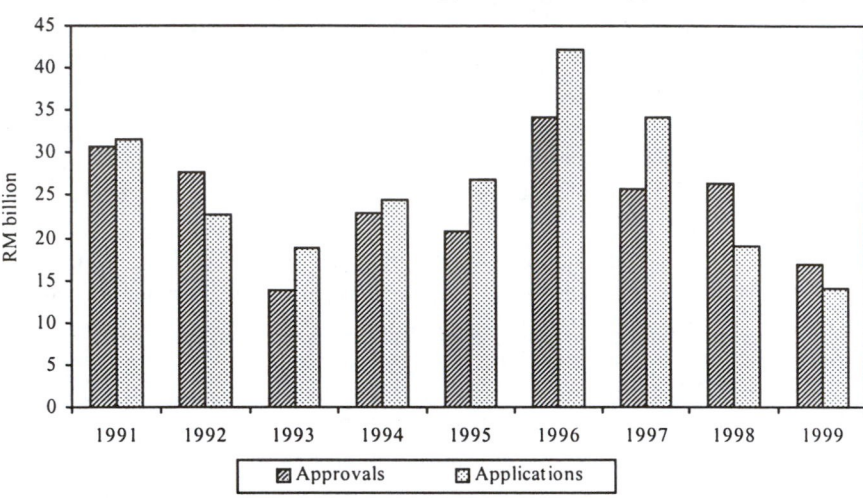

Monetary Stimulus for Stock Market Recovery

While the capital control measures may not have done much for the real economy, it is likely that associated measures have contributed to the stock market's recovery. Many foreign portfolio investors are now attracted to Malaysia by the very capital controls they may once have condemned soon after they were first introduced in September 1998. For them, Malaysia now offers a portfolio investment haven relatively sheltered from the volatility of global capital markets.

The ringgit peg against the greenback — ironically, tantamount to quasi-dollarisation of the currency — and the strict foreign exchange controls has also allowed the Malaysian authorities to pursue expansionary monetary policy while minimising its usual adverse consequences, e.g. price inflation. Despite significant increases in M1 money supply, price inflation has actually been brought down. The loose monetary policy has brought down the cost of credit, generating 'apparent profits and a sense of prosperity' (Shostak 2000), i.e. a wealth effect, which the authorities probably hope will generate a virtuous cycle leading to sustained recovery. As Figures 7.3a to 7.3c suggest, the Kuala Lumpur Stock Exchange Composite Index (KLCI) seems to have been responsive to changes in M1, rather than M2 or M3. However, Figures 7.4a and 7.4b does not suggest a very strong and consistent relationship.

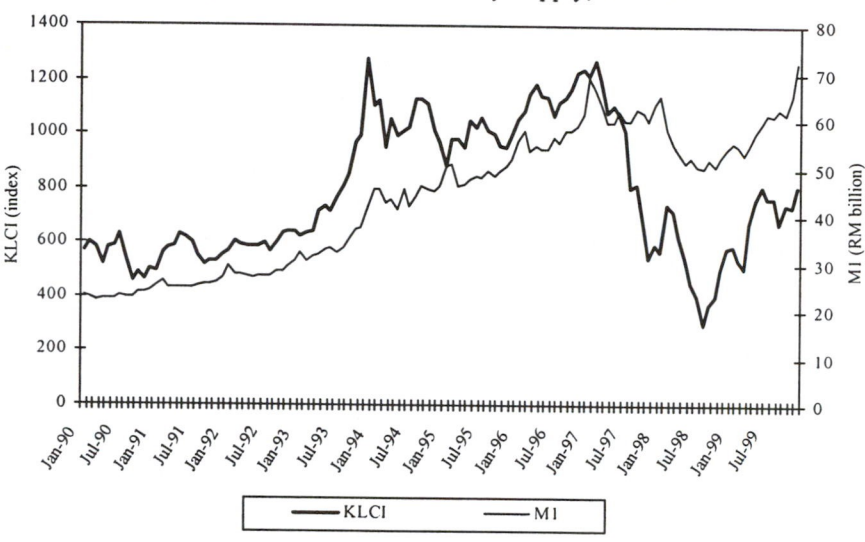

Figure 7.3a
Malaysia: KLCI and M1 Money Supply, 1990-1999

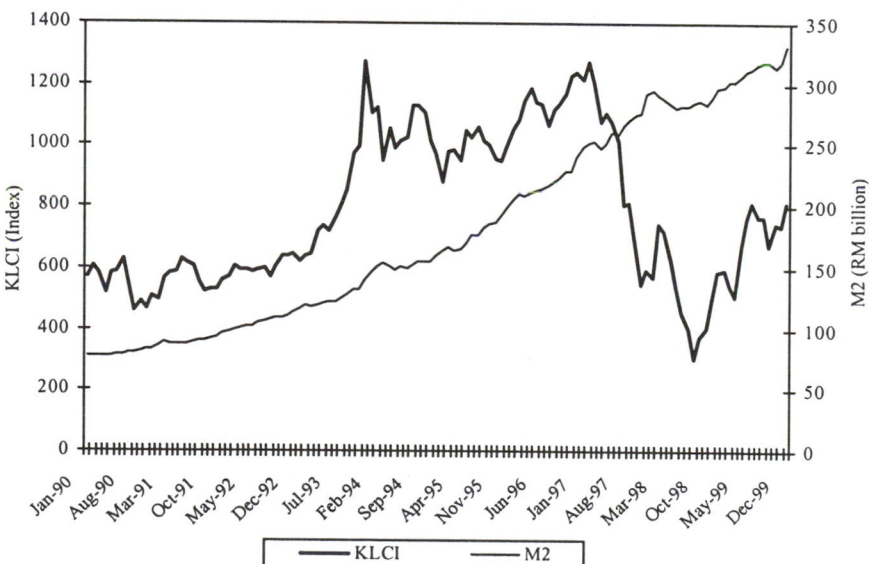

Figure 7.3b
Malaysia: KLCI and M2 Money Supply, 1990-1999

Figure 7.3c
Malaysia: KLCI and M3 Money Supply, 1990-1999

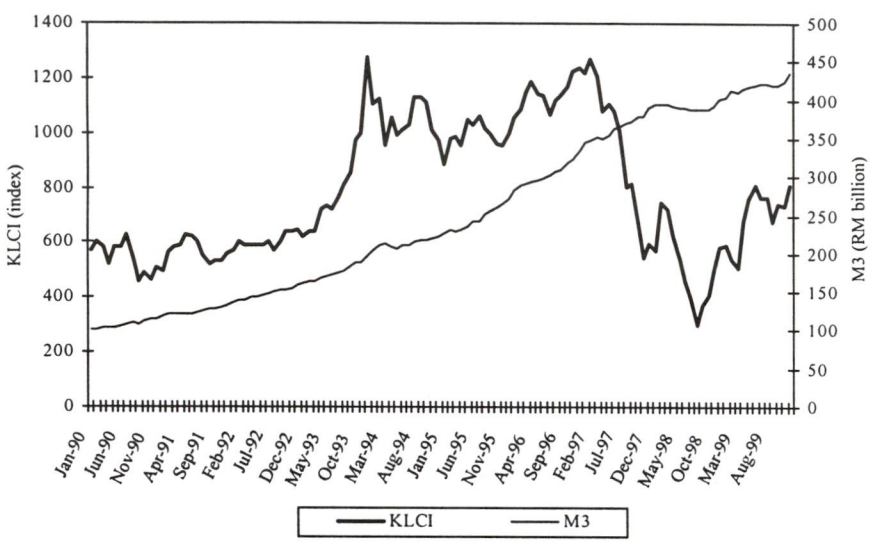

Figure 7.4a
Malaysia: Changes in KLCI and M1, 1990-1999

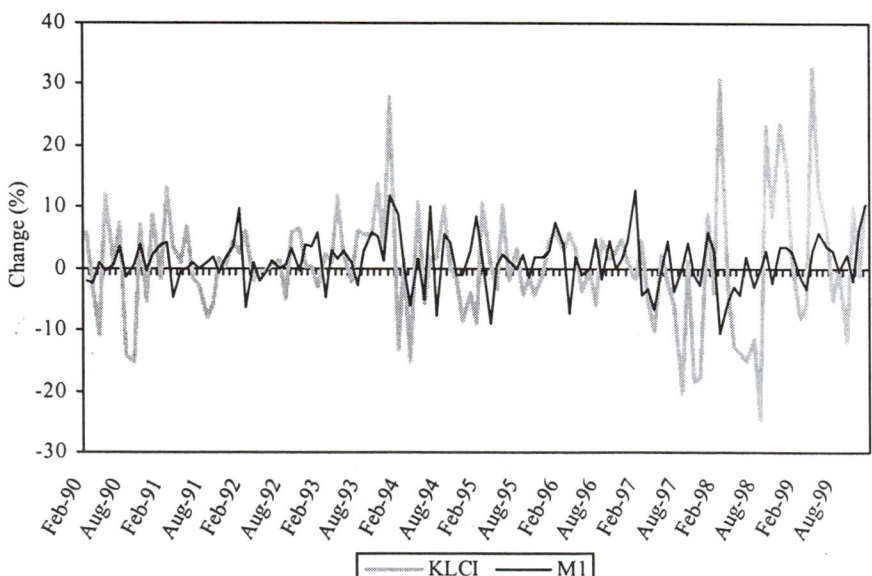

Figure 7.4b
Malaysia: Changes in KLCI and M2, 1990-1999

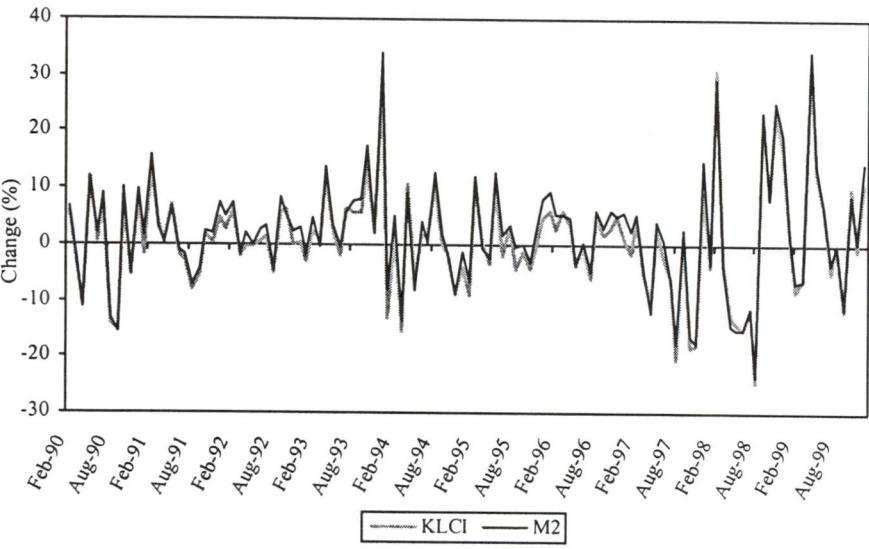

Figure 7.5
Kuala Lumpur Stock Exchange: Market Capitalisation and Composite Index

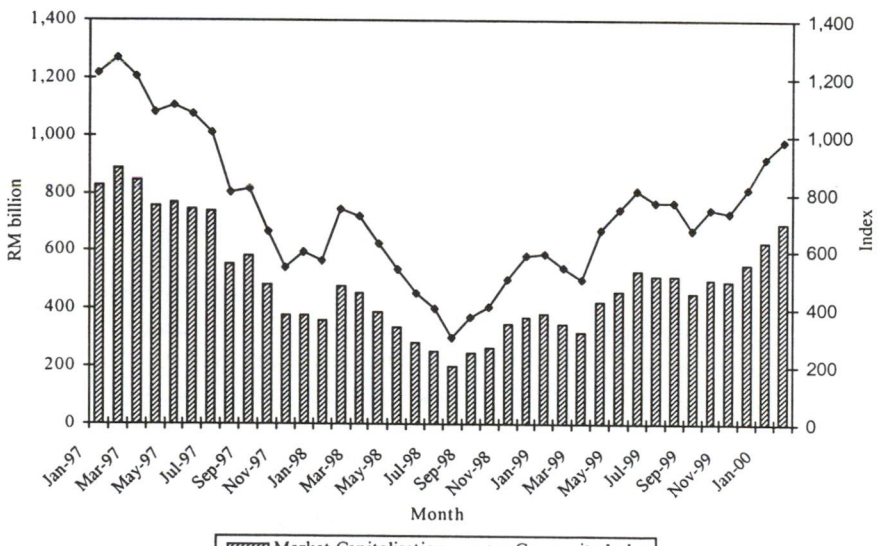

While this strategy has undoubtedly had some success in boosting the stock market since September 1998 (see Figure 7.5), it also exacerbates certain vulnerabilities. The stock market recovery is now more vulnerable than ever to a weakening of the money supply growth momentum. Since M1 cannot indefinitely race well ahead of other monetary growth indicators without exacerbating inflationary and other pressures, this money supply-led recovery strategy could well sow the seeds for the next bust when the central bank inevitably has to tighten monetary policy to stem growing inflationary expectations. Despite low interest rates (the three-month Kuala Lumpur inter-bank rate fell to 3.2 per cent at the end of December 1999 from the pre-controls post-crisis high of 11.05 per cent in April 1998), loan growth remains very low (barely above one per cent in 1999) despite considerable central bank pressure on the banks to increase lending; ominously, a higher pro-portion than ever before has been lent in recent months for share purchases, thus fuelling yet another share price bubble.

Thus, contrary to the claims of the Malaysian government, there is no clear evidence that the capital control measures have contributed decisively to economic recovery. All the other crisis-affected economies turned around during the first quarter of 1999, while Malaysia was the only one to do so in the second quarter of 1999, when some of the other countries registered even higher growth rates. (Hong Kong, the only other place with an even more tightly pegged currency, has been the worst laggard.) On the other hand, Malaysian capital controls have certainly not been the unmitigated disaster that many of its most vociferous and ideological opponents predicted.

There are now three remaining elements left of the controls introduced in September 1998, namely the ringgit peg, non-convertibility on the capital account and restricted convertibility on the current account, and the capital gains tax, though no longer with the higher rate on capital staying for less than a year.

With respect to the peg and convertibility, regional currency volatility has largely abated, and there is little risk in the near to medium-term of another round of sustained attack; hence, there is now little need to maintain the peg for this reason. In any case, it is unclear that the Malaysian peg would stand in the event of a sustained attack on neighbouring currencies, as evidenced by the need for Taiwan to devalue its currency in 1997. The evidence from Hong Kong, with its rigid peg, is far from encouraging — it's upturn has been the weakest in the region. Ironically, despite the regime's strong anti-Western rhetoric, the *status quo* leaves Malaysian exchange rate determination in the hands of the US Federal Reserve and, to a lesser extent, of the Japanese and European central banks.

Some Policy Lessons

Capital controls have not caused the recovery in Malaysia to be slower than in the other crisis countries. The 1998 collapse was less deep in Malaysia than in Thailand and Indonesia, while the recovery in Malaysia has been faster since early 1999, though of course, the pre-crisis problems in Malaysia were less serious to begin with. The Malaysian controls were intended to provide monetary policy independence to reflate the economy, though international developments from August 1998 also created new international monetary conditions that facilitated the adoption of reflationary policies in the rest of the region. While Malaysia missed out on most of the renewed capital flows to the region from the last quarter of 1998, it is not clear that such easily reversible capital inflows are all that desirable. The more serious problem has been the future credibility of government policies, which seems to have adversely affected foreign direct investments into the country (despite official protestations to the contrary) as well as risk premiums for Malaysian securities.

The currently undervalued pegged ringgit has negative implications for a broad recovery, which depends upon imported inputs. It appears that the peg has not really given a major boost to exports, as the official export figures suggest. The regime has also not had other desired effects, as the export base remains narrow, with the most significant growth coming in electronics, i.e. due to fortuitous external demand, while the welcomed increase in the foreign reserves situation has largely resulted from massive import compression. There are costs to maintaining an under-valued ringgit, especially in the context of an economic upturn of what is still a very open economy. An under-valued ringgit may help some exports in the short term, but it also makes imports of capital and intermediate goods more expensive, thus impeding recovery and capacity expansion in the medium term. (Before the crisis, imports were equivalent to more than 90 per cent of GDP.) There are already some early indications of a declining trade surplus as the import compression due to the collapsed ringgit declines. This, together with an apparently stubborn negative services balance, will mean a shrinking current account surplus if the economic upturn continues.

While there is a need to continue to press ahead for international financial reform as well as for new regional monetary arrangements in the absence of adequate global reform, there is little to be gained by retaining the current regime of controls. Instead, if it succeeds in attracting short-term portfolio capital as the various amendments to the regime have sought to do, it would be largely ineffective in the event of another currency and financial panic.

The controls should be dismantled while ensuring an adequate and effective regulatory framework to reduce financial vulnerability and to moderate capital flow surges into and out of the country. Malaysia should not be completely defenceless against another round of speculative attacks. While Malaysia can afford to return to ringgit convertibility, this should be phased in with effective measures to ensure the non-internationalisation of the ringgit to reduce vulnerability to external currency speculation. This can include measures such as not permitting off-shore ringgit accounts as well as non-resident borrowing of ringgit.

Contrary to the official claim that the controls have had no adverse impacts, it appears to have had negative effects, among others, on desired long-term foreign direct investments. Even if this has been due to mis-perceptions, the authorities have nonetheless had to spend inordinate energy and resources trying to correct this misunderstanding. Confidence in the Malaysian government's policy consistency and credibility has been seriously undermined, as have been years of investment promotion efforts. This has not been helped by unnecessarily hostile and ill-informed official rhetoric.

The current regime is now counter-productive and will probably have adverse medium-term, indeed long-term, consequences if it is the intention, as declared by the Prime Minister, to retain the regime until such time as the international financial system is reformed. Hence, it would be desirable to phase out the existing measures in light of their ambiguous contribution to economic recovery and the adverse consequences of retaining the measures. While recognising the utility of portfolio inflows, there is increasing recognition of the need to have protection against rapid massive outflows. Part of that protection has to involve oversight of bank lending to avoid the creation of asset bubbles, which are then used to leverage other activity. Ultimately, however, there are no foolproof guarantees in an increasingly volatile globalised economy.

Since the desired reforms to the international financial architecture are unlikely to materialise in the foreseeable future, the Malaysian government should institute a permanent, but flexible, market-based regime of prudential controls to moderate capital inflows and deter speculative surges, both domestic and foreign, to avert future crises. This would include a managed float of the currency with convertibility, but no internationalisation, meaning, minimally, no off-shore ringgit accounts and limits on off-shore foreign exchange accounts, and limits on foreign borrowings. There is clearly an urgent need for some degree of monetary co-operation in the region. It is now clear that currency and financial crises have a primarily regional character. Hence, regional co-operation is a necessary first step towards the establishment of an East Asian monetary facility. Only responsible Malaysian relations with its neighbours will contribute to realising such regional co-operation.

The window of opportunity offered by the capital controls regime has been abused by certain powerfully-connected business interests, not only to secure publicly funded bail-outs at public expense, but even to consolidate and extend their corporate domination, especially in the crucial financial sector. Capital controls have been part of a package focussed on saving friends of the regime, usually at the public expense. While ostensibly not involving public funds, the government-sponsored 'restructuring' of the ruling party-linked Renong conglomerate will cost the government, and hence the public, billions of ringgit in foregone toll and tax revenue. Also, non-performing loans (NPLs) of the thrice-bankrupted Bank Bumiputra — to be taken over by politically well-connected banking interests — have not been heavily discounted like other banks' NPLs, although it has long abandoned its ostensible 'social agenda' of helping the politically dominant Bumiputera community.

Other elements in the Malaysian government's economic strategy since then reinforce the impression that the capital control measures were probably motivated by political considerations as well as the desire to protect politically well-connected businesses. For example, the Malaysian ringgit's exchange rate was pegged against the US dollar in the afternoon of 2 September 1998, hours before Deputy Prime Minister and Finance Minister Anwar Ibrahim was sacked, probably to pre-empt currency volatility and speculation after the firing. The Malaysian experiment with capital controls has been compromised by political crisis, vested interests and inappropriate policy instruments. Hence, it would be a serious mistake to reject capital controls on account of the flawed Malaysian experience.

Capital controls on outflows and other such efforts to prop up a currency already under attack may ultimately be ineffective and may actually unwittingly subsidise further speculative actions. Instead, measures to insulate the domestic banking system from short-term volatility through regulatory measures and capital controls on easily reversible short-term inflows as well as stricter prudential regulation and supervision may be far more effective and sustainable. International co-operation and co-ordination have often not only provided the best responses during crisis episodes, but have also been important for effective prudential and regulatory initiatives as well as to reduce 'policy arbitrage'.

8

SOCIAL IMPACTS

Jomo K. S. and Lee Hwok Aun

The financial nature of the crisis, the relatively brief (year long) duration of the recession and the largely fortuitous external sources of the recovery have affected the crisis' social or welfare impact. There is no denying that the Malaysian economy experienced an economic downturn from late 1997, with severe contraction through 1998, as the currency crisis developed into a financial crisis, and then, economic recession. Several consequences of the currency and financial crises — e.g. loss of investor confidence, sudden and massive capital outflows, credit crunch — had various adverse effects on the real economy and on social welfare. Like the early debate on the origins of the financial crisis, initial discussion on the social impacts of the recession tended toward extremes of either denial or alarm.

This chapter's review of the main social consequences of the 1997-8 economic crisis in Malaysia does not consider the origins and nature of the currency and financial crises from mid-1997, already covered in preceding chapters. However, it is now generally agreed that the Malaysian economy and population were not as adversely affected as their counterparts in Thailand, South Korea and Indonesia. This is not the place to engage in a comparative analysis of the nature and impact of the crisis in the region. Nevertheless, it has to be noted that the financial crisis was not as severe in Malaysia for various reasons discussed elsewhere in this volume, especially in the first, fourth and seventh chapters.

While the pre-crisis level of indebtedness in Malaysia was very high, the level of foreign exposure was less — as a share of GDP, and especially, as a share of export earnings. Unlike the other three crisis-hit economies that had to seek emergency IMF credit facilities, and were therefore obliged to accept the Fund's conditionalities, the level of foreign liabilities in Malaysia did not exceed its foreign exchange reserves. After the severe banking crisis of the late 1980s, Malaysian prudential regulation was improved and had not been as badly undermined by liberalisation pressures as in the other three economies. There is an ongoing debate about the actual effects of the unusual policy responses associated with capital controls from September 1998. As chapter seven suggests, while the Malaysian government's claims about the success of the controls seem rather exaggerated, the prophecies of doom by its influential monetarist critics have also not been realised.

The 1997-8 crisis reversed the preceding decade-long boom, taking the economy into its most severe recession of the post-war era. In chapter one, consideration was given to some macroeconomic impacts of the crisis. This chapter will look more closely at the impact of the crisis on employment, prices and earnings. Other factors affecting economic welfare, including government expenditures and social transfers during this period, are considered next. Limited mention is made of various official policy responses — much discussed by other studies (Ishak *et al.* 1999; Haflah *et al.* 1999) — because of the uncertain social impacts of most such policy initiatives thus far. Lastly, several conclusions are drawn, giving some consideration to the uneven impact of the crisis as well as of official policy responses. Thus, this chapter also considers some other social implications of the recent crisis which have not received much attention in the literature so far.

This study is constrained by many factors, including the paucity of reliable data and the Malaysian authorities' general reluctance to release socio-economic statistics it deems sensitive. In some respects also, the apparent confusion over the social impacts of the recession mirrors the difficulty and complexity of such inquiry. The actual impact of the economic recession on society — individuals, households and communities — is difficult to empirically measure and assess with accuracy and objectivity. At another level, the causes of recession are also difficult to identify, because the links between causes and effects are not always direct or obvious, and also subject to considerable theoretical dispute.

There is also a need to distinguish other economic trends from the direct social impacts of the crisis even though they might occur simultaneously. For this study, for example, it is difficult to separate out the adverse impacts of international price movements from those of other non-economic changes (e.g. weather) on the Malaysian economy during the period of the crisis.

Income

The earlier chapters on macroeconomic and financial aspects of the recession lays the foundation for more specific discussion of the impact and transmission of the crisis and contraction to individuals and households in society. The Asian Development Bank has suggested four channels through which the financial and economic crisis has produced adverse social impacts:

1) decreased employment, earnings and incomes;
2) inflation of consumption items;
3) reduced government transfers and weakened crisis-alleviating programs; and
4) decline in demand for migrant labour (Haflah *et al.* 1999: 6).

While this list is limited, it provides a starting point for our discussion.

Employment and Wages

With full employment by the mid-1990s, real income gains increased in Malaysia before 1998. The recession, therefore, came as a shock to an economy that had grown accustomed to plentiful job opportunities and labour shortages. The number of net additional contributors to the Employees Provident Fund (EPF) — an indicator of employment creation/contraction — dropped by 17.5 per cent from January-September 1997 to January-September 1998. While the most devastating impact of the recession was on those who lost their jobs, the recession also impacted on others who did not lose their jobs. Wages form a significant proportion of total household incomes. For many households, especially those with low and medium incomes, wages are the principal incomes. In a recession, reductions in economic activity — and consequently, in demand for labour — push wages down. Malaysian labour unions have limited membership and influence, often failing to safeguard workers' wages. While the welfare of the low-income groups may not receive much media coverage or policy attention, their plight is nonetheless real. Most have experienced reduced real incomes because of reduced overtime work opportunities (on which many workers depend for their supplementary incomes), lower nominal wage rates and price inflation, exacerbated by currency depreciation (Ishak *et al.* 1999: 42).

The impact of the economic recession on private sector wages may be inferred from production and employment data. Juxtaposing Tables 1.2 and 1.3 on GDP growth with Table 8.1 on employment growth, one confirms the expected relationship between the two. In the pre-crisis boom years,

Table 8.1
Malaysia: Employment by Sector, 1994-1999 (% annual change)

	1994	*1995*	*1996*	*1997*	*1998*	*1999*[*]
Total	1.4	5.5	5.3	4.6	-2.5	1.7
Agriculture, forestry and fishing	3.2	2.9	-0.1	-1.6	-4.6	-0.1
Mining and quarrying	5.5	-0.5	1.2	1.6	1.2	-0.7
Manufacturing	8.6	6.4	10.0	6.5	-4.1	4.0
Construction	9.9	20.2	11.0	10.1	-7.6	-0.7
Finance, insurance, real estate and business services	6.0	12.3	5.1	9.5	-2.6	0.6
Transport and communications	6.4	7.3	3.7	5.8	0.4	1.5
Government services	0.5	0.1	0.2	0.2	0.2	0.2
Other services	2.1	8.4	5.3	5.8	2.1	2.1

Note: [*] Estimate.
Source: *Economic Report*, various issues, Table 6.1.

Malaysian workers enjoyed an environment of burgeoning employment. Table 8.1 shows how high rates of employment generation — of close to five per cent per annum — were sustained from 1995 to 1997. Yet, these rates remained lower than the corresponding economic activity growth rates — around eight per cent per annum — implying growth in GDP per worker or productivity. Employment in manufacturing, construction and non-government services grew most in the latter half of the 1990s. Employment in construction fell most sharply in 1998, while manufacturing, agriculture, as well as financial and business services were also hard hit; manufacturing continued to experience severe job losses in 1999 as well. The 1999 employment figures suggest some generation of new jobs as well as abatement of job losses, with a net increase in employment, reflecting the end of the recession and the onset of recovery.

Table 8.2 summarises data on jobs created or lost in Malaysia from 1997 to 1999. It is worth noting that the sectoral distribution of employment did not experience any significant shift, except for the increase in manufacturing's share of total employment, from 26.4 per cent in 1998 to 27.0 per cent in 1999. As expected, the impact of the financial crisis on employment was

Table 8.2
Malaysia: Employment by Sector, 1996-1999

Sector	Employment ('000)				Jobs Created ('000)		
	1996	1997	1998	1999	1997	1998	1999
Agriculture, Forestry, Livestock and Fishing	1,492 (17.5)	1,468 (16.5)	1,401 (16.2)	1,399 (15.9)	-23	-67	-2
Mining and Quarrying	41 (0.5)	42 (0.5)	42 (0.5)	42 (0.5)	1	0	0
Manufacturing	2,230 (26.4)	2,375 (26.9)	2,277 (26.4)	2,368 (27.0)	144	-97	91
Construction	796 (9.4)	876 (9.9)	810 (9.4)	804 (9.2)	80	-66	-6
Transport, Storage and Communications	410 (4.8)	434 (4.9)	435 (5.0)	442 (5.0)	24	2	7
Finance, Insurance, Real Estate, and Business Services	392 (4.6)	429 (4.8)	418 (4.8)	420 (4.8)	37	-11	3
Government Services[a]	871 (10.3)	873 (9.8)	875 (10.1)	877 (10.0)	2	2	2
Other Services[b]	2,195 (25.8)	2,321 (26.1)	2,339 (27.0)	2,389 (27.1)	127	18	50
Total	8,465	8,891	8,669	8,813	426	-221	144

Notes: Figures in parentheses denote percentage share of total.
[a] Includes public administration, health, education and defence.
[b] Includes electricity, gas and water, wholesale and retail trade, hotel and restaurants and other services.

Source: *Economic Report 1999/2000*, Table 6.1.

most pronounced in construction and manufacturing. However, the economy as a whole did not experience much structural change despite the huge loss of 221,000 jobs in 1998. In 1998, many jobs were lost in sectors badly hit by the financial crisis: 97,000 in manufacturing, 66,000 in construction, and 11,000 in finance, insurance and business services. The severity of the volatility of employment is underscored by the many jobs created in these same sectors in 1997: 144,000 in manufacturing, 80,000 in construction, and 37,000 in finance, insurance and business services. Agriculture, forestry and fishing also saw employment down by 67,000 in 1998, but other factors un-related to the crisis had affected the production of and demand for primary commodities. Indeed, agriculture has experienced job losses before and throughout the 1997-9 period.

The impact on employment is reflected by other indicators as well. As noted above, changes in EPF contributions broadly parallel formal sector employment. Comparing the first eight months of 1997 with 1998, the number of net additional contributors to the EPF declined from 186,805 to 154,029, i.e. by 17.5 per cent. The number of defaulters probably reflects the economic resilience of employers. During the first half of 1998, 15,561, or 5.4 per cent of total registered employers defaulted on EPF contributions. In contrast, for the whole of 1997, 13,143, or 4.4 per cent of total registered employers defaulted (Ishak *et al.* 1999, Table 3, p. 20). The total amount contributed to the EPF increased slightly from RM14.6 billion in 1997 to RM14.8 billion in 1998, i.e. at an annual growth rate of 1.05 per cent, which was much lower than the growth rate of 13.30 per cent between 1996 and 1997. Meanwhile, the amounts withdrawn from the EPF increased from RM3.6 billion (1996) to RM5.7 billion (1997) and RM8.4 billion (1998), i.e. at annual growth rates of 56.1 per cent and 47.6 per cent. Prior to 1996, EPF withdrawals grew by 15.1 per cent annually on average (BNM, Table IV.1). Meanwhile, the excess of contributions over withdrawals decreased from RM9.3 billion in 1996 to RM8.9 billion in 1997 and RM6.4 billion in 1998, reversing the previously steady growth dating back to 1987. Since the mid-eighties, there have been growing fears that EPF investments in the stock market have been used to support certain politically well connected share counters or to serve public policy objectives other than the contributors' interest in maximising returns to their savings. Such fears gained greater currency in the aftermath of the crisis, especially after the government announced its intention in September 1997 to support certain investors to save them from financial distress.

The relationship between production and employment decreases are not consistent or straightforward (see Tables 1.2 and 8.1), though output decreases give some idea of how wages have been affected by the downturn. During 1998, in manufacturing and construction, the drops in output (-13.7 and -23.0 per cent) considerably exceeded the declines in employment (-4.1 and -7.6 per cent). In contrast, the drop in agricultural employment (-5.4 per cent) exceeded output decline (-4.0 per cent). More detailed data on wage trends suggest varying impacts of the recession on different sub-sectors owing to different conditions. According to the Ministry of Human Resources' *Labour Market Report*, employment in certain non-manufacturing sub-sectors rose in 1998: coconut (4.5 per cent), oil palm (4.8 per cent), insurance, real estate and business services (4.2 per cent), retail (3.6 per cent) and wholesale trade (0.8 per cent). Within the manufacturing sector, the following sub-sectors recorded employment growth: crude oil refining (10.9 per cent), industrial chemicals (4.3 per cent), wood and cork products except furniture (3.3 per cent), textiles (1.5 per cent) and rubber products (0.3 per cent).

According to the *Economic Report, 1998/1999*, the average nominal wage per worker increased by 6.4 per cent in the first seven months of 1998, compared with an increase of 11.1 per cent for the corresponding period in 1997. Wage increases in negotiated agreements averaged around 10 per cent during the first seven months of 1998 — compared with 13.1 per cent in 1997. In the manufacturing sector, where 53 per cent of agreements were concluded, average wages grew at a slower rate of 8.4 per cent in 1998 — as against 15.0 per cent in 1997. Overall wage growth in manufacturing slowed down markedly in 1998 to 0.3 per cent, from 8.4 per cent in 1996 and 7.3 per cent in 1997 (BNM, *Annual Report 1998*, Appendix Table 1.1). Surveys found that workers on oil palm estates fared better in 1998 due to higher palm oil prices (see Ishak 1999, Chapter 2).

Labour union members comprise a small proportion of all wage earners and have limited influence in Malaysia. Nonetheless, collective agreements are signed every year, which, to an extent, reflect prevailing trends in the formal labour market and the relative bargaining power of management versus labour (see Table 8.3). Wage increases in collective agreements in most sectors were smaller in 1998 than in 1997. In manufacturing, where most collective agreements were signed (146 out of 284 in 1998), negotiated increases averaged 8.0 per cent in 1998, compared to 15.0 per cent in 1997. The increases were also smaller, notably in transportation (6.1 per cent in 1998 compared to 10.0 per cent in 1997) and services (10.1 per cent in 1998, 14.1 per cent in 1997). But collective wage agreements in some other sectors involved higher increases, e.g. wholesale and retail trade (13.8 per cent in 1998, 11.8 per cent in 1997) and mining (10.6 per cent in 1998, 7.7 per cent

Table 8.3

Malaysia: Number of Collective Agreements Signed by Sector, 1994-1998

	1994	*1995*	*1996*	*1997*	*1998*	*1999*
Total	348	257	398	412	284	268
	(112.8)	(79.3)	(113.3)	(130.0)	(142.5)	(133.1)
Agriculture, forestry and	15	8	32	18	11	30
fishing	(1.5)	(0.1)	(1.3)	(36.0)	(6.7)	(54.3)
Mining and quarrying	0	0	6	7	4	6
	(0)	(0)	(1.3)	(0.4)	(0.2)	(0.5)
Manufacturing	199	196	210	241	146	134
	(54.9)	(53.5)	(47.7)	(63.4)	(37.3)	(27.6)
Construction	–	–	1	–	1	2
	(–)	(–)	(0.1)	(–)	(0.2)	(0.1)
Finance, insurance, real estate	44	53	42	106	75	17
and business services	(6.7)	(10.1)	(4.9)	(18.8)	(54.7)	(10.1)
Transport and	31	31	55	31	37	31
communications	(3.6)	(3.1)	(9.9)	(0.7)	(42.4)	(5.0)
Government services	–	–	–	–	–	–
Other services	40	52	53	32	7	n.a.
	(10.0)	(44.5)	(36.5)	(6.5)	(0.1)	(n.a.)

Note: Figures in parentheses indicate thousands of workers involved.
Sources: *Economic Report, 1998/1999*, Table 6.1, pp. lx-lxi, BNM, *Annual Report 1998*,
        Table A.29, p. 284, Ministry of Human Resources, http://www5.jaring.my/jppm/
        Contents.htm.

in 1997). The smaller number of collective agreements concluded in 1998 reflects the reduced bargaining clout of workers in recessionary times. Importantly, only one collective agreement was signed between construction workers and employers between 1994 and 1998, denoting the low level of unionisation in the sector, now dominated by foreign, often undocumented contract workers.

Worker-management relations remained stable during 1997 and 1998. In 1997, five strikes, involving 812 workers, were recorded, resulting in a loss of 2,396 workdays. In 1998, the number of strikes and workers involved increased to 12 and 1,777 respectively, though the number of workdays lost only rose slightly to 2,635. In 1999, one less strike was recorded, although the 11 strikes involved more workers (3,452), all of whom were in the agriculture or manufacturing sectors. Workdays lost amounted to 10,554, of which agriculture, forestry and fishing accounted for 5,219 and manufacturing 5,335. Only 14 pickets were recorded in 1998, down from 34 in 1997. The number increased to 21 in 1999. Industrial disputes were also slightly less numerous in 1998 than in 1997, but involved far fewer workers. Disputes in 1997 totalled 463, involving 139,187 workers, while 442 in 1998 involved 95,530 workers. 1999 saw 496 disputes, involving 90,278 workers. On the whole, data on labour disputes do not show clear trends reflecting either recession or recovery.

Not long after the onset of the financial crisis, wages in the public sector were reduced or frozen, as part of the early government response to the crisis. Ministers' salaries were cut by 10 per cent, senior civil servants' by 5 per cent, while a freeze was imposed on salary increments for those in the higher ranks of the civil service. Public Service Department data, updated in April 1999, show the majority of government employees in the second lowest rung on the salary scale, with 44.5 per cent receiving RM500-1,000 monthly; 29.6 per cent receiving RM1,001-1,500, while 12.4 per cent were paid RM1,501-2,000. As the majority of civil servants receive relatively low remuneration, a significant fraction encountered difficulties making ends meet with the inflation of 1998. However, lower wages, exacerbated by higher inflation, was compensated for by the financial and psychological security of public sector employment. Public sector employment was generally protected from the recession. Government employees later gained from the government's counter-cyclical spending increases from mid-1998, including a RM7 billion fiscal stimulus package (*White Paper 1999*). Civil servants also benefited from government inducements for political support in the wake of the economic and political crises, before the November 1999 general elections and the May 2000 ruling party elections.

Unemployment and Retrenchment

According to official estimates, unemployment in Malaysia rose, but did not increase as much as in Thailand, South Korea or Indonesia. The total number of layoffs reported for 1998 was 81,672. The official unemployment rate for 1998 was 3.2 per cent, compared to 2.6 per cent for 1997 and 2.5 per cent for 1996. These percentages correspond to the estimated increase in unemployed persons, rising from 233,100 in 1997 to 443,200 in 1998. A total of 83,865 retrenchments were officially recorded in Malaysia in 1998, a remarkable 345 per cent rise from 18,863 in 1997 and 7,773 in 1996. With general economic recovery, total retrenchments in 1999 also decreased to 37,357 (*Labour Market Report, 1999*).

However, these figures should be taken with circumspection, since reporting retrenchments only became mandatory from 1 February 1998. In addition, reporting employers tend to be more law-abiding and responsible, i.e. more inclined to be concerned with employee welfare. These statistics obviously do not include unreported cases of retrenchment, let alone other job losses (e.g. of contract labour) or harsh treatment of employees. Employees have reported (to the MTUC and the Ministry of Human Resources) intimidation and coercion to accept lower wages and heavier work schedules (Ishak *et al.* 1999: 22). The situation has probably improved, since such strong-arm tactics appear to have coincided with the worst stages of the recession, and there is little evidence of prolonged opportunistic behaviour by employers after labour market conditions improved. Correspondingly, Table 8.4 shows that official registered retrenchments increased rapidly by 345 per cent in 1998, before falling back by 55 per cent in 1999. Table 8.5 shows total retrenchments remaining high throughout 1998 and peaking in the third quarter before declining. This pattern was also true of manufacturing, whereas construction peaked earlier in the first quarter and services in the second quarter.

The sectoral and temporal distribution of retrenchments sheds some more light on the impacts of the crisis on labour. Manufacturing was clearly worst hit, accounting for 54.0 per cent of total retrenchments in 1998 (Table 8.6). Services also suffered, with workers retrenched from retail and wholesale trade, restaurant and hotel comprising 12.4 per cent of total retrenched workers, and 7.8 per cent from finance, insurance, property and business services. Officially recognised retrenched construction workers came up to

Table 8.4
Malaysia: Retrenchments, 1996-1999

Year	Total	Percentage Change
1996	7,773	–
1997	18,863	143%
1998	83,865	345%
1999	37,357	-55%

Source: *Mid-Term Review of the 7MP*, Table 4-3, p. 100; Ministry of Human Resources, *Labour Market Report 1999*.

Table 8.5
Malaysia: Retrenchment of Workers by Quarter, 1998-2000

	98Q1	98Q2	98Q3	98Q4	99Q1	99Q2	99Q3	99Q4	00H1*
Total	20,818	18,693	26,238	18,116	11,454	10,304	7,690	7,909	11,221
Sector:									
Agriculture, forestry and fishing	1,177	676	1,698	1,557	358	842	527	2,089	300
Mining	159	338	272	108	298	133	21	21	895
Manufacturing	12,273	7,602	15,382	9,894	6,336	5,584	4,976	3,589	7,881
Construction	2,665	2,584	2,152	1,933	1,269	927	382	291	895
Services	4,437	7,493	6,727	4,623	3,191	2,818	1,784	1,919	2,001
of which:									
Wholesale and retail trade, hotel and restaurant	2,220	2,725	3,304	2,185	1,301	1,160	803	1,056	593
Transport and communications	373	845	408	381	189	209	246	46	462
Finance, insurance, real estate and business services	1,389	2,038	2,290	879	1,040	1,007	338	404	518
Social and private services	455	1,885	724	1,178	661	404	299	412	428
Others	107	0	7	1	2	38	0	0	0

Note: * 1 January until 20 May 2000.
Sources: BNM, *Quarterly Economic Bulletin (QEB), Second Quarter 1998*, p. 96; *QEB, First Quarter 1999*, p. 38; *QEB, Third Quarter 1999*, p. 157; *QEB, Fourth Quarter 1999*, p. 230; and *QEB, First Quarter 2000*, p. 13. Ministry of Human Resources, Malaysia, *Labour Market Report*, Table 2 or URL: www.jaring.my/ksm/synopsis.htm.

Table 8.6
Malaysia: Number of Registered Retrenchments by Sector, 1998

Sector	No. of Retrenchments	% of Total
Manufacturing	45,021	54.0
Construction	9,294	11.1
Retail and wholesale trade, restaurant and hotel	10,355	12.4
Finance, insurance, property and business services	6,502	7.8
Agriculture, forestry and fishing	5,108	6.1
Social services	4,223	5.1
Other services	2,938	3.5
Total	83,441	100.0

Source: Ministry of Human Resources, *Labour Market Report*, 26 December 1998.

only 11.1 per cent of the total retrenched. Termination of work and, in many cases, deportation, were attractive cheaper options.

The rise in the official unemployment rate amidst the crisis was surprisingly small, considering the scale of the downturn, possibly because undocumented workers dominated the most hard-hit sector, construction. The docile labour force generally had no choice but to accept retrenchment, pay cuts and reduced working hours. Pre-crisis full employment and limited government registration of the unemployed are among other main reasons why the official unemployment rate in 1998 was not as high as expected. Notably, the total number of job vacancies reported by employers at the end of 1998 was 74,610, many of which were in the plantation sector. The dearth of interest in these jobs partly reflects the poor wage and working conditions in the sector.

When other factors are taken into account, it appears that the low official unemployment figure may be misleading. First, the official definition of employment in Malaysia — i.e. working at least one hour per week — understates the extent of under-employment. Many people are merely under-employed, and not unemployed by this definition of employment. Thus, the extent to which official unemployment figures reflects workers' conditions is questionable. Still, changes in the official unemployment rate roughly reflect actual economic conditions. The reduction of the annual official unemployment rate to 3.0 per cent in 1999 (from 3.2 per cent in 1998) was slight. However, recovery is better reflected by monthly unemployment rates, which fell from 4.5 per cent in March, to 3.3 per cent in June and to 2.9 per cent in September.

Second, the majority of workers in the construction sector, which was the most devastated by the crisis, were foreigners; approximately 80 per cent of construction workers were believed to be foreign immigrants (see Wong 1999). For the calendar year 1998, the official data states that 89.2 per cent of the retrenched workers were Malaysian citizens or residents. However, it seems most likely that very few foreign workers who lost their jobs would have registered as unemployed. The majority of them are believed to be illegally present in the country, with most remaining undocumented.

The Home Ministry estimated that 207,946 illegal foreign workers returned to their home countries between January and August 1998, though there is evidence of considerable re-entry. According to the authorities, 48.1 per cent returned voluntarily, 27.9 per cent were deported and 24.0 per cent were 'repatriated under the government's amnesty program, which allowed them to leave without being penalized' (Ishak *et al*. 1999: 32). These numbers are sizeable, but may not even represent a tenth of the foreign labour presence in Malaysia. The total number of foreign workers in Malaysia at the outbreak of the crisis has been estimated to be well over two million. Some evidence of re-entry, or new entry, may be garnered from official sources, which again, probably only reflect a fraction of total foreign worker flows. The Ministry of Human Resources reported that in 1999, the Technical Committee on Foreign Workers at the Ministry of Home Affairs approved the importation of 232,270 foreign workers — including extension of work permits and redistribution of workers. These workers were primarily designated for plantations, manufacturing and selected services (*Labour Market Report 1999*).

Most of the registered retrenchments were located in the major urban centres. Hence, the states contributing most to the total number of registered layoffs were: Selangor with 23.8 per cent, Penang with 20.2 per cent and Kuala Lumpur with 13.0 per cent. However, there appears to have been significant variation over time. For example, for the week 20-26 December 1998, the states that reported the largest shares of all layoffs were Kedah and Perlis with 47.6 per cent, Penang with 23.7 per cent and Johor with 17.0 per cent.

The Employment Act, 1955, stipulates that employers are obliged to compensate employees at between 1.25 to 1.75 of the last drawn monthly pay for each year of service to give retrenched workers some respite while searching for new jobs. Compliance with these regulations has not been commendable. On 5 October 1998, the Human Resources Minister announced that RM56.7 million due as compensation to 43,889 workers retrenched during the first seven months of 1998 had not been paid by their 2,094 employers. In other words, about 23 per cent of the legally prescribed compensation was still due to the workers (Ishak *et al.* 1999: 20).

Retrenchment was not always the most preferred means of adapting to adverse labour market conditions; for example, if the employer anticipated that imminent economic recovery would necessitate reemployment. It is usually also not the desirable option from the perspective of worker welfare. Other options for employers to cut labour costs include pay cuts, voluntary lay-offs and voluntary separation schemes. From 1 August 1998, pay-cuts, voluntary lay-offs and voluntary separation also became subject to mandatory reporting. The government amended the Employment Act 1955 and introduced guidelines on alternatives to retrenchment such as pay cuts and work hour reductions. Employers were also encouraged to encourage and provide for part-time employment and flexible working hours, and to raise wages in line with productivity. From August to December 1998, pay cuts (67.2 per cent) exceeded voluntary separation schemes (28.4 per cent) and voluntary lay-offs (4.4 per cent). The alternative to retrenchment most frequently used by employers in 1999 was still the pay-cut. But pay-cuts were preferred (by employers) over voluntary separation schemes by a smaller margin than in 1998, with 50.5 per cent of employers opting for pay-cuts, 45.5 per cent choosing voluntary separation schemes, and 4.0 per cent choosing voluntary lay-offs. As to reasons for retrenchment, in 1998, 59.9 per cent of employers cited reduction in demand for their products or services, while 11 per cent cited high production costs, 8.1 per cent company reorganisation, 6.4 per cent closure and 2.4 per cent sale of the companies (MHR 1999). Quarterly findings of the main reasons for retrenchments varied significantly over the year (Table 8.7).

While job losses and retrenchments both rose sharply in 1998, 74,610 unfilled vacancies were reported in 1998, compared to 64,463 at the end of 1997 (MHR 1999). A high proportion of the unfilled vacancies was in the plantation sector. The two main explanations for this anomaly were the skill mismatches of unemployed workers with the job vacancies and worker unwillingness to take available jobs — especially on plantations — because of low pay, poor working or living conditions, and other reasons (see Haflah *et al* 1999: 38). In 1999, 108,318 vacancies were reported, signifying some improvement in economic conditions (*Labour Market Report 1999*).

Table 8.7
Malaysia: Employers' Reasons for Laying Off Workers, 1998-2000 (percentages)

Reason	98Q2	98Q3	1998	99Q1	99Q2	99Q3	99Q4	1999	00Q1
Decline in demand	10.0	60.0	52.2	28.0	–	15.0	21.3	45.0	–
Business slowdown	57.0	–	–	–	–	–	–	–	–
Reduce production costs	–	10.0	–	–	–	11.0	–	–	–
Corporate restructuring	–	–	8.1	12.0	–	–	11.2	12.9	41.6
Winding-up	14.0	10.0	6.4	–	–	48.0	28.7	11.0	–
Sale of company	–	–	–	15.0	–	–	–	–	–

Notes: Such data only became available after retrenchments increased in the wake of the crisis. The *Quarterly Economic Bulletin* seems only to report the three main reasons in any particular quarter. There was no *QEB* for the fourth quarter of 1998, as such quarterly information would previously have been incorporated in the BNM's *Annual Report*. Hence, the information for the fourth quarter of 1999 was made available for the first time. It also seems that BNM data categorised as due to 'slowdown in business activity' were classified under 'Other Reasons' by the Ministry of Human Resources' *Labour Market Report*, 26 December 1998. The 1998 figures used here are from BNM, *Annual Report, 1999*, p. 73; these figures differ from those presented in BNM, *Annual Report, 1998*, p. 76, as well as those presented in Ministry of Human Resources, *Labour Market Report*, 26 December 1998.

Sources: BNM, *Quarterly Economic Bulletin (QEB), Second Quarter 1998*, p. 96; *QEB, First Quarter 1999*, p. 38; *QEB, Third Quarter 1999*, p. 157; *QEB, Fourth Quarter 1999*, p. 230. BNM, *Annual Report, 1999*, p. 73.

Households experiencing declining wage incomes would presumably reduce savings or even draw on their savings. But Malaysia's savings rate, which has been among the highest in the world, did not decline much in 1998, remaining above 40 per cent. Access to and availability of savings varies among households, especially among those with different income levels. Accordingly, for example, middle- and high-income strata households may have more savings to draw upon. In contrast, lower income households tend to have little left over from consumption to channel into savings. The increase in inflation probably adversely affected savings. Those with fixed incomes, including pensioners, saw their real incomes dwindle in the face of higher living costs and lower deposit interest rates.

Due to the economic slowdown, the job market for graduates became more competitive. The number of registered job-seekers holding degrees or diplomas increased from 5,634 in 1997 to 12,938 in 1998 (by 129.6 per cent), and to 15,396 in 1999 (by 19.0 per cent) (*Labour Market Report 1999*). The number of registered unemployed graduates was 4,592 in September 1998, much more than the 2,150 in September 1997 (Ishak *et al*. 1999: 19). Table 8.8 suggests that white collar workers (professional and technical, clerical, others) were most likely to register themselves as unemployed. Table 8.9 suggests a generally higher proportion of registered female unemployed as well as a greater increase in male registered unemployed during 1998. The number of unemployed females, however, increased proportionally more in the first half of 1999. Table 8.10 shows that the number of officially registered unemployed in the 20-24 age category increased more relative to other age

Table 8.8
Malaysia: Registered Unemployed by Occupational Group, 1994-1999

	1994	*1995*	*1996*	*1997*	*1998*	*1999*[*]
Total job-seekers	26,445	25,546	21,747	23,762	33,345	37,315
Production related workers	9,198	8,210	6,989	8,156	9,845	8,828
Agriculture	132	98	87	67	95	88
Services	584	674	574	437	823	678
Clerical	13,589	13,181	11,219	11,066	14,712	18,637
Professional and technical	2,149	2,629	2,237	2,797	5,281	6,150
Others	793	754	641	1,239	2,589	2,934

Note: [*] Until end of July only.
Source: *Economic Report, 1999/2000*, Table 6.2, pp. lii-liii.

Table 8.9
Malaysia: Registered Unemployed by Gender, 1994-1999

End of Period	Total Job Seekers	Male		Female	
		No.	%	No.	%
1994	26,445	15,095	57.1	11,350	42.9
1995	25,546	13,935	54.5	11,611	45.5
1996	21,747	11,863	54.6	9,884	45.4
1997	23,762	12,680	53.4	11,082	46.6
1998	33,345	18,832	56.5	14,513	43.5
1999*	37,315	19,948	53.5	17,367	46.5

Note: * Until end of July only.
Sources: *Economic Report, 1998/1999*, Table 6.2, pp. lxii-lxiii; *Economic Report, 1999/2000*, Table 6.2, pp. lii-liii.

Table 8.10
Malaysia: Registered Unemployed by Age Cohort, 1994-1999

End of Period	Total Job Seekers	15-19 years		20-24 years		25-29 years	
		No.	%	No.	%	No.	%
1994	26,445	7,557	28.6	11,315	42.8	3,998	15.1
1995	25,546	7,800	30.5	10,967	42.9	3,576	14.0
1996	21,747	6,640	30.5	9,336	42.9	3,044	14.0
1997	23,762	5,904	24.8	11,251	47.3	3,371	14.2
1998	33,345	7,778	23.3	15,334	46.0	5,209	15.6
1999*	37,315	10,586	28.4	16,412	44.0	5,294	14.2

Note: * Until end of July only.
Sources: *Economic Report, 1998/1999*, Table 6.2, pp. lxii-lxiii; *Economic Report, 1999/2000*, Table 6.2, pp. lii-liii.

groups, i.e. from 44.8 per cent of total registered unemployed in 1997 to 48.7 per cent at the end of July 1998. One factor should be noted in interpreting this observation. Mid-1998 saw two cohorts of Malaysian university graduates come on the job market because of an earlier reduction of non-medical university education from four to three years. This untimely adjustment doubled the number of fresh graduate job applicants from these universities, unfortunately at a time of low or negative employment generation.

Labour force participation rates declined from 85.7 to 83.4 per cent for males, from 47.4 to 44.2 per cent for females, and from 67.0 to 64.3 per cent in aggregate between 1997 and 1998 respectively. These rates probably improved in 1999, and should continue to rise with economic recovery. The official annual unemployment figures in Table 8.11 show a 1998 unemployment rate similar to that for 1995, suggesting that official unemployment statistics probably understate the actual impact of the crisis on workers, especially those casually employed, particularly undocumented foreign workers.

Women

Table 8.11 shows how labour force participation rates for women did not decrease significantly in 1998. Retrenchment figures, however, reveal some discrepancy in the impact of the recession on men and women (also see Table 8.9). Women comprise about two-fifths of the labour force, but comprised 42.3 per cent of retrenched workers in 1998 and 48.1 per cent in 1999. The majority (64.5 per cent, or 23,387)) of retrenched women were from the manufacturing sector, where weaker unionisation among women and other factors made them more vulnerable to coercion and exploitation. Female-

Table 8.11
Malaysia: Labour Force Participation and Unemployment Rates, 1991-1999

Year	Labour Force Participation Rate			Unemployment Rate
	Total	Male	Female	
1991	66.6	85.7	47.5	4.6
1992	66.7	85.7	47.6	3.7
1993	66.8	87.0	46.1	3.0
1994	66.8	87.1	46.5	2.9
1995	64.5	83.8	44.3	3.1
1996	65.8	84.8	45.8	2.5
1997	67.0	85.7	47.4	2.4
1998	64.3	83.4	44.2	3.2
1999[*]	64.3	83.4	44.2	3.0

Note: [*] Estimate.
Source: *Economic Report*, various issues, Table 6.1.

headed households, of which there are an estimated 630,500 in Malaysia, or 16.6 per cent of all households, also warrant special concern (Ishak *et al.* 1999: 47). These women — who typically perform most, if not all household chores in addition to earning incomes for themselves and their families — tend to have little in terms of support facilities or networks to fall back on.

Human Resource Development

Malaysia's human resources have been widely credited as a major contributor to economic development. A healthy and educated labour force is a pre-requisite for rapid and successful assimilation of new technologies, and for increasing productivity and efficiency. In this respect, the impact of the recession on human resources may be more long term, due to the cumula-tive effects of poorer provision of and access to quality education and less employee training. The Human Resources Development Fund (HRDF), established by the Ministry of Human Resources, is meant to help retrain retrenched workers, among other things. Only 572 workers benefited from this fund in 1998, and another 426 in 1999. On 12 February 1999, the gov-ernment announced exemptions from payment of the Human Resources Development Fund levy for employers facing financial difficulties (MHR 1999). The government claims that RM40 million has been allocated to firms that have contributed substantially in the past to the HRDF to defray training costs (*White Paper*: 47).

Economic Welfare

Available evidence suggests that the groups most badly affected by the economic recession were mainly in urban areas. The worst hit sectors, construction and manufacturing, are both mainly concentrated in urban areas, as are the highly leveraged or indebted middle- and upper-income businesses and households affected by the financial crisis.

Consumption

Private consumption fell drastically as the financial crisis and recession deepened. Household consumption declined, as lower incomes reduced consumption besides encouraging some substitution in consumption. Lower incomes caused consumers to buy less, reflected, for example, in the massive drops in passenger car sales in 1998 (-54.8 per cent), sales tax (-37.8 per cent) and consumption credit extended by the banking system (-14.6 per cent) compared to the previous year. The relative prices of goods and services also affected consumption. In the Malaysian Institute of Economic Research *Quarterly Report on Consumer Sentiments* (for the fourth quarter of 1998), an increasing number of respondents indicated a preference for deferring consumption of durable and semi-durable goods to cope with their new financial constraints (Haflah *et al.* 1999: 31).

The substitution effect due to decreased incomes is also of concern, particularly when it adversely affects the nutrition of families, especially children. Poor households typically spend larger proportions on food and 'basic needs', and are more vulnerable to nutritional decline or illness. Poor parents may also take their children out of schools to save on out-of-pocket expenses, or to supplement family incomes with income from child labour. The uncertainty induced by the financial crisis, and subsequent spending and savings behaviour, point to the critical role of sentiments and confidence in conditioning the decision-making of individuals and households.

Cost of Living

Households have had to bear with cost of living increases. Table 8.12 shows the consumer price index (CPI) for Malaysia. Inflation rates rose markedly to 5.3 per cent in 1998 from 2.7 per cent in 1997. The price of food increased by more than any other category of consumer expenditure. Accounting for 34.9 per cent of the CPI, it is the main determinant of the CPI level. However, other items also became more expensive. Medical care and health expenses increased by 6.2 per cent in 1998, up from 3.6 per cent in 1997. Health care costs have tended to rise relatively more than the CPI since 1996. Gross rent, fuel and power expenditures also increased significantly, rising by 4.4 per cent in 1998. These also account for major portions of consumer budgets.

How price inflation has impacted on household consumption at different income levels has not been assessed empirically in Malaysia. However, household expenditure surveys seem to concur with Engel's Law, which postulates that households with lower incomes allocate proportionally more of their household budgets to food than to other consumption items. A nation-wide survey found that rural households earning less than RM300 per month spent up to 45 per cent of their incomes on food. In urban areas, households earning less than RM200 spent 38.6 per cent on food, while households earning RM200-299 spent an average of only 29.7 per cent (Shireen 1998: 159).

Table 8.12

Malaysia: Consumer Price Index, 1993-1999 (1994 = 100) (percentage annual change)

	1993	1994	1995	1996	1997	1998	1999
Total	3.6	3.7	3.4	3.5	2.7	5.3	2.8
Components:							
Food	2.2	5.3	4.9	5.7	4.1	8.9	4.6
Beverages and tobacco	14.8	5.0	2.3	2.2	1.3	4.3	7.9
Clothing and foot-ware	0.5	-0.7	0.0	-0.7	-0.5	0.4	-2.0
Gross rent, fuel and power	3.5	2.4	3.4	3.2	3.2	4.4	1.6
Furniture and household equipment	1.3	1.4	2.8	1.1	0.1	3.9	1.3
Medical care and health expenses	5.1	3.3	3.1	3.7	3.6	6.2	3.1
Transport and communication	5.6	4.6	1.8	1.4	0.6	-0.1	0.5
Recreation, entertainment, education and cultural services	0.5	0.7	2.5	3.3	0.4	3.3	2.6
Miscellaneous goods and services	0.5	0.7	2.5	3.3	4.6	7.1	1.5

Sources: *Economic Report*, various issues; BNM, *Annual Report 1999*, Table A.28, p. P35; Department of Statistics, *Monthly Consumer Price Index*.

Table 8.13
Malaysia: Consumer Price Index for Food Items,
1997-1999 (% annual change)

Food Items	March 1997	Sept. 1997	March 1998	Sept. 1998	May 1999
Sugar	0.4	0.3	14.1	18.9	n.a.
Fruits and vegetables	1.9	2.1	13.0	14.2	5.6
Coffee and tea	0.1	0.7	5.5	9.6	6.4
Fish	7.0	7.1	7.6	9.3	10.5
Meat	11.7	3.7	5.7	8.5	n.a.
Rice, bread and other cereals	7.3	4.1	n.a.	6.4	7.4
Oils and fats	2.7	-1.6	5.1	5.6	n.a.
Food at home	5.6	3.6	n.a.	9.1	6.3
Food away from home	7.0	5.6	n.a.	8.3	4.5
Total	6.0	4.3	6.6	8.9	5.8

Note: n.a. — not available.
Source: Department of Statistics, *Monthly Consumer Price Index*, various months,
         p. 3.

Table 8.13 shows the inflation rates for various food items. The total inflation rate did not change significantly from March 1997 to March 1998. However, certain food items witnessed considerable price increases, e.g. sugar (14.1 per cent annual increase up to March 1998) and fruits and vegetables (13.0 per cent over the same period). Price hikes for food items have, in some instances, been associated with price controls, e.g. in February 1998 (Haflah *et al.* 1999: 12). The severity of food price inflation seems to have been associated with the collapse of the ringgit and the high import content of food consumed. Macroeconomic data indicate the recession was at its worse in late 1998, while the inflation rate for food was highest in September 1998 (8.9 per cent). In that month, all components of the food CPI witnessed large increases. Another worrying characteristic of the food price inflation has been the rise in the cost of home-cooked food.

Savings and Financial Security

Malaysia's gross national savings during 1993-97 averaged 36.5 per cent, and was on the increase from 1995 to 1997, rising steadily from 35.3 per cent to 39.4 per cent. Despite the recession, gross national savings amounted to 41.2 per cent of GNP in 1998, indicating a continuing increase in the savings rate despite the drop in income. Meanwhile, the expected growth in EPF contributions decreased in the aftermath of the financial crisis that will also have adverse consequences for future retirees withdrawing their EPF savings.

Debt Burden

Interest rates initially rose in Malaysia after the crisis began to stem capital flight, and to thus protect the ringgit from depreciation. This adversely affected those with debt to service. Households and businesses faced difficulties paying higher interest on their loans as incomes declined. In particular, non-performing loans for the purchase of homes, transport vehicles, credit card and consumer goods increased markedly in 1998. It has been estimated that a borrower servicing a housing loan or overdraft facility of RM100,000 had to pay 20 per cent more for their monthly repayments as a result of interest rate hikes in wake of the financial crisis (*White Paper 1999*). According to a BNM survey, from the onset of the crisis to October 1998, 7,393 cars — worth RM258.5 million — were repossessed (Ishak *et al.* 1999: 23).

Tables 4.16, 4.17 and 4.18 reflect this trend of growing un-serviced loans. For commercial banks, non-performing loans increased from RM1,119 million in September 1997 to RM3,058 million (by 173 per cent) in September 1998 for the purchase of residential property, from RM805 million to RM2,492 million (by 210 per cent) for consumption credit, and from RM436 million to RM8,273 million (by 1,797 per cent) for the purchase of securities. For finance companies, NPLs for the purchase of transport vehicles swelled from RM1,164 million in September 1997 to RM5,101 million in September 1998 (by 338 per cent). A considerable number of highly leveraged households and individuals have come under great pressure to service their debts, and may have had their homes or cars repossessed.

The increase in interest rates, however, should not be overstated. Base lending rates (BLR) for banks, for instance, never rose more than three per cent, and certainly by much less than neighbouring Thailand (see Figures 4.1 and 7.1, and Table 4.15). The commercial banks average BLR increased from 9.61 per cent at the end of September 1997 to 12.21 per cent at the end of May 1998. The finance companies' average BLR increased relatively more, but still by less than four percentage points, rising from 11.22 per cent at the end of September 1997 to 14.70 per cent at the end of June 1998. Obviously, highly leveraged businesses and households are more vulnerable to shocks to the financial system. The decrease in interest rates since September 1998 has reduced the weight of such debt, though rates in Malaysia became higher than Thai rates.

Health and Education

Social expenditures on health and education arguably contribute significantly to economic development. Some aspects of health care have been severely affected by the crisis. There has been an average 30 per cent increase in prices of imported drugs, which comprise 60 per cent of pharmaceutical drugs used in the country. As the prices of medicines increased rapidly, household welfare, especially for the low income social segments, have been adversely affected. An estimated 75 per cent of hospital equipment is imported; hence, in the long term, one can expect a lagged adverse impact on health care due to the ringgit depreciation and development spending cutbacks in purchasing or upgrading medical equipment (Abu Bakar 1998: 7). Private hospitals and clinics reported drops of between 15 to 50 per cent in the number of patients seeking treatment. At the same time, the Ministry of Health reported a 10-18 per cent increase in patient load of public hospitals and clinics (Haflah *et al.* 1999: 19). The decline in allocations for public health — despite rising federal health expenditure — and increased health service charges has reduced access of low-income households to affordable healthcare. Many of those previously able to pay for private medical treatment have turned to public services. As a result, various government health services have become overloaded and overcrowded. The relative scarcity of doctors in government hospitals and clinics — 4,719 compared to 6,051 in private practice — aggravates the pronounced shortage due to under-provision and over-subscription (Haflah *et al.* 1999: 6).

Primary school enrolment appears to have been fairly unaffected by the downturn. According to Ministry of Education data, the number of under-enrolled primary schools (i.e. with less than 150 pupils) declined from 1,538 in January 1997 to 1,511 in January 1998 and 1,407 in January 1999; i.e. at the beginning of each school year. The states of Sabah and Pahang accounted for most of these under-enrolled schools; Sabah's total fell from 378 to 320, and Pahang's from 99 to 71. Secondary school enrolment at the start of the 1998 and 1999 school years did not undergo significant declines either. Unfortunately, data on drop-out rates — which are more reliable (than enrolment rates) in indicating household means for and commitment to schooling — are not publicly available. Other impacts of economic recession on the quality of education are also difficult to identify and assess. Presumably, for instance, reduced learning capability — e.g. due to under-nourishment, chronic illness or inadequate facilities — affects the present performance and future prospects of students.

The impact of recession on education may not be reflected in enrolment rates. For example, a major financial burden to low-income households, who tend to have larger families, is the cost of buying textbooks. In December 1998, the government announced that it would pay RM400 to civil servants, in lieu of a bonus, and as financial assistance for the purchase of school textbooks. In addition, the eligibility ceiling for the government's book loan scheme was raised from RM1,000 to RM1,001-1,500, so that more families would be entitled to this benefit. These concessions were made after much pressure from low-income parents, who asserted that rising costs and con-stant or dwindling financial resources made it more difficult for them to support schooling expenses. The RM1,000 ceiling applies to all national primary and secondary schools, while the new relaxed ceiling only applies to national primary and public religious secondary schools. National-type (Chinese and Tamil language) schools have been excluded from this scheme (Ishak *et al.* 1999: 30-31).

Tertiary level education has probably been worst affected. The sudden increase in foreign education costs, due to the collapse of the ringgit, has compelled many students to seek alternatives locally. Malaysia has long had a very high proportion of tertiary students studying abroad, especially in the UK, Australia, US, Canada, India and Taiwan. For Malaysian public uni-versities' 1998 intake, 112,000 candidates vied for 40,220 places, i.e. only 35.9 per cent of applicants managed to enrol. Universities have increased enrolment to accommodate the increased demand, but without significantly increasing teaching staff and other university facilities. Ironically, understaffed Malaysian universities with inadequate facilities may have been granted some relief, with lower enrolment (36,373 students) in the 1999/2000 session. Still, under-provision of university places is a long-standing issue, with complex implications in Malaysian society. Private higher education institutes — which have proliferated since the mid-1980s — have also reported increased enrolments. Despite the availability of new options, there have been those who have had to postpone or cancel their study plans. According to the British Council, Malaysian student enrolment in UK universities fell from 18,015 in 1996-97 to 16,791 in 1997-98 and an estimated 14,000 in 1998-99. For the 1999-2000 session, enrolment was estimated to have increased to 15,000, with a forecasted further increase to 16,500 in 2000-2001. While these figures are rebounding and indicate recovery on the part of families and the government to sponsor children's or scholars' higher education abroad, the weak ringgit implies that many of those paying for this education are facing, or will face, financial strains. On the public side, federal government allocations for scholarships and educational aid increased from RM669 million in 1997 to RM769 million in 1998. This was probably due to currency depreciation requiring larger ringgit allocations, and not necessarily a reflection of additional support for students.

Marginalised and Vulnerable Groups

Some brief mention should be made of certain groups particularly vulnerable to the economic downturn. This is not to suggest that these groups are unimportant, but data on the actual impacts of the recession are difficult to obtain. Unfortunately, systematic information from charitable organisations, affected by declines in donations, is not available on a wide scale. The extent and adequacy of community support — in lieu of adequate state-provided social safety net — is quite unclear. However, a few groups can be singled out:

1. The elderly, especially those dependent on pension incomes or remittances from family members, including those residing in old folk's homes, face various problems. Surveys suggest that many of the rural elderly have been adversely affected by the lower earnings of and transfers from children or relatives working elsewhere (Ishak *et al.* 1999: 23-24).
2. People with special needs, the disabled and orphans. Organisations that care for these groups seem to be facing dwindling resources.
3. Single-parent households, mostly headed by women, face particular problems and pressures, as mentioned above.
4. Rural farmers, rice cultivators, fishermen and plantation workers are vulnerable to shifts in commodity and food prices, as well as input costs. For instance, tenant rice farmers, endure severe cost fluctuations, mainly accruing to rent. For small-scale fishermen, on the other hand, equipment and fuel have risen, reducing their net incomes (Ishak *et al.* 1999: 54-56).

Poverty

The 1997 currency and financial crises and the ensuing recession did not result in widespread unemployment, extensive impoverishment and a groundswell of social discontent in Malaysia. Nonetheless, the recession caused more households to slip into poverty (see Table 8.14). The poverty rate increased from 6.1 per cent in 1997 to 7.0 per cent in 1998, reversing

Table 8.14
Malaysia: Incidence of Poverty and Number of Poor Households, 1995-2000

	1995			1997			1998	2000		
	Total	*Urban*	*Rural*	*Total*	*Urban*	*Rural*	*Total*	*Total*	*Urban*	*Rural*
Malaysian Citizens										
Incidence of poverty	8.9	3.7	15.3	6.1	2.1	10.9	–	5.5	1.9	10.0
No. of poor households	370.2	84.6	285.6	294.4	55.4	239.0	–	276.0	53.2	222.8
Incidence of hardcore poverty	2.1	0.8	3.7	1.4	0.4	2.5	–	0.5	0.1	1.0
No. of hardcore poor households	88.4	19.2	69.2	67.3	11.6	55.7	–	25.4	2.8	22.6
Overall										
Incidence of poverty	9.6	4.1	16.1	6.8	2.4	11.8	8.0	6.0	2.2	10.7
No. of poor households	417.2	95.9	321.3	346.0	67.4	278.6	399.1	323.7	64.7	259.0
Incidence of hardcore poverty	2.2	0.9	3.7	1.4	0.5	2.4	1.7	0.5	0.1	1.0
No. of hardcore poor households	93.5	20.5	73.0	70.3	13.8	56.5	82.9	27.3	3.0	24.3

Notes: 1) Poverty estimation for 1997 is based on the following poverty line incomes: RM460 per month for a household
size of 4.6 in Peninsular Malaysia, RM633 for a household size of 4.9 for Sabah, and RM543 for a household
size of 4.8 for Sarawak.
2) Figures for 1998 are based on National Economic Action Council (NEAC) estimates.
3) Hardcore poverty is estimated using half the poverty line income.
4) Figures for 2000 are projections.
Source: *Mid-term Review of the Seventh Malaysia Plan, 1996-2000*, reproduced in Haflah *et al.* 1999, Table 4, p. 16.

the long-standing trend of declining poverty, e.g. from 8.9 per cent in 1995 (*White Paper*: 21). Another estimate suggests that the poverty rate rose from 6.7 per cent in 1997 (involving 346,000 households) to 8.0 per cent in 1998 (involving 422,100 households), i.e. the number of impoverished households increased by 22 per cent. Dislocation and dispossession as direct results of the crisis — due to job loss, reduced working hours, inflation, etc. — are estimated to have pushed an additional 53,100 urban households into poverty. The incidence of hardcore poverty — defined as households receiving less than half the poverty line income — also rose, from 1.2 per cent to 1.7 per cent (Ishak *et al.* 1999: x). The efficacy of official policies in addressing poverty is difficult to ascertain, though such efforts may well have increased during the downturn. A sum of RM100 million was allocated to Amanah Ikhtiar Malaysia (AIM) for the provision of interest-free loans to the very poor, and RM200 million for a micro-credit scheme to assist petty traders and hawkers in urban areas (*White Paper*: 48).

As the Malaysian economy and rural incomes continue to recover, poverty can be expected to decline. Many issues surrounding social policy still need to be addressed in the long term, in particular, to ensure more egalitarian access to education and health services. Malaysia has made much progress in terms of human development in the last few decades. Health, education and other social indicators continue to show positive trends in spite of the recession. While access to health services is high by developing country standards, and primary schooling is virtually universal, there are growing concerns regarding the quality of education and health services. The ongoing plans to privatise and commercialise tertiary education institutions and health services will have long term consequences for social welfare, especially in the aftermath of the recession. It is difficult to identify and quantify, with great certainty, the impacts of the 1997-98 crisis on human development. Unfortunately, there is little evidence of much progress in social policies despite, or perhaps because of the severity of the crisis and recession.

Government Expenditure and Social Programs

Malaysia has been lauded in the international development discourse for its success in providing public services, especially health and education. Many lower income households have enjoyed some government transfers and services, and have even become dependent on and continue to expect of government subsidies. Generally, therefore, changes in government social expenditure tend to be felt more by lower-income households. Government intervention, especially for interethnic economic redistribution, has extended such expectations of government transfers to higher-income Bumiputera households.

Rising medical, food and other costs, and the relatively higher expenses and opportunity costs of sending children to school have made education for children of the poor more vulnerable to the crisis and its consequences. One of the early policy responses to the financial crisis was to reduce government spending. Facing declining government revenue and financial market hostility to fiscal deficits, expenditure was cut in order to limit the budgetary deficit through a series of austerity measures. However, such fiscal conservatism was abandoned by mid-1998 in favour of a counter-cyclical fiscal strategy. Total government revenue shrank by 13.7 per cent between 1997 and 1998, but only by 0.04 per cent between 1998 and 1999 (Tables 1.10 and 1.11). Direct taxes collected by the federal government in 1998 were 1.4 per cent lower than in the preceding year; in 1999, there was a decrease of 10.3 per cent. Other tax revenue declined by larger margins: 40.8 per cent for export duties, 40.7 per cent for import duties, and 37.7 per cent for sales tax. As shown in Table 1.11, the first major fiscal deficits of the 1990s — of 1.8 per cent and 4.9 per cent of GDP respectively — were recorded in 1998 and 1999.

Tables 8.15 and 8.16 show various recent changes in allocations of public funds for government operating and development expenditure by sector. Aggregate expenditure for social services — education, health and housing — remained quite constant between 1997 and 1998, although housing expenditure dropped relatively. Social services operating expenditure rose from RM15.1 billion in 1998 to RM16.4 billion in 1999, or by 9.2 per cent. Social services expenditure accounted for 30.9 per cent of the total operating budget in 1995, 33.1 per cent in 1997 and 28.5 per cent in 1998. Within this category, funds designated for education rose from RM10.4 billion in 1997 to RM10.5 billion in 1998 and then RM11.3 billion in 1999, an increase of 6.9 per cent. Economic services operating expenditure remained at around RM4.1 billion in 1997 and 1998, before jumping to RM4.9 billion in 1999, i.e. rising by 20.7 per cent. It is worth noting the reductions in allocation for agricultural and rural development in 1997 and 1998.

Federal government development expenditure continued to grow in the face of the crisis (*Economic Report, 1999/2000*, p. xxxiv, Table 4.6). Total development expenditure rose by 14.9 per cent in 1998 and by 38.2 per cent in 1999, after rising by 4.1 per cent in 1996 and 7.7 per cent in 1997. Social services development expenditure grew by 13.4 per cent in 1996, 23.5 per

Table 8.15

Malaysia: Federal Government Operating Expenditure by Sector, 1995-2000
(RM million; percentage annual change)

Selected sectors	1995	1996		1997		1998		1999		2000*	
	RM	RM	%	RM	%	RM	%	RM	%	RM	%
Security:											
Defence	3,647	4,030	10.5	4,063	0.8	3,528	-13.2	3,602	2.1	3,920	0.1
Internal security	2,357	2,592	10.0	2,544	-1.9	2,369	-6.9	2,406	1.6	2,667	10.8
Social services:											
Education	8,559	10,398	21.5	10,360	-0.4	10,528	1.6	11,251	6.9	11,937	6.1
Health	2,384	3,015	26.5	3,278	8.7	3,331	1.6	3,627	8.9	4,040	11.4
Housing	80	201	151.3	121	-39.8	88	-27.3	87	-1.1	113	29.9
Total	12,141	14,824	22.1	15,051	1.5	15,063	0.1	16,446	9.2	17,774	8.1
Economic services:											
Agriculture & rural devt.	1,135	1,436	26.5	1,300	-9.5	1,121	-13.8	1,238	10.4	1,243	0.4
Public utilities	53	222	318.9	105	-52.7	397	278.1	193	-51.4	35	-81.9
Trade and industry	624	1,468	135.3	1,277	-13.0	1,279	0.2	2,124	66.1	1,665	-21.6
Transport	996	1,087	9.1	1,378	26.8	1,040	-24.5	1,247	19.9	1,257	0.8
Communications	30	36	20.0	32	-11.1	38	18.8	98	157.9	34	-65.3
Total	2,869	4,285	49.4	4,125	-3.7	4,086	-0.9	4,931	20.7	4,266	-13.5
Total	21,014	25,731	22.4	25,783	0.2	25,046	-2.9	27,385	9.3	28,627	4.5

Note: * Federal Budget allocation.
Source: *Economic Report*, various issues, Table 4.5.

Table 8.16
Malaysia: Federal Government Development Expenditure by Sector, 1995-2000
(RM million, % annual change)

Selected sectors	1995	1996		1997		1998		1999		2000[*]	
	RM	RM	%	RM	%	RM	%	RM	%	RM	%
Defence and security	2,888	2,438	-15.6	2,314	-5.1	1,380	-40.4	3,122	126.2	2,634	-15.6
Social services:											
Education	2,044	2,091	2.3	2,521	20.6	2,915	15.6	3,865	32.6	3,695	-4.4
Health	388	459	18.3	449	-2.2	716	59.5	835	16.6	908	8.7
Housing	403	501	24.3	735	46.7	1,030	40.1	1,081	5.0	1,145	5.9
Social and community services	678	933	37.6	1,214	30.1	1,122	-7.6	1,155	2.9	1,504	30.2
Total	3,513	3,984	13.4	4,919	23.5	5,783	17.6	6,936	19.9	7,252	4.5
Economic services:											
Agricultural and rural development	1,360	1,182	-13.1	1,105	-6.5	960	-13.1	1,089	13.4	1,288	18.3
Public utilities	654	733	12.1	1,496	104.1	1,968	31.6	1,850	-6.0	1,013	-45.0
Trade and industry	1,218	1,212	-0.5	1,285	6.0	3,227	151.1	2,798	-13.3	3,762	34.4
Transport	3,151	4,530	43.8	3,578	-21.0	3,062	-14.4	2,893	-5.5	4,643	60.5
Total	6,440	7,693	19.5	7,501	-2.5	9,243	23.2	8,970	-3.0	10,875	21.2
Total	12,841	14,115	9.9	14,734	4.4	16,406	11.3	19,028	16.0	23,674	24.4

Note: [*] Ministry of Finance forecasts.
Source: BNM, *Monthly Statistical Bulletin*, Table VII.4; Ministry of Finance, *Economic Report 1999/2000*, Table 4.6, p. xxxiv.

cent in 1997, 17.5 per cent in 1998 and an allocated 20.9 per cent in 1999. However, the share of total government development expenditure for social services has fared less well, rising from 27.2 per cent in 1996 to 31.2 per cent in 1997 and 31.9 per cent in 1998, before falling to 27.9 per cent in 1999. While the relative shares for education, health and housing did not suffer badly, other social services experienced a drop from 7.7 per cent in 1997 to 3.7 per cent in 1999. As Table 8.16 shows, allocations to most sectors increased in 1997 and 1998. Notably, defence and security allocations fell in successive years, but increased by an incredible 126.2 per cent in 1999 — perhaps to compensate for much more modest increases in earlier allocations for defence and security operating budgets. Education, health and housing development expenditure have risen at considerable rates, except for a small decline for health in 1997. The allocation of funds for education and health is shown in greater detail in Tables 8.17 and 8.18.

The government increased its expenditure once again from mid-1998 and again in its 1999 and 2000 Budgets, in line with its counter-cyclical measures to revive the economy. One notable increase in the first half of 1999 was for education, which rose to RM5.6 billion from RM5.1 billion in January-June 1997 — an increase of 8.9 per cent (BNM, *MSB*, Table VII.3). Aggregate social services spending in the first halves of 1998 and 1999 came to RM6.8 billion and RM7.5 billion respectively, equivalent to a 9.8 per cent

Table 8.17

Malaysia: Government Budget Allocations for Education, 1997-1999

	1997	*1998*		*1999*	
	RM mil.	*RM mil.*	*% change*	*RM mil.*	*% change*
Education (total)	9,924.7	12,510.4	26.05	13,520.0	8.07
Level/type					
Pre-school, Primary, Secondary	6,281.7	6,838.1	8.87	7,302.0	4.64
Tertiary	73.6	77.8	5.79	87.9	12.90
Technical	223.7	289.9	29.61	304.7	5.09
Private	1.3	1.9	53.54	1.3	-33.83
Special	25.0	28.9	15.62	26.6	-7.94

Source: Haflah *et al.* 1999, Table 6, p. 18, compiled from *Federal Government Budget Report 1998/1999*.

Table 8.18
Malaysia: Government Budget Allocations for Health, 1997-2000

	1997	*1998*		*1999*	
	RM mil.	*RM mil.*	*% change*	*RM mil.*	*% change*
Health (total)	3,703.2	4,238.0	14.4	4,512.3	6.47
Public Health	675.2	661.5	-2.02	653.6	-1.20
Medical Treatment	1,628.8	1,656.3	1.69	1,642.8	-0.81

Source: Haflah *et al.* 1999, Table 7, p. 21, compiled from *Federal Government Budget Report 1998/1999.*

annual increase. RM664 million was spent on agriculture and rural development in January-June 1999, compared to RM627 million for the corresponding period the year before, making for a rise of 5.9 per cent.

Specific Social Programs for Crisis Alleviation

The following specific programs and funds were designated for certain sectors or needy groups in response to the crisis (Haflah *et al.* 1999: 34-35). These were primarily credit schemes, also referred to in other contexts in this study:

- Under the auspices of the Ministry of Health and the Ministry of Education, an additional RM200 million was set aside for rural social infrastructure facilities.
- The Fund for Food program, worth RM300 million, was established to increase food production through provision of low-interest loans to small farmers and Farmers' Associations.
- An additional allocation of RM100 million for the Hardcore Poverty Development Program was designed to provide loans to the hard-core poor for income-earning activities through Amanah Ikhtiar Malaysia (AIM).
- The Small-Scale Entrepreneur Fund (RM100 million) and Economic Business Group Fund (RM150 million) were set up to provide assistance to petty traders, hawkers and small entrepreneurs — including women entrepreneurs — in urban areas. The former provides project financing for up to RM20,000, while the latter provides loans for up to a maximum of RM10,000.

- The Small and Medium-Scale Industry (SMI) Fund, with start-up financing of RM750 million, was mandated to aid small and medium scale businesses to expand production. Loans were mainly channelled for the purchase of equipment and machinery.
- The National Higher Education Fund, with an initial RM320 million allocation, is meant to provide financial assistance to students in local universities and colleges.

Funding for and implementation of immediate aid and crisis-response programs has generally been disappointing. The Fund for Food Program, which provides low-interest loans to farmers, saw only RM199 million — out of an allocated RM700 million — approved as loans. Similarly, the Special Scheme for Low and Medium Cost Housing approved only RM241 million (out of an available RM2,000 million), while the Small-Scale Entrepreneur Fund approved RM882 million out of an available RM1.5 billion (Haflah *et al*. 1999: 46). Whatever the reasons, substantial proportions of the credit program allocations have not been taken up, when they could have generated much needed economic activity or boosted demand.

Small and medium size industries (SMIs) have been afflicted by the recession, but have not been given as much official attention as politically well connected big business interests. The number of insolvencies partly reflects the extent of the impact of the financial crisis and recession on businesses. For about a year from July 1997, more than 2,000 businesses declared bankruptcy. In contrast to the limited attention to SMIs, conglomerates and large businesses have attracted much more official attention as well as media coverage, with many enjoying considerable support and protection from government policies. Limited financial resources and access, intense competition, poor political connections, and limited government support, *inter alia*, have made SMIs more vulnerable to crisis and contraction.

To aid floundering SMIs, the government set up a Rehabilitation Fund for Small and Medium Industries (RFSMIs) in 1998, with an initial endowment of RM750 million. This measure is intended to assist viable SMIs that face credit constraints; 30 per cent of total loans approved from this fund may be used to restructure problematic existing loans (*White Paper*, p. 36). The adequacy and effectiveness of this fund have yet to be ascertained, but the modest funds committed to SMIs contrast with the RM55 billion already committed to financing Danaharta and Danamodal bank rescue operations involving NPL restructuring and bank re-capitalisation. The speed with which financial assistance has been made available to privileged groups

also contrasts markedly with the tardiness, inadequacy and poor administration of funds for the poor.

Concluding Remarks

It is probably still too early to assess the full socio-economic impact of the
1997-8 economic crisis. This review of the social impact in Malaysia of the
1997-8 crisis has also been handicapped by several other factors. Most
importantly, much relevant data has not been made available in the public
domain. This is particularly true of socioeconomic data, especially involving
labour. There also seems to be a considerable lag-time of several years before such data is published even if it is eventually made available. There are
also considerable doubts about the reliability of some official data, e.g. of
government estimates of foreign labour in the country or of the size of the
informal sector.

It has also been difficult to accurately assess the actual social impact of
the crisis itself because of contemporaneous developments with social
consequences. Before the crisis began in mid-1997, there was already
considerable evidence of significant commodity price deflation, involving
not only primary products, but also generic manufactures not enjoying
monopolistic rents due to exclusive intellectual property rights held by
transnational corporations (TNCs). In 1997 and 1998, agricultural output,
especially in peninsular Southeast Asia, was adversely affected by the El Nino
and then La Nina weather phenomena of drought followed by floods. Forest
fires due to land clearance activity by plantation interests in Sumatra and
Kalimantan resulted in tall palls of smoke in neighbouring Malaysia for
several months, also affecting agricultural output as well as public health and
labour productivity.

Hence, the full impact of the 1997-8 economic crisis in Malaysia is difficult to assess for various reasons. First, various concurrent developments
complicate careful assessment of the actual impact of the crisis. These
included the El Nino drought, La Nina heavy rains, heavy smoke palls from
forest fires in neighbouring Indonesia as well as commodity price deflation
(and presumably adverse terms of trade trends) since the mid-1990s. Second,
there is still considerable debate over the origins, nature and consequences
of the crises; more prudent bank regulation, a more stock market oriented
financial system as well as different policy responses, especially from
September 1998, distinguishes the Malaysian experience rather profoundly.
Third, a great deal of relevant data has not been made available to the public.

Fourth, much available data is widely considered suspect. The employment impact of the crisis is especially difficult to measure because of the unreliability of labour data, especially for undocumented immigrant workers, as well as the widespread 'casualisation' of employment relations in recent years, e.g. the increasingly widespread use of contract labour.

Employment data suggest that those employed in construction and manufacturing were hardest hit by job losses. Consumer price trends suggest that low-income groups probably suffered most due to large increases in the consumer price index mainly due to the ringgit depreciation, especially for food. Producer price trends suggest that agricultural producers have suffered heavily due to agricultural price trends, especially for rubber, and more recently, for palm oil. However, it may be wrong to attribute lower agricultural incomes to the financial crisis alone owing to the effects of drought and forest fires. Also, the adverse wealth effect of the asset price deflation have cut incomes and consumption of the top decile or quintile of Malaysian households, with negative multiplier effects throughout the economy, e.g. in terms of demand for services and consumer durables. Easy and cheap credit fostered by government policy since September 1998 may well have helped reverse such effects.

Government data suggest that construction and manufacturing were the two sectors most adversely affected by the downturn in terms of recession and unemployment. Despite the recession through 1998 and into the first quarter of 1999, it is remarkable that the national savings rate was barely affected, remaining above 40 per cent despite the worst recession in post-war history. The government's adoption of a counter-cyclical deficit budgetary strategy from 1998 meant the substitution of government dis-savings for previous government savings, implying the increase in private savings. And since we can presume household savings to have been adversely affected by the recession as well as lower wages and property incomes due to the negative wealth effect, one can only presume an increase in corporate savings. This is not contradicted by the lower investment rate, owing to the end of the availability of foreign savings for investment in Malaysia as well as the much slower credit growth, especially for productive investments.

The modest increase in unemployment in Malaysia is probably largely due to the exclusion of undocumented workers from official employment statistics. Foreign workers are probably most widespread in construction, agriculture, manufacturing and lower-end services, with illegal labour most likely outside manufacturing. The growing casualisation of labour relations since the late 1980s, e.g. as reflected in the growth of contract labour arrangements, probably also limits the comprehensiveness of official measures of unemployment. Since the eighties, a growing proportion of construction labour, especially involving relatively unskilled work, had come to involve immigrant workers, many of whom are believed to have been undocumented or illegal. Hence, it is believed that the official data on the construction sector, especially of labour, grossly underestimates its actual size and significance. Job losses in the sector are believed to be much greater than suggested by official data.

Another likely reason for the low unemployment figures has been the likely increase in underemployment instead, especially with the widespread preference by workers for reduction of wages and other labour remuneration instead of job losses. While there is considerable anecdotal evidence to this effect, the poor official labour data does not allow any meaningful assessment of these different trends that have moderated the impact of the economic crisis on employment.

The most obvious victims of the crisis would be those who lost their jobs, mainly in the construction, manufacturing and financial services sectors. A second identifiable group would include businesses, households and individuals who experienced drops in real incomes for various reasons. These could include lower prices and output (not necessarily due to the crisis), job losses, pay cuts, reduced working hours, reduced overtime work opportunities as well as higher consumer prices. A third group would be those who became insolvent due to the crisis, e.g. highly leveraged businesses that have sunk with their debt burdens. Many of these victims would include middle- and high-income individuals and households most affected by higher interest rates, asset (stock, property) price drops as well as more difficult access to credit. A fourth group would include beneficiaries of government spending, especially on social expenditure, particularly social welfare transfers.

The increased incidence of retrenchments, lay-offs, and other means of cost reduction that have hurt employees draws attention to Malaysian labour laws which by and large favour management and capital at the expense of labour. Union membership is low, partly because of the inefficacy of the unions — which is, in turn, mainly due to severe strictures on labour organisation. At various levels, authorities have the leeway to exercise considerable discretionary power. In times of recession, when cost reduction became a paramount concern, labour is especially vulnerable to measures undermining their welfare.

A system that has consistently sought to weaken labour cannot be expected to adequately safeguard its welfare during a downturn, when its bargaining power is further depleted and management interests try to impose the main burden of cost cutting on labour. Malaysia does not have a national minimum wage, although the Wages Councils Act (1947) provides for minimum wages in sectors or regions when the need arises (Jomo and Vijayakumari 1999: 6-7). Wage reduction measures, therefore, lack guidelines and minimal levels to be adhered to. Human resource development efforts have been more pro-active. The Human Resource Development Council, initiated in 1993, has managed to train 800,000 workers by 1999 when 247,785 training places involving RM106 million in financial assistance were approved (*Labour Market Report 1999*).

The issue of social safety nets — or their absence — has also come to the fore in the wake of the financial crisis. Government responses to the crisis have revealed some commitment to key social sectors, perhaps because abandonment of these sectors may be politically hazardous. The slowness of government response, as Haggard (1999) points out, mirrors lack of ex-perience in providing social safety nets. This tardiness is all the more sur-prising when many 'initiatives' are, in fact, extensions of existing programs (p. 23). The small number that the Training Scheme for Retrenched Workers managed to assist (572 in 1998 and 426 in 1999) at considerable expense (RM2.5 million and RM2 million respectively), is unfortunate in a situation where many more could have benefited. The preponderance of more advanced and expensive types of training reflects its bias toward highly-skilled labour and professional work: 31 per cent of workers on the scheme were in the computer field, 27 per cent in technical engineering fields, and 42 per cent in management fields.

So far, there has been little auditing of the government expenditure in the wake of the crisis. Most of the dedicated funds set up during Anwar's tenure after the crisis began were for small businesses and the self-employed, with nothing for adversely affected workers except enforcement of existing labour laws to deter retrenchments. It is also unclear how much of the allocations have actually been spent. Hence, there is little evidence of government establishment or strengthening of social safety nets, let alone social insurance schemes, in Malaysia. There is also considerable anecdotal evidence that the suspension of regulations on government spending — ostensibly to stimulate the economy — was probably abused to ensure the re-election of the ruling coalition in November 1999 and the consolidation of the leadership of the ruling UMNO in May 2000.

Instead, far more has been allocated to rescuing and bailing-out the private sector. At least RM45 billion has been utilised by Danaharta so far, while an additional RM20 billion has been used by Danamodal. As rescuer of the financial sector, the government has sought to push through financial sector consolidation plans that will greatly enhance the status and profitability of favoured interests. Also, the actual costs — to the government or to the public — of corporate bail-outs arranged or facilitated by the official Corporate Debt Restructuring Committee (CDRC) are difficult to assess.

The growing bias in favour of politically well connected big businessmen over the last two decades may well have been reinforced by the policy responses to the crisis. This is especially clear from the nature and beneficiaries of various officially sanctioned — if not initiated — bail-outs, including business interests closely associated with the Prime Minister and Finance Minister, as well as various businesses privatised to well-connected 'cronies'. As noted earlier, although the original forced bank merger scheme was revised, the identities of the additional bankers accommodated have only reinforced this impression of cronyism at the highest level.

Small and medium sized enterprises have actually received greater official attention in recent years in line with government efforts to promote a broad-based Malay business community. Such efforts have also been politically important for reinforcing the changing political patronage considered necessary to retain political hegemony for the ruling UMNO and particular political leaders. More so than in the late 1980s, various support measures were initiated in the wake of the crisis by then Finance Minister Anwar Ibrahim, and later extended by the National Economic Action Council (NEAC) run by current Finance Minister Daim Zainuddin. Such efforts have met with mixed success, but more importantly, their financing has been far more modest than the funding for bailing-out the banking system, which is now in excess of RM65 billion.

Finally, while there is likely to have been some increase in the official incidence of poverty due to the recession, it is not likely to have been catastrophic, in so far as many victims are likely to have been foreign workers. It is also likely that the economic crisis may well have reduced income inequality owing to the impact of the crisis on the financial sector and many other businesses as well as professionals. Although the onset of the recent crisis was not due to cronyism, it appears that such influences have greatly shaped the government's policy responses. Hence, it is likely that such interests will not have their positions significantly eroded by the crisis, although the eventual outcome is subject to a variety of factors, many of which have not been fully played out.

But, as noted earlier, regardless of the actual success of the September 1998 measures, effective media control has ensured that much of the business community has been appreciative of such government initiatives in response to the crisis. In contrast, much of the ethnic Malay community — including its fast growing and influential middle class — have been increasingly alienated by the growing concentration of power and influence among the politically well connected elite, as well as by some of its social consequences and cultural manifestations. Not surprisingly then, the ruling coalition managed to secure additional political support from the non-Malay business community while alienating much more of the Malay middle class in the November 1999 general election.

9

EAST ASIAN COMPARISONS

Jomo K. S.

Although there has been considerable work critical of the East Asian economic growth record and potential, none actually anticipated the East Asian debacle of 1997-98 (e.g. see Krugman 1994). Although some of the weaknesses identified in this critical literature did make the region economically vulnerable, none of the critical writing seriously addressed one crucial implication of the greater role of foreign capital in Southeast Asia, especially with international financial liberalisation, which became more pronounced in the 1990s. As previously noted (Jomo 1998), dominance of manufacturing — especially the most technologically sophisticated and dynamic activities — by foreign transnationals subordinated domestic industrial capital in the region, allowing finance capital, both domestic and foreign, to become more influential in the region.

In fact, finance capital developed a complex symbiotic relationship with politically influential rentiers, now dubbed 'cronies' in the aftermath of 1997-98. Although threatened by the full implications of international financial liberalisation, Southeast Asian financial interests were quick to identify and secure new possibilities of capturing rents from arbitrage as well as other opportunities offered by gradual international financial integration. In these and other ways (e.g. see Gomez and Jomo 1999; Khan and Jomo 2000), transnational dominance of Southeast Asian industrialisation facilitated the ascendance and consolidation of financial interests and politically influential rentiers.

This increasingly powerful alliance was primarily responsible for promoting financial liberalisation in the region, both externally and internally.

However, in so far as the interests of domestic financial capital did not entirely coincide with those of international finance, the process of international financial liberalisation was necessarily partial. The processes were necessarily also uneven, considering the variety of different interests involved and their varying lobbying strengths in various parts of the region.

History too was not unimportant. For example, the banking crisis in Malaysia in the late 1980s served to ensure a prudential regulatory framework which checked the process from becoming more like Thailand's, where caution was thrown to the wind as early external liberalisation measures succeeded in securing capital inflows. Yet, in both countries, such flows were desired to finance current account deficits. These were principally due to service account deficits (mainly for imported financial services as well as investment income payments abroad), growing imports for consumption, speculative activity in regional stock markets, and output of non-tradeables, mainly in the property (real estate) sector. There is little evidence that such capital inflows contributed significantly to accelerating the pace of economic growth, especially of the tradeable sectors of the economy. Instead, it is likely that they contributed greatly to the asset price bubbles, whose inevitable deflation was accelerated by the advent of crisis with such devastating economic, social and political consequences.

The objectives of this chapter are modest. The first part will review the causes of the crises in the region. Macroeconomic indicators in Malaysia and the three most crisis-affected economies — i.e. Thailand, Indonesia and South Korea — are briefly reviewed to establish that despite some misdemeanours, the crises cannot be attributed to macroeconomic profligacy. Instead, the consequences of the reversal of short-term capital inflows are emphasised. In this regard, Malaysia will be shown to have been less vulnerable owing to pre-crisis restrictions on foreign borrowings as well as stricter central bank regulation, but more vulnerable due to the greater role of capital markets compared to the other three economies. The role of the IMF and financial market expectations in exacerbating the crises is also considered.

The second part will seek to advance the emerging discussion of economic recovery in the region. It begins by asserting that the recovery in the region, especially in Korea and Malaysia, has been principally due to successful Keynesian reflationary efforts, both fiscal and monetary. This implies that the emphasis by the IMF and the financial media on corporate governance reforms has been misguided and such reforms are not a pre-condition for economic recovery. Instead of the Anglo-American or neo-liberal-inspired reforms being proposed, it is suggested that reforms should create new conditions for further catching up throughout the region. Finally, although pessimistic about prospects for international financial system reform, the chapter concludes by outlining a reform agenda in the interests of the South.

Causing Crises

Rapid economic growth and structural change, mainly associated with export-led industrialisation in the region, can generally be traced back to the mid-1980s. Then, devaluation of the currencies of Thailand, Indonesia and Malaysia, as well as selective deregulation of onerous rules helped create attractive conditions for the relocation of production facilities in these countries and elsewhere in Southeast Asia and China. This was especially attractive for Japan and the first-tier or first-generation newly industrialising economies of South Korea, Taiwan, Hong Kong and Singapore, most of which experienced currency appreciations, tight labour markets and higher production costs. This sustained export-oriented industrialisation well into the 1990s, and was accompanied by the growth of other manufacturing, services as well as construction activity.

High growth was sustained for about a decade, during much of which fiscal surpluses were maintained, monetary expansion was not excessive and inflation was generally under control. Table 9.1 shows various summary macroeconomic indicators for the 1990s with greater attention to the period from 1996 (also see Table 9.2). Before 1997, the savings and investment rates were high and rising in all three Southeast Asian economies. Foreign savings supplemented high domestic savings in all four economies, especially in Thailand and Malaysia. Unemployment was low while fiscal balances generally remained positive before 1997/8.

This is not to suggest, however, that the fundamentals were all alright in East Asia (Lim 1999; Rasiah 1998). As Table 9.1 also shows, the incremental capital-output ratio (ICOR) rose in all three Southeast Asian economies during the 1990s before 1997, with the increase greatest in Thailand and least in Indonesia. The rising ICOR suggests declining returns to new investments before the crisis. Export-led growth had been followed by a construction and property boom, fuelled by financial systems favouring such 'short-termist' investments — involving loans with collateral which bankers like — over more productive, but also seemingly more risky investments in manufacturing and agriculture. The exaggerated expansion of investment in such 'non-tradeables' exacerbated their current account deficits. Although widespread in East Asia, for various reasons, the property-finance nexus was particularly

Table 9.1
East Asian Four: Macroeconomic Indicators, 1990-1999

Unemployment Rate						Savings/GDP				
	1990	1996	1997	1998	1999	1990-95	1996	1997	1998	1999
Indonesia	n.a.	4.1	4.6	5.5	6.3	31.0	26.2	26.4	26.1	23.7
Malaysia	6.0	2.5	2.4	3.2	3.0	36.6	37.1	37.3	39.6	38.0
Korea	2.4	3.0	2.6	6.8	6.3	35.6	33.7	33.3	33.8	33.5
Thailand	4.9	1.1	0.9	3.5	4.1	34.4	33.0	32.5	34.9	31.0

Investment/GDP						(Savings-Investment)/GDP				
	1990-95	1996	1997	1998	1999	1990-95	1996	1997	1998	1999
Indonesia	31.3	29.6	28.7	22.1	19.3	-0.3	-3.4	-2.3	4.0	4.4
Malaysia	37.5	42.5	43.1	26.8	22.3	-0.9	-5.4	-5.8	12.8	15.7
Korea	36.8	36.8	35.1	29.8	28.0	-1.2	-3.1	-1.8	4.1	5.5
Thailand	41.0	41.1	33.3	22.2	21.0	-5.6	-8.1	-0.9	12.8	10.0

Incremental Capital-Output Ratios								Fiscal Balance/GDP				
	1987-89	1990-92	1993-95	1996	1997	1998	1999	1990-95	1996	1997	1998	1999
Indonesia	4.0	3.9	4.4	2.6	1.7	-6.0	0.0	0.2	1.4	1.3	-2.6	-3.4
Malaysia	3.6	4.4	5.0	2.0	3.9	-2.8	2.4	-0.4	0.7	2.4	-1.8	-3.2
Korea	3.5	5.1	5.1	1.8	4.2	-2.2	4.0	0.2	0.5	-1.4	-4.2	-2.9
Thailand	2.9	4.6	5.2	1.6	-1.3	-4.7	2.0	3.2	2.4	-0.9	-3.4	-3.0

Sources: Radelet and Sachs (1998: Table 11); ADB (1999); Bank of Thailand; Bank Indonesia; Bank of Korea; Bank Negara Malaysia.

Table 9.2
East Asian Four: Macroeconomic Change, 1990-1999 (year-on-year % change)

	1990	*1991*	*1992*	*1993*	*1994*	*1995*	*1996*	*1997*	*1998*	*1999*
Malaysia										
Real GDP	9.7	8.2	7.8	8.4	9.2	9.5	8.6	7.5	-7.5	5.4
Private Consumption	13.1	9.5	3.0	4.6	9.8	9.4	6.9	4.3	-10.8	2.5
M2	12.8	14.5	19.1	22.1	14.7	24.0	21.4	22.6	1.5	11.6
M3	18.2	15.3	19.6	23.5	13.1	22.3	21.2	18.5	2.73	8.25
Inflation	3.1	4.4	4.8	3.6	3.7	3.4	3.5	2.7	5.3	2.8
C.A. Deficit/GDP	2.1	8.9	2.8	4.8	6.3	8.5	4.9	-5.0	12.9	14.0
Foreign Reserves[a]	9,327	10,421	16,784	26,814	24,888	22,945	26,156	20,013	24,728	30,853
Korea										
Real GDP	9.0	9.2	5.4	5.5	8.3	8.9	6.8	5.0	-6.7	11.0
Private Consumption	9.6	8.0	5.5	5.6	8.2	9.6	7.1	3.5	-11.4	10.3
M2	17.2	21.9	14.9	16.6	18.7	15.6	15.8	14.1	27.0	27.4
M3	28.7	23.6	21.8	19.0	24.7	19.1	16.7	13.9	12.5	8.0
Inflation	8.5	9.3	6.3	4.8	6.2	4.5	4.9	4.5	7.5	0.8
C.A. Deficit/GDP	-0.8	-2.8	-1.3	0.3	-1.0	-1.7	-4.4	-1.7	12.8	6.1
Foreign Reserves[a]	14,459	13,306	16,640	19,704	25,032	31,928	32,402	19,710	51,963	73,700

(continued…)

	1990	1991	1992	1993	1994	1995	1996	1997	1998	1999
Thailand										
Real GDP	11.6	8.4	7.8	8.3	8.9	8.7	6.4	-1.8	-10.4	4.1
Private Consumption	12.8	6.6	7.8	8.7	8.3	8.6	6.6	-1.3	-2.2	n.a.
M2	26.7	19.8	15.6	18.4	12.9	17.0	12.6	16.4	9.5	2.1
M3	–	19.9	18.5	19.7	17.6	18.7	13.4	3.2	8.9	1.6
Inflation	6.0	5.7	4.1	3.3	5.0	5.8	4.8	5.6	8.1	0.3
C.A. Deficit/GDP	8.3	7.5	5.5	5.5	5.6	8.0	7.9	-2.1	12.7	9.1
Foreign Reserves[a]	13,247	17,287	20,012	24,078	28,884	35,463	37,192	25,697	28,434	34,781
Indonesia										
Real GDP	7.2	7.0	6.5	6.5	7.7	8.2	7.8	4.7	-13.2	0.2
Private Consumption	17.2	8.0	3.1	11.8	4.7	9.7	9.2	5.3	-2.1	1.5
M2	44.2	17.1	20.2	22.0	20.2	27.6	29.6	23.2	62.3	11.9
Inflation	7.4	9.4	7.5	9.7	8.5	9.4	6.5	6.6	58.5	20.5
C.A. Deficit/GDP	3.4	3.8	2.1	1.6	1.7	3.6	3.3	-2.3	4.1	3.5
Foreign Reserves[*]	7,353	9,151	10,181	10,988	11,820	13,306	17,820	16,088	22,401	27,160

Notes: [*] Foreign exchange, US$ million.

Sources: Asian Development Bank; Bank Negara Malaysia, *Economic Report*; Bank of Thailand; International Monetary Fund, *International Financial Statistics*; Monetary Authority of Singapore.

strong in Thailand, which made it much more vulnerable to the inevitable bursting of the bubble (Jomo 1998; Pasuk 2000).

Capital Flows

There has been growing acknowledgement of the role of reversible capital flows into the East Asian region as the principal cause of the 1997-98 crisis. It is increasingly widely accepted that the national financial systems in the region did not adapt well to international financial liberalisation (e.g. Jomo 1998). The bank-based financial systems of most of crisis-hit East Asia were especially vulnerable to the sudden drop in the availability of short-term loans as international confidence in the region dropped suddenly during 1997. Available foreign exchange reserves were exposed as inadequate to meet financial obligations abroad, requiring the governments to seek temporary credit facilities to meet such obligations mainly incurred by their private sectors.

Bank of International Settlements data show that the banks were responsible for much of this short term debt, though of course, some of this debt consisted of trade credit and other short-term debt deemed essential to ensuring liquidity in an economy. However, the very rapid growth of short-term bank debt during stock market and property boom periods suggests that much short-term debt was due to factors other than trade credit expansion. In Malaysia, the temporary capital controls introduced in early 1994 by the central bank momentarily dampened the growth of such debt. However, by

Table 9.3
East Asian Four: Lending by BIS Reporting Banks by Sector,
as of end-June 1997 (US$ billion)

	South Korea	Thai-land	Indo-nesia	Malay-sia	Developing Countries
Total Borrowings	103.4	69.4	58.7	28.8	744.6
Banks	67.3	26.1	12.4	10.5	275.3
(%)	(65.1)	(37.6)	(21.1)	(36.5)	(37.0)
Private Non-bank	31.7	41.3	39.7	16.5	352.9
(%)	(30.6)	(59.5)	(67.6)	(57.3)	(47.4)
Government	4.4	12.0	6.5	1.9	115.6
(%)	(4.3)	(17.3)	(11.1)	(6.6)	(15.5)

Source: Bank for International Settlements.

1996 and early 1997, a new short-term borrowing frenzy was quite evident, involving not only the banks, but also other large private companies with enough political influence to circumvent central bank guidelines.

As Table 9.3 shows, in Thailand, Indonesia and Malaysia, the non-bank private sector was the major recipient of international bank loans, accounting for more than 50 per cent of total foreign borrowings by the end of June 1997, i.e. well above the developing country average of slightly under half. In contrast, 65 per cent of Korean borrowing was by banks, with only 31 per cent by the non-bank private sector. Government borrowings were low, and lowest in Korea and Malaysia, although the data does not allow us to differentiate the state-owned public companies or partially private, but corporatised former fully state-owned enterprises.

Tables 9.4a, 9.4b, 9.4c and 9.4d show the remarkable growth of (mainly private) foreign debt in the early and mid-1990s, especially in the three most externally indebted economies of Thailand, Indonesia and Korea. While foreign direct investment (FDI) grew in all four economies in the 1990s, it was most modest in Korea. Profit remittances on FDI were least from Korea and Thailand, and highest from Malaysia, reflecting its greater role historically, although FDI in Indonesia was actually higher in 1995-96. Portfolio equity flows into all four economies grew tremendously in the mid-1990s.

External debt as a share of export earnings rose from 112 per cent in 1995 to 120 per cent in 1996 in Thailand and from 57 per cent to 74 per cent over the same year in Korea, but actually declined in Indonesia and grew more modestly in Malaysia. By 1996, reserves as a share of external debt were only 15 per cent in Indonesia, 30 per cent in Korea, 43 per cent in Thailand and 70 per cent in Malaysia. By 1997, this ratio had dropped further to 15 per cent in Korea, 29 per cent in Thailand and 46 per cent in Malaysia, reflecting the reserves lost in futile currency defence efforts. Despite recessions in 1998, reserves picked up in all four economies, mainly due to the effects of currency devaluations on exports and imports. Short-term debt's share of total external debt in 1996 stood at 58 per cent in Korea, 41 per cent in Thailand, 28 per cent in Malaysia and 25 per cent in Indonesia.

Table 9.5 shows that much of BIS bank lending to developing countries was from Japanese, German and French banks, with US and UK banks proportionately less significant. This was quite different from the pattern of lending before the 1980s' debt crises, and suggests that Anglo-American banks were generally more reluctant to lend in the 1990s after their previous experiences in the 1980s. There is little evidence to suggest that such banks

Table 9.4a
Thailand: Foreign Debt Indicators, 1970-1998 (US$ million)

	1970	*1980*	*1990*	*1992*	*1993*	*1994*	*1995*	*1996*	*1997*	*1998*
Total debt stock (EDT)		8,297	28,165	41,865	52,717	65,597	83,093	90,777	93,731	86,172
Long-term debt (LDOD)	726	5,646	19,842	27,138	30,083	36,418	41,998	53,164	56,466	59,410
Short-term debt		2,303	8,322	14,727	22,634	29,179	41,095	37,613	34,836	23,523
Net flow on debt	365	1,808	3,534	4,132	11,112	10,474	18,226	6,755	5,796	-10,998
of which short-term debt		-37	2,210	2,235	7,907	6,545	11,916	-3,482	-2,777	-11,313
Aggregate Resource Flows and Net Transfers (Long-term)										
Net resource flows (long-term)	139	2,087	4,691	4,175	8,226	4,863	10,630	14,220	9,615	8,987
Foreign direct investment (net)	43	190	2,444	2,113	1,804	1,366	2,068	2,336	3,746	6,941
Portfolio equity flows	0	0	449	4	3,117	-538	2,154	1,551	-308	2,341
Profit remittances on FDI	19	38	312	350	420	465	480	510	550	580
Major Economic Aggregates										
Gross national product (GNP)	7,096	32,091	84,272	108,975	122,790	141,500	164,619	176,593	149,257	112,720
Exports of goods & services (XGS)		8,575	31,289	42,919	49,596	58,679	74,093	75,385	76,157	69,227
International reserves (RES)	911	3,026	14,258	21,183	25,439	30,280	36,939	38,645	26,897	29,537
Current account balance		-2,076	-7,281	-6,303	-6,364	-8,085	-13,554	-14,691	-3,024	14,241
Debt Indicators										
EDT/XGS (%)		96.8	90.0	97.5	106.3	111.8	112.1	120.4	123.1	124.5
EDT/GNP (%)		25.9	33.4	38.4	42.9	46.4	50.5	51.4	62.8	76.4
RES/EDT (%)		36.5	50.6	50.6	48.3	46.2	44.5	42.6	28.7	34.3
RES/MGS (months)		3.3	4.4	5.1	5.4	5.4	5.0	5.1	4.1	6.4
Short-term/EDT (%)		27.8	29.5	35.2	42.9	44.5	49.5	41.4	37.2	27.3

Key: MGS – Imports of goods and services.
Source: World Bank, *Global Development Finance 2000*.

Table 9.4b
Indonesia: Foreign Debt Indicators, 1970-1998 (US$ million)

	1970	1980	1990	1992	1993	1994	1995	1996	1997	1998
Total debt stock (EDT)		20,938	69,872	88,002	89,172	107,824	124,398	128,940	136,173	150,875
Long-term debt (LDOD)	2,948	18,163	58,242	69,945	71,185	88,367	98,432	96,710	100,338	121,672
Short-term debt		2,775	11,135	18,057	17,987	19,457	25,966	32,230	32,865	20,113
Net flow on debt	890	2,280	7,216	9,331	-1,124	5,066	9,941	12,346	10,087	-4,935
of which short-term debt		667	3,160	3,742	-70	1,470	6,509	6,264	635	-9,750
Aggregate Resource Flows and Net Transfers (Long-term)										
Net resource flows (long-term)	686	1,902	5,901	7,945	3,622	9,594	12,901	15,564	11,592	-808
Foreign direct investment (net)	83	180	1,093	1,777	2,004	2,109	4,348	6,194	4,677	-356
Portfolio equity flows	0	0	312	119	2,452	3,672	4,873	3,099	298	250
Profit remittances on FDI	128	3,234	2,192	2,623	2,577	2,800	3,000	3,400	3,300	2,800
Major Economic Aggregates										
Gross national product (GNP)	9,698	74,806	109,209	132,938	151,992	170,284	192,474	221,277	209,438	85,486
Exports of goods & services (XGS)			29,870	38,234	41,940	46,517	54,880	58,793	65,819	57,470
International reserves (RES)	160	6,803	8,657	11,482	12,474	13,321	14,908	19,396	17,487	23606
Current account balance			-2,988	-2,780	-2,106	-2,792	-6,431	-7,663	-4,889	3972
Debt Indicators										
EDT/XGS (%)			233.9	230.2	212.6	231.8	226.7	219.3	206.9	262.5
EDT/GNP (%)		28.0	64.0	66.2	58.7	63.3	64.6	58.3	65.0	176.5
RES/EDT (%)		32.5	12.4	13.0	14.0	12.4	12.0	15.0	12.8	15.6
RES/MGS (months)			3.1	3.3	3.4	3.2	2.9	3.5	3.0	5.3
Short-term/EDT (%)		13.3	15.9	20.5	20.2	18.0	20.9	25.0	24.1	13.3

Key: MGS – Imports of goods and services.
Source: World Bank, *Global Development Finance 2000*.

Table 9.4c
Malaysia: Foreign Debt Indicators, 1970-1998 (US$ million)

	1970	1980	1990	1992	1993	1994	1995	1996	1997	1998
Total debt stock (EDT)		6,611	15,328	20,018	26,149	30,336	34,343	39,673	47,228	44,773
Long-term debt (LDOD)	440	5,256	13,422	16,379	19,197	24,147	27,069	28,605	32,289	36,117
Short-term debt		1,355	1,906	3,659	6,951	6,189	7,274	11,068	14,939	8,656
Net flow on debt	63	1,592	-1,851	2,041	5,470	2,220	5,138	6,387	8,397	-3,361
of which short-term debt		481	-367	1,565	3,312	-762	1,085	3,974	3,871	-6,283
Aggregate Resource Flows and Net Transfers (Long-term)										
Net resource flows (long-term)	99	2,052	1,183	6,093	10,923	8,680	10,495	12,031	9,152	8,529
Foreign direct investment (net)	94	934	2,333	5,183	5,006	4,342	4,132	5,078	5,106	5,000
Portfolio equity flows	0	0	293	385	3,700	1,320	2,299	4,353	-489	592
Profit remittances on FDI	166	1,190	1,926	2,713	2,985	3,250	4,000	4,000	4,200	4,500
Major Economic Aggregates										
Gross national product (GNP)	4,089	23,607	40,902	55,166	60,969	68,918	83,101	94,563	94,833	68,581
Exports of goods & services (XGS)		14,836	34,514	46,421	54,656	68,526	85,992	94,065	95,387	71,900
International reserves (RES)	667	5,755	10,659	18,024	28,183	26,339	24,699	27,892	21,470	26,236
Current account balance		-266	-870	-2,167	-2,991	-4,520	-8,469	-4,596	-4,792	9,683
Debt Indicators										
EDT/XGS (%)		44.6	44.4	43.1	47.8	44.3	39.9	42.2	49.5	62.3
EDT/GNP (%)		28.0	37.5	36.3	42.9	44.0	41.3	42.0	49.8	65.3
RES/EDT (%)		87.1	69.5	90.0	107.8	86.8	71.9	70.3	45.5	58.6
RES/MGS (months)		4.6	3.6	4.4	5.8	4.3	3.2	3.4	2.6	5.2
Short-term/EDT (%)		20.5	12.4	18.2	26.6	20.4	21.2	27.9	31.6	19.3

Key: MGS – Imports of goods and services.
Source: World Bank, *Global Development Finance 2000*.

Table 9.4d
Korea: Foreign Debt Indicators, 1970-1998 (US$ million)

	1970	1980	1990	1992	1993	1994	1995	1996	1997	1998
Total debt stock (EDT)		29,480	34,986	44,156	47,202	72,415	85,810	115,803	136,984	139,097
Long-term debt (LDOD)	1,991	18,236	24,186	32,236	35,002	40,802	39,197	49,221	72,128	94,062
Short-term debt		10,561	10,800	11,920	12,200	31,613	46,613	66,582	53,792	28,139
Net flow on debt	847	6,415	1,058	4,698	2,262	28,321	22,706	33,300	16,774	7,190
of which short-term debt		3,396	1,000	720	280	19,412	15,001	19,969	-12,790	-1,653
Aggregate Resource Flows and Net Transfers (Long-term)										
Net resource flows (long-term)	411	2,440	1,369	7,753	8,603	12,244	13,045	19,358	22,382	13,201
Foreign direct investment (net)	66	6	788	727	588	809	1,776	2,325	2,844	5,415
Portfolio equity flows	0	0	518	3,045	6,029	2,525	3,559	3,700	1,257	4,096
Profit remittances on FDI	5	64	266	247	253	270	295	320	350	375
Major Economic Aggregates										
Gross national product (GNP)	8,997	60,801	252,384	314,337	345,232	401,782	487,918	518,501	473,939	316,195
Exports of goods & services (XGS)		22,050	76,679	89,858	97,860	114,850	151,237	157,229	168,928	160,061
International reserves (RES)	610	3,101	14,916	17,228	20,355	25,764	32,804	34,158	20,465	52,100
Current account balance		-5,312	-2,003	-3,944	990	-3,867	-8,507	-23,006	-8,167	40,552
Debt Indicators										
EDT/XGS (%)		133.7	45.6	49.1	48.2	63.1	56.7	73.7	81.1	86.9
EDT/GNP (%)		48.5	13.9	14.0	13.7	18.0	17.6	22.3	28.9	44.0
RES/EDT (%)		10.5	42.6	39.0	43.1	35.6	38.2	29.5	14.9	37.5
RES/MGS (months)		35.8	30.9	27.0	25.9	43.7	54.3	57.5	39.3	20.2
Short-term/EDT (%)		35.8	30.9	27.0	25.8	43.7	54.3	57.5	39.3	20.2

Key: MGS – Imports of goods and services.
Source: World Bank, *Global Development Finance 2000*.

Table 9.5
Exposure of BIS Reporting Banks to Non-BIS Borrowers,
end-June 1997 (US$ bn)

Total	*1,054.9*
Germany	178.2
Japan	172.7
USA	131.0
France	100.2
UK	77.8
% of private non-bank borrowers	45%

Source: Bank for International Settlements

have been more averse to lending either to governments or to developing economies. The pattern of lending in the late 1970s and early 1980s suggests the contrary.

From the beginning of the 1990s, Thailand and Malaysia sustained significant current account deficits. Over-investment of investible funds in 'non-tradeables' made things worse. In so far as such investments — e.g. in power generations and telecommunications — did not contribute to export earnings, they aggravated the problem of currency mismatch, with foreign borrowings invested in activities not generating foreign exchange. An additional problem of 'term mismatch' also arose as a high proportion of these foreign borrowings were short-term in nature (Table 9.6), but were deployed to finance medium to long-term projects.

Foreign capital inflows into East Asia augmented the high domestic savings rate to raise the domestic investment rate as well as East Asian investments abroad in the 1990s. Thus, though there is some evidence that foreign capital inflows may have adversely affected the domestic savings rate indirectly, foreign capital inflows generally supplemented, rather than substituted for domestic savings (see Wong with Jomo 1999). It is difficult to be conclusive on this point as the nature of foreign capital inflows has changed significantly over time. Hence, even if earlier foreign capital inflows may once have adversely affected domestic savings, it is also possible that the changed composition of foreign capital inflows just before the crisis no longer adversely affected domestic savings.

Increased foreign capital inflows have also reduced foreign exchange constraints, allowing the financing of additional imports, but thus, also

Table 9.6
East Asian Four: Maturity Distribution of Lending by
BIS Reporting Banks, 1996 (US$ million)

	South Korea	*Thailand*	*Indonesia*	*Malaysia*
All Loans				
June 1996	88,027	69,409	49,306	20,100
Dec. 1996	99,953	70,147	55,523	22,234
June 1997	103,432	69,382	58,726	28,820
Under 1 Year				
June 1996	62,332	47,834	29,587	9,991
Dec. 1996	67,506	45,702	34,248	11,178
June 1997	70,182	45,567	34,661	16,268
1-2 Years				
June 1996	3,438	4,083	3,473	834
Dec. 1996	4,107	4,829	3,589	721
June 1997	4,139	4,592	3,541	615

Source: Bank of International Settlements (BIS).

inadvertently encouraging current account deficits. Finally, foreign capital inflows most certainly adversely affected factor payment outflows, export and import propensities, the terms of trade as well as capital flight, and thus, the balance of payments. These results suggest caution in determining the extent to which foreign capital inflows should be encouraged. Also, the Southeast Asian three's heavy dependence on foreign direct investment in gross domestic capital formation, especially for manufacturing investments, has probably also limited the development of domestic entrepreneurship as well as many other indigenous economic capabilities by requiring greater reliance on foreign capabilities, usually associated with some types of FDI (Jomo *et al.* 1997).

After mid-1995, the Southeast Asian currency pegs to the US dollar — which had enhanced the region's competitiveness as the dollar declined for a decade after the 1985 Plaza accord — became a growing liability as the yen began to depreciate once again. The overvalued currencies became attractive targets for speculative attacks, resulting in the futile, but costly defences of the Thai baht and Malaysian ringgit, and the rapid regional spread of herd panic termed contagion. The resulting precipitous asset price collapses —

as the share and property market bubbles burst — undermined the East Asian four's heavily exposed banking systems, for some (e.g. Malaysia), for the second time in little over a decade, undermining financial system liquidity, and causing economic recession.

Undoubtedly, international financial liberalisation succeeded in temporarily generating massive net capital inflows into East Asia, unlike many other developing and transitional economies, some of which experienced net outflows. But it also exacerbated systemic instability and reduced the scope for the developmental government interventions responsible for the region's economic miracle. In Southeast Asia, FDI domination (well above the average for developing countries) of internationally competitive manufacturing had weakened domestic industrialists, inadvertently enhancing the dominance of finance capital and its influence over economic policy making.

As noted earlier, three major indicators began to cause concern from the mid-1990s. The current account of the balance of payments and the savings-investment gap were recording large imbalances in the Southeast Asian economies, especially Thailand and Malaysia. However, as Table 9.7 shows, short-term foreign debt and the current account deficit as proportions of international reserves in Malaysia were better than in South Korea, Thailand and Indonesia, thereby later averting the need for IMF emergency credit. Domestic credit expansion had also soared in all four countries by the mid-1990s. Prior to the crisis, there had been a steady trend towards financial liberalisation in East Asia, dating back to the mid-1980s. This had included bank liberalisation, considerable promotion of the region's 'newly emerging' stock markets and greater capital account convertibility. Thus, East Asia succeeded in attracting a great deal of capital inflows.

Whereas the other three crisis-affected East Asian economies succeeded in attracting considerable, mainly short-term US dollar bank loans into their more bank-based financed systems, Malaysia's vulnerability was mainly due to the volatility of international portfolio capital flows into its stock market. As a consequence, the nature of Malaysia's external liabilities at the beginning of the crisis was quite different from that of the other crisis-stricken East Asian economies. A greater proportion consisted of equity, rather than debt.

Much more of the liabilities, including the debt, were private — rather than public — compared to foreign debt exposure in the mid-eighties. Also, compared to the other three, much more of Malaysian foreign debt in the late 1990s was long-term — rather than short-term — in nature. Monetary policy as well as banking supervision in Malaysia had generally been much more prudent compared to the other crisis victims. Banks in Malaysia had

Table 9.7
East Asian Four: Debt Service and Short-term Debt, 1980-1996

	Debt Service as a Proportion of Exports (%)			Short-term Debt (US$ billion)[a]				Current Account Deficit Plus Short-term Debt as Share of International Reserves (%)[b]			
	1980	1992	1995	1992	1994	1995	1996	1992	1994	1995	1996
Indonesia	13.9	32.1	30.9	18.2	14.0	16.2	17.9	191	139	169	138
Malaysia	6.3	6.6	7.8	3.6	7.6	7.5	8.5	29	46	60	55
South Korea	14.5	6.9	5.8	11.9	31.6	46.6	66.6	133	125	131	127
Thailand	18.9	14.1	10.2	14.7	29.2	41.1	44.0	101	127	152	153

Notes: [a] Year-end figures.
[b] As a percentage of reserves, measured by dividing the current account deficit plus short-term debt by international reserves (1992 figures computed from World Bank data).
Sources: UNCTAD (1997: Table 14); World Bank (1994: Tables 20, 23; 1997: Table 17).

not been allowed to borrow heavily from abroad to lend in the domestic market, as in the other economies. Such practices involved currency and term mismatches, which increased financial system vulnerability to foreign bankers' confidence as well as pressure on the exchange rate pegs.

These differences have lent support to the claim that Malaysia was an 'innocent bystander' which fell victim to the regional contagion for being in the wrong part of the world at the wrong time. Such a view takes a benign perspective on portfolio investment inflows, and does not recognise that such inflows are even more easily reversible and volatile than bank loan inflows. The magnitude of the gross inflows and outflows reflect the much greater volatility of these flows, often obscured by focussing on net flows. However, contrary to the 'innocent bystander' hypothesis, Malaysia's experience actually suggests greater vulnerability due to greater reliance on the capital market. As a consequence, the Malaysian economy became hostage to international portfolio investor confidence. Hence, when the government leadership engaged in fiery rhetoric and market-insensitive policy initiatives that upset such investor confidence, Malaysia paid a heavy price as capital flight accelerated.

Role of the IMF

Critical consideration of the causes and consequences of the East Asian crises requires close and careful attention to the nature and implications of IMF 'rescue' programs and conditionalities, as well as policies favoured by the international as distinct from the domestic financial communities and others affected. IMF prescriptions and conventional policy-making wisdom favoured bank closures, government spending cuts and higher interest rates in the wake of the crisis. Such contractionary measures transformed what had started as a currency crisis, and become a full-blown financial crisis, into a crisis of the real economy. Thus, Indonesia, Malaysia and South Korea — all had previously enjoyed massive capital inflows in the form of short-term bank loans or portfolio investments — went into recession during 1998, following Thailand, which went into recession in 1997.

Not only did the IMF underestimate the severity of the collapse in all the East Asian economies, it also under-estimated the speed and strength of the recovery (IMF 1997, 1998; Lane *et al.* 1999). This suggests that the IMF not only did not understand the causes of the crises but was also incapable of designing optimal policies in response. There is still considerable doubt as to whether the IMF actually recognised the novel elements of the crisis and their implications ('old medicines for a new disease'), especially at the outset. The apparent failures of the IMF — to anticipate the current crisis in its generally glowing recent reports on the region, and also to effectively check, let alone reverse the situation despite interventions in Thailand, Indonesia and Korea — certainly did not inspire much confidence. And though the Philippines had long been under IMF programs and supervision, it was not spared the contagion.[1]

There is considerable international scepticism about the IMF's role in and prescriptions for the East Asian crisis. Most economists now agree that the early IMF programs for Thailand, Indonesia and South Korea were ill conceived, though there is little agreement over why the IMF made such mistakes. Perhaps partly out of force of habit in dealing with situations in Latin America, Africa, Eastern Europe and elsewhere, where fiscal deficits had been part of the problem, the IMF insisted on the same prescription of deflationary policies in its early policy responses to the East Asian crisis.

Thus, many of its programs were effectively contractionary in consequence, although this was sometimes disguised by poorly conceived measures to provide social safety nets for the poor. Hence, what started of as currency and financial crises, led — partly due to IMF-recommended or imposed policy responses — to economic recessions in much of the region in 1998. The accounts, of course, vary with the different countries involved, e.g. see Jomo 1998; *Cambridge Journal of Economics*, November 1998 for accounts of the East Asian experiences.

The early IMF policy prescription to raise domestic interest rates[2] not only failed to stem the capital flight, but instead exacerbated the impact of the crisis, with financial pain caused by currency depreciation, stock market collapse and rising interest rates. But even if higher interest rates succeeded in doing so, such capital flight can only be temporarily checked, and even so, at great and permanent cost to productive investments in the real economy. And when inflows are eventually reversed in the precipitous manner experienced by East Asia from the second half of 1997, much collateral damage is inevitable.

Despite their sound fiscal balances before the crisis, the East Asian economies were also asked to cut government spending to restore confidence in their currencies, despite the ominous implications for economic recovery. Although all the affected East Asian economies had been running fiscal surpluses in the years before the crises (except Indonesia, which had a small deficit in 1996), the IMF expected the governments to slash public expenditure. With the possible exception of Indonesia (which could not raise the financing required), the other crisis-affected economies eventually ignored this advice and began to undertake Keynesian-style reflationary counter-cyclical measures from the second half of 1998, which have been primarily responsible for economic recovery since.

Incredibly, the Fund did not seem to be very cognisant of the subjective elements contributing to the crisis, and seemed to approach the crises as if they were solely due to macroeconomic or financial system weaknesses. Examining the changing risk premiums on Eurobonds issued by East Asia, Woo (2000b) found evidence of 'irrational exuberance', implying that the potential for investor panic also existed. Also, though the risk premiums on Thai Eurobonds increased by 10 basis points following the July 1997 devaluation, they jumped by four times as much with the acceptance of the IMF program for Thailand in August 1997. This suggests that the latter's deflationary macroeconomic policies and abrupt closure of financial institutions had undermined — rather than restored — investor confidence.

Insolvent financial institutions should have been restructured in ways so as to avoid the possibility of triggering bank runs and consequent social instability. By insisting on closing down banks and other financial institutions in Thailand, Indonesia and South Korea, the IMF undermined much of the remaining confidence there, inducing further panic in the process. Anwar Nasution (2000) points out that the IMF way of taking insolvent banks out of the Indonesian financial system in late 1997 exacerbated the country's economic crisis. He argues that the Indonesian government should have taken over the insolvent banks temporarily —rather than have them closed them down suddenly — to sustain credit to solvent borrowers and retain depositors' confidence. Also, while the IMF insisted on greater transparency by the affected host governments and those under their jurisdiction, it continued to operate under considerable secrecy itself.

Such IMF double standards, also reflected by its priority in protecting the interests of foreign banks and governments, also compromised its ostensible role as an impartial agent working in the interests of the host economy. The burden of IMF programs invariably fell on the domestic financial sector and, eventually, on the public at large who have borne most of the costs of adjustment and reform. The social costs of the public policy responses have been very considerable, usually involving bail-outs of much of the financial sector and the corporate sector more generally.

There has also been considerable unhappiness in East Asia about how differently the IMF had responded to the East Asian crises compared to the earlier Mexican crisis. It is widely believed that the IMF was far more generous in helping Mexico due to US interest in ensuring that the tequila crisis would not be seen as an adverse consequence of Mexico's joining the North American Free Trade Agreement (NAFTA). In contrast, East Asians saw the IMF as far less generous and also more demanding with Thailand, Indonesia and South Korea which had long seen themselves as US and Western allies.

Liabilities and other commitments to foreign banks have invariably been given priority by the Fund, even though both foreign and domestic banks may have been equally irresponsible or imprudent in their lending practices. As the Bank of International Settlements (1998) noted, "In spite of growing strains in Southeast Asia, overall bank lending to Asian developing countries showed no evidence of abating in the first half of 1997" (also see Raghavan 1998). In the year from mid-1996 to mid-1997, South Korea received US\$15 billion in new loans, while Indonesia received US\$9 billion from the banks. Short-term lending continued to dominate, with 70 per cent of lending due within a year, while the share of lending to private non-bank borrowers rose to 45 per cent at the end of June 1997. The banks were also actively acquiring 'non-traditional assets' in the region, e.g. in higher yielding local money markets and other debt securities. Most of this lending was by Japanese and continental European banks.

Thus, Western and Japanese banks will emerge from the crisis relatively unscathed and stronger than the domestic financial sectors, which have taken the brunt of the cost of adjustment. Some merchant banks and other financial institutions will also be able to make lucrative commissions from marketing sovereign debt as the short-term private borrowings — which precipitated the crisis — are converted into longer-term government-guaranteed bonds under the terms of the IMF programmes. Hence, the IMF programmes have been seen as primarily benefiting foreign banks, rather than the East Asian economies or people.

Recovery and Reform

For the first year after the East Asian crises began in mid-1997, there was limited interest in the West with respect to growing calls from East Asia and elsewhere for reforms to the international monetary and financial systems. A Japanese government initiative from the third quarter of 1997 to set up a regional monetary facility with US\$100 billion to deal with the crisis was opposed by the IMF. This opposition was endorsed by the Western powers as well as China, which was suspicious of Japanese intentions to take advantage of the crisis to secure regional leadership.

However, the situation changed dramatically a year later as the East Asian crisis seemed to be spreading West, via Russia and Brazil. In the USA, there was a scare on Wall Street after the collapse of the LTCM hedge fund, subsequently rescued thanks to an initiative of the US Federal Reserve Bank. The second half of 1998 saw much greater Western concern about the international financial system, and the possible damage its vulnerability might cause. Various government leaders began a briefly animated international discussion about the need for a new international financial architecture, leading to some initiatives to promote greater international financial stability.

Macroeconomic Recovery

As noted earlier, before the East Asian crisis, there were no clear macroeconomic warnings of imminent crisis. The countries sustained high growth with low inflation. Their public finances were sound, with both the external debt and the current account deficit manageable. Thus, East Asian government officials kept reiterating 'healthy fundamentals' up to the outbreak of the full-scale crisis. Many attempts have since been made to explain the causes and consequences of the crisis, but there has been relatively little attention to the recovery.

With the possible exception of Indonesia, largely due to its complicated political transition, the other three East Asian economies are now clearly on a path of recovery from financial crisis, with the pace of economic recovery far quicker than most early forecasts, including those by the IMF. Hence, the speed of the recovery has been as surprising as the earlier spread and deepening of the crisis (see the official IMF publications during 1997-2000). Initial IMF predictions were that growth would be stagnant for at least three to four years after the crisis (U-shaped recovery). In late 1997 and early 1998, the IMF failed to anticipate the sharp downturns of 1998. Then, once deep recession was evident, it anticipated continued recession in 1999 and very modest recovery from 2000. Instead, the Korean, Malaysian and, arguably, Thai economies have quickly recovered after sharp drops in 1998 (V-shaped recovery).

The turnaround in economic performance can mainly be attributed to Keynesian[3] macroeconomic measures. Both the Korean and Malaysian economies recovered due to reflationary macroeconomic policies. Also, among financial reform measures, the swift recapitalisation of commercial banks from mid-1998 in both Malaysia and South Korea is now acknowledged as having been crucial for their recoveries. However, a much lower share of recent Malaysian bank lending is going to productive purposes compared to the other three economies with their more bank-based financial systems. As shown in Tables 9.8a, 9.8b, 9.8c and 9.8d, in 1999, only 19 per cent of commercial bank loans and advances went to manufacturing in Malaysia, compared to 35 per cent in Korea (in 1998), 30 per cent in Thailand and 36 per cent in Indonesia. However, the restoration of bank liquidity through such measures is not what is usually meant by the structural reforms desired by the IMF. In fact, such measures have been much criticised as likely to perpetuate, if not exacerbate the problem of moral hazard in the economy. After all, as Shin (2000) notes, "the injection of public money is necessary to revive its financial sector whether a government is committed to reform or not."

Interest rates were reduced drastically — almost in defiance of IMF prescriptions — to boost corporate recovery. The IMF's initial macroeconomic policy emphasis involved retrenchment. By insisting on sharply higher interest rates, corporate failures soared, making voluntary corporate reforms even more difficult. Figure 9.1 shows interest rates peaking in Thailand in September 1997, in Korea in January 1998, in Malaysia in April 1998 and in Indonesia in August 1998. Of the East Asian four, interest rates had risen least in Malaysia, by less than three percentage points. And although capital controls introduced in September 1998 succeeded in consolidating the downward trend in interest rates, Thai interest rates soon fell below the Malaysian rates from much higher levels earlier. Interest rates fell throughout the region in the second half of 1998. This was helped by changed monetary policies in the West, and it is not clear whether Malaysia's capital controls were really necessary for bringing down interest rates by the third quarter of 1998.

The depreciation of the region's currencies due to the crisis (see Table 9.9 and Figure 9.2) may also have helped corporate recovery and contributed to improved trade balances as well as foreign reserves among the four economies (Figures 9.3a, 9.3b, 9.3c and 9.3d). Figure 9.2 also shows that exchange rate volatility declined significantly after mid-1998 except in Indonesia due to political instability. Figures 9.4a, 9.4b, 9.4c and 9.4d show that interest rates were highest when exchange rates were lowest, indicating that all four governments responded similarly by raising interest rates in response to the contagion of spreading currency crises and falling foreign exchange rates. The self-fulfilling nature of such crises suggests that little else could be done in the face of such capital flight with open capital accounts. It is also difficult to determine how futile these initial monetary policy responses actually were.

Table 9.8a
Thailand: Loans and Advances by Commercial Banks, 1989-1999 (% of Total Loans)

	1989	1990	1991	1992	1993	1994	1995	1996	1997	1998	1999
Agriculture	6.5	6.6	7.0	6.2	5.5	4.4	3.7	3.4	2.7	2.8	2.6
Manufacturing	25.8	25.1	25.3	23.7	24.0	24.2	25.8	27.1	30.9	30.7	30.1
Construction	3.8	4.0	4.0	4.0	3.8	4.1	4.4	4.9	4.5	4.7	4.3
Trade and Transportation	19.5	19.3	19.1	18.9	20.0	18.4	20.3	20.9	20.4	20.2	19.3
Finance and Real Estate	14.8	17.0	17.0	17.6	17.3	17.6	17.4	15.9	16.1	14.7	17.7
Service Industries	5.7	6.1	6.8	7.3	7.7	7.8	7.8	7.8	7.6	8.0	7.5
Households	10.8	10.6	11.2	12.3	12.6	12.7	12.3	12.6	10.8	11.4	11.0
Others	13.0	11.3	9.7	9.9	9.0	10.9	8.2	7.6	7.1	7.6	7.4
Total Loans (Dom. Credit)	100.0	100.0	100.0	100.0	100.0	100.0	100.0	100.0	100.0	100.0	100.0
Change (growth yoy %)	29.9	32.7	21.0	20.7	23.5	28.3	22.9	14.2	24.8	-13.6	-2.0
Total Loans (% of GDP)	60.6	68.4	72.1	77.1	85.0	95.2	101.5	103.5	125.5	113.0	109.1

Sources: Computed from *SEACEN Financial Statistics* and Bank of Thailand data.

Table 9.8b
Indonesia: Loans & Advances by Commercial Banks, 1989-1999 (% of Total Loans)

	1989	1990	1991	1992	1993	1994	1995	1996	1997	1998	1999
Agriculture	8.3	7.3	7.5	8.3	8.0	7.3	6.6	6.0	6.9	8.1	8.1
Manufacturing	32.0	31.3	29.2	30.1	34.2	31.9	30.7	26.9	29.5	35.2	36.4
Construction	n.a.	n.a.	n.a.	n.a.	n.a.	n.a.	n.a.	n.a.	n.a.	n.a.	n.a.
Trade and Transportation	31.6	30.4	29.1	26.6	25.1	23.5	23.1	24.1	21.8	19.8	19.6
Finance and Real Estate	n.a.	n.a.	n.a.	n.a.	n.a.	n.a.	n.a.	n.a.	n.a.	n.a.	n.a.
Service Industries	16.4	18.3	18.3	21.5	23.8	26.9	28.4	31.3	30.0	28.5	26.5
Households	n.a.	n.a.	n.a.	n.a.	n.a.	n.a.	n.a.	n.a.	n.a.	n.a.	n.a.
Others	11.7	12.7	16.0	13.4	8.9	10.5	11.2	11.7	11.8	8.4	9.5
Total Loans (Dom. Credit)	100.0	100.0	100.0	100.0	100.0	100.0	100.0	100.0	100.0	100.0	100.0
Change (growth yoy %)	38.0	50.0	49.9	47.6	45.6	49.5	51.6	55.0	60.5	49.3	
Total Loans (% of GDP)	44.6	53.8	16.2	8.9	21.6	25.6	24.2	24.8	29.1	28.9	-24.8

Sources: Computed from *SEACEN Financial Statistics* and Bank Indonesia data.

Table 9.8c
Malaysia: Loans and Advances by Commercial Banks, 1989-1999 (% of Total Loans)

	1989	1990	1991	1992	1993	1994	1995	1996	1997	1998	1999
Agriculture	5.4	5.2	4.8	4.4	3.5	2.6	2.2	2.1	2.0	2.0	2.3
Manufacturing	20.9	23.2	24.2	24.0	23.0	24.0	24.2	22.0	20.1	18.8	18.8
Construction	7.1	6.8	3.8	8.1	7.9	7.7	8.0	8.9	10.1	10.3	9.6
Trade and Transportation	17.6	16.1	15.3	13.6	13.4	13.0	12.6	12.1	13.1	13.7	13.5
Finance and Real Estate	23.7	22.6	22.1	23.3	24.2	20.7	22.7	25.2	24.1	13.9	13.1
Service Industries	n.a.	n.a.	n.a.	n.a.	n.a.	n.a.	n.a.	n.a.	n.a.	n.a.	n.a.
Households	n.a.	n.a.	n.a.	n.a.	n.a.	n.a.	n.a.	n.a.	n.a.	n.a.	n.a.
Others	25.3	26.1	29.7	26.5	28.0	31.9	30.2	29.7	30.5	41.3	42.6
Total Loans (Dom. Credit)	100.0	100.0	100.0	100.0	100.0	100.0	100.0	100.0	100.0	100.0	100.0
Change (growth yoy %)	18.1	20.3	20.4	8.8	10.9	14.4	30.5	24.5	32.9	7.2	3.5
Total Loans (% of GDP)	65.5	67.8	71.9	70.2	68.1	68.6	78.7	85.8	102.8	109.1	107.4

Source: Computed from *Quarterly Economic Bulletin*, Bank Negara Malaysia data.

Table 9.8d
Korea: Loans and Advances by Commercial Banks, 1989-1999 (% of Total Loans)

	1989	1990	1991	1992	1993	1994	1995	1996	1997	1998	1999
Agriculture	9.8	10.0	9.9	8.7	9.0	9.5	10.2	9.7	9.6	9.8	n.a.
Manufacturing	41.4	42.0	46.7	43.8	43.4	42.1	40.9	39.2	37.1	35.3	n.a.
Construction	9.6	8.7	7.5	6.7	6.7	6.6	7.5	7.4	6.9	7.1	5.9
Trade and Transportation	7.0	7.2	7.8	7.3	7.5	7.6	8.0	8.8	9.3	9.3	n.a.
Finance and Real Estate	6.5	5.6	0.5	6.3	4.7	3.3	2.1	2.1	2.9	5.0	6.8
Service Industries	n.a.	n.a.	n.a.	n.a.	n.a.	n.a.	n.a.	n.a.	n.a.	n.a.	n.a.
Households	2.7	3.1	3.1	2.4	2.2	2.0	2.2	2.3	2.6	2.9	n.a.
Others	22.9	23.4	24.5	24.7	26.6	29.0	29.1	30.5	31.6	30.6	n.a.
Total Loans (Dom. Credit)	100.0	100.0	100.0	100.0	100.0	100.0	100.0	100.0	100.0	100.0	100.0
Change (growth yoy %)	28.2	18.4	15.4	20.3	12.0	18.0	12.2	16.2	13.1	-0.1	24.9
Total Loans (% of GDP)	41.9	41.4	39.5	41.8	41.5	42.0	40.4	42.3	44.2	44.6	n.a.

Sources: Computed from *SEACEN Financial Statistics* and Bank of Korea data.

East Asian Comparisons

Figure 9.1
East Asian Four: Monthly Interest Rates,
January 1997 - May 2000

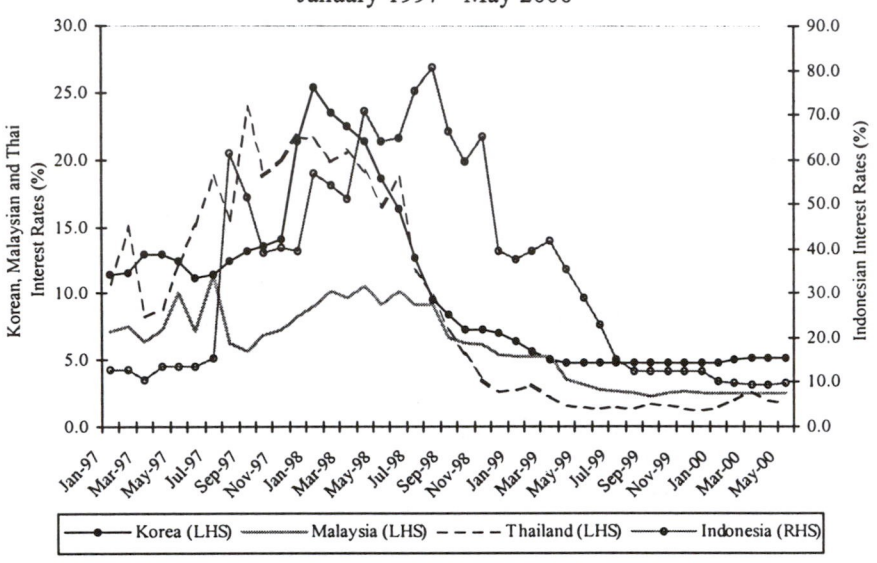

Figure 9.2
East Asian Four: Monthly Foreign Exchange Rates, January 1996 - June 2000

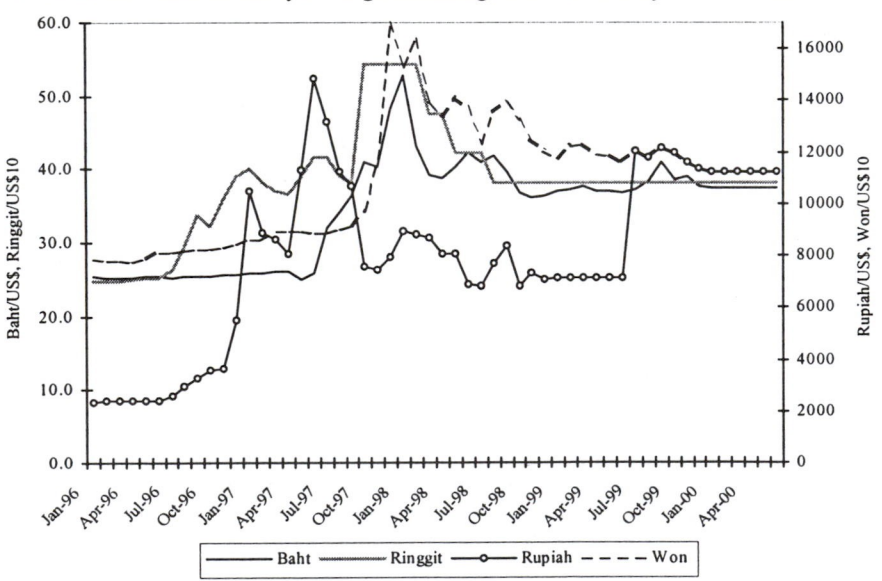

Figure 9.3a
Thailand: Quarterly Trade Balance and Reserves, 1996Q1 - 2000Q1

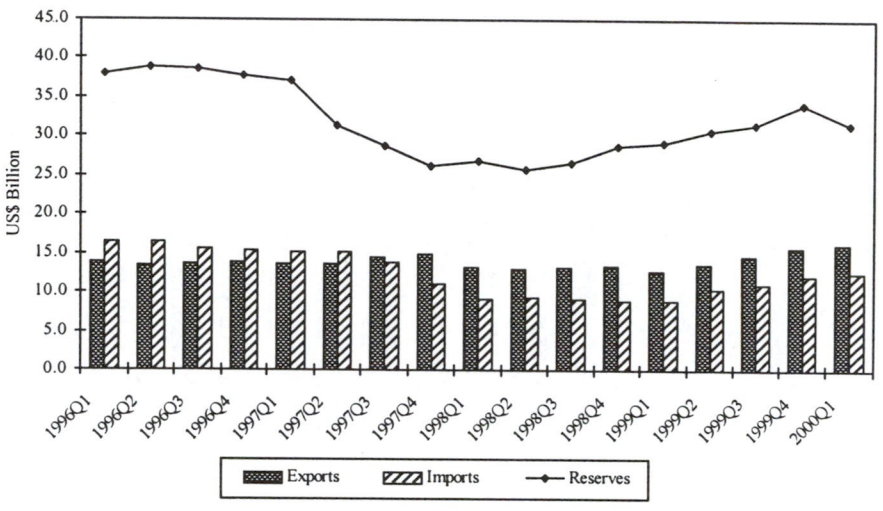

Figure 9.3b
Indonesia: Quarterly Trade Balance and Reserves, 1996Q1 - 1999Q4

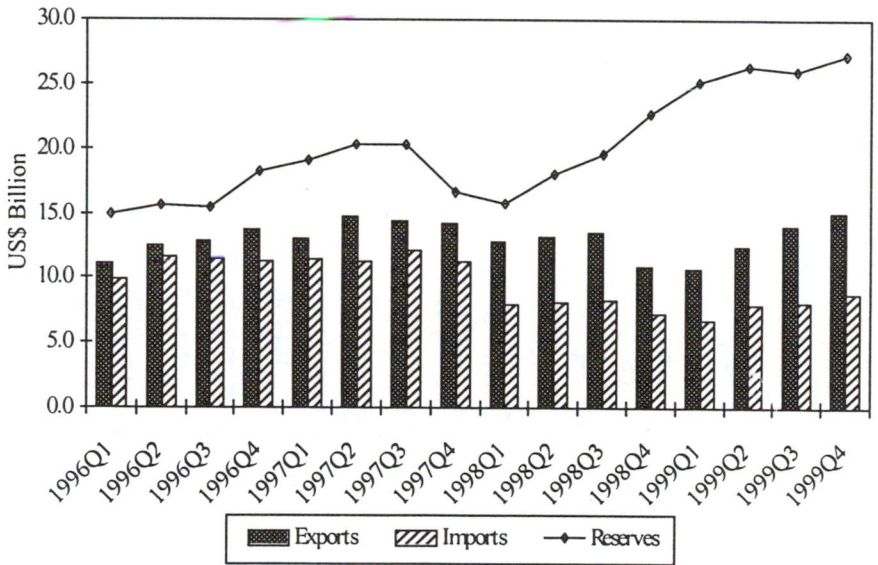

Figure 9.3c
Malaysia: Quarterly Trade Balance and Reserves, 1996Q1 - 1999Q4

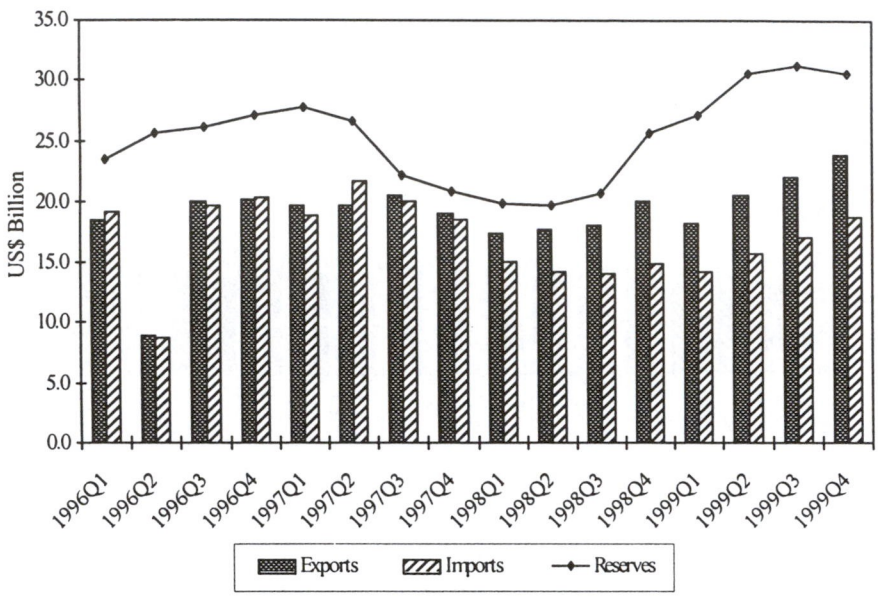

Figure 9.3d
Korea: Quarterly Trade Balance and Reserves, 1996Q1 - 2000Q1

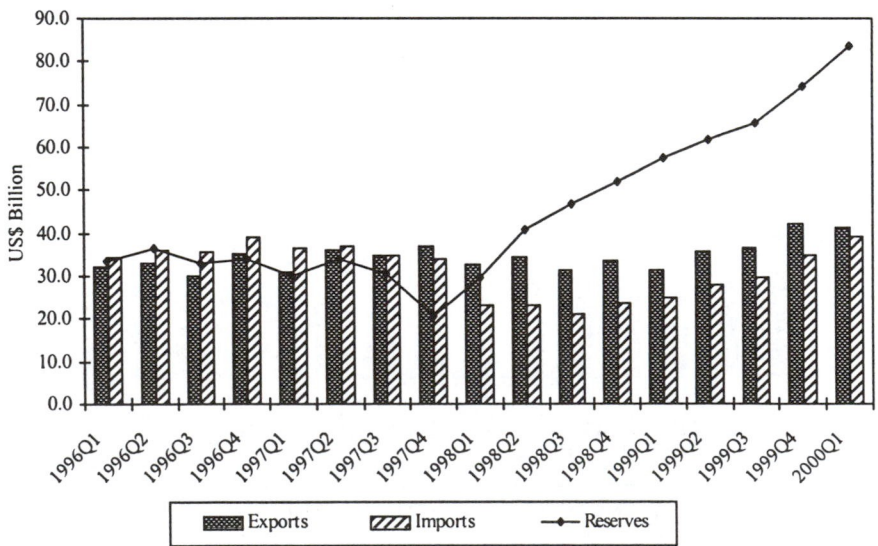

Figure 9.4a
Thailand: GDP Growth, Foreign Exchange and Interest Rates,
1997Q1 - 2000Q1

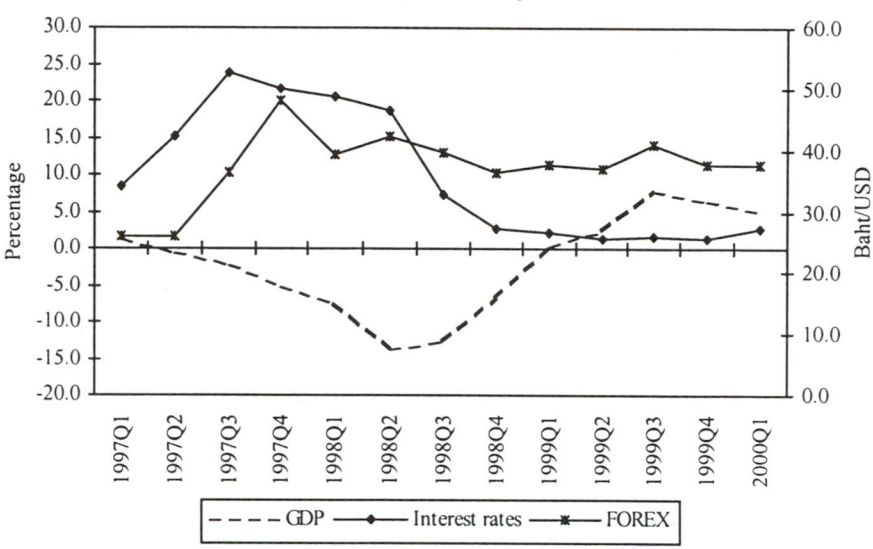

Figure 9.4b
Indonesia: GDP Growth, Foreign Exchange and Interest Rates,
1997Q1 - 2000Q1

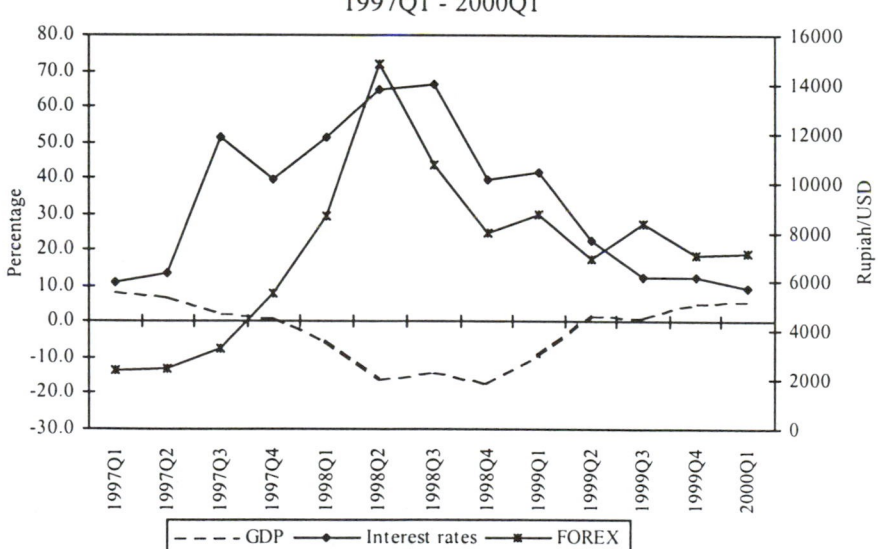

Figure 9.4c
Malaysia: GDP Growth, Foreign Exchange and Interest Rates,
1997Q1 - 2000Q1

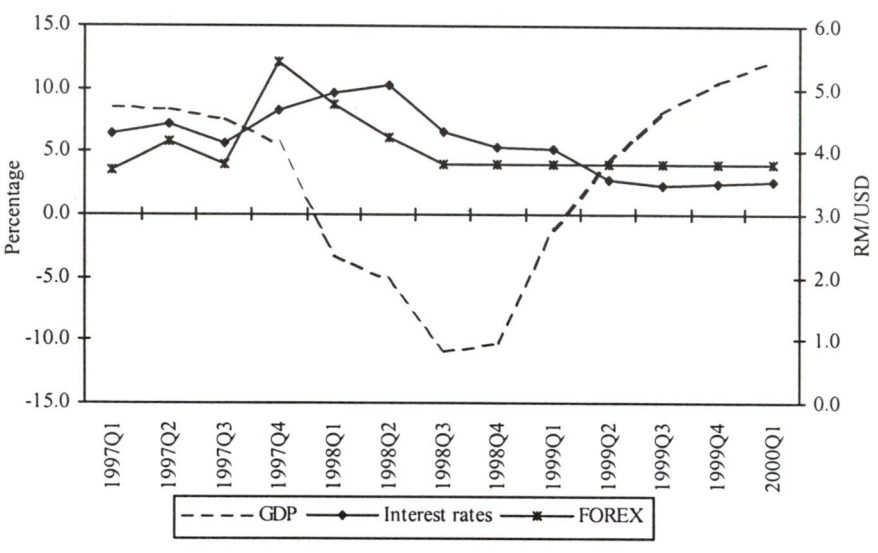

Figure 9.4d
Korea: GDP Growth, Foreign Exchange and Interest Rates,
1997Q1 - 2000Q1

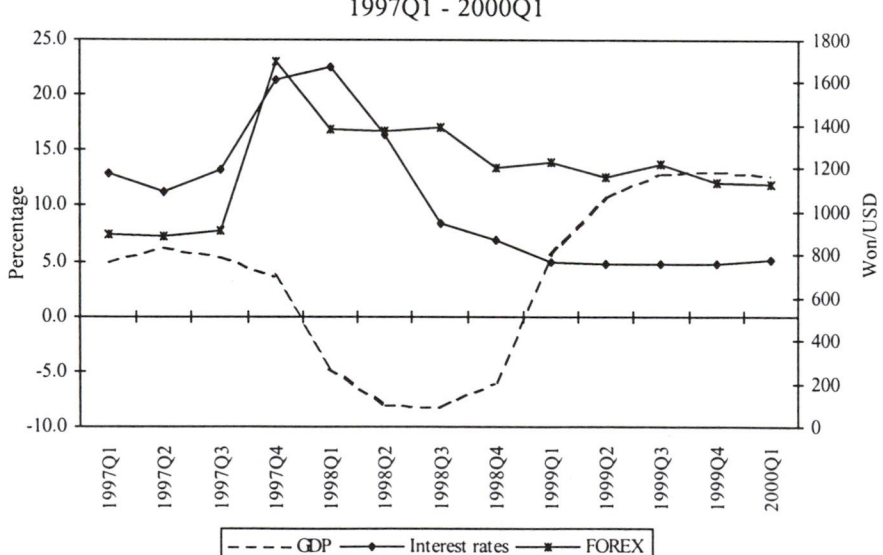

Table 9.9
East Asian Four: Exchange Rates and
Depreciation Against US$, 1997-2000

	Exchange Rate (monthly average)				Depreciation (%)		
	Jan. 1997	Jan. 1998	July 1998	July 2000	Jan. 1997-Jan. 1998	Jan. 1997-July 1998	Jan. 1997-July 2000
Indonesia Rupiah	2,369	9,767	14,233	8,249	312.2	500.7	248.2
Thailand Baht	25.72	53.12	41.22	39.29	106.5	60.3	52.8
Malaysia Ringgit	2.491	4.363	4.151	3.800	75.2	66.7	52.6
Korea Won	850.6	1,700	1,294	1,119	99.9	52.1	31.5

Source: Computed from *Financial Times*, Extel data.

The currency depreciations generally more than compensated for the declining export prices due to global price deflation of both primary and manufactured commodities associated with international trade liberalisation. The Malaysian ringgit was fixed to the US dollar from early September 1998 in an effort originally intended to strengthen its value. Fortuitously, lower US interest rates in the aftermath of the Russian, Brazilian, LTCM and Wall Street crises of August 1998 served to strengthen other East Asian currencies, causing the ringgit to be undervalued instead from late 1998. To ensure Korean exchange rate competitiveness, the Seoul authorities intervened in the foreign exchange market to slow down the pace of won appreciation from late 1998.

As Figures 9.5a and 9.5b show, budget deficits substantially increased in 1998, especially in the second half. While government revenues were probably adversely affected by the economic slowdown, government expenditure also rose with efforts to reflate the economy from around mid-1998. Government funds went to re-capitalise financial institutions and for increased spending, especially for public works and to provide the 'social safety nets' advocated by the Fund and the Bank. The re-capitalisation of financial

Figure 9.5a
Indonesia, Korea, Thailand and Malaysia: Annual Budget Balances
(% of GDP), 1996-1999

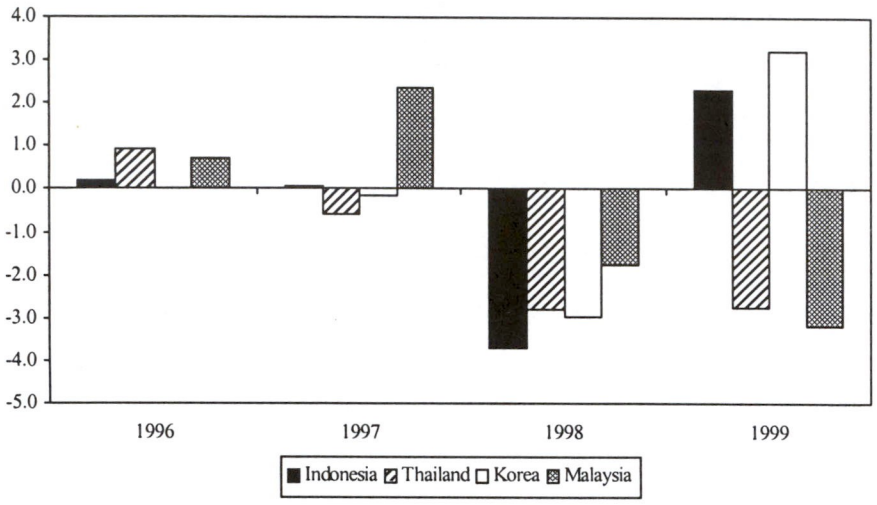

Figure 9.5b
Thailand, Korea and Malaysia: Quarterly Budget Balances
(% of GDP), 1997Q1 - 1999Q4

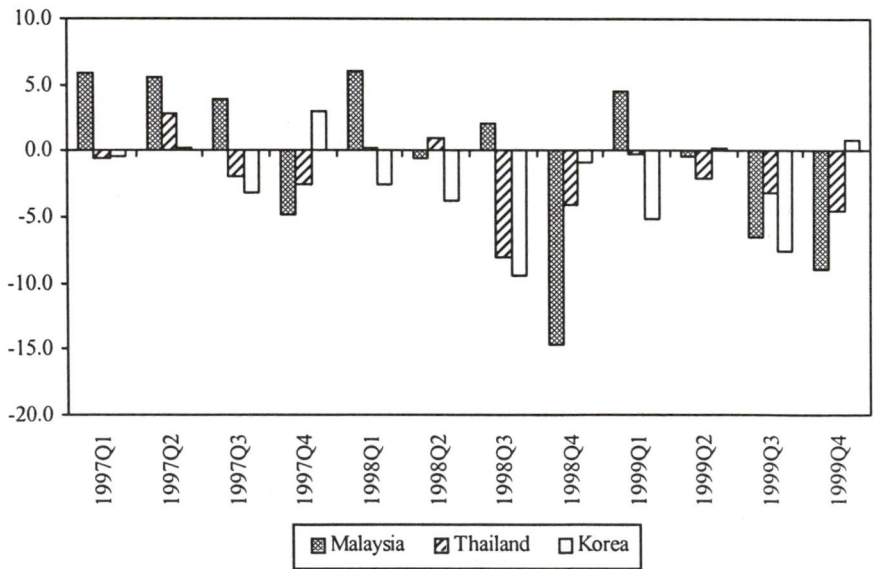

institutions[4] has been crucial for recovery by taking out inherited systemic risk from the banking system, thus restoring liquidity. The modest budget surpluses during the early and mid-1990s before the crisis were replaced by significant budgetary deficits to finance counter-cyclical measures. Thus, the balanced budgets of the pre-crisis period were crucial to helping overcome the crisis. It should be emphasised that such Keynesian policies were not part of the IMF programs.

Without capital controls, the East Asian economies could not reverse monetary policy without further adverse effects due to international exposure. Hence, monetary policy remained cautious until mid-1998. Thus, regional macroeconomic policies could only be changed after conducive changes in the international economic environment. Interest rates could only be lowered after the G7 took concerted action to lower interest rates and increase money supply to avoid financial turmoil after the Russian crisis led to the collapse of Long Term Capital Management (LTCM) hedge fund. In other words, East Asian Keynesian policies were made possible by international responses to the fear of global financial collapse from the third quarter of 1998. Ironically, this only became possible over a year after the East Asian crisis began when it seemed to threaten the rest of the world, especially Wall Street.

Reform of Corporate Governance[5]

Many institutional arrangements in the most affected economies probably at least once contributed significantly to 'catching-up', and while many features may no longer be desirable or appropriate, corporate reform advocates usually fail to even acknowledge that they were at least once conducive to rapid accumulation and growth. This is largely due to ideological presumptions about what constitutes good corporate governance, usually inspired by what has often been termed the Anglo-American model of capitalism. From this perspective, pre-crisis economic institutions were undesirable for various reasons, especially in so far as they departed from such a model. Worse still, with minimal evidence and faulty reasoning, the 1997-98 crises in the region have been blamed on these institutions as if they were crises just waiting to happen. Not surprisingly then, from this perspective, thoroughgoing reforms should be the top priority and the pre-crisis systems need to be abandoned altogether.

The IMF pushed for radical corporate reforms claiming that corporate structure was at the root of the crisis, with some reform-minded East Asian governments agreeing. However, it is doubtful that corporate structure was a major cause of the crisis though there were some symptoms of corporate distress in all the crisis-affected economies before the crisis. First, corporate profitability was deteriorating, more rapidly in Thailand, but also elsewhere in East Asia. Second, indices of investment efficiency, such as the ICOR, were rapidly deteriorating. Some of the economies (especially Thailand and South Korea) began to experience corporate failures from early 1997.

After Thailand, South Korea and Indonesia went to the IMF for emergency credit facilities, the Fund kept emphasising microeconomic reform as central to its recovery program, especially in Thailand and South Korea (e.g. Neiss 1999; Lane *et al.* 1999). The newly elected reformist Thai and South Korean governments, led by Chuan Leekpai and Kim Dae Jung, agreed with the IMF's insistence on the urgency of comprehensive corporate reforms, although there was some dissent over the Fund's punitive macroeconomic policies. These reforms generally sought to transform existing corporate structures, regarded as having caused over-investment and other ills, in line with ostensibly 'global' Anglo-American standards. Shin (2000) describes how Korean corporate reforms sought to remould its corporate structure along more American lines.

From recent East Asian experiences, it was clearly better to first improve the macroeconomic environment and remove systemic risks in the financial system. There is no evidence whatsoever that the simultaneous attempts at radical corporate reforms helped recovery in any decisive way. The agenda for corporate reform needs to be determined after careful consideration of existing weaknesses, rather than by presumptions about what may be best according to some textbook, ideological or policy driven agenda. An economy's corporate structure is inevitably the consequence of evolutionary developments including cultural heritages as well as colonial inheritances. Most economies accommodate a diversity of corporate structures. Inappropriate arrangements would have perished unless propped up by patrons such as the state. While others may have become dysfunctional due to changing circumstances, there is no universally optimum corporate structure (Chandler 1990).

The East Asian experiences also suggest that the IMF programs were generally not conducive to corporate reforms. The programs tended to exacerbate corporate failures sharply and made corporate as well as financial adjustments more difficult. The East Asian experiences, especially those of South Korea and Malaysia, suggest that improvements in macroeconomic conditions, especially interest rate reductions and appropriate increases in government spending, were necessary to facilitate adjustments and reforms.

New stock issues, asset sales and foreign capital investments, all necessary for corporate restructuring, only became possible with the more buoyant economic conditions from 1999.

It has also been argued that in all the East Asian cases, corporate reform efforts thus far have hardly succeeded in achieving their objective of correcting the structure of high debt and low profitability, but have instead imposed large costs on the economy. This view is seen as self-evident in the case of Malaysia, owing to the regime's approach, and for Indonesia owing to the political uncertainties since the crisis, but is also held to be true, albeit to lesser degrees, for Korea (Shin 2000) and Thailand (Pasuk 2000).

Enterprises anywhere that are otherwise well managed and profitable may find themselves in serious financial distress owing to developments beyond their control. During the East Asian crisis, sudden and steep currency devaluations increased firms' import costs and unhedged external liabilities denominated in foreign currencies, usually the US dollar. As these devaluations were accompanied by financial crises, limited access to emergency finance threatened the very survival of firms in the affected countries, especially small and medium-sized enterprises. Such firms face insolvency or being taken over at 'bargain basement' or 'fire sale' prices, usually by foreign interests unaffected by the crisis. For a whole variety of microeconomic reasons, such take-overs are unlikely to result in superior management. Such elimination of otherwise viable enterprises would most certainly undermine the processes of capacity and capability building deemed essential for catching-up development.

Shin (2000) argues for building a second stage catching-up system for Korea, instead of IMF and other proposed transitions on ostensibly Anglo-American lines. Other similar arguments from elsewhere in the region acknowledge that there were considerable abuses of the pre-crisis system by politically powerful rentiers, and these should, of course, be eliminated (e.g. Gomez and Jomo 1999). Nevertheless, the other crisis-affected Southeast Asian economies still need reforms to ensure more appropriate developmentalist regimes in line with changing circumstances and challenges. States need to develop a new range of institutions for more effective selective intervention to accelerate the development of new industrial, technological, organisational and managerial capabilities to face the various new challenges associated with accelerated globalisation in the last decade and a half.

There are also grave doubts as to whether the reforms have improved corporate resilience for the long term. Shin (2000) has argued that foreign capital returned to Korea because the economy began picking up from

November 1998, after uncertainties were substantially reduced, rather than the return of foreign investment having led the recovery, as hoped for by the IMF. The recovery has been mainly driven by typically Keynesian policies, and certainly not by reforms in corporate governance.

In light of the basis for and nature of the recent recovery, the earlier and ongoing emphasis on the urgency of corporate reform was clearly ill informed and ill advised. Corporate profitability has undoubtedly improved. But there is no clear evidence that corporate reform was key to bringing about these recoveries. In fact, it has been noted that many corporate reform measures have been intended to prevent future crises, even at the cost of short-term economic recovery. With their earlier predictions of imminent 'doom without corporate reform' not realised, those insisting on such reforms as a prerequisite for recovery have now switched to warning of a second downturn for countries like Malaysia where resistance to reform has been officially articulated.

New International Financial Architecture[6]

As noted earlier, recent trends in the IMF and the WTO after the East Asian crises began are unlikely to make prevention of future crises any easier. By keeping open the capital account and allowing freedom for trans-border movements of funds, it becomes difficult not only to have measures to prevent financial crises, but also to introduce effective financial safety nets at the national level. Past IMF consultations with various governments have been unable to prevent major financial turmoil, with the frequency of currency and financial crises increasing, rather than decreasing with financial liberalisation in the last two decades. Despite its grudging acceptance of the efficacy of capital controls in Chile, Colombia and elsewhere, the Fund has been reluctant to urge countries to control short-term inflows before a crisis occurs.

Too little attention is being paid to the policies of the developed countries, especially the major economic powers, despite their impact on exchange rates in the rest of the world, especially in developing countries. Akyuz (2000a) has noted that all emerging-market crises of the last two decades have been associated with large changes in the exchange rates of the major industrial economies. Developing countries seem generally incapable of maintaining exchange rate stability while the major currencies experience big fluctuations. Hence, currency co-ordination among the US, Europe and Japan is desperately needed for the stability of their own currencies as well as other currencies in the world today. Despite frequent G7 meetings, existing arrangements leave much to be desired. Consequently, there are fluctuations of up to 20 per cent within a week. The effects of such huge swings on smaller open economies are not well understood, though they are expected to simply adjust to such changes.

Since the East Asian crisis, the international discussion on international financial reform to prevent future crises has emphasised questions of transparency and greater supply of information. However, there is no evidence that having more information will be enough to prevent crises. Also, efforts seem to be directed mainly to getting more information from governments, especially from the developing countries, with little done to get information on the various financial markets, especially the most volatile and vulnerable ones such as those involving highly-leveraged institutions and offshore markets.

A global system of prudential controls should accommodate the existing diversity of national conditions as well as regional arrangements. However, the currently favoured approach to prudential regulation is to formulate international standards for countries to implement and enforce. In the recent past, such standards have usually been set by the Bank of International Settlements (BIS), which serves banks in the OECD economies. There are several problems with this approach (Akyuz 2000a; 2000b). First, such standards do not specifically take into account the risks associated with international lending. Currently, credit rating agencies are relied upon to fill the vacuum, but they have a tendency to be pro-cyclical, thus exacerbating — rather than checking — fluctuations. Second, the standards have mainly been designed to protect creditors, not debtors, and the countries they belong to. A similar level of exposure may imply different risks to different creditors as well as debtors. Third, the one-size-fits-all approach implicit in setting standards tends to gloss over important variations, thus undermining the efficacy of this approach. Although there is currently agreement that the IMF should not set standards, it is likely to be involved in policing the enforcement of such standards, which would raise similar concerns.

After the East Asian crises, there seemed to be agreement that short-term capital flows needed to be regulated. But while developing countries currently have the right to control short-term capital flows, the lack of international endorsement for such measures serves as a major deterrent for those considering their introduction.

Instead, developing countries are currently being encouraged to either fix (through a currency board system or even dollarisation) or freely float their currencies, but are being discouraged from considering intermediate alternatives. However, studies have shown that a float system is associated with the same degree of volatility as a fixed system (Akyuz 2000a; 2000b), with the principal difference between the two being that of how external shocks work themselves out. It is crucial to insist that countries should be allowed to choose their own exchange rate regime, which should not be imposed as an IMF conditionality.

In managing crises, the recent East Asian experiences highlight the crucial importance of ensuring international liquidity by quickly providing foreign funds to economies experiencing crisis. Currently, such international liquidity provision is being frustrated by the following factors:

- Multilateral institutions generally do not have the necessary finances readily at their disposal. Although the IMF nominally has the requisite facilities, it lacks the required funds, which have to be raised with the approval and active support of its principal shareholders. This de facto requirement subjects the process to undue political influence, as was clear in the international financial community's changing responses to the East Asian crises as it unfolded from mid-1997.
- The IMF-imposed policy conditionalities accompanying the provision of such emergency liquidity have also been onerous. The East Asian experiences suggest that these conditionalities actually exacerbated the macroeconomic crises.
- Such funds should be used to support a currency against speculation, but instead, currencies were allowed to collapse first with the emergency funds going to pay off creditors.

Recent experiences underline the crucial importance of facilitating fair and orderly debt workouts to restructure debt payments due. Existing arrangements tend to treat debtor counties as if they are bankrupt without providing the protection and facilities of normal bankruptcy procedures[7]. With such a bankruptcy procedure, a debtor would have certain rights, including getting a temporary standstill on debt payments, continued financing for on-going operations, and orderly debt restructuring. While the IMF's Articles of Agreement allow for such temporary standstills, this has never actually been exercised.

During the recent South Korean crisis, creditors got together and struck an agreement with the government after a private meeting, causing three problems:

- The government was thus coerced to take over responsibility for private debt.

- The creditors thus got better debt restructuring terms, whereas debtors would be more likely to get better terms in a bankruptcy court.
- The new finance went to the creditors, instead of supporting the debtor.

Closing Remarks

The Malaysian experience has been compared and contrasted with those of the three most-affected economies, namely Thailand, Indonesia and South Korea, which sought IMF emergency credit facilities and were thus subjected to its conditionalities. The review of macroeconomic indicators in the four economies clearly shows that despite persistent current account deficits in Thailand and Malaysia, the crises cannot be attributed to macroeconomic profligacy. Instead, investor sentiment, herd behaviour, transborder contagion and the reversal of short-term capital inflows were primarily responsible for the crises throughout the region. Fortunately, Malaysia was less vulnerable thanks to pre-crisis restrictions on foreign borrowings as well as stricter central bank regulation. Unfortunately, however, but it was more vulnerable due to the greater role of its capital market unlike the other three economies with more bank-based financial systems. IMF policy conditionalities clearly exacerbated the economic contraction in the other economies. While deflationary fiscal and monetary policies were temporarily introduced in late 1997, they were less severe and of shorter duration. Instead, as the introduction suggested, contrarian rhetoric and policy initiatives were probably far more important in exacerbating the economic decline in Malaysia. In this regard, financial market expectations also served to exacerbate the crises.

More recently, recovery in the region, especially in Korea and Malaysia, has been principally due to successful Keynesian reflationary efforts. The recovery suggests that the emphasis by the IMF and the financial media on the prior necessity of corporate governance reforms has been misguided, i.e. such reforms are not a pre-condition for economic recovery. Instead of the Anglo-American-inspired reforms proposed, reforms should create new conditions for further catching up. Since the Malaysian experiment with capital controls has attracted considerable international attention, the chapter ends by outlining an agenda for international financial system reform in the interests of developing countries, although reform prospects have worsened with economic recovery and the apparently receding threat of fresh crises.

Notes

1. Arguably, the Philippines currency has not taken quite as hard a hit, in part because their (colonial-inherited) banking and accounting standards are considered

relatively better, but also because short-term capital inflows have been relatively lower.

2. Furman and Stiglitz (1998) have critically reviewed the relevant literature to argue against raising interest rates to protect the exchange rate. Especially where leveraging is high, as in East Asia, high interest rates will take a huge toll by weakening aggregate demand and increasing the likelihood and frequency of insolvencies. Unexpected interest rate hikes tend to weaken financial institutions, lower investments and hence, output. They offer three main reasons why keeping interest rates low while letting the exchange rate depreciate may be preferable option in the face of the trade-off involved:

   • To avoid crisis, there should be greater concern about interest rate increases than exchange rate declines (Demirguc-Kunt and Detragiache 1998).
   • Invoking a moral hazard argument, they suggest that any government intervention to stabilise the exchange rate is likely to encourage economic agents to take positions they would otherwise not take, later compelling the government to support the exchange rate to avoid the now larger adverse effects.
   • Invoking an equity argument, they ask why borrowers, workers, firms and others adversely affected by higher interest rates, should be compelled to pay for speculators' profits. When a government defends its currency, it is often making a one-way bet, where the expected loss is speculators' expected gain. In contrast, if the government does not wager any reserves, the gains of some speculators are simply the losses of others" (Furman and Stiglitz 1998: footnote 132).

3. As Keynes (1973: 322-323) argued, the remedy for crisis is lowering, rather than increasing interest rates:

   "The right remedy for the trade cycle is not to be found in abolishing booms and thus keeping us permanently in a semi-slump; but in abolishing slumps and thus keeping us permanently in a quasi-boom. ...[A] rate of interest, high enough to overcome the speculative excitement, would have checked, at the same time, every kind of reasonable new investment. Thus an increase in the rate of interest... belongs to the species of remedy which cures the disease by killing the patient."

4. For instance, the re-capitalisation of Korean commercial banks in September 1998 involved an injection of 64 trillion won. Similarly, the Malaysian effort involved over RM47 billion to take non-performing loans out of the banking system and another RM5-7 billion to re-capitalise the most distressed banks.

5. This sub-section and the next draw from Furman and Stiglitz (1998).

6. This section draws heavily on Akyuz (2000a; 2000b).

7. Henderson (1999) has argued that rather than invoke US bankruptcy procedures for private firms (Chapter 11) (see Cui 1996), the more relevant and appropriate reference point for developing country governments are the provisions for municipal authorities (Chapter 14).

REFERENCES

Abang Zainal Abidin (1986). "Financial Reform and the Role of Foreign Banks in Malaysia", in Cheng H.S. (ed.) *Financial Policy and Reform in Pacific Basin Countries*. Lexington Books, Lexington, MA.: 305-09.

Abu Bakar Suleiman, *et al.* (1998). "Impact of the East Asian Economic Crisis on Health and Health Care: Malaysia's Response". *Asia-Pacific Journal of Public Health*, 10(1): 5-9.

ADB (2000a). *Asian Recovery Report 2000*, March, Regional Economic Recovery Unit, Asian Development Bank, Manila.

ADB (2000b). *Asian Recovery Report 2000*, May, Regional Economic Recovery Unit, Asian Development Bank, Manila.

Agosin, Manuel R. and Ricardo Ffrench-Davis (1997). "Financial Liberalization and Development: A View for Emerging Economies". *Estudios de Economia*, 24(2), December: 207-218.

Agosin, Manuel R. and Diana Tussie (1993). *Trade and Growth: New Dilemmas in Trade Policy*. Macmillan, London.

Akyüz, Yilmaz (1995). "Taming International Finance", in J. Michie and J. G. Smith (eds) *Managing the Global Economy*. Oxford University Press, New York.

Akyüz, Yilmaz (2000a). *The Debate on the International Financial Architecture: Reforming the Reformers*. UNCTAD Discussion Paper No. 148, Geneva, April.

Akyüz, Yilmaz (2000b). "On Financial Instability and Control". Paper presented at a FONDAD conference on Crisis Prevention and Response, The Hague, 26-27 June.

Akyüz, Yilmaz and Charles Gore (1994). "Investment-profits Nexus in East Asian Industrialization", *UNCTAD Discussion Paper*, No. 91, Geneva, October.

Akyüz, Yilmaz and Andrew Cornford (1999). "Capital Flows to Developing Countries and the Reform of the International Financial System", *UNCTAD Discussion Paper*, No. 143, Geneva, November.

Al'Alim Ibrahim (ed.) (1994). *Generating a National Savings Movement*. ISIS, Kuala Lumpur.

Amadeo, E. J. (1996). "The Knife-edge of Exchange Rate-based Stabilization: Impact on Growth, Employment and Wages", *UNCTAD Review*.

Amsden, Alice (1989). *Asia's Next Giant: South Korea and Late Industrialization.* Oxford University Press, New York.

Anwar Ibrahim (1996). *The Asian Renaissance.* Times Books International, Singapore.

Asian Wall Street Journal, 19 June 1995.

ASEAN Economic Bulletin, Special issue, April 2000.

Awang Adek Hussin (1997). "Offshore Financial Centre: The Labuan Experiment", MIER 1997 National Outlook Conference, Kuala Lumpur, 2-3 December.

Aziz Zariza Ahmad (1997). *Mahathir's Paradigm Shift: The Man Behind the Vision.* Firma, Taiping.

Backman, Michael (1999). *Asian Eclipse: Exposing the Dark Side of Business in Asia.* Wiley, Singapore.

Bank Negara Malaysia, *Annual Report,* various issues, Bank Negara Malaysia, Kuala Lumpur. http://www.bnm.gov.my

Bank Negara Malaysia (1989). *Central Banking in an Era of Change: Landmark Speeches, 1959-1988.* Bank Negara Malaysia, Kuala Lumpur.

Bank Negara Malaysia (1994). *Money and Banking in Malaysia, 1959-1994.* 35th Anniversary Edition 1959-94. Bank Negara Malaysia, Kuala Lumpur.

Bank Negara Malaysia (BNM). *Monthly Statistical Bulletin (MSB),* various issues, Bank Negara Malaysia, Kuala Lumpur. http://www.bnm.gov.my

Bank Negara Malaysia, *Quarterly Economic Bulletin,* various issues, Bank Negara Malaysia, Kuala Lumpur. http://www.bnm.gov.my

Bank of International Settlements (1998). *Report on the Maturity and Nationality of International Bank Lending.* Bank of International Settlements, Basel, January.

Banker's Journal Malaysia, October/November, 1995, Kuala Lumpur.

Bello, Walden (1998). "The End of a 'Miracle': Speculation, Foreign Capital Dependence and the Collapse of the Southeast Asian Economies". *The Multinational Monitor*, 19(1) [http://www.essential.org/monitor].

Bhagwati, Jagdish (1998). "The Capital Myth". *Foreign Affairs*, 77(3), May/Jun: 7-12.

Booth, Anne (1999). "Education in Southeast Asia". Paper presented at the Second International Malaysian Studies Conference, Malaysian Social Science Association, Kuala Lumpur. To be published in Jomo K. S. (ed.) (2001b). *Paper Tigers in Southeast Asia? Behind Miracle and Debacle.* Macmillan, Basingstoke.

Bosworth, Barry and Susan Collins (1999). "From Boom to Crisis and Back Again: What Have We Learned". Asian Development Bank Institute Second Anniversary Workshop on Development Paradigms, Tokyo, 10 December.

Bowie, Alasdair (1988). *Crossing the Industrial Divide: State, Society and the Politics of Economic Transformation in Malaysia.* Columbia University Press, New York.

Bowie, Alasdair (1994). "The Dynamics of Business-government Relations in Industrialising Malaysia", in Andrew MacIntyre (ed.) *Business and Government in Industrialising Asia*. Cornell University Press, Ithaca: 167-94.

Cailloux, Jacques and Stephany Griffith-Jones (1999). "International Capital Flows, What Do We Know About Their Volatility? Evidence from Latin American Countries". Processed, Institute of Development Studies, University of Sussex.

Calvo, G. A. and C. M. Reinhart (1999). "Capital Flow Reversals, the Exchange Rate Debate and Dollarization". *Finance & Development*, 36(3), September: 13-15.

Camroux, David (1994). *"Looking East"... and Inwards: Internal Factors in Malaysian Foreign Relations during the Mahathir Era, 1981-1994.* Griffith University, Australia — Asia Working Paper No. 72, Brisbane.

Cardenas, Mauricio and Felipe Barrera (1997). "On the Effectiveness of Capital Controls: The Experience of Colombia during the 1990s". *Journal of Development Economics*, 54: 27-57.

Case, William (1993). "UMNO Paramountcy: A Report on Single-party Dominance in Malaysia". *Party Politics*, 2(1): 115-27.

Case, William (1996). *Elites and Regimes in Malaysia: Revisiting a Consociational Democracy.* Monash Asia Institute, Clayton, Victoria.

Chakravarty, B. (1997). "ASEAN Market Shadow Over the WTO Financial Talks". *Third World Resurgence*, 86: 22-24.

Chang H. J. (1994). *The Political Economy of Industrial Policy*. Macmillan, Basingstoke.

Cheong, Sally (1997). *Bumiputera Enterprises in the KLSE*. Volume 2. Corporate Research Services, Kuala Lumpur.

Chin Kok Fay (1999). *The Stock Market and Economic Development in Malaysia*, IKMAS Working Paper 16, March, Universiti Kebangsaan Malaysia, Bangi.

Chin Kok Fay (2000). "Financing Manufacturing in Malaysia: Experience, Issues and Challenges", in Jomo K. S. (ed.) *Southeast Asia's Ersatz Industrialisation*. Macmillan, Basingstoke.

Chin Kok Fay and Jomo K. S. (1996). "Financial Liberalization and Economic Development in Malaysia". Paper presented to the International Conference on 'Globalisation and Development', Faculty of Economics and Administration, University of Malaya, August.

Chin Kok Fay and Jomo K. S. (1999). "Financial Reform and Crisis in Malaysia". Paper for Hosei University workshop on the 'Big Bang in East Asia', March.

Chin Kok Fay and Jomo K. S. (2000). "Financial Sector Rents in Malaysia", in Mushtaq Khan and Jomo K. S. (eds) *Rents, Rent-seeking and Economic Development: Theory and Evidence in Asia*. Cambridge University Press, Cambridge: 304-26.

Chin Kok Fay with Jomo K. S. (2001). "Financial Intermediation and Restraint", in Jomo K. S. and Shyamala Nagaraj (eds.) *Globalisation versus Development: Heterodox Perspectives.* Macmillan, Basingstoke.

Chossudovsky, Michel (1997). "The Global Financial Crisis", *Third World Resurgence,* 86: 9-13.

Chowdhury, Anis and Islam, Inayatul (1993). *The Newly Industrialising Economies of East Asia.* Routledge, London.

Chuah Lay Lian (2000) "The Impact of Real Exchange Rates on Exports: The Malaysian Case". M.Ec. Research Paper, University of Malaya, Kuala Lumpur.

Chung Kek Yoong (1987). *Mahathir Administration: Leadership and Change in a Multiracial Society.* Pelanduk Press, Petaling Jaya.

Classens, Stijn, Simeon Djankov and Daniela Klingebiel (1999). "Financial Restructuring in East Asia: Halfway There?" Financial Sector Discussion Paper No. 3, World Bank, Washington, D.C., September.

Daim Zainuddin (1994). *Daim Speaks His Mind.* Pelanduk Publications, Kuala Lumpur.

Demirgüç-Kunt, Asli and Enrica Detragiache (1998a). "The Determinants of Banking Crises in Developing and Developed Countries". *IMF Staff Papers* 45(1): 81-109.

Demirgüç-Kunt, Asli and Enrica Detragiache (1998b). "Financial Liberalization and Financial Fragility". Paper prepared for the 1998 World Annual Bank Conference on Development Economics.

Diaz-Alejandro, Carlos (1985). "Good-bye Financial Repression, Hello Financial Crash". *Journal of Development Economics,* 19(1/2), September-October.

Doh Joon Chien (1985). *Tan Sri Ahmad Noordin: Kampung Boy to Auditor-General.* Pelanduk Publications, Petaling Jaya.

Drake, P. J. (1969). *Financial Development in Malaya and Singapore.* Australian National University Press, Canberra.

Drake, P. J. (1975). "The New-Issue Boom in Malaya and Singapore, 1961-64". Reprinted in David Lim (ed.), *Readings on Malaysian Economic Development.* Oxford University Press, Kuala Lumpur.

Dwor-Frecaut, Dominique, Francis Colaco and Mary Hallward-Driemeier (eds) (2000). *Asian Corporate Recovery: Findings from Firm-Level Surveys in Five Countries.* World Bank, Washington, D. C.

East Asia Analytical Unit (1999) *Asia's Financial Markets: Capitalising on Reform.* Department of Foreign Affairs and Trade, Canberra.

Eatwell, John (1997). *International Financial Liberalization: The Impact on World Development,* Discussion Paper Series, Office of Development Studies, United Nations Development Program, New York, May.

Eatwell, John and Lance Taylor (1999). "Towards an Effective Regulation of International Capital Markets". *International Politics and Society,* 3: 279-86.

Economic Planning Unit, Prime Minister's Office, Malaysia (2000). "The Asian Financial Crisis: Impact at the Firm Level — the Malaysian Case", in Dominique Dwor-Frecaut, Francis Colaco and Mary Hallward-Driemeier (eds), *Asian Corporate Recovery: Findings from Firm-Level Surveys in Five Countries*. World Bank, Washington, D. C.

Edison, Hali J. and Carmen M. Reinhart (2000). "Capital Controls during Financial Crises: The Case of Malaysia and Thailand". Processed, Federal Reserve Bank.

Edwards, C. B. (1996). "Foreign Labour in Malaysian Development: A Strategic Shift?" IKMAS Working Paper No. 6, Universiti Kebangsaan Malaysia, Bangi, Selangor.

Edwards, Sebastian (1986). "The Order of Liberalization of the Current and Capital Accounts of the Balance of Payments", in A. M. Choksi and D. Papageorigiou (eds), *Economic Liberalization in Developing Countries*. Basil Blackwell, Oxford.

Emery, R. (1970). *The Financial Institutions of Southeast Asia: A Country-by-Country Study*. Praeger, New York.

Esman, Milton (1972). *Administration and Development in Malaysia: Institution Building and Reform in a Plural Society*. Cornell University Press, Ithaca.

Euromoney (1996). *Thailand: Reaping the Rewards of Growth*. Euromoney Books, London.

Fan Yew Teng (1990). *The UMNO Dilemma: Power Struggles in Malaysia*. Egret Publications, Kuala Lumpur.

Fane, G. (1998). "The Role of Prudential Regulation", in R. McLeod and R. Garnaut (eds), *East Asia in Crisis: From Being a Miracle to Needing One?* Routledge, London: 287-303.

Federation of Malaya (1956). *Report of the Committee on Malayanisation of the Public Service*. Government Press, Kuala Lumpur.

Felix, David (1996). "Financial Globalisation versus Free Trade: The Case for the Tobin Tax". *UNCTAD Review*.

Felker, Greg and Jomo K. S. (1999). "New Approaches to Investment Policy in the ASEAN 4". Asian Development Bank Institute Second Anniversary Workshop on Development Paradigms, Tokyo, 10 December.

Fischer, Stanley (1997). "IMF — The Right Stuff". *Financial Times*, 17 December.

Flassbeck, Heiner (2000). "Wanted: An International Exchange Rate Regime — The Missed Lesson of the Financial Crisis". *International Politics and Society*, 3: 282-91.

Frankel, Jeffrey A. (1997). "Sterilization of Money Inflows: Difficult (Calvo) or Easy (Reisen)?" *Estudios de Economia*, 24(2), December: 263-286.

Fransman, M. (1985). "Conceptualising Technical Change in the Third World in the 1980s: An Interpretative Survey". *Journal of Development Studies*, 21(4): 572-652.

Freeman, Chris (1987). *Technology Policy and Economic Policy: Lessons from Japan*. Frances Pinter, London.

Fukasaku, Y. (1992). *Technology Development in Pre-war Japan*. Routledge, London.

Furman, Jason and J. E. Stiglitz (1998). "Economic Crises: Evidence and Insights from East Asia", in *Brookings Papers on Economic Activity, 2: 1998*, Brookings Institute, Washington DC: 1-135.

Gan Wee Beng (2000). "The Perils of the Fixed Exchange Rate Systems (Even in the Presence of Capital Control)", *Ekonomika*, 12(3), July: 6-8.

Ganesan (1998). "Malaysia-Singapore Relations: Some Recent Developments", *Asian Affairs*, 25(1), (Spring): pp. 21-36.

Gill, Ranjit (1998). *Anwar Ibrahim: Mahathir's Dilemma*. Epic Management Services, Singapore.

Gomez, E. T. (1990). *Politics in Business: UMNO's Corporate Investments*. Kuala Lumpur, Forum.

Gomez, E. T. (1991). *Money Politics in the Barisan Nasional*. Forum, Kuala Lumpur.

Gomez, E. T. (1994). *Political Business: Corporate Involvement of Malaysian Political Parties*. James Cook University of North Queensland, Townsville, Queensland.

Gomez, E. T. (1996). "Electoral Funding of General, State and Party Elections in Malaysia". *Journal of Contemporary Asia*, 26(1): 81-99.

Gomez, E. T. (1999). *Chinese Business in Malaysia: Accumulation, Ascendance, Accommodation*. Curzon, London and University of Hawaii Press, Honolulu.

Gomez, E. T. and Jomo K. S. (1997). *Malaysia's Political Economy: Politics, Patronage and Profits*. Cambridge University Press, Cambridge.

Gomez, E. T. and Jomo K. S. (1999). *Malaysia's Political Economy: Politics, Patronage and Profits*. 2nd Edition. Cambridge University Press, Cambridge.

Malaysia (1999). *White Paper: Status of the Malaysian Economy*. Government of Malaysia, Kuala Lumpur.

Griffith-Jones, Stephany (1997). "Regulatory Challenges for Source Countries of Surges in Capital Flows". Paper prepared for FONDAD Conference, 18-19 November. Available from URL: http://www.ids.ac.uk/ids/research/easia.html

Griffith Jones, Stephany (1999). "A New Financial Architecture for Reducing Risks and Severity of Crises". *International Politics and Society*, 3: 263-78.

Haflah Piei, Musalmah Johan, Syarisa Yanti Abubakar (1999). "The Social Impact of the Asian Crisis: Malaysian Country Paper", Malaysian Institute of Economic Research for Asian Development Bank, Manila, July.

Haggard, Stephan (2000). *The Political Economy of the Asian Financial Crisis*, Institute for International Economics, Washington, D.C.

Haggard, Stephan (with Nancy Birdsall) (1999). "The Social Fallout: Safety Nets and Recrafting the Social Contract". Processed.

Haggard, Stephan and Low, Linda (1999). "The Political Economy of Malaysia's Capital Controls". Processed.

Hamada Koichi (2000). "On the Emergence of Currency Crises and Their Recovery Processes". *JBIC Review*, 1, May: 68-82.

Hamilton-Hart, Natasha (1999). "States and Capital Mobility: Indonesia, Malaysia and Singapore in the Asian Region". PhD dissertation, Cornell University, Ithaca, New York.

Hellmann, T., K. Murdock and J. Stiglitz (1995). "Financial Restraint: Towards a New Paradigm". Processed, Stanford University.

Hellmann, T., K Murdock and J. Stiglitz (1997). "Financial Restraint: Towards a New Paradigm", in M. Aoki, Kim Hyung-Ki and Okuno-Fujiwara (eds.) *The Role of Government in East Asian Economic Development: Comparative Institutional Analysis*. Clarendon Press, Oxford.

Hill, Hal (1998). "Malaysia's Risky Gamble." *Asian Wall Street Journal*, October 9-10.

Hing Ai Yun (1987). "The Financial System and Industrial Investment in West Malaysia". *Journal of Contemporary Asia*, 17(4): 409-435.

Hino Hiroyuki (1998). "Maintaining a Sound Banking System: New Lessons of the Asian Miracle". Processed, Kobe University.

Ho Ting Sing (1990). *The Financial Industry of Malaysia: Toward a New Era of Technological Change*. Malaysian Institute of Economic Research Discussion Paper No. 33, September, Kuala Lumpur.

International Finance Corporation (IFC) (1997). *Emerging Stock Market Factbook, 1997*, Washington, D.C.

IMF (International Monetary Fund). *International Financial Statistics*. Various years, International Monetary Fund, Washington, D. C.

Investors Digest, February 1997, Kuala Lumpur.

Ishak Shari *et al.* (1999). "Social Impact of Financial Crisis: Malaysia". Report submitted to the United Nations Development Program, Kuala Lumpur.

Ito Takatoshi, Ogawa Eiji and Y. N. Sasaki (1998). "How Did the Dollar Peg Fail in Asia?". National Bureau of Economic Research (NBER) Working Paper No. 6729, Cambridge, MA.

Jesudason, James (1989). *Ethnicity and the Economy: The State, Chinese Business and Multinationals in Malaysia*. Oxford University Press, Singapore.

Johnson, Chalmers (1982). *MITI and the Japanese Miracle*. Stanford University Press, Stanford.

Jomo K. S. (1986). *A Question of Class: Capital, the State, and Uneven Development in Malaya*. Oxford University Press, Singapore.

Jomo K. S. (1990). *Growth and Structural Change in the Malaysian Economy*. Macmillan, London.

Jomo K. S. (1994). *U-Turn? Malaysian Economic Development Policies After 1990*. Centre for Southeast Asian Studies, James Cook University, Cairns.

Jomo K. S. (ed.) (1995). *Privatizing Malaysia: Rents, Rhetoric, Realities.* Westview Press, Boulder, CO.

Jomo K. S. (ed.) (1998a). *Tigers in Trouble: Financial Governance, Liberalisation and Crises in East Asia.* Zed Books, London.

Jomo K. S. (1998b). "Malaysia's Debacle: Whose Fault?" *Cambridge Journal of Economics*, 22(6): 707-722.

Jomo K. S. (1999a). "Globalization and Human Development in East Asia", in UNDP, *Globalization with a Human Face: Human Development Report 1999, Background Papers*, Vol. 2, Human Development Report Office, United Nations Development Programme, New York: 81-123.

Jomo K. S. (1999b). "Beyond Crony Capitalism: Rent-Seeking, Financial Restraint and Economic Development", Centre for Development and Enterprise (Johannesburg) project on 'Entrepreneurship and Expanding the Business Sector in South Africa'. Processed.

Jomo K. S. (ed.) (2000). *Malaysian Eclipse: The Economic Crises of 1997-98.* Zed Books, London.

Jomo K. S. (ed.) (2001a). *Southeast Asia's Ersatz Industrialisation.* Macmillan, Basingstoke.

Jomo K. S. (ed.) (2001b). *Paper Tigers In Southeast Asia? Behind Miracle And Debacle.* Macmillan, Basingstoke.

Jomo K. S. *et al.* (1997). *Southeast Asia's Misunderstood Miracle: Industrial Policy and Economic Development in Thailand, Malaysia and Indonesia.* Westview, Boulder.

Jomo K. S. with E. T. Gomez (1997). "Rents and Development in Multiethnic Malaysia", in Masahiko Aoki, Hyung-Ki Kim and Masahiro Okuno-Fujiwara (eds) *The Role of Government in East Asian Economic Development*, Oxford University Press, New York: 342-72.

Jomo K. S. and Greg Felker (eds) (1999). *Technology, Competitiveness and the State: Malaysia's Industrial Technology Policies.* Routledge, London.

Jomo K. S. and Vijayakumari Kanapathy (1999). *Economic Liberalization and Labour in Malaysia: Efficiency and Equity Considerations in Public Policy Reform.* Report for International Labour Office, Geneva.

Kahler, Miles (ed.) (1998). *Capital Flows and Financial Crises.* Cornell University Press, Ithaca, NY.

Kahn, Joel S. and Loh Kok Wah, Francis (eds) (1992). *Fragmented Vision: Culture and Politics in Contemporary Malaysia.* Allen & Unwin, Sydney.

Kaminsky, Graciela and Carmen M. Reinhart (1998). "The Twin Crises: The Causes of Banking and Balance of Payments Problems". Processed.

Kanapathy, V. and Ismail Muhd Salleh (1994). *Malaysian Economy: Selected Issues and Policy Directions.* ISIS, Kuala Lumpur.

Kaplinsky, Raphael (1999). "'If You Want to Get Somewhere Else, You Must Run at Least Twice as Fast as That!': The Roots of the East Asian Crisis".

Competition and Change: The Journal of Global Business and Political Economy, 4(1).

Keynes, J. M. (1936). *The General Theory of Employment, Interest and Money*. Harcourt Brace and Company, New York.

Khalid Ibrahim, Abdul (1994). "Role of Unit Trusts in Mobilising Private Individual Savings", in Al'Alim Ibrahim (ed.), *Generating a National Savings Movement*. ISIS, Kuala Lumpur: 167-78.

Khan, Mushtaq (2000). "Rent-seeking as Process", in Mushtaq Khan and Jomo K. S. (eds), *Rents, Rent-seeking and Economic Development: Theory and Evidence in Asia*. Cambridge University Press, Cambridge: 70-144.

Khan, M. S. and C. M. Reinhart (eds) (1995). *Capital Flows in the APEC Region*, IMF Occasional Paper 122, Washington, D.C.

Khasnor Johan (1984). *The Emergence of the Modern Malay Administrative Elite*. Oxford University Press, Kuala Lumpur.

Khoo Boo Teik (1995). *Paradoxes of Mahathirism: An Intellectual Biography of Mahathir Mohamed*. Oxford University Press, Kuala Lumpur.

Khor K. P., Martin (1997). "SEA Currency Turmoil Renews Concern on Financial Speculation". *Third World Resurgence*, 86: 14-16.

Khor Kok Peng (1987). *Malaysia's Economy in Decline*. Consumers' Association of Penang, Penang.

KLSE (Kuala Lumpur Stock Exchange) (1997). *KLSE Statistics*. Various years, Kuala Lumpur Stock Exchange, Kuala Lumpur.

Kindleberger, Charles (1987). *International Capital Markets*. Cambridge University Press, Cambridge.

Kornai, Janos (1962). "Appraisal of Project Appraisal", in Boskin M. J. (ed.), *Economics of Human Welfare: Essays in Honour of Tibor Scitovsky*. Academic Press, New York.

Kregel, Jan (1998). "East Asia is not Mexico: The Differences between Balance of Payments Crises and Debt Deflation", in Jomo, pp. 44-62.

Krugman, Paul (1998a). "Saving Asia: It's Time to Get Radical". *Fortune*, 138, 5 (September 7): 74-80.

Krugman, Paul (1998b). "Malaysia's Opportunity?" *Far Eastern Economic Review*, 161, 38 (September 17): 32.

Krugman, Paul (1998c). "A Letter to Malaysia's Prime Minister". *Fortune*, 138, 6 (September 28): 35-6.

Krugman, Paul (1998d). "What Happened to Asia?" January, [http://web.mit.edu/krugman/www/DISINTER/html].

Krugman, Paul (1999a). *The Return of Depression Economics*. Allen Lane, London.

Krugman, Paul (1999b). "Capital Control Freaks: How Malaysia Got Away with Economic Heresy", *Slate*, September 27; also posted on http://wed.mit.edu/krugman/www/

Lane, Timothy (1999). "The Asian Financial Crisis: What Have We Learned?" *Finance & Development*, 36(3), September: 44-47.

Lee Hock Lock (1981). *Public Policies, Commercial Banks and Other Deposit Institutions in Malaysia: A Study in Resource Mobilization and Utilization.* UMBC Publications, Kuala Lumpur.

Lee Hock Lock (1987). *Central Banking in Malaysia: A Study of the Development of the Financial System and Monetary Management.* Butterworths, Singapore.

Lee Hock Lock (1992). *Regulation of Banks and Other Depository Institutions in Malaysia: A Study in Monetary, Prudential and Other Controls.* Butterworths, Singapore.

Lee Kuan Yew (1998). *The Singapore Story: Memoirs of Lee Kuan Yew.* Times Editions, Singapore.

Lee S. Y. (1990). *The Monetary and Banking Development of Singapore and Malaysia.* 3rd edition, Singapore University Press, Singapore.

Leigh, Michael (1992). "Politics, Bureaucracy and Business in Malaysia: Re-aligning the Eternal Triangle", in A. MacIntyre and K. Jayasuriya (eds), *The Dynamics of Economic Policy Reform in South-East Asia and the South-West Pacific.* Oxford University Press, Singapore: 115-23.

Lin S. Y. (1993). "The Institutional Perspective of Financial Market Reforms: The Malaysian Experience", in S. Faruqui (ed.), *Financial Sector Reforms in Asian and Latin American Countries: Lessons of Comparative Experience.* World Bank, Washington, D.C.: 215-48.

Lopez-Mejia, Alejandro (1999). "Large Capital Flows: Causes, Consequences, and Policy Responses". *Finance & Development*, 36(3), September: 28-31.

MacIntyre, Andrew (ed.) (1994). *Business and Government in Industrialising Asia.* Allen & Unwin, Sydney.

Mahani Zainal Abidin (2000). "Implications of the Malaysian Experience on Future International Financial Arrangements". *ASEAN Economic Bulletin*, Special issue, April.

Mahathir Mohamad (1998). *Currency Turmoil.* Prime Minister's Department, Kuala Lumpur.

Mahathir Mohamad (1999). *A New Deal for Asia.* Pelanduk, Petaling Jaya.

Malayan Law Journal (1999). *The Anwar Ibrahim Judgement.* Malayan Law Journal, Kuala Lumpur.

Malaysia (1991). *Second Outline Perspective Plan, 1991-2000.* Government Printers, Kuala Lumpur.

Malaysia (1994). *Mid-Term Review of the Sixth Malaysia Plan, 1991-1995.* Government Printers, Kuala Lumpur.

Malaysia, (1999). *Mid-term Review of the Seventh Malaysia Plan, 1996-2000.* Government Printers, Kuala Lumpur.

Malaysia (1999). *White Paper: Status of the Malaysian Economy.* Government of Malaysia, Kuala Lumpur.

Malaysia, Civil Service Department (1999). http://www.jpa.gov.my

Malaysia, Department of Statistics. http://www.statistics.gov.my

Malaysia, Ministry of Education. http://www.moe.gov.my

Malaysia, Ministry of Finance. *Economic Report.* http://www.treasury.gov.my

Matthias, Rudolph C. (1999). "An Analysis of Industrial Finance Systems: A Comparision of Malaysia and Thailand", PhD thesis, Faculty of Economics and Politics, University of Cambridge, Cambridge, UK, September.

Mansor Md. Isa (1995). "Malaysian Capital Market: Recent Development and Future Challenges". Paper prepared for the Fifth Tun Abdul Razak Conference, Ohio University, Athens, Ohio, April 21-23.

MASTIC (1994). "Basic Information", Malaysian Science and Technology Information Centre, Kuala Lumpur.

McLeod, R. (1998). "Indonesia", in R. McLeod and R. Garnaut (eds), *East Asia in Crisis: From Being a Miracle to Needing One?* Routledge, London: 31-48.

McLeod, R. and R. Garnaut (eds) (1998). *East Asia in Crisis: From Being a Miracle to Needing One?* Routledge, London.

Mehmet, Ozay (1986). *Development in Malaysia: Poverty, Wealth and Trusteeship.* Croom Helm, London.

Merican, Omar (1997). "Structural Weaknesses in Lending: Using Volatile Assets as Collateral". *Malaysian Journal of Economic Studies*, 34(1&2), June & December: 61-66.

Miller, V. (1998). "The Double Drain with a Cross-border Twist: More on the Relationship between Banking and Currency Crises". *American Economic Review*, 88(2): 439-43.

Ministry of Human Resources, Malaysia. (1999). *Labour Market Report, 1998.* Available at URL: http://www.ksm.gov.my

Mohamed Ariff *et al.* (1993). "A Market Micro-Structure Explanation for the Excessive Underpricing in Malaysian IPOs". Paper presented at a seminar on 'Underpricing of New Issues: International Comparison', KLSE Research Division, 20 September.

Montes, Manuel F. (1998). *The Currency Crisis in Southeast Asia.* Institute of Southeast Asian Studies (ISEAS), Singapore.

Morais, Victor, J. (1994). *Anwar Ibrahim: Resolute in Leadership.* Arenabuku, Kuala Lumpur.

Munro-Kua, Anne (1996). *Authoritarian Populism in Malaysia.* Macmillan Press, London.

Mussa, M., A. Swoboda, J. Zettelmeyer and O. Jeanne (1999). "Moderating Fluctuations in Capital Flows to Emerging Market Economies". *Finance & Development*, 36(3), September.

Nesadurai, Helen E. S. (2000). "In Defence of National Economic Autonomy? Malaysia's Response to the Financial Crisis". *The Pacific Review*, 13(1): 73-113.

Ng Beoy Kui (ed.) (1989). *The Development of Capital Markets in the SEACEN Countries*. South East Asian Central Banks (SEACEN) Research and Training Centre, Kuala Lumpur.

Obiyathulla Ismath Bacha (1997). "The Asian Currency Crisis — *A Fait Accompli*". *Malaysian Journal of Economic Studies*, 34(1&2), June & December: 67-91.

Ong H. C. (1996). "Exchange Rate Fluctuations and Macroeconomic Management, 1980-1995: A Malaysian Perspective". Paper presented at the PEO/Structure Specialists' Meeting, 27-28 September, Osaka.

Ong H. C. (1998). "Coping with Capital Flows and the Role of Monetary Policy: The Malaysian Experience, 1990-95", in Kwan C. H., Donna Vandenbrink and Chia Siow Yue (eds) *Coping with Capital Flows in East Asia*. Institute of Southeast Asian Studies, Singapore and Nomura Research Institute, Tokyo.

Oo Yu Hock (1991). *Ethnic Chameleon: Multiracial Politics in Malaysia*. Pelanduk Press, Petaling Jaya.

Park Yung Chul (1994). "Concepts and Issues", in H. T. Patrick and Y. C. Park (eds), *The Financial Development of Japan, Korea and Taiwan: Growth, Repression and Liberalisation*. Oxford University Press, New York.

Pasuk Phongpaichit (1990). *The Recent Wave of Japanese Investment in Southeast Asia*. Singapore: ISEAS.

Pempel, T. J. (ed.) (1999). *Politics of the Asian Economic Crisis*. Cornell University Press, Ithaca and London.

Pempel, T. J. (2000). "International Finance and Asian Regionalism". *The Pacific Review* 13(1): 57-72.

Perkins, Dwight H. and Woo Wing Thye (2000). "Malaysia: Adjusting to Deep Integration with the World Economy", in W. T. Woo, J. D. Sachs and Klaus Schwab (eds) *The Asian Financial Crisis: Lessons for a Resilient Asia*. MIT Press, Cambridge, MA.

Philippine Statistical Yearbook. National Statistical Coordinating Board, Manila, 1997.

Pindyck, Robert S. and Daniel L. Rubinfeld (1997). *Econometric Models and Economic Forecasts*. 4th edition. McGraw-Hill, Singapore.

Polanyi, Karl (1957). *The Great Transformation*. Beacon Press, Boston.

Puthucheary, Mavis (1978). *The Politics of Administration: The Malaysian Experience*. Oxford University Press, Kuala Lumpur.

Radelet, Steven and Jeffrey Sachs (1998a). "The Onset of the East Asian Financial Crisis". Paper prepared for the NBER Currency Crisis Conference, Feb 6-7. NBER Working Paper Series, No. 6680, Cambridge. [www.stern.nyu.edu/~nroubini/asia/].

Radelet, S. and J. Sachs (1998b). "The East Asian Financial Crisis: Diagnosis, Remedies, Prospects". *Brookings Papers on Economic Activity, 1998(1)*: 1-90.

Rasiah, Rajah (1988). "The Semiconductor Industry in Penang: Implications for NIDL Theories". *Journal of Contemporary Asia*, 18(1): 24-46.

Rasiah, Rajah (1992). "Foreign Manufacturing Investment". *Economic Bulletin for Asia Pacific*, 63(1): 63-77.

Rasiah, Rajah (1994a). "Flexible Production Systems and Local Machine Tool Subcontracting: Electronics Component Transnationals". *Cambridge Journal of Economics*, 18(3): 279-298.

Rasiah, Rajah (1994b). "Capitalist Industrialization in ASEAN Economies". *Journal of Contemporary Asia*, 24(2): 197-216.

Rasiah, Rajah (1995). *Foreign Capital and Industrialization in Malaysia*. Macmillan, Basingstoke.

Rasiah, Rajah (1996a). "Institutions and Innovations: Moving Towards the Technology Frontier in Malaysia's Electronics Industry". *Industry and Innovation*, 3(2).

Rasiah, Rajah (1996b). "Changing Organisation of Work in Malaysia's Electronics Industry". *Asia Pacific Viewpoint*, 37(1): 21-38.

Rasiah, Rajah (1997). "Class, Ethnicity and Economic Development in Malaysia", in G. Rodan, K. Hewison and R. Robison (eds), *The Political Economy of South-East Asia*. Oxford University Press, Melbourne.

Rasiah, Rajah (1998a). "Export-Manufacturing Experience of Indonesia, Malaysia and Thailand: Lessons for Africa", UNCTAD Discussion Papers, No. 136, Geneva.

Rasiah, Rajah (1998b). "Slowdown and Bust: Causes of the Southeast Asian Financial Crisis". EIAS Briefing Paper 98/01, European Institute of Asian Studies, Brussels.

Rasiah, Rajah (1998c). "The Malaysian Financial Crisis: Capital Expansion, Cronyism and Contraction". *Journal of Asia Pacific Economy*, 3(3): 358-378.

Rasiah, Rajah (1999). "Malaysia's National Innovation System", in Jomo K. S. and Greg Felker (eds.), *Technology, Competitiveness and the State: Malaysia's Industrial Technology Policies*. Routledge, London.

Rasiah, Rajah (2000). "Southeast Asia's Ersatz Miracle: The Dubious Sustainability of Its Growth and Industrialisation", in Jomo K. S. (ed.) *Southeast Asia's Ersatz Industrialisation*. Macmillan, Basingstoke.

Rasiah, Rajah (2001). "Proton: Building a National Car Industry in Malaysia", in Jomo K. S. (ed.), *Manufacturing Competitiveness*, Macmillan, Basingstoke.

Rasiah, Rajah and Anuwar Ali (1996). "Governing Industrial Technological Change in Malaysia". Processed, Universiti Kebangsaan Malaysia.

Rasiah, Rajah and Osman-Rani H. (1997). "Enterprise Training and Productivity in Malaysia's Manufacturing Sector". IKMAS Working Paper No. 12, Universiti Kebangsaan Malaysia, Bangi, Selangor, Malaysia.

Reinhart, Carmen M. and Vincent Raymond Reinhart (1998). "Some Lessons for Policy Makers Who Deal with the Mixed Blessing of Capital Inflows," in Miles Kahler (ed.), *Capital Flows and Financial Crises*. Cornell University Press, Ithaca.

Root, H. L. (1996). *Small Countries, Big Lessons: Governance and the Rise of East Asia*. Oxford University Press, Hong Kong for Asian Development Bank.

Rosenberger, L. (1997). "Southeast Asia's Currency Crisis: A Diagnosis and Prescription". *Contemporary Southeast Asia*, 19(3): 223-51.

Rugayah Muhamad (1995). "Public Enterprises", in Jomo K. S. (ed.) *Privatizing Malaysia: Rents, Rhetoric and Realities*. Westview, Boulder.

Ruzita Mohd. Amin and Rokiah Alavi (1997). "The Contagion and Public Effects on Financial Markets Behaviour in Malaysia". *Malaysian Journal of Economic Studies*, 34(1&2), June & December: 123-141.

Rybczynski, T. (1984). "Industrial Finance Systems in Europe, US and Japan". *Journal of Economic Behaviour and Organisation*, 5: 275-86.

Sakakibara Eisuke (2000). "Thai Crisis Played Part in IMF Idea". *Yomiuri Shimbun*, 25 November.

Scherer, F. (1992). *International High Technology Competition*. Harvard University Press, Cambridge.

Schumpeter, Joseph (1934). *Theory of Economic Development*. MIT Press, Cambridge.

Searle, Peter (1999). *The Riddle of Malaysian Capitalism: Rent-Seekers or Real Capitalists?* Allen & Unwin and University of Hawaii Press, Sydney and Honolulu.

Securities Commission, Malaysia (1996). *Annual Report, 1996*. Kuala Lumpur.

Sheng, Andrew (1989). *Bank Restructuring in Malaysia 1985-88*. Policy, Planning and Research Working Papers, WPS54, September, World Bank, Washington, D.C.

Sherwood, P. W. (1966). "The Watson-Caine Report on the Establishment of a Central Bank in Malaya", in P. J. Drake (ed.) *Money and Banking in Malaya and Singapore*. Malaysia Publications Ltd., Singapore: 5-19.

Shirai Sayuri (2000). "Draft Technical Background Paper for Asian Policy Forum Report". Document No. 5, APF Brainstorming Workshop on 'How to Prevent Another Crisis', Asian Development Bank Institute, 10-11 March, Tokyo.

Shireen M. Hashim. (1998). *Income Inequality and Poverty in Malaysia*. Rowman and Littlefield, Lanham, Maryland.

Singh, Ajit (1992). *The Stock Market and Economic Development: Should Developing Countries Encourage Stock Markets?* UNCTAD Discussion Paper No. 49, October.

Singh, Ajit (1995). *Corporate Financial Patterns in Industrialising Economies: A Comparative International Study*, IFC Technical Paper No. 2, International Finance Corporation, Washington, D.C.

Singh, Hari (1997). "The 1995 Malaysian Elections: Reaffirmation of Barisan Nasional Dominance". *The Round Table*, 343: 389-409.

Singh, Hari (1998). "Tradition, UMNO and Political Succession in Malaysia. *Third World Quarterly*, 19(2): 241-25.

Singh, S. (1984). *Bank Negara Malaysia: The First 25 Years, 1959-1984.* Bank Negara Malaysia, Kuala Lumpur.

Skully, M. and G. Viksnins (1987). *Financing East Asia's Success: Comparative Financial Development in Eight Asian Countries.* St. Martin's Press, New York.

Stiglitz, Joseph (1998). "The Role of International Financial Institutions in the Current Global Economy". Address to the Chicago Council on Foreign Relations, Chicago, 27 February. [http://www.worldbank.org/html.extme/jssp022798.htm]

Stiglitz, Joseph (1999). "What Have We Learned from the Recent Crises: Implications For Banking Regulation". Remarks at the Conference on 'Global Financial Crises: Implications for Banking and Regulation', Federal Reserve Bank of Chicago, Chicago, IL, May 6.

Suresh Narayanan, Lai Yew Wah, Abdul Rahim Ibrahim, Chua Soo Yean and Chan Huan Chiang (1997). "The East Asian Economic Crisis: Why was Malaysia Vulnerable?". *Malaysian Journal of Economic Studies*, 34(1&2), June & December: 93-112.

Tan Eu Chye (1997). "The Present Malaysian Economic Crisis with Reference to the Crisis of the Mid-1980s". *Malaysian Journal of Economic Studies*, 34(1&2), June & December: 113-122.

Tham Siew Yean (1997). "Can the Malaysian Manufacturing Sector Survive the Asian Financial Crisis and Its Aftermath?". *Malaysian Journal of Economic Studies*, 34(1&2), June & December: 143-63.

Tham Siew Yean (1998). "Policy and Productivity". Processed, Analytical Economics Department, Universiti Kebangsaan Malaysia, Bangi, Selangor, Malaysia.

Thillainathan, R. (1997). "The Malaysian Banking Crisis and the Way Forward". *Malaysian Journal of Economic Studies*, 34(1&2), June & December: 33-59.

Thillainathan, R. (2000). "Malaysian Financial and Corporate Sector Under Distress — A Mid-term Assessment of Restructuring Efforts". Processed, revised version of paper originally prepared for a World Bank conference, Tokyo, January 2000.

Tilman, Robert (1964). *Bureaucratic Transition in Malaya.* Duke University Press, Durham, NC, and Cambridge University Press, Cambridge.

Tourk, Khairy Ahmed (2000). "Challenging the IMF Orthodoxy: The Malaysian Experience". Processed, Eighth Pacific Basin Finance, Economics and Accounting Conference, Bangkok, 1-2 June.

UNCTAD (1996). *World Investment Report, 1996.* United Nations Conference for Trade and Development, Geneva.

UNCTAD. *Trade and Development Report.* Various years, United Nations Conference for Trade and Development, Geneva.

UNCTAD and International Chamber of Commerce (ICC) (1998). "Financial Crisis in Asia and Foreign Direct Investment". Available from URL: http://www.unctad.org/en/press/bg9802en.htm

UNDP (1995). *1995 Human Development Report*. Oxford University Press, New York for United Nations Development Program.

Wade, Robert (1990). *Governing the Market*. Princeton University Press, Princeton.

Wade, Robert and Frank Veneroso (1998). "The Asian Crisis: The High Debt Model vs. the Wall Street-Treasury-IMF Complex". *New Left Review*, March-April.

White Paper: Malaysia (1999). *White Paper on Status of the Malaysian Economy*. Government Printers, Kuala Lumpur, 6 April.

Williamson, John (1997). "Prospects for Avoiding Crises with Liberalized Capital Flows". *Estudios de Economia*, 24(2), December: 287-296.

Wong Hwa Kiong with Jomo K. S. (1999). "The Impact of Foreign Capital Inflows on the Malaysian Economy, 1966-1996". Processed, Faculty of Economics and Administration, University of Malaya, Kuala Lumpur.

Wong, Diana (1998). "Social Consequences of the Economic Crisis". Paper presented at a seminar on 'The Economic Crisis in Malaysia and the Role of the Media', Asian Institute for Development Communication, Kuala Lumpur, 22 July.

World Bank (1993). *The East Asian Miracle*, Oxford University Press, New York.

World Bank (1998). *East Asia: The Road to Recovery*. World Bank, Washington, D.C.

World Bank, *World Development Report*, various issues. Oxford University Press, New York for World Bank.

Yamabe Taku and Megumi Suto with Junichi Yamada (1999). "The Effectiveness and Major Issues of Capital Controls Policy in Malaysia". *OECF Research Papers*, No. 33, Research Institute of Development Assistance, Overseas Economic Cooperation Fund, Tokyo, June.

Zainal Aznam Yusof et al. (1994). "Financial Reform in Malaysia", in G. Caprio et al. (eds), *Financial Reform: Theory and Experience*. Cambridge University Press, Cambridge: 276-320.

Zainuddin Maidin (1994). *The Other Side of Mahathir*. Utusan, Kuala Lumpur.

Zeti Akhtar Aziz (1989). "Development of Capital Market in Malaysia", in Ng Beoy Kui (ed.) *The Development of Capital Markets in the SEACEN Countries*. South East Asian Central Banks (SEACEN) Research and Training Centre, Kuala Lumpur.

Zeti Akhtar Aziz (forthcoming). "Managing Capital Flows in Malaysia", Processed, World Institute for Development Economics Research (WIDER), Helsinki.

INDEX